Travel Adventures

Leeward Islands

Anguilla, Antigua St Barts, St Kitts & St Martin

3rd Edition

K.C. Nash

D1125818

HUNTER PUBLISHING, INC.
80 Northfield Ave, Edison, NJ 08837
☎ *732-225-1900 / 800-255-0343 / fax 732-417-1744*
www.hunterpublishing.com
E-mail comments@hunterpublishing.com

IN CANADA:
Ulysses Travel Publications
4176 Saint-Denis, Montréal, Québec, Canada H2W 2M5
☎ *514-843-9882 ext. 2232 / fax 514-843-9448*

IN THE UNITED KINGDOM:
Windsor Books International
5, Castle End Park, Castle End Rd, Ruscombe
Berkshire, RG10 9XQ England, ☎ *01189-346-367/fax 01189-346-368*

ISBN 978-1-58843-642-9

© 2008 Hunter Publishing, Inc.

Cover photo: Pinney's Beach, Nevis (© Bill Brooks/Alamy)

Maps © 2008 Hunter Publishing, Inc.

For complete information about the hundreds of other travel guides offered by Hunter Publishing, visit us at www.hunterpublishing.com.

Most of our guides are also available in digital form as e-books through NetLibrary.com, ebrary.com, Ebooks.com, Overdrive.com and other partners. For more information, e-mail comments@ hunterpublishing.com.

4   3   2   1

Contents

About the Author

K.C. Nash is a professional travel writer with years of experience in writing feature stories for magazines and newspapers. She lives in Antigua, one of the Leewards, and frequently travels throughout the region to explore new developments and share them with her readers.

Before moving to Antigua in 2005, K.C. lived in the East Bay area of San Francisco, and served as a special sections editor and feature writer for the Contra Costa Times newspaper chain. She also contributed articles to Diablo Magazine, an award-winning regional publication based in the East Bay.

Most recently, she has been a contributor to the Caribbean Edge website, and now hosts her own site, www.leewardislands.net, where she will be updating the information contained in this book on a continuous basis.

Acknowledgments

I would like to thank my husband Willie Nash, Jr. for his patient support over the last year as I researched each island. I truly enjoyed his company as we visited hotels, restaurants and various attractions on each island. He always had insightful questions and cogent observations to add—especially when I completely missed the obvious or got too cranky and out of sorts to think of good questions.

I would also like to thank the professional staff members of the tourism boards and authorities on each island who were so helpful in arranging tours and visits, and generally supporting the publication of this book. They include Director Amelia Vanterpool-Kubisch and Merlyn Rogers of the Anguilla Tourist Board; Director General Lorraine Headley and U.S. Director of Tourism Derede Samuel-Whitlock of the Antigua and Barbuda Ministry of Tourism; Director Ernestine Cassell, Ishwar Persad and Jadine Glitzenhirn of the Montserrat Tourist Board; Director Glenn Holm of the Saba Tourism Office; Director Christine Walwyn and her capable staff members Diannille Taylor and Wendell Pemberton of St. Kitts; Chief Executive Officer Helen Kidd and Angelique France of the Nevis Tourism Authority; and Director of Tourism Elise Magras of St. Barths for their kind assistance.

I appreciate the time each of the hotel and restaurant managers and staff took to tell me about their properties and take me on tours. Without their patient guidance, this book would be a lot shorter and half as valuable.

The Caribbean

Gulf of Mexico

Florida

Bahama Islands

Cuba

Jamaica

Haiti

Dominican Republic

Virgin Islands

Puerto Rico

Anguilla

Barbuda

Antigua

Guadeloupe

DOMINICA

St. Kitts & Nevis

Martinique

ST. LUCIA

Barbados

St. Vincent

Grenada

Trinidad & Tobago

Margarita

Tortuga

Curaçao

Aruba

Atlantic Ocean

Caribbean Sea

HONDURAS

NICARAGUA

COSTA RICA

PANAMA

COLOMBIA

VENEZUELA

GUYANA

N

HUNTER PUBLISHING

NOT TO SCALE

© 2007 HUNTER PUBLISHING, INC.

Introduction
What Type Are You?

Before you decide where to go in the Leeward Islands, you should examine your needs and desires – and especially your traveling style. Take a look at the suggested styles below, and see which description fits you best.

The Perfect Cruise Passenger

Your idea of the perfect vacation is settling into one place and having the world come to you. Your idea of heaven includes multiple restaurants to choose from, loads of entertainment, fun activities and shopping... all within a short distance from your room. And you still want to explore different cultures, albeit in quick glimpses that can be had on an organized tour, so that you can return to your little haven on or by the sea.

The Boots-On Adventurer

To you, the world is one big hiking trail supplemented by huge pools for your kayaking, sailing, parasailing or diving activities. The more explorations you can cram into a day the better – and then at the end of the day you want to see what the local culture has to explore in the way of cuisines and entertainment. Beach-sitting, lazy swimming in a warm pool, or sitting on a balcony reading a good book are not among your preferred activities.

The Cultural Explorer

The world is a fascinating place, and you want to know as much about it as you can. You love talking to hotel owners, restaurateurs, tour operators and just ordinary people to hear what they like best about their country. You are game to try native cuisines (although monkey brains may not be to your liking), dances, games and anything different from your own culture. You'd prefer to stay in places that don't remind you of home, but give you a new view of the world at large.

The "I Like What I Like" Traveler

You still expect all the comforts of home when you travel – including the foods you normally eat, the type of bed you sleep in, and the media you are accustomed to. You would like a little adventure, but for the most part you don't want to be inconvenienced by a lot of unfamiliar things flying at you while you are abroad. Your favorite activities, like golfing, horseback riding, or tennis, are easily available in a form similar to what you get at home.

The Incurable Romantic

Faraway places inspire you to new romantic heights. You love finding panoramic vistas that bring out your joy, intimate restaurants that delight your palate, and local music and entertainment that stir your soul. You prefer hotels with room décors that offer glimpses of past cultures, and tours that bring you into a world of historical intrigues and swashbuckling adventures. You want to return home with gorgeous photos and special memories to savor.

The Family Social Director

While you may resemble one of the above types of travelers, you have a spouse, children, relatives or friends to consider. Your idea of heaven is a place where everyone gets what they need – whether it's special dietary requirements, activities suited to their age levels and interests, or the right-sized bed. The ideal place would allow you time to yourself as well as opportunities for quality family time together. You want everyone to head home with happy memories and the desire to do it all again next year.

The Ultimate Shopper

Vacations to you are an opportunity to discover some incredible deals or to pick up artifacts and treasures no one else in your social set will have. Your accommodations should be nice, the restaurants should be interesting, but most of all, you want a duty-free port where the prices are impressively low and the goods are of the highest quality. The beach is there primarily to keep your spouse or traveling companions happy while you prowl the streets, looking for that unique bibelot, sexy outfit, or incredible piece of jewelry that will set you off from the crowd.

If you and your traveling partner or family happen to be different types, maybe you should examine your relationships. Or decide which is the alpha dog who gets to have what he or she wants. Or be mature and compromise, deciding to stay a few nights at places that make you happy and other nights at those that make the partner happy (okay, so this doesn't work for Cruise-ites). But you get the idea. These categories will give you guidance as you make your way through this book. In each chapter, I've indicated the accommodations, restaurants and activities that should intrigue each type. Decide who you really are, and then make your plans accordingly. If you don't find a description that matches your style, then you are on your own – but I would like to hear about what you came up with.

Pick Your Island

Before you go to the chapters, let's make it even easier by looking at the big picture, analyzing what Leeward Island locations hold the most appeal for each type.

Anguilla

With its glamorous new super-luxury resorts and high-end villas, this island is the **Incurable Romantic**'s dream. Most of the resorts also accommodate children with special activities and room arrangements, so the **Family Social Director**'s job is made easy here as well. The array of villas also offers the **"I Like" Traveler** an opportunity to adopt a home in another land and make it his or her own for a little while.

Antigua & Barbuda

This two-island nation offers something for everyone, and basically pleases pretty much every type of traveler. It's one of the major Caribbean seaports for cruise ships, and it offers a wide range of accommodations, restaurants and activities for longer stays. **Ultimate Shoppers** will enjoy downtown St. John's, especially Heritage Quay and Redcliffe Quay, along with the many boutiques and galleries nearby. Antigua & Barbuda have recently added some rainforest activities to their growing list of "into the bush" type adventures which should please the Boots On Adventurer.

Montserrat

With its active volcano, and more than half the island looking like a moonscape, this is the perfect place for the Boots On Adventurer. You can get up close and personal with a volcano that puts on a pyroclastic display every few months, as well as see how the plucky natives survive in the face of adversity. This also makes it an interesting place for the **Cultural Explorer**. But it's definitely not for the **Incurable Romantic or "I Like" Traveler.**

St. Kitts

St. Kitts & Nevis are fast becoming the capital of five-star resorts, as evidenced by the massive and glitzy palace on the sea built by Marriott overlooking a well-maintained and scenic golf course. Villas are going up like mushrooms after the rain, so Cruise Passengers and **"I Like" Travelers** will find something here that makes them very comfortable. For **Incurable Romantics**, the lovely small plantation inns will transport them back to British colonial times. **Ultimate Shoppers** will love downtown Basseterre in St. Kitts and the sparkling new Port Zante complex where cruise ship passengers can browse an outstanding collection of duty-free shops; shoppers will also enjoy Charlestown in Nevis.

Nevis

This cool little island, sister state to St. Kitts, is just coming into its own and has a little bit of everything. The plantation inns will delight the **Incurable Romantics**, the sleek Four Seasons will satisfy the most discerning **"I Like" Traveler** or Cruise Passenger. The smaller beachside resorts are perfect for families. And the kids can spend hours looking for a glimpse of the wild monkeys or snorkeling around looking for the underwater behaviors described by Barbara Whitman, a marine biologist and animal behaviourist who runs tours in Oualie Bay.

Saba and St. Eustatius

These are the islands for the Boots On Adventurer, who can explore the heights of the rainforests and dive in some of the deepest canyons in the Caribbean. For the **Cultural Explorer**, most of the hotels and restaurants are small places where you get to know the owners and can satisfy your delight in all things native. But, other than diving and hiking, and the interesting diversion of an archaeological dig, activities are few and the other types of travelers should not consider this a "must-do" destination.

St. Barthelemy

This haven of celebrities and the ultra-rich is low on native culture and high on all things American and French. Although the perception is that all hotels here are five-star havens, there is a range of other accommodations, including villas. The high-end resorts and villas cater to the **"I Like" Travelers**, but also offer enough variety to keep the **Family Social Director** happy. Rooms at well-known resorts like Eden Rock overlook spectacular beaches and turquoise seas, offering the **Incurable Romantic** a perfect setting. St. Barts is also a duty-free port so the shopping in Gustavia and St. Jean's is the **Ultimate Shopper's** dream come true – although be prepared for a preponderance of high-style shops with designer clothes and accessories. **Boots On Adventurers** should look for another island.

St. Martin/Sint Maarten

Catering to both French and Dutch sensibilities (with a lot of American influences), this island is great for those who want a European or American vacation in a tropical location. The wealth of casinos, night spots and restaurants make this a no-brainer for Cruise Passengers and **"I Like" Travelers**. There are a few top-end resorts and a lot of French bistros to delight the **Incurable Romantics**. And, with the array of watersports at Orient Beach, the zoo and the Butterfly Farm, the **Family Social Director** will find it easy to plan outings for the kids. The duty-free havens of Phillipsburg and Marigot are enough to send the **Ultimate Shopper** into absolute ecstasy. There's not much here to attract the **Cultural Explorer** or the **Boots-On Adventurer**, unless they take a day-trips to Saba or St. Eustatius.

Now get into each destination chapter, and see what best suits your traveling type. Have fun, and make your next vacation the one you'll remember for the rest of your life!

JUST A WORD BEFORE YOU START

From what I've experienced in traveling through the Leeward Islands, the people are friendly and welcoming, eager to have you experience their own special island. Many of them are also freewheeling, hardworking entrepreneurs (shooting down the whole "island time" mythology). So be aware that, while all the restaurants, hotels, tours and attractions are current as of my creation of the book, by the time you see this many things may have changed.

Websites

In the chapters on each island, you'll find names of companies, phone numbers and locations. Where they were available, I also included websites. In addition, you may want to consult the following websites specific to each island.

To update the information contained in this guide, one of your easiest paths will be to go to www.leewardislands.net. This website will have current information, with the latest about what's happening on each island.

General Caribbean

www.caribbean.com

www.caribbean.travel

www.caribbean.worldweb.com

www.caribbeanedge.com

www.caribbeanhotels.com

www.caribbeaninns.com

www.caribbeanmag.com

www.caribbean-on-line.com

www.caribbeantravelmag.com

www.caribseek.com

www.definitivecaribbean.com

www.doitcaribbean.com (Caribbean Tourism Organization site)

www.luxurylink.com

www.turq.com

www.wiol.com

Villas in the Leeward Islands

www.caribbeanway.com

www.caribbeans.com

www.caribbeanvillas.org

www.cvillas.com

www.villascaribe.com – Anguilla

www.wimco.com – Anguilla, St. Martin, St. Barth, and Nevis

Anguilla

www.anguilla-vacation.com – Tourism Authority

www.anguillaguide.com

www.gov.ai

www.anguilla-beaches.com

Antigua & Barbuda

www.antigua-barbuda.org – Tourism Authority

www.antigua-barbuda.tv

www.antiguanet.net

Introduction

www.antiguanice.com
www.antigua-resorts.com
www.everytingantigua.com
www.myantigua.org
www.barbudaful.com

Montserrat

www.visitmontserrat.com – Tourism Authority
www.mvo.ms – volcano tracking

Nevis

www.nevis1.com
www.nevisisland.com – Tourism Authority
www.nevisvillaholidays.com

Saba

www.sabatourism.com – Tourism Authority

St. Barts

www.sbhonline.com
www.st-barths.com – Tourism Authority
www.stbartstalk.com
www.frenchcaribbean.com/St-Barthelemy

St. Eustatius

www.statiatourism.com – Tourism Authority

St. Kitts

www.stkitts-tourism.com – Tourism Authority
www.sknvibes.com

St. Martin/St. Maarten

4funstmartin.com
www.everythingstmaarten.com
www.experiencestmaarten.com
www.gobeach.com
www.k-pasa.com – daily listing of events
www.sint-maarten.net
www.st-maarten.com – Tourism Authority Dutch side
www.st-maarten-info.com

www.st-martin.org – Tourism Authority French side
www.sxm-activities.com
www.sxmvibes.com www.sxmrestaurants.com

Following the Symbols

To make things easier, we use some visual codes that will help you along.

Hotels

Everyone has a budget in mind, even when planning the perfect vacation. The range of prices in each category differs from island to island, and is indicated in each chapter . Hotels are ranked by cost categories, according to the following:

HOTEL PRICE CHART	
$	Inexpensive, but be prepared to forego amenities
$$	Good value
$$$	Moderate
$$$$	Expensive, a mix of all-inclusives and European plans
$$$$$	Very expensive, usually all-inclusive

Meal Plans

Various hotels offer meal plans according to four different standards:

AI – Includes breakfast, lunch, dinner (and in the British West Indies, afternoon tea), plus all drinks (usually not premium brand liquor), watersports and activities.

MAP – Includes breakfast and dinner, plus watersports and activities; also called "half board."

BP or **CP** – Includes breakfast only; CP indicates continental breakfast, rather than full breakfast.

EP – Reflects rate of room only, with no meals.

RESTAURANT PRICE CHART	
$	Cheap eats, normally quick meals or take-out foods; US$8 or less per entrée
$$	Good value, lots of West Indian cuisine; US$9-$14 for a plate of food.
$$$	A nice place with gourmet aspirations; US$15-$24 for a satisfying entrée.
$$$$	Positively elegant, usually requiring some dressing up; entrées range from US$25 to $50, depending on the island.

A Word of Caution

Sunscreen/sun intensity: Although everyone will tell you this, somehow it doesn't sink in. So I'll say it one more time: the sun down here is more intense than in the northern climes. You can burn quickly and won't even know it until you come in and start getting ready for dinner and find that putting on clothes feels like wrapping your body in heated sandpaper. Get several strengths of suntan lotion. Start with SPF 50 for the first two days, then go down to SPF 30, then maybe SPF 15 if you are staying for more than one week. You may also want to bring along aloe gel to help with burns (the ones with menthol feel great when you are suffering). Some of the beach bars put aloe leaves in a refrigerator and have them ready to help. Even better, if you have serious burns, head for the nearest spa where they offer body treatments to help calm down the heat and ease the pain – as well as make you feel pampered.

Ciguatera: This is a natural toxin that shows up occasionally in warm-water fish, resulting in numbness and tingling in the facial area, which may spread to the extremities, causing nausea, vomiting, severe headache and diarrhea. The headaches and neurological symptoms are what set this nasty reaction apart from run-of-the-mill food poisoning. Onset of the symptoms comes within six hours of ingesting the poisoned fish. The bad news is that there are no tests for it in humans or fish, and no unified records of incidents to track. The good news is that it shows up on a not-too-frequent basis in the Caribbean. The best way to avoid it is by not eating native-caught fish such as grouper, barracuda, snapper, jack, mackerel, and triggerfish (so just watch these beauties while snorkeling and leave them in the water). If you begin to feel ill after eating fish, contact a local doctor to see if there are any reported ciguatera outbreaks in the area.

Coral: While coral is indeed beautiful, it is a living creature and will inflict pain if you get close enough to touch. So be aware of your surroundings when snorkeling or diving, and don't let your arms or legs stray into danger. The environmentalists will thank you too, because many people think nothing of damaging these fragile habitats by standing on the reefs or breaking off pieces of coral that have been growing for years.

Manchineel trees: In this case Mother Nature put trees that are poisonous and drip caustic sap right at the edge of beaches where people are looking for shade or protection from a sudden shower. These short trees, with small round fruit that look like apples and shiny round leaves, are pretty to look at, but don't eat the fruit or mess with the leaves. And if it starts raining, fight your natural instincts to take cover. Instead, quickly move your towels, gear and body away from the branches.

Mosquitos: These buggers are everywhere, and I'm thoroughly convinced they know the difference between natives and visitors. People who live on the island are seemingly oblivious to the bites that plague tourists. And, because it's so fashionable to have open-air dining and living areas, you cannot escape them. The mosquito nets some hotels provide are not there to add colonial ambiance – use them at every opportunity. Think of repellent as necessary, and apply it every time you go out in the evening – even during the day if you don't anticipate putting on a lot of sun block. If you forget to use it, check with the bar or restaurant you are visiting to see if they have a repellent on hand you can borrow.

Sand Flies or "No-See-Ums": Another plague on mankind, these little critters are also sneaky. If you linger on a beach to take photos of a sunset, be aware that you may be under siege, but you won't realize you've been bitten until the middle of the night when your ankles suddenly feel like they are on fire and your legs start looking like you have smallpox. It's wise to stay off the beach sand at dusk when they are most active.

PASSPORT ALERT!

It used to be that if you were traveling to the Caribbean from the US, you only needed a driver's license to get in and out, and children under 12 needed only birth certificates. But, as of Dec. 31, 2006, all US citizens, including children, returning to the US from any Caribbean destination other than Puerto Rico or the US Virgin Islands must have a valid passport. It's all part of additional security requirements put in place after 9/11. Many islands have followed suit and now require them for entry.

To find out how to get a passport, visit the State Department's travel website at www.travel.state.gov, or call the US National Passport Information Center at ☎877-487-2778. For a list of the more than 7,700 post offices, town clerk's offices and other facilities where passport applications are processed, type in your ZIP code at www.iafdb.travel.state.gov.

Essential Packing List

To all but the die-hard traveler, packing is half the challenge of traveling. It's hard to remember everything, so here is a checklist of the most needed items that really should be in your suitcase:

- Mandatory documents such as passports, itineraries, airline tickets, traveler's checks, cash, credit cards, ATM cards, driver's licenses (if planning to rent a car or scooter)

- Prescription drugs
- Glasses, sunglasses, contact lens solution and backup lenses
- Important phone numbers
- Clothes and swimwear
- Sandals, sneakers and good hiking shoes
- Hats for sun protection
- Lots of sunscreen and lip block
- Bug repellent, bug repellent, and more bug repellent
- Toiletries
- A 220-to-110 voltage converter and set of plug adapters for appliances (necessary for Montserrat, St. Barts and St. Martin)
- Cell phone
- Camera and film or extra digital storage media
- Special film bag to protect high-speed film from airport X-rays, if you haven't gone digital
- Good map of your destination, although there are usually excellent, up-to-date ones free at the destination
- A copy of this guidebook, plus any articles or website info you've found
- A French mini-phrase book/dictionary (for St. Barts and St. Martin)
- Those books you've been meaning to read
- Small umbrella, just in case
- A rain poncho if you plan to hike in the rain forest
- Small alarm clock
- Plastic bags in gallon size (zip-locks are best) for wet clothes as well as a couple of quart-sized bags that always come in handy for something
- Sports gear (snorkel, mask, etc.)
- Binoculars
- Spare batteries for cameras, clocks, etc.
- Small flashlight
- Travel candles in small metal or glass containers, preferably with citronella or other mosquito-repelling ingredients
- MP3 or CD player with CDs plus portable speakers, or iPod
- Names & addresses for postcards, preferably on mailing labels to make it easy

US DUTY-FREE REGS

Before you go shopping in the duty-free paradise of the Caribbean, you should know what you can bring back at no extra cost.

US citizens, regardless of age, who have been out of the US for at least 48 hours are entitled to an $800 duty-free tax exemption. Families traveling together can pool their exemptions, so even though the kids don't buy jewelry, they give you another $800 in

Introduction

exemptions. You can also bring in one quart of liquor per person, but the person needs to be at least 21 years of age. The value of the liquor is included in the $800 exemption. Also, purchasing and bringing in Cuban cigars is a big no-no.

For more details, see www.cbp.gov, and click on the "Travel" tab at the top. Go to the publication "Know Before You Go."

Lesser Antilles

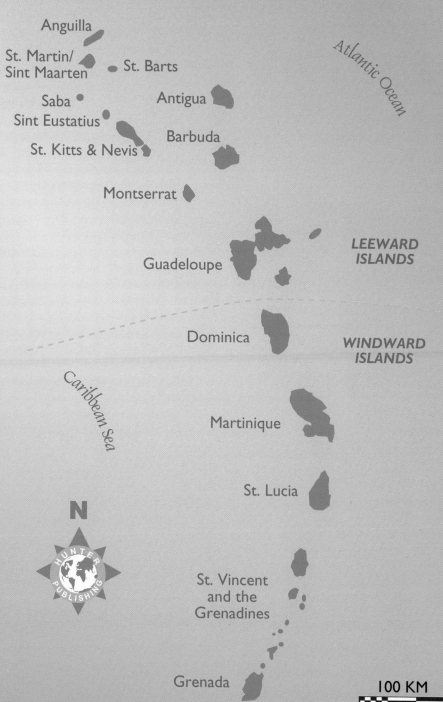

Anguilla

St. Martin/ Sint Maarten   St. Barts

Saba
Sint Eustatius

St. Kitts & Nevis

Antigua

Barbuda

Montserrat

Atlantic Ocean

LEEWARD ISLANDS

Guadeloupe

Dominica

WINDWARD ISLANDS

Caribbean Sea

Martinique

St. Lucia

N

St. Vincent
and the
Grenadines

Grenada

100 KM

60 M

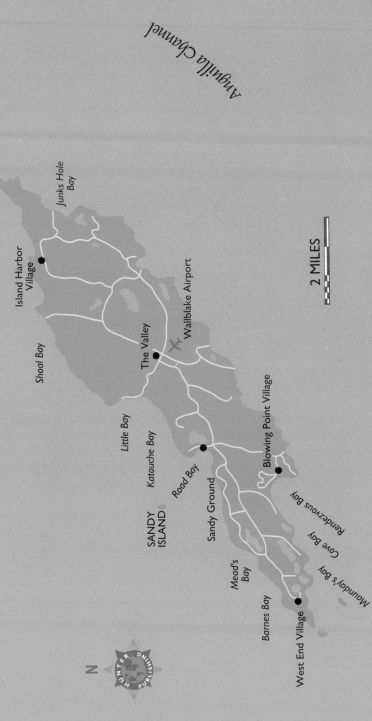

Anguilla

SCRUB ISLAND

Anguilla Channel

Junks Hole Bay

Island Harbor Village

Shoal Bay

The Valley

Wallblake Airport

Little Bay

Katouche Bay

SANDY ISLAND

Road Bay

Sandy Ground

Blowing Point Village

Rendezvous Bay

Cove Bay

Maunday's Bay

Mead's Bay

Barnes Bay

West End Village

N

2 MILES

Anguilla
The Allure of the Island

The continually expanding popularity of Anguilla, especially with the rich and famous, has caught everyone by surprise. After all, at first glance Anguilla looks to be nothing special. It's a long, narrow flat island, 16 miles long by three miles wide, with constant droughts and a notable absence of the lush rainforests, beautiful mountains, rushing rivers or deep canyons that normally provide all the activities today's tourist clamors for.

But Anguilla's trump card is its beaches. Spectacular even in this region where above-average beaches are the norm, Anguilla's wide swaths of sparkling white sand and bright turquoise waters teeming with tropical fish are indeed something special. It's a point well taken by island planners and developers who have built luxury resorts on those beaches. Many of those resorts quickly qualified as prime hotels of the world. Properties like Cap Juluca, CuisinArt and Malliouhana are routinely ranked at the top of the "best" lists in *Caribbean Travel & Life*, *Conde Nast Traveler*, and *Travel & Leisure*.

Besotted visitors have created a market for luxury villa and home sales

Sandy Ground Beach

Anguilla's southern coast

that have developers madly working to provide choices for them. Covecastles and Altamer were among the first individual-owner villas; their units are sold and now are available for vacation rentals. They have since been joined by other impressive developments, among them the St. Regis Temenos, the Viceroy and Cerulean, and there are a number of private individual villas dotting the landscape all over the island. These new homes not only add to the available rooms for visitors, but also provide a significant boost to the local economy as contractors, interior designers and support service providers keep employment and retail sales high.

What is the reaction of native Anguillians to all this? Gratefully, a welcoming one. Anguillians have a long history of looking after each other and visitors. They enjoy sharing their island with visitors, and you'll find you are received with warmth and goodwill. Their history is rich with examples of "jollifications" or merry festivities where a whole village gathered to plant crops, raise a house or build a boat as a team. Everyone was there to help each other, and money was never exchanged. This spirit of oneness extended into an understanding of hospitality in the truest sense of the word. Make sure you plan activities that take you out of your hotel and into the villages so you can meet some of "the belongers," as they call themselves.

More than any other Leeward Island, Anguilla has a wealth of beautiful villas in all sizes and shapes, along with world-class hotels, five-star restaurants, lots of activities and incredible beaches. If there aren't enough activities, shopping, restaurants or nightlife for you, St. Martin is only a short ferry ride away.

Here's What to Look For According to the Type of Traveler You Are:

The Perfect Cruise Passenger will love the luxury and all-inclusive feel of Cap Juluca, CuisinArt or Malliouhana resorts, where you can arrange for a MAP or FAP plan to make your stay truly all-inclusive. The concierges at those hotels are glad to arrange day-long excursions and direct you to pretty much anything you would want to do. Do make a point of going off the property, if only to enjoy the night life at the Dune Preserve or the Pumphouse.

The Boots-On Adventurer will enjoy exploring Anguilla's seven marine parks and other spectacular sites. To get away from the crowds, take a picnic lunch to Scrub Island and wander through the airplane wreck site and abandoned resort. If you are really up for an exploration, charter a fishing boat to take you to Sombrero Island, 40 miles to the north, to see the lighthouse and then spend the day pursuing marlin or tuna in the waters off that island. For basic accommodations, Alamanda Beach Club, Anguilla Great House or Arawak Beach Inn have reasonable prices.

The Cultural Explorer should include a visit to the Anguilla Arts & Crafts Center in the Valley and the Heritage Collection Museum in East End Village. If you love collecting art from local artisans, see the section *Finding Great Finds* for a list of art galleries. For a stay with an authentic Anguillian feel, look at Lloyd's Bed & Breakfast or Nathan's Cove.

The "I Like What I Like" Traveler has a number of choices of luxurious villas that can be arranged to suit your particular needs, or you can choose a luxury resort with lots of dining options and attentive service. The restaurants offer a great variety of cuisines, and you'll be happy to find that even the beach shacks and West Indian restaurants have hamburgers and other American staples to fall back on if you don't want to be gastronomically adventurous.

The Incurable Romantic can find a real home in Anguilla. The high-end hotels offer beautiful settings at every turn, with service that will make you feel pampered. The island also has a wealth of beach restaurants where you can watch the sunset and enjoy a great meal. In some, like Jazz'eez or Johnno's, you can stay after dinner to listen to the bands and take a turn on the dance floor. For true solitude, get a picnic lunch from Fat Cat Gourmet and hire a boat to take you to Scrub Island or Dog Island, where you can find a beach with no one else lying about.

The Family Social Director will love the selection of private villas where you can set up your kitchen and dining to accommodate children's needs. One outstanding resort for families with children is Malliouhana, where they have a pirate ship and playground as well as a video arcade for older children. For family adventures, see the section on *Family Fun* for information on the Dolphin Discovery and the Play-A-Round amusement center. Take the kids on one of the glass-bottom boat tours, and then plan a visit to a day spa for a little quiet time and rejuvenation on your own.

The Ultimate Shopper will find some quality shops on the Main Road at West End, where there is a collection of galleries and clothing and souvenir stores in one area. The boutiques at Cap Juluca, CuisinArt and Malliouhana are also great places to find some unique and beautiful items. Want more? Hop a ferry and take a day to visit the duty-free shops in St. Martin, where you'll find an incredible array of jewelry, clothing, perfume and electronics.

A Brief History

The history of Anguilla is the history of a people who have faced hardships not known on other islands – such as drought and famine – and survived with an amazingly resilient and independent spirit. The first settlers, as in most of the Caribbean, were the Arawak Indians, a peaceful, agrarian society that left

Arawak Spirit Eues carving at Big Spring

behind artifacts and petroglyphs in the caves of Big Springs at Island Harbour and The Fountain at Shoal Bay. They first called the island "Malliouhana," a type of sea serpent, because of the island's shape.

Although Christopher Columbus sailed by Anguilla, he did not set foot on it or name it as he so freely did throughout the rest of the Leewards. However, when they made their maps, the Europeans called the island Anguilla, a genus of eel, again in reference to the island's shape.

The first British settlers came to the island in 1650, and although lack of fresh water presented a problem for farming, the settlers found the soil well suited to tobacco and corn. When the British arrived there were no Arawaks living on the island, but Caribs from neighboring islands attacked and destroyed the settlement in 1656. The settlers persisted in spite of this.

The French captured the island in 1666. It was returned to British control by the Treaty of Breda in 1667. A joint Irish and French attack in 1688 forced most of the inhabitants to immigrate to Antigua. Those that remained faced severe hardship as neither the tobacco nor the cotton crops produced much revenue. This led to further migration, and by 1694, many had left the island for the Virgin Islands and other neighbors.

The hardy lot that remained replaced tobacco and cotton with sugar, which, in turn, paved the way for the growth of the plantation system and its demand for slave labor. Progress was frequently halted by European political conflicts, which led to raids and attacks by nations interested in controlling whatever parts of the Caribbean they could.

An old prison of coral stone still stands in South Hill

In 1744, in a move to improve their conditions and exert more control over their fate, 300 Anguillians captured the French portion of St. Martin. The French retaliated, but their troops were repelled by the local militia. The French attacked again in 1796, but this time a British frigate, the HMS *Lapwing*, came to the Anguillians' rescue and repelled the French.

The British finally took real control, and in 1825 grouped Anguilla with St. Kitts and Nevis in a federation allowing the Anguillians to send one delegate to the St. Kitts House of Assembly. The island lived in relative peace from then on, with occasional mass migrations when droughts and famines peaked.

But, while other islands were flourishing with large sugar plantations, the thin soil and infrequent rain left Anguilla with small estates that could not use many slaves. Those that were employed tended to their own garden plots, and eventually developed into individual peasant farmers or took to the sea as fishermen or sailors. By the time slavery officially ended, the population had dwindled to less than 2,000 people, as many Anguillians had left the island to work in the cane fields of Santo Domingo or the oil refineries of Aruba and Curacao.

As with the other British-controlled islands, Anguilla was granted universal adult suffrage in 1952. In 1958, the island became part of the Federation of the West Indies, remaining under British control. In 1962, the federation fell apart, and the individual islands of Antigua, St. Kitts, Nevis and Anguilla were granted statehood in association with Great Britain. The creation of the Associated State of St. Kitts-Nevis-Anguilla was finalized in 1967, without endorsement of the Anguillian population.

On May 30th, 1967, now celebrated as Anguilla Day, a crowd demanding independence from the St. Kitts-Nevis confederation marched on police headquarters and physically expelled the police. A peacekeeping committee was set up to run the affairs of the island until elections could take place. That committee approved another attack on the Defense Force camp and police headquarters, which resulted in a draw. After several years of negotiation with the British government, Anguilla became a separate British Dependent Territory on December 19, 1980.

The Facts

Population: 13,500, with 90% black ethnicity and a large expat community of American, British and Canadian origin.

Language: English, with a West Indian lilt.

Main City: The Valley, in the center of the island.

Government & Economy: The official head of state for Anguilla is Queen Elizabeth II, who is represented on the island by an appointed governor. Elections are held every five years (the next being in 2010), where seven of the 11 House of Assembly members are popularly elected. The other members are ex officio and appointed. The head of the majority coalition is usually appointed chief minister by the governor, and he (no she, so far) heads an executive council appointed by the governor from members of the Assembly. Justice is meted out by a High Court, with a judge provided by the Eastern Caribbean Supreme Court.

The economy depends heavily on tourism, lobster fishing and remittances from those Anguillians living elsewhere. Over the past few years the construction sector has grown considerably because of the impressive investment in tourism infrastructure and properties.

The government recognized the importance of the offshore financial sector of the economy and instituted the world's first online company registration system, known as ACORN. Authorized users can file company documents electronically from anywhere in the world, in six languages, across time zones, 365 days a year. Advantages of doing business in Anguilla include low registered office fees, low filing fees for International Business Corporations and free continuance into the jurisdiction. To support this business registration, the government also passed a number of acts to protect trademarks, copyrights and designs and to legislate mutual funds and insurance activities.

People & Culture: The Anguillians are very hospitable and proud people. They have a good sense of their history, which they celebrate in events such as the Summer Festival (akin to other islands' carnivals). They also reflect their British heritage through observance of the Queen's Birthday and other public holidays. You can see the British influence in cultural markers such as the afternoon tea observed at many of the hotels. Primarily Christian, the population enjoys access to many churches, with approximately one church for every two square miles.

One of the island's prime activities is boat racing. During the annual Heineken Cup Race held in August, big fancy boats come from other islands to race. But the real heart of Anguillian racing revolves around home-made boats in races usually sponsored by a village or a community group. The boats are simple wooden sailing craft, with open hulls, colorfully painted to distinguish one from another (to see some of these boats, check out the Anguilla Sailing Association website at www.sailanguilla.com). Most holidays are not complete without a race, and everyone turns out at the shore to watch.

Anguilla also has a flourishing artists' community of native painters, potters and woodworkers, as well as foreign-born artists who have made their home here. There are many galleries where you will find their work on sale (see the *Finding Great Finds* section below for more on these).

Sailing in the Anguilla Regatta

Geography: The eel-shaped island is 16 miles long and three miles wide. Once lush with dense rainforests, the island is now flat and dry, with an irregular coastline edging numerous bays and beaches. In addition, there are several uninhabited islands fringing the coastline, including Scrub Island, Anguillita Island, Sandy Island, Seal Island and Prickly Pear Cays.

Climate: With an 80°F monthly mean temperature and trade winds from the Atlantic keeping it pleasantly cool at night, the climate is ideal any time of the year. Rain is relatively scarce and fresh water is precious, gathered primarily in the rainy summer months. Hurricane season runs from June through November, but the island, like most of the Leewards, has been blessed with relatively few storms over the past 10 years.

Flora & Fauna: The dry climate provides a hospitable place for typical tropical plants, flowers, trees and wildlife. Around the hotels and villas are bougainvilleas, oleanders, croton, Indian lilac, and hibiscus. Drought-tolerant plants including sea cotton, aloe, green agave and organ pipe cactus thrive in the native brush.

Anguilla is home to more than 100 species of land, sea and wetland birds, both resident and migratory. The many salt ponds throughout the island provide good breeding grounds for wetland birds, including the egret, banana quit, frigate bird,

Oleander

Island orchid

West Indies whistling duck, Antillean crested hummingbird, and brown pelican. In a census done of the outer islands in 2004, species such as brown boobies, red-billed tropicbirds, laughing gulls, brown noddies and several species of terns were observed.

Visit the **Anguilla National Trust** office on Albert Lake Drive in the Valley to purchase a bird-watching guide and other helpful publications.

Also living on Anguilla are iguanas, corn snakes and a variety of

lizards. Hawksbill, leather-back, loggerhead and green sea turtles are frequently spotted in areas all around the island and are the subject of active conservation measures. The peak season for sighting them is April through November, and the best beaches for sightings are Maunday's Bay, Mead's Bay, Captain's Bay and Limestone Bay.

Laughing gull

Travel Information

When to Go

 The climate in Anguilla is delightful year-round, although many travelers prefer going to the Caribbean when northern temperatures turn cold and they are facing the prospect of traveling to work on snow-covered streets. However, summer is a good time to visit all the Leewards because the hotel rates are lower and the sea water is clear, calm and warm; summer is also the time when major events take place. In Anguilla, the special summer attractions include the Summer Carnival and the Heineken Cup Regatta.

Getting There

As with all islands, there are two ways to get to Anguilla – by air and by sea. While no major US airlines have direct flights to the island, there are many connecting flights from San Juan, Antigua and Sint Maarten to the Wallblake Airport on Anguilla. A more picturesque way to arrive is on one of the many ferries that run between Anguilla and St. Martin/Sint Maarten daily. Departure tax from the airport is US$20, and at the ferry terminal it is US$3.

> Note that American citizens are required to have a passport to get into Anguilla and to return to the US, as well as to enter St. Maarten/St. Martin.

By Air

 Wallblake Airport, near the Valley in the center of the island, underwent significant renovation in 2004. It now has a 5,400-ft runway, a new ground lighting system, an upgraded terminal and more parking. It is serviced by a number of airlines, including:

American Eagle, with flights to and from San Juan twice a day. ☎ 800-433-7300, www.aa.com.

LIAT, with a daily flight to and from Antigua. ☎ 264-497-5002, www.liatairline.com.

Rainbow International Airways, with private jet charter service non-stop from Miami and Atlanta for up to eight passengers. ☎ 264-476-4367, info@tgvconsulting.com.

Anguilla

TransAnguilla, with a daily flight to and from St. Maarten as well as charter flights to many Caribbean destinations. ☎ 264-497-8690, www.transanguilla.com.

WinAir, with several flights a day to and from St. Maarten. ☎ 264-497-2748, www.fly-winair.com.

Island Charters, with private jet charters between St. Maarten/St. Martin and Anguilla. ☎ 264-497-4064.

By Water

One of the more scenic ways to arrive on Anguilla is by ferry from St. Martin run by The Link (www.link.ai). Boats run roughly three times a day between Blowing Point, Anguilla and either Marigot Bay, St. Martin or the dock near the Princess Juliana Airport, St. Maarten. From St. Martin the first departure is at 8:45 am and the last at 4 pm; from Anguilla the first departure is at 10 am and the last at 5 pm. Costs range from US$12 to $15 each way, plus a $5 departure tax from each island. Schedules constantly change, so be sure to call the Link office for updates, ☎ 264-581-4152/264-497-2231.

Reservations are not necessary, so you can plan the crossing at your convenience. Simply check in at the ferry terminal, where you will receive a boarding pass, and then go to a separate window to pay the departure tax (be sure to bring your passport – Anguilla requires them for entry). The ferry fare will be collected while you are en route. The boats are spacious and comfortable. Luggage is permitted on board.

Funtime Charters operates a powerboat transfer service between the Stop & Shop dock near Princess Juliana Airport in Sint Maarten and Blowing Point. The 46-ft boat, capable of carrying 20 passengers, makes three trips a day between the two islands. ☎ 264-497-8106, www.funtimeai.com.

Another way to arrive by water is on a private yacht or boat charter. Many of these are run by the regular charter boat operators (see the section on *Exploring* for specifics), and some are recommended by the resorts. Again, you will need to provide your passport when the boat pulls into the Anguillian port.

Customs

The customs requirements are relatively simple and straightforward. Each visitor is allowed to bring into Anguilla food for their own consumption plus one bottle of spirits duty-free.

Special Events & Holidays

January

New Year's Day, January 1 – Public holiday.

National Arts & Craft Exhibition – At the Anguilla Craft Shop.

Police Week.

February

St. Gerard's Garden Party – At the Church Grounds.

ABC Annual Flower Show.

March

Annual Moonsplash Music Festival – Occurs on the weekend of the full moon in March. The festival showcases Caribbean and international talent at the Dune Preserve, Rendezvous Bay West. ☎ 264-497-6219, dunepreserve.com.

April

Good Friday – Public holiday.

Easter Monday – Public holiday. Easter Monday Boat Racing and Beach Party with Fun Day rallies, sport meets, family gatherings & picnics.

May

Whit Monday – Public holiday.

Annual "Go...Mix It Up" Yacht Regatta.

Anguilla Day, May 30 – Commemorates the beginning of the Anguillian Revolution (May 30, 1967); parade and around-the-island Boat Race that ends in Sandy Ground.

June

Anguilla Day Gospel Explosion.

Miss Venus Swimsuit Competition.

Celebration of Her Majesty Queen Elizabeth's Birthday, May 12 – Public holiday. Parade at Ronald Webster's Park.

July

John T. Memorial Annual Cycling Race – Starts in the Valley, sponsored by the Anguilla Cycling Association.

Miss Tiny Tot Pageant – Pre-Summer Festival Event.

Ms. Ecstasy Regional Talent Pageant – Pre-Summer Festival Event.

Miss Anguilla Swimsuit Competition – Pre-Summer Festival Event.

August

Anguilla Summer Festival – Cultural celebration including parades, boat races, calypso and soca competitions, pageants, street jam and fireworks. ☎ 264-497-8458, axasummerfestival.com.

Heineken Cup Boat Race at Sandy Ground – Sponsored by the Anguilla Sailing Association. ☎ 264-584- 7245, www.sailanguilla.com.

Constitution Day – Colorful parade of troupes through the Valley.

November

Tranquility Jazz Festival – Event features regional and international jazz musicians, with venues throughout the island. ☎ 264-497-2759, 800-553-4939 US, www.anguillajazz.org.

Optimist Race Against AIDS – Sponsored by the Optimist Club of Anguilla. www.optimistaxa.org.ai.

December

Biennial Arts Festival.

Separation Day, December 19 – Public holiday.

Annual Christmas Tree Lighting – Coronation Avenue adorned with special festive lighting and representations of the Nativity. Sponsored by the Valley Community Group. Each night sees the hosting of various cultural activities. Begins approximately a week before Christmas.

Christmas Day, December 25 – Public holiday.

Boxing Day, December 26 – Public holiday.

Health

The island's primary medical facility is **Princess Alexandra Hospital**, located in the Valley. ☎ 264-497-2551. In addition, the **Hughes Medical Center** offers private medical care and is particularly noted for its plastic surgery practitioners. ☎ 264-497-3053. For more serious cases, the hospital can arrange for transport to a medical facility in Miami.

There is also a **Dental Health Unit** in the Valley that is available for routine and emergency procedures. ☎ 264-497-2343/3342. For over-the-counter and first aid supplies, there are several pharmacies on the island.

AN HERBAL REMEDY FOR CANCER AND AIDS?

Anguilla is also known for its strong orientation to holistic health care, as witnessed by the many yoga teachers, massage therapists and other types of practitioners on the island. An alternative caregiver getting international attention is **John E. Edwards**, an herbalist known as Dr. John or "Thunder." Although he has no formal medical training, he has extensive native training and instinctual knowledge of the healing properties of herbs. Dr. John has been prescribing cures for Anguillians and visitors for over 40 years.

In the mid-1990s, Dr. John's growing reputation for curing various types of cancer and managing HIV/AIDS caused the government to provide him with a building for his "practice," which he has called Nature's Gift Clinic. International researchers – including the Harvard AIDS Institute – are probing his herbal cures. Medical doctors in Anguilla, St. Maarten and other islands have also begun verifying anecdotal evidence claiming that his remedies have put AIDS patients into remission.

Appointments can be made with Dr. John at the Nature's Gift Clinic in South Hill ☎ 264-497-8220.

Pets

Visitors traveling with pets should contact the Agricultural Department for the Import Permit form that your veterinarian must complete (☎ 264-497-2615). The form must be dated 10 days or less before your arrival on Anguilla, and indicate when your pet had its last rabies vaccination. Since Anguilla does not honor the two-year cycle used in the US, the pet must have had its shot within a year of your arrival.

Crime

There is very little crime on Anguilla because the island is so small and everyone knows everyone else (or is related in some way). However, tourists are urged to take the usual precautions of safeguarding valuables and locking doors.

Electricity

Voltage throughout the island is 110, so Americans don't need converters.

Tipping

By and large, the island follows the US style of tipping, with no automatic addition. A range of 10 to 15% is welcomed for all services, including those of restaurants, taxis, hotel bellmen and others.

Money Matters

 Anguilla's economy is based on the Eastern Caribbean dollar, or EC, with a set exchange rate of EC$2.70 to US$1. However, visitors from the US could spend their entire stay without ever seeing an EC dollar, because most of the restaurants, hotels and shops take US dollars and major credit cards. The four banks on the island, **ScotiaBank**, **National Bank of Anguilla**, **Caribbean Commercial Bank** and **First Caribbean Bank**, all have ATMs where you can get cash advances in US dollars on your Visa or MasterCard, or by using any card in the Cirrus or Plus networks. In addition, there are ATM machines at Wallblake Airport and in many of the grocery stores.

> **Tip:** To determine the US dollar equivalent of a price given in EC, just divide the EC cost in half, and then take away another 25% or one-fourth of that figure. Example: EC$68 would be US$34 minus $8, for a rough estimate of US$26 (if you used a calculator, the exact amount is US$25.18).

Weddings

 If you want a wedding on the beach, you have the right island. Most of the hotels offer wonderful settings for that special occasion as well as services to support the bride and groom.

Government regulations on obtaining a license are fairly straightforward. License application can be obtained from the **Judicial Department** in the Valley (☎ 264-497-2377/3347) on weekdays from 8:30 am to noon, and 1 to 2:30 pm; the license takes 48 hours to process. Applicants must have valid passports or proof of identification with a photo and, if married before, some documentation that they are now single, such as a divorce decree or death certificate of a deceased spouse and previous marriage certificate. All documents must be in English.

The fees vary by length of residence. If one of the partners has resided in Anguilla for at least 15 days prior to registering for the license, the cost of the license is waived but a stamp duty of EC$100 is required. This means one of the partners has to go to the Anguillian post office and purchase that amount of stamps. If the stay is shorter, the total cost is US$279, which includes the stamp duty.

Internet Access

Because of the number of US tourists, the island is quite advanced in technology. Most hotels offer in-room high-speed Internet access (for an additional fee). High-speed Internet access providers include Cable and Wireless and Caribbean Cable broadband connections.

Communications

The island's cell phones are provided by **Cable & Wireless** (☎ 268-480-4000 or 800-804-2994, www.anguillanet.com) and **Digicel** (☎ 264-498-7500, www.digicalanguilla.com). Some US cell phones work in Anguilla because of reciprocal arrangements with local providers. For example, Cable & Wireless has a relationship with T-Mobile and Digicel is connected with Cingular, so phones using those carriers work in Anguilla. You can also purchase SIM cards locally for your phone, if it is compatible with the local system.

Media

If you have to have news from the world outside this paradise, the *Wall Street Journal* and *London Financial Times* are available at some of the grocery and drug stores and at the airport. Local media include *The Anguillian*, a weekly publication (also found at www.anguillian.com), and *The Light*, another weekly paper. The St. Martin newspaper, *The Daily Herald*, is available as well in many places on the island.

The television cable system, **Caribbean Cable Television**, carries primarily US stations and cable networks. ☎ 264-497-3600.

Sources of Information

For more information, go to the Anguilla Tourist Board website at www.anguilla-vacation.com, or contact the offices below.

In the US: Mrs. Marie Walker, Anguilla Tourist Board, 246 Central Ave., White Plains, NY 10606, ☎ 914-287-2400, toll free 1-877-4-ANGUILLA, fax 914-287-2404, mwturnstyle@aol.com.

In Canada: William & Sari Marshall, Xybermedia, 33 Hazelton Ave., Suite 400, Toronto, Ontario, Canada M5R 2E3, ☎ 416-923-9813, toll free 1-877-GO ANGUILLA, fax 416-944-3191, info@go-anguilla.com.

In the UK: Carolyn Brown, CSB Communications, 7A Crealock St., London SW18 2BS, ☎ 011-44-208-871-0012, fax 011-44-207-207-4323, anguilla@tiscali.co.uk.

In France: Gerard Germin, c/o Sergat SARLl, 745 av. Du General Leclerc, 92100 Boulgne, France, ☎ 011-33-1-4608-5984, fax 011-33-1-4609-9676, anguillaparis@wanadoo.fr.

In Germany: Ms. Rita Morozow, c/o Sergat Deutschland IM Guldenen Wingert 8-C D-64342 Seeheim, Germany, ☎ 011-49-6257-962920, fax 011-49-6257-962919, rmorozow@t-online.de.

In Italy: **Anguilla Tourist Board**, c/o De Paoli Associate Communications, via Del Mare, 47 20142 Milan, Italy, ☎ 39 02 89 53 41 08, fax 39 02 84 60 841, anguilla@depaoliassociati.com.

In Anguilla: **The Anguilla Tourist Board**, Coronation Avenue, The Valley, Anguilla, BWI, ☎ 264-497-2759, toll free 800-553-4939, fax 264-497-2710, atbtour@anguillanet.com.

Getting Around

Like most of the islands once under British rule, Anguilla is a country where driving is done on the left. It's not difficult to get used to, once you train yourself to know the correct way to look for oncoming traffic. If you are willing to try, there are many car rental companies on the island. But remember, the speed limit in Anguilla never exceeds 30mph, and West Indians are prone to not only the speed limit, but also the usual cautions against passing on a curve or when there is a line of traffic. So be careful.

Street signs aren't plentiful, but everyone knows the island, so don't hesitate to stop and ask for directions. It's only three miles wide, and the roads lead to the resorts in a sort of loop, so you really can't get lost. If you opt out of driving, the taxi drivers are great guides as well as competent drivers. Make friends with one you like, and he'll try to accommodate all your requests during your stay.

Airport

The modernized **Wallblake Airport** is small but welcoming, and you should have little problem going through customs and getting your baggage.

Taxi Service

You can easily pick up a taxi at the airport or at Blowing Point where the ferry arrives. If you want to arrange something in advance, call the **Anguilla National Taxi Association** for a referral. They have offices at the airport (☎ 264-497-5054) and Blowing Point (☎ 264-497-6089).

The fares are set by the government and usually include the first two people, with a surcharge for extra passengers. The typical two-hour island tour is US$40 for two. Here are some point-to-point fares (all in US dollars) from the major points of entry:

Airport to Meads Bay $16
Blowing Point to Meads Bay. $14
Airport to West End hotels $22
Blowing Point to West End $20
Airport to Sandy Ground $10
Blowing Point to Sandy Ground $10
Airport to Shoal Bay East. $15
Blowing Point to Shoal Bay East $20

Car Rentals

The many car rental agencies on the island offer everything from 'jeeps' (any SUV) to compact cars. You will need to obtain an Anguillian drivers' license, available through any of the car rental agencies. The fee is US $20, and you must be able to show a valid driver's license from your home area.

Car Rental Agencies

Avis Rent-A-Car . . . . . 264-497-2642, avisasa@anguillanet.com
Bass Car Rental 264-497-2361
Carib Rent-A-Car. 264-497-6020
Connor's Car Rentals 264-497-6433
Freeway Car Rental. 264-497-6621, flemingw@anguillanet.com
Hertz. 264-497-2934
Highway Rent-A-Car . . . . 264-497-2183, www.rentalcars.ai
Island Car Rental 264-497-2723
Junie's Car Rental . . 264-497-7114, juniorconnor@hotmail.com
Pete's Car Rental . . . . 264-497-6296, petesrentacar@yahoo.com
Richardson's Agency 264-498-8900, sandra_d@anguillanet.com
Summer Set Car Rental . . . . 264-497-5278, www.summerset.ai
Wendell Connors Car Rental 264-497-6894

Exploring

On Foot

As you wander the various beaches in Anguilla, you may notice lines of weathered gray fences partially covered with sand. These are part of a national effort to recover the sand dunes that were drastically over-mined for sand, which is used in construction and renewal of other beaches, effectively destroying beach habitats. The Anguilla National Trust has mounted an effort to rebuild the dunes to protect the coast from sea surges and hurricanes and create a safe habitat for plant and animal life – particularly the sea turtles. The Trust asks that you don't touch or lean on the fences and do not use the fences to tie up your pet or even to drape your towel. They are part of Anguilla's future, and must be kept in good condition today.

Hiking

Although Anguilla is flat and scrubby, many people enjoy hiking through the natural and historical sites of the island's interior. Maps to the various destinations can be obtained from the Anguilla National Trust. If you are looking for a guide, contact the Anguilla Tourism Board (☎ 264-497-2759) or the Trust to see who may be available when you are on the island.

If you want to strike out on your own, The Anguilla Guide website (www.anguillaguide.com) outlines five hikes of different parts of the island, as well as simple maps.

SPELUNKING YOUR WAY THROUGH THE ISLAND

Anguilla is mostly flat, but it has some interesting contours below ground. All over the island, there are holes and caves where gaps in the coral bed left air pockets and the surrounding rock eroded away or collapsed.

Some of the most interesting and accessible holes are:

■ **Abadam Hole**, near Windward Point. This hole descends 20 feet and is fed by underground streams so it is filled with water.

■ **Big Spring National Park** in Island Harbour. This collapsed cave has a natural spring and decorations courtesy of the

Arawak Indians. The government recently opened a new walking area through the springs.

■ **Pitch Apple Hole**, near Brimmigan, about one mile from the Valley. It's easy to tell where this hole is – a big Pitch Apple tree is growing out of the entrance.

■ **Iguana Cave**, at the beginning of the Katouche Trail. This simple cave has two rooms and a fig tree that grows through an opening towards the light.

■ **Blackgarden Hole**, east of Blackgarden. With underground access to the sea, the surges that come up through the hole make for some dramatic wind spray photos.

Two other caves, **The Fountain** and **Old Ta**, are not open to the public at this time. To see photos and get detailed directions, go to www.anguillaguide.com.

On Horseback

For a gallop across the beach and around the salt ponds, two stables offer horses for riding: **El Rancho del Blues** at Blowing Point, ☎ 264-497-6164; **Seaside Stables**, ☎ 264-235-3667, seashorses@caribcable.com.

On Wheels

By Car or Jeep

Most of the taxi drivers are available for guided tours, and many have mini-vans and larger vehicles to accommodate a crowd. Ask at your hotel for a referral, or talk to any driver you meet at the airport or at your hotel. Or see the *Car Rental* section above for an alternative to taxis.

On Water

Scuba Diving

Anguilla is building a solid reputation within the diving community as the sunken ships that began as artificial reefs in the marine parks have grown into natural structures. The marine parks are **Dog Island, Prickley Pear, Seal Island Reef System, Little Bay, Sandy Island, Shoal Bay Harbour Reef System** and **Stoney Bay Marine Park**. All divers in these parks must be accompanied by a certified Anguillian dive operator. For specifics on the sites, see the Anguilla Tourism Board's website at www. anguilla-vacation.com or the two dive operator websites listed below.

Divers agree that among the most commonly seen living treasures are turtles, sting rays, conchs, lobsters, reef fish and garden eels. Scrub Island is a favorite for those who like seeing sharks, and barracudas are said to like swimming around the wrecks.

Prickley Pear

Anguilla Dive Sites & Wreck Moorings
1. Mepel. 2. Sarah. Lady Vi. Commerce. 5. Ida Maria. 6. Oster Diep. 7. Cathley H. 8. Paintcan Reef. 9. Deep South. 10. Dougies Corner. 11. Sandy Deep. 12. Sandy Shallow. 13. No Name. 14. Prickley Pear. 15. Grouper Bowl. 16. Sandy Canyon. 17. Ritas Wall. 18. Little Bay. 19. Frenchman's Reef. 20. Authors Deep. 21. The Coliseum.

Dive Operators

Anguillian Divers conducts dives leaving from Cove Bay every morning in *Adventure*, a 31-ft specially equipped dive boat. They offer the usual range of PADI classes (including Discover Scuba for the beginner conducted in their own pool), plus snorkeling cruises, and diving trips to Sandy Island and Prickly Pear. The dive shop is behind La Sirena Hotel in the West End. ☎ 264-497-4750, www.anguilliandivers.com.

Shoal Bay Scuba is another PADI-certified dive operator that offers dive instructions and dive packages and trips. They operate from Shoal Bay in a custom-fitted boat named *Karma*. They also have a well equipped dive shop on Shoal Bay East next to Ku Hotel. ☎ 264-497-4371, www. shoalbayscuba.com.

Snorkeling

Snorkeling the coral reefs ringing the main island and the shoals around the offshore islands are ideal for those who love to peer into the deep without going *too* deep. Beaches that offer the ingredients to make snorkeling fun – close-in reefs, shallow water and calm seas – include **Shoal Bay East** (an easy snorkel), **Turtle Bay** (flat sea, lots of life), **Crocus Bay** (along a cliff wall), **Sandy Hill Bay** (a small area), **Savannah Bay** (can be rough at times), **Forest Bay** (rock formations right off shore), **Elsie Bay** (again, good snorkeling right off shore), **Barnes Bay** (with three good areas) and **Sea Feather's Bay** (very popular). More experienced snorkelers can find a boat at **Crocus Bay** that will take them over to **Little Bay** for a great underwater display.

In addition to Shoal Bay Scuba, you'll find other vendors who rent equipment and supply boats for off-shore trips to reefs. Dive operators also offer snorkeling trips to the outer islands and some of the reefs too far off shore to swim to comfortably.

Kayaking, Windsurfing, Sailing

One look at the bright turquoise water and white sand beaches, and you know you're destined to hit the waves on something that floats. Most of the hotels offer equipment for activities such as kayaking and Sunfish sailing on a complimentary basis; for a fee, you can rent things that go fast like windsurfing boards, water skis and towable

Windsurfing

floats. If you are staying in a villa, head to Shoal Bay East where **Shoal Bay Scuba** offers kayaks, Sunfish boats, windsurfing and Boogie boards, water skis and towable water toys. ☎ 264-497-4371, www.shoalbayscuba.com.

Deep-Sea Fishing

Anguilla offers a variety of fishing opportunities, from shallow bottom fishing to deep-sea excursions where the big ones lurk. The shallow areas surround the main island and extend to the reefs around the outer islands. You have to travel to Sombrero Island in the north and beyond to find deep water fish like tuna, marlin and wahoo.

Fishing Boat Operators

Bevis Rogers (nicknamed "Keg") takes sport fishermen out in the 28-ft *Keg 2* for a half-day or full day of deep-sea and bottom fishing. His boat, moored at Island Harbour, includes downriggers for deep-sea trawling. ☎ 264-497-4487.

Ed Carty offers the 31-ft Bertram called *Miss Daisy* for a half-day of fishing from Sandy Ground to the tuna bank off shore. Carty is said to be very knowledgeable and a great guide. ☎ 264-497-2337.

Captain Johnno, owner of Johnno's Restaurant at Sandy Ground, has been operating fishing charters for 20 years, and really knows the waters of Anguilla. He provides all the gear, including poles, lures and lunch. ☎ 264-497-2728, www.johnnos.com.

Shaun Liburd shares his deep-sea fishing expertise on trips aboard *No Mercy*; he also does island tours and snorkeling tours. ☎ 264-235-6283.

Shoal Bay Scuba offers the *Thomas B*, a Panga Classic specifically selected for deep-sea fishing because of its stability and adaptability. They offer half-day and full-day trips from Shoal Bay East. ☎ 264-497-4371, www.shoalbayscuba.com.

Water Tours

One of the preferred ways to see the shores and reefs of Anguilla is on a glass-bottomed boat, where little ones don't need to use snorkeling gear to see the wondrous world below the surface. A good choice for families.

Water Tour Operators

Junior's Glass Bottom Boat operates from Shoal Bay East. The captain leads guests on a multifaceted trip that includes snorkeling, touring the coast and visiting Scrub Island. He also teaches snorkeling, so first-timers in the family can get instructions before going out. ☎ 264-497-4456, www.junior.ai.

Mike's Glass Bottom Boat, run by Mike's father Hilton Fleming, operates out of Shoal Bay. He takes families out for an interesting view of the many reefs in the area. He also does trips to Scrub Island. ☎ 264-497-5641.

DAY TRIPPING TO THE OUT ISLANDS

Anguilla is a small island surrounded by even smaller islands offering beautiful, secluded beaches as well as lively restaurants, live music and a general good time. Be sure to visit one of them during your stay on the mainland.

Scilly Cay. This tiny coral-based island in the middle of Island Harbour features a restaurant owned by Sandra and Eudoxie Wallace and a great beach. To get there, go to the end of the dock in Island Harbour and wave to the boat person sitting and waiting on the island. He'll speed over to pick you up and take you to this island paradise. Your most difficult exertion will be getting all the luscious meat out of the grilled lobster. The restaurant is open Wednesday, Friday and Sunday for lunch, with live music on Wednesday and Sunday. ☎ 264-497-5123.

Prickly Pear Island. The restaurant here is run by the same people who own Johnno's Restaurant, so you know the food will be good. Bring your snorkel and beach towels and spend the day. The restaurant is open Tuesday through Sunday, and you reach the island on the *PP Express*, a 32-ft speedboat. The package tour offered by Johnno's includes boat transport, lunch and drinks, kayaks, beach lounges and snorkeling gear. ☎ 264-235-5864, www.johnnos.com.

Dog Island. This deserted island sits about one mile north of Prickly Pear. Some catamarans drop anchor in the coves to spend an afternoon on the beach, but the water is not great for snorkeling. There are no scheduled or regular boat trips to the island, but you can sometimes convince a boat captain headed to Prickly Pear to make a side-trip.

The reef off Dog Island

Scrub island

Scrub Island. The beaches on this three-square-mile island are good for sunning and snorkeling, but there are no facilities. The beach on the leeward side, closest to the mainland, is protected from the wind. You may also want to explore the interior, where you'll find an airplane wreck near the old airstrip, and an abandoned resort wrecked by Hurricane Luis. **Junior's** or **Mike's Glass Bottom Boats** at Shoal Bay provide transport to the island, or you can just go to Island Harbour and check at **Smitty's on the Beach** for a way to get across the water on any given day. Smitty's will also supply drinks and food to take along for your picnic.

Sandy Island. This island offshore at Sandy Ground is a major luncheon spot, due to the presence of the **Sandy Island Barbecue**, run by the same people who own Oliver's. You can pick up the shuttle boat *Shauna*, which leaves from the pier next to Johnno's every half-hour. The restaurant is open from noon to 4 pm every day except Saturday, so plan to go a little early. That way you can enjoy the beach and snorkel before lunch. It's a major limin' spot on Sundays with the draw being live entertainment. ☎ 264-497-8780, www.olivers.ai.

Sandy Island

Sombrero Island. This farthest point of Anguilla, 40 miles north of the mainland, is a rocky outcrop formerly used for phosphate mining. It is deserted now except for a lighthouse and the animals that live there, including the black lizard and many species of water birds. Birds you can encounter include the brown booby, brown noddy, bridled and sooty terns. Several years ago, a US aerospace company wanted to use the island for a rocket launching facility. The idea (an unpopular one with Anguillians and other environmentalists) was abandoned when the company realized that the island occasionally gets fully swamped by the ocean, with only the lighthouse standing out of the water. So the island is still deserted, and the waters around it have some of the best sport fishing spots in the area.

Boat Charters

There is no better way to set your own agenda for tooling around the beaches, reefs and offshore islands than by chartering your own boat.

Charter Boat Operators

Sail Chocolate catamaran

Sail Chocolate offers day charters and tours on a 35-ft Edel catamaran out of Sandy Ground for a quiet and pleasant day of sailing, snorkeling and swimming. ☎ 264-497-3394, www.sailinganguilla.com.

Funtime Charters has five powerboats, ranging from 32 to 38 feet, available for day-trips out of Cove Bay. They also offer airport charters and shopping trips to St. Martin. ☎ 264-497-6511, 264-235-8106, funtimeai.com.

Gotcha! Garfield's Sea Tours, based in Sandy Ground, has four powerboats in the 31- to 48-ft range for hire. ☎ 264-497-2956, 264-235-7902, gotcha@caribcable.com.

Offshore Sunsations offers powerboat package tours to the outer islands and sunset cruises; you can also ask for a customized trip or a ride to St. Martin's for dinner. *No Fear* is a 38-ftCigarette with 1,200 hp Chevy Cobra engines (think *Miami Vice*) that seats up to 10 people. The *Zippity Do Da*, a 42-ftChris Craft, runs a more sedate 700 hp engine, but is equally stylish. ☎ 599-552-6026 Saint Martin, 330-431-8722 US, www.offshoresunsations.com.

Eco-Travel

Being a flat island with many salt ponds, Anguilla is a bird haven. These ponds serve as sanctuary for more than 130 species of birds, including various species of pelicans, falcons, gulls, terns and herons. In 2006, the **Anguilla National Trust** opened the East End Pond Conservation Area as a prime bird-watching site, offering two observation facilities. This is one of the highlights of a guided bus tour the Trust conducts on Tuesdays and Thursdays for a minimal fee. To make reservations, call ☎ 264-497-5297. The organization also offers two valuable guides, *Bird Identification Cards* (US$5) and *A Field Guide to Anguilla's Wetlands* (US$10), that can be purchased at the Trust headquarters in the Valley. For more information, see www.axanationaltrust.org

At Sandy Ground, **Emile Gumbs** leads a walking tour that highlights the avian life and includes a short tour of Wallblake House. ☎ 264-497-2711.

Other ponds with sizeable bird populations can be easily observed at East End, West End and Little Harbour ponds.

Playing & Watching Sports

Regattas & Races

Anguilla Day boat race

With the island's love of boats and boat building, national holidays such as the May 30 Anguilla Day and the early August Carnival mean everybody pulls out the boats and gets onto the water. There's a flotilla of other major races, including:

The annual **"Go Mix It Up" Anguilla Yacht Regatta**, sponsored by the Anguilla Sailing Association, takes place in mid-May. It involves local races and other events, plus a lot of partying and prize-giving. ☎ 264-497-5438 or 264-235-8300, www.sailanguilla.com.

Another big one is the **Heineken Cup Race**, held during the Summer Festival in August. It's one of the highlights of that fortnight celebration of all things Anguillian. Find out more at the Festival's website, www.axasummerfestival.com.

If you're in Anguilla in early March, you may want to observe the activities of the **St. Maarten Heineken Regatta** in the waters between the two islands. This is a major international/Caribbean boat race that attracts family boats, bare boats, sports boats and other classes, all intertwined with entertainment and parties. ☎ 599-544-2079, fax 599-544-2091, www.heinekenregatta.com.

Golf

Golf is an ever-growing and popular activity on Anguilla. The **Temenos Anguilla Golf Club** opened in 2006, and offers a Greg Norman-designed, 18-hole, 7,200-yd. championship course with great views to the sea. The corporations are already lining up for tournaments at what is becoming known as one of the best courses in the Caribbean. Greens fees are steep, heading up to US$415 in high season. The course borders the tony St. Regis Residences and has its own clubhouse and restaurant. ☎ 264-498-7000, www.stregisresidences.com.

Tennis

One of the hardest-working sports groups in the Caribbean is the **Anguilla Tennis Academy**. In addition to offering courses to get young people involved in the sport from an early age, it is the force driving construction of a world-class tennis facility in Blowing Point. The complex will have seven courts (including one stadium court), lockers and administrative offices. Fundraising is underway and the projected completion date is still uncertain. For updates, see www.tennis.ai.

In the meantime, the ATA uses the two public courts at the **Ronald Webster Park** in the Valley, which means these courts are maintained and are ready for play. Many of the hotels also have courts and pros available.

Family Fun

Anguilla is a great place to keep children busy having fun. If they tire of the beach and pool, offer them a swim with dolphins (sure to excite even adults) at **Dolphin Discovery** at Mead's Bay. The facility houses two large tanks that allow all ages to get close enough for a kiss from one of these dolphin darlings. Older children and adults can ride the gentle water creatures, and there's an education program explaining the dolphins' special talents and needs. Be aware that for safety reasons pregnant women are not allowed in the water with the animals. ☎ 264-497-7946, 800-293-9698 US and Canada, www.dolphindiscovery.com.

Another lively place for the amusement of young and old is the **Play-A-Round** at Rendezvous Bay West, an 18-hole, par 43 miniature golf course where you'll play through waterfalls and fountains. For the endlessly energetic, there's a 24-ft-high rock climbing wall, bumper boats and an inflatable obstacle course for children. For a little educational recreation, take the kids through the Tiki huts that display highlights in Anguillian history. The clubhouse features a snack bar with live music on Fridays and can accommodate birthday parties and other events. ☎ 264-498-PLAY.

Seeing the Sights

Sampling the Culture

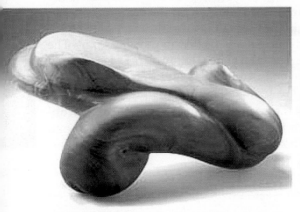

Sculpture by Courtney Devonish

One of the best ways to enjoy Anguilla's rich cultural history is to join in the revelry known as the **Summer Festival**, held each August. It goes on for weeks, and you'll be hard-pressed to catch all the activities and events. Beauty pageants for all ages, soca, reggae and calypso competitions and concerts, boat races, parades, and beach parties are just some of the festivities offered. This is a great time to taste a variety of homemade West Indian delicacies available at the local food vendor booths that line the streets during the festivities. It's the greatest concentration of culture in one place that you'll ever find.

By Cheddie Richardson

The visual arts are also a very popular pursuit in this island of beautiful vistas and gorgeous seas. Some works to look for as you peruse the galleries are those by Anguillians Roland Richardson, Cheddie Richardson, Michelle Owen-Vasillis, Louise Brooks, Courtney Devonish, Carolle Devonish and Daryl Thompson, and St. Lucian Kizzy Garconnette. The works of American transplants Lynne Bernbaum and Peg Gregory, and French-born Lydia Semeria are also worthy of note. The **Anguilla Arts & Crafts Center** in the Valley, next to the public library, is a good and reliable place to see and purchase locally made pottery, paintings, bags, hats, t-shirts,

Painting by Marjorie Morani

wood carvings, textile works and jewelry. The building is open from 9 am to 4 pm Monday through Friday. ☎ 264-497-2200.

Reliving History

For an overview of the history of Anguilla, visit the **Heritage Collection Museum**, across from the East End Pond bird sanctuary in East End Village. Colville Petty, an Officer of the British Empire (OBE), published writer and occasional Deputy Governor and Governor of the island, has filled this typical Anguillian wood structure with national treasures. A grand promoter of all things Anguillian, Petty can often be found at his museum, offering commentary and answering questions on his impressive collection of artifacts, photographs and documents tracing the history of the country. The museum is open Monday through Saturday from 10 am to 5 pm. ☎ 264-497-4092.

Wallblake House

For a look into the colonial side of Anguilla's past, you'll want to stop in the Valley to tour **Wallblake House.** Wallblake is the oldest surviving plantation house on the island and, perhaps more remarkably, it is one of the few plantation houses in the Caribbean with surviving outbuildings. Create your own stories as you wander through the kitchens, stables and workers' quarters original to the house. The house has been substantially restored and tours are conducted Monday, Wednesday and Friday from 10 am to 2 pm. See www.wallblake.com.

Big Spring Heritage Site in Island Harbour honors the contributions of the island's earliest settlers, the Amerindians. The site is jointly operated by the government and the Anguilla National Trust. Trust docents are available for guided tours of the ceremonial cavern and its rock markings. A walkway is provided for access. ☎ 264-497-5297, www. axanationaltrust.org.

Where to Stay

Luxe Resorts

$$$$$ – These are some of the best hotels in the world, not just in the Caribbean. Daily EP/BP rates in junior suites for two range from US $850 to more than $1,000 in high season, and from US$485 to $550 in low.

Cap Juluca

 This grand Moorish collection of villas by the sea appears regularly in *Travel & Leisure*'s list of the top hotels of the world and *CondeNast Traveler*'s Gold List routinely recognizes it as one of the outstanding resorts of the Caribbean. The setting is romantic and luxurious and the large, open rooms face the sea. Amenities include beautiful gardens, great restaurants, and a gorgeous white sand beach. The furnishings are contemporary, with Middle Eastern accents, and the service is ever-present but never overbearing. Those that return to Cap Juluca year-after-year delight in the little things, like the beach crew that anticipates the precise moment you need a cooling drink, a cup of sherbet or a cold-water face towel. It's an experience not to be missed.

Cap Juluca

Location: At the West End, on Maunday's Bay.

Rooms: 98 in all, with 18 buildings housing superior and luxury rooms, junior suites, one- and two-bedroom patio or private pool suites, and three- and five-bedroom villas. All have large marble baths, refrigerator, mini-bar, telephone and AC. Internet available for a fee.

Rates: BP, MAP or FAP.

Features: Continental breakfast served in room or on patio, three restaurants, three tennis courts, pool, beach, watersports, Golf Aqua driving range, putting green and bunker, spa, fitness center, croquet lawn, library, children's program, twice daily maid service, and daily eight-hour butler service in pool suites and villas.

☎ 264-497-6666, 888-8JULUCA US, fax 264-497-6617, www.capjuluca. com.

CuisinArt Resort & Spa

Gleaming white buildings set against a turquoise backdrop, surrounded by intense green tropical foliage – it's the image that remains in the mind of all who behold this beautiful resort. But CuisinArt is more than a collection of pretty buildings. The service is some of the best in the world, the accom-

CuisinArt Resort

modations are spacious, serene and luxurious, and the password here is indulgence. The emphasis is, of course, on cuisine. The resort offers weekly cooking classes in their special demonstration dining room as well as culinary weekend escapes and gourmet holiday packages. Be sure to ask for a tour of the hydroponics garden, the only one in the Caribbean.

Location: In West End, on Rendezvous Bay.

Rooms: 93 total, including luxury, junior suites, luxury junior suites, one-bedroom suites, luxury bedroom suites, and two penthouses. All have *luxe* marble baths, living areas, private balconies or terraces and TV/VCRs (some with Bose Wave Music System CD players).

Rates: BP, MAP and FAP.

Features: Two restaurants, three tennis courts, beach, watersports, fitness training classes, Venus Spa, children's playground and activities program during holidays, bocce court, croquet, billiards room, Internet access in lobby.

☎ 264-498-2000, 800-943-3210 US, fax 264-498-2010, www. cuisinartresort.com.

Malliouhana

While other luxury hotels in Anguilla go for Mediterranean styling, this one stays true to its roots with West Indian ambience and luxury. The walnut wood accents, light walls and tile offset the lush tropical greenery and sea views in a way that no other décor could. The resort is a regular on

Malliouhana

CondeNast Traveler Reader's Awards as a Best Caribbean Resort for many reasons. The service is accommodating and discreet, and the activities are plentiful. The resort's three beaches span a mile in front of the resort from Meads Bay to Turtle Cove. Children delight in a special beachside play with pirate ship (with water cannons), and a 60-ft waterslide. There is a toddler's pool and a covered area with a ping pong table, TV and video games. It's definitely a place that everyone will enjoy.

Location: On Meads Bay.

Rooms: 55, including garden-view doubles and one-bedroom suites, ocean-view doubles, junior, Jacuzzi and honeymoon pool suites, one- and two-bedroom suites, and beach-front double rooms. All have spacious marble baths, patios or terraces, TV, AC, and Internet access (for fee).

Rates: EP.

Features: Two restaurants, three pools, outdoor Jacuzzi, four lighted tennis courts, half-court basketball, 15,000-sq-ftspa and fitness center, children's play area, watersports, library, and TV room.

☎ 264-497-6111, fax 264-497-6011, www.malliouhana.com.

Luxury with Limits

$$$$ – The following hotels are designed as villa units, but are part of a resort setting offering other services. Rates for a beachfront double range from US$475 to $650 in high season; US$250 to $450 in low.

Frangipani

This beautiful Spanish-styled resort has undergone massive renovation to convert it from a traditional hotel into private owner-held units that are then rented out as hotel rooms – a trend increasingly found throughout the Caribbean. The renovation has preserved the trademark pink buildings with red tile roofs, but added a new look and ambience of luxury. The accommodations now have Caribbean rattan furniture, stone floors, and large mosaic tile baths with cave showers. The service has also been refreshed with more guest-centered offerings such as room service, cell phone rentals, concierge services and in-room Internet access.

Location: On Mead's Bay.

Rooms: Eight units, including a one-bedroom suite, five two-bedroom suites and two three-bedroom suites, all with full kitchens, living rooms, dining areas, DVD and CD players, flat panel TV, Internet access and AC.

Rates: EP.

Features: Restaurant with room service, bar, beach activities center with watersports, pool, in-room spa services.

☎ 264-497-6442, 866-780-5165 US, fax 264-497-6440, www. frangipaniresort.com.

Carimar Beach Club

This hotel is also a hybrid of privately owned units maintained and offered as hotel rooms. The resort is 20 years old, but significant upgrades have been made, including refurbishing of the rooms and adding air conditioning to all rooms. The resort is on spectacular Mead's Bay beach, which is centrally located near some of the best restaurants and shopping destinations on the island.

Location: On Mead's Bay.

Rooms: 24 two-bedroom, two-bath units, which can be divided into one-bedroom accommodations. All have full kitchens, living rooms, balconies with outdoor dining, grills, daily housekeeping, ceiling fans, AC (additional charge), Internet access (additional charge).

Rates: EP.

Features: Beach with watersports, recreation room with TV, tennis court.

☎ 264-497-6881, 800-235-8667 US, fax 264-497-6071, www.carimar.com.

Reasonable & Comfortable Hotels

$$$ – These hotels represent good value with pleasant surroundings in great locations. Daily double rates for oceanfront rooms run from US$325 to $400 in high season, and US$200 to $275 in low.

Ku Hotel

This bright, breezy newcomer to the Anguilla hospitality scene sets a new standard for mid-priced hotels (it is a sister property to the more upscale Cap Juluca). There's a serious South Beach sensibility going on here; rooms are done in a wash of white with blue and green accents that mirror the seascapes surrounding the property. The main check-in area is enveloped in a billowing white canopy. The beachfront bar runs 75 feet along the shore, a new benchmark in bar size for Anguilla. It's a relaxed, cool, hip kind of place to be.

Location: On Shoal Bay, at the eastern end of the island.

Rooms: 27 one-bedroom suites with full kitchens, living rooms, ceiling fans, DVD and CD players, TV, AC, Internet.

Rates: EP.

Features: Restaurant, bar, pool, 'petit' spa and gym, store/boutique, concierge, beach, adjacent to Shoal Bay Divers for watersports.

☎ 264-497-2011, 800-869-5827 US, fax 264-497-3355, www.ku-anguilla. com.

Madeariman Beach Club

Madeariman Beach Club

A tiny but charming hotel, Madeariman sits on Shoal Bay East, one of the favorite beach spots on the island, hence its popularity. It's also an intimate hotel where guests feel like family and return year after year. Built in 2000, it's furnished in Mexican pine furniture with bright colorful accents all around, and the grounds are lushly landscaped. But it's really the beach that everyone comes here for.

Location: On Shoal Bay East.

Rooms: Five, including beach studio, beach suite, and beach suite with kitchen. All have queen beds, microwaves, mini-fridges, coffee/tea service, TV and AC.

Rates: EP.

Features: Restaurant and bar, beach, adjacent to Shoal Bay Scuba for watersports.

☎ 264-498-3833, fax 264-497-5751, www.madeariman.com.

Paradise Cove Resort

This small resort makes up for the inland location (i.e., no beach) with comfortable, bright and airy accommodations. It's just a short walk to

Cove Bay beach, and the location is central to the attractions of Rendezvous Bay to the east, Mead's Bay to the northwest, and Maunday's Bay to the west.

Paradise Cove Resort

Location: Inland near Cove Bay, on Paradise Drive.

Rooms: 29 studio, one- and two-bedroom and penthouse suites with kitchens, living and dining areas, baths with double vanities, powder rooms, patios, ceiling fans, AC and TV.

Rates: EP.

Features: Café, pool, two Jacuzzis, kiddies' pool, children's playground, fitness center, croquet court, barbecue area, boutique, Internet cafe.

☎ 264-497-6603, fax 264-497-6927, www.paradise.ai.

Rendezvous Bay Hotel & Villas

Rendezvous Bay

The two-mile long white powder sand beach of Rendezvous is a perfect setting for this sprawling resort. The rooms are located in two areas: beach*f*ront on the western side and oceanfront on the eastern side (called the snorkeling side because there is no beach but lots of reefs). The standard rooms were built a while ago and are nothing special, but that's outweighed by the great beach and a chance to stay at one of the friendliest and most relaxed hotels on the island.

Location: On Rendezvous Bay, western end of the island.

Rooms: 24 deluxe villa rooms, 19 standard garden rooms and seven three- or four-bedroom villas. All have coffee/tea service, refrigerators, dial-up Internet access and TV/VCRs (no cable). Villa rooms are air conditioned; villas have full kitchens and AC.

Rates: EP.

Features: Restaurant, two tennis courts, watersports, hammocks, picnic tables, game room, library, entertainment room with cable TV, art gallery, boutique, in-room spa services, high speed Internet access.

☎ 264-497-6549, 800-274-4893 US, fax 264-497-6026, www. rendezvousbay.com.

Sirena Resort

Sirena Resort

On the hill above Mead's Bay sits this beauty of a resort surrounded by landscaped gardens. But fear not, beach access is only a short walk through those gardens, and there's access to chairs and umbrellas, as if you were staying right on the beach. With the coming of a new owner in 2006, the rooms were refurbished, a new reception area was built, and overall the resort was upgraded. The welcoming rooms are done in white with dark wicker furniture, and the ambience is invitingly cool and contemporary.

Location: Above Mead's Bay.

Rooms: 20 single, standard and superior rooms, plus six suites. All have ceiling fans, minibars and daily maid service, cable TV/VCR is available for an extra charge. Some standard and all superior rooms have AC. Suites have living/dining areas, kitchenettes and whirlpool baths.

Rates: EP.

Features: Restaurant, two pools, in-room massage services, dive shop, Internet access in lobby.

☎ 264-497 6827, 800-331 9358 US, fax 264-497 6829, www.sirenaresort. com.

Good Value Hotels

$$ – These budget hotels are well loved by many loyal visitors who return year-after-year. Rates for a deluxe double run from US$190 to $290 in high season, US$150 to $225 in low.

Allamanda Beach Club

This family favorite, budget hotel on Shoal Bay Beach is fondly regarded by those who value the great beach. The hotel has a friendly, down-home atmosphere, and the rooms are certainly adequate for vacationers.

Location: On Shoal Bay East.

Rooms: 16, including studio, standard and deluxe rooms and apartments with ocean or garden view. All have

Allamanda Beach Club

microwaves, toaster ovens, coffee/tea service, TVs and ceiling fans. Apartments have full kitchens.

Rates: EP.

Features: Restaurant, pool, beach.

☎ 264-497-5217, www.allamanda.ai.

Anguilla Great House Beach Resort

The gingerbread cottages and long grassy arcade leading to a perfect white-powder beach here typify the romantic, airy side of Anguilla. A long-standing favorite, the hotel could do with some upgrading but still offers simple and comfortable accommoda-

Anguilla Great House

tions in rooms touched with colorful stencils and bright bouquets of silk flowers.

Location: On Rendezvous Bay.

Rooms: 35, with choice of garden or ocean view and king or queen beds. All have private patios, ceiling fans, cable TVs and AC.

Rates: EP.

Features: Restaurant, pool, beach, watersports, WiFi in lobby area.

☎ 264-497-6061, fax 264-497-6019, www.anguillagreathouse.com.

Arawak Beach Inn

This collection of brightly colored chattel houses on the waterfront at Island Harbour offers low-cost, simple accommodations in a great location; two beaches are just a short walk away.

Location: At Island Harbour, eastern end of the island.

Rooms: 17 oceanfront standard or deluxe. All have refrigerators and private baths. Deluxe rooms have cable TVs and Internet access, and some have full kitchens. Air conditioning available at extra cost.

Rates: EP.

Features: Restaurant and bar, store/boutique.

☎ 264-497-4888, fax 264-497-4889, www.arawakbeach.com.

Villa Resorts or "Villatels"

$$$$$ – *Anguilla is rapidly becoming the star attraction of the Leewards, with gorgeous privately owned luxury villas, part of a larger development that includes hotels and hotel amenities. To rent a five-bedroom villa with luxury appointments and plunge pools at these beauties, you'll pay $30,000-$50,000 a week in low season, and $50,000-$75,000 in high season.*

Altamer

This collection of three very special villas designed by world-renowned architect Myron Goldfinger cater to the most discriminating and demanding of visitors. They are huge (up to 14,000 sq ft), with interiors described as of "museum quality." The villas offer unexpected amenities, such as home theaters, full offices with computers and faxes, gyms, and treatment rooms. If you have a crowd, and are used to the best, Altamer is for you.

Location: On Shoal Bay West, at the West End.

Rooms: Three villas, two with five bedrooms, one with eight. Each villa is unique and has distinct features.

Rates: Weekly EP.

Features: Award-winning restaurant, tennis courts, beach volleyball, croquet, watersports, children's activities.

☎ 264-498-4000, 888-652-6888 US, fax 264-498-4010, www.altamer.com.

Altamer

Temenos Anguilla, a St. Regis Resort

Altamer

St. Regis Resorts set a worldwide standard for luxury. The Temenos Anguilla hits that benchmark with grand success. The three villa residences (with more in the works) have price tags in the millions. This brand new property offers 120 guest rooms to well-heeled travelers.

Location: On Merrywing Bay.

Rooms: Three 6,500- to 7,000-sq-ft villas with private infinity-edge pools and Jacuzzis, outdoor dining pavilions, and oceanfront beach houses

Rates: Weekly EP.

Features: Spa and fitness center, beach, tennis courts, golf course, butler and concierge services.

☎ 264-498-7000, www.stregisresidences.com.

Viceroy Resort & Residences

Viceroy Resort

This large-scale resort is in the construction phase, with units becoming available as they are purchased and built. The plan includes beachfront resort residences, oceanfront town homes, bluff-top resort residences, bluff-top villas and beachfront villas, all spread across 3,200 feet of ocean frontage.

Location: Between Mead's Bay and Barnes Bay.

Rooms: Four- and five-bedroom villas, three- and four-bedroom town homes, one-, two- and three-bedroom resort residences (hotel suites), and luxury penthouses, all with private pools, gourmet kitchens, and spacious luxury baths.

Rates: To be determined.

Features: Restaurant, spa and fitness center, tennis courts, Kids' Club, conference center, and beach club with watersports.

☎ 264-497-0757, 800-357-1930 US, www.viceroyanguilla.com.

$$$$ – Here you'll pay a pretty penny, although not quite as much as in the above villas. Expect weekly rates of $17,000-$22,500 in low season, and $26,000-$37,000 in high season for a five-bedroom. Most of these offer smaller villas or the opportunity to rent a one-bedroom villa sectioned off from a larger one.

Cove Castles

This elegant, high-style resort was designed by Myron Goldfinger and has been featured in *Architectural Digest*. The stark, modern white buildings house eminently livable villas whose attributes have been heralded in just about every publication or program about luxury accommodations on Anguilla.

Location: On Shoal Bay West, in West End.

Rooms: Eight two-bedroom beach houses, four three-bedroom villas, two four-bedroom grand villas and one five/six-bedroom grand villa, all fully equipped with state-of-the-art kitchens, elegant baths, private pools and many amenities.

Rates: Weekly EP.

Features: Restaurant, tennis courts, beach, bicycles, watersports, concierge service.

☎ 264-497-6801, www.covecastles.com.

One of the Cove Castles

Anguilla

Little Harbour Estates

These three villas share three acres of tropical landscape. They sit at the ocean's edge with a protective reef in front and views to St. Martin and St. Barts. Each villa is unique in size, décor and amenities. All have private pools and share small beaches.

Location: In Little Harbour.

Rooms: A five-bedroom villa, a four-bedroom villa with an adjoining two-bedroom villa, all with luxury appointments, full kitchens, and private pools.

Rates: Weekly EP.

Features: Maid and laundry service, chef service and babysitting available for a fee.

☎ 264-497-0357, 44 (0) 1530 249719 UK, fax 44(0) 1530 249729 UK, www.littleharbourestates.com.

Sheriton Estates

This villa enclave on Cove Pond stands out because of the elegance of the three waterfront "super villas" and amenities such as trendy baths, lush gardens, a private chef, and seven pools distributed among the residences. The interiors are influenced by Caribbean and Asian styles. The living spaces are spacious and distinguished.

Location: On Cove Pond, West End.

Rooms: Two villas with seven bedrooms each that can be broken up into a three-bedroom villa, a loft suite, an executive suite, and a two-bedroom pool suite; one grand villa with five bedrooms and three pools. All include media areas with large-screen TVs, DVD and CD players, WiFi Internet, fitness equipment, gourmet kitchens, indoor and outdoor dining areas and large marble baths with special features.

Rates: Weekly EP.

Features: Concierge services, private chef, shuttles to Maunday's Bay and Temenos Golf Course, in-villa spa treatments, fitness instructors and other personal services.

☎ 264-498-9898, fax 264-498-9595, www.sheritonestates.com.

$$$ – This category gets to be a little more reasonable, with a five-bedroom going for just under $7,000 weekly in low season or $9,800 in high. This is also a villatel where you can book a room for two to four people, unlike some of the larger ones.

Yacht Club Villas at Callaloo Club

This collection of 12 villas is near Blowing Point on the Cul-de-Sac Peninsula. The largest and most luxurious villa has 12½ bedrooms on three floors with two private pools and two waterfalls, plus private mooring and a private beach. All guests have access to the Tiny Bay Beach and the Antigua Yacht Club restaurant and boutique, which are adjacent to the property. The interiors are bright and airy, with contemporary furniture.

Yacht Club Villas at Callaloo Club

Location: Near Blowing Point.

Rooms: 12 villas and condo units ranging in size from the one-bedroom Seapool Gazebo to the 12-bedroom Rosamaris Villa. All have full kitchens, en-suite baths, and luxury appointments.

Rates: EP.

Features: Beach, restaurant, beach bar, watersports, pool, private chef services available.

☎ 284-498-8600, office@callalooclub.com, www.callalooclub.com.

Small Inns & Guest Houses

If you are on a budget, or like a vacation in simple settings where you are close to the local scene, these are a good bet. Expect to pay US$100-150 per night in low season, and $125-250 in high season.

Ferryboat Inn

This family-run private house with apartments is on the beach near Blowing Point, with the ferry dock a short walk away. The restaurant on-site features West Indian food, or you can cook your own meals in fully equipped kitchens in the units.

Ferryboat Inn

Location: Near Blowing Point.

Rooms: Six apartments with one bedroom, full kitchen and living/dining area, one beach house with two bedrooms, kitchen, living and dining areas, plus air conditioning. All units have patios and cable TV.

Rates: EP.

Features: Restaurant, beach, location close to ferry.

☎ 264-497-6613, fax 264-497-6713, www.ferryboatinn.ai.

Lloyd's Bed & Breakfast

Created by David Lloyd back in the early 1950s, this historic property was the first hotel on the island, as well as the epicenter of the Anguillian Revolution in 1967. It is now a charming guest house run by David Lloyd Jr., who has sustained the original and welcoming vision of his father. The center living room leads to a gracious dining room where guests eat family-style at one table.

Location: On Crocus Hill, in The Valley.

Rooms: The nine guest rooms offer all amenities, including cable TV, air conditioning and en-suite bathrooms.

Rates: BP.

Features: Dining room, central location, near Crocus Bay Beach.

☎ 264-497-2351, fax 264-497-3028, www.lloyds.ai.

Nathan's Cove

One of the few small inns on the beach, this gem is owned by the renowned Gumbs family of Anguilla. The two-story building is 40 feet from Mead's Bay beach, and offers a great view out to the sea from every unit.

Location: On Mead's Bay.

Rooms: Two two-bedroom, two-bath units on ground floor; one four-bedroom, five-bath unit on second floor; all have full kitchens, living and dining rooms, full laundry, daily maid service, TV with VCR, AC.

Rates: EP.

Features: Verandahs with furniture and hammocks overlooking beach, direct beach access.

☎ 732-566-3838, 718-783-2759, or 301-630-3040 (all in US), www.nathanscove.com.

The Pavilion Inn

This three-story building in Blowing Point offers comfortable apartment units as well as a two-bedroom, two-bath penthouse suite with cathedral ceilings, a large patio and a Jacuzzi. All have front terraces with views to the ocean and St. Martin. The ferry, Sandy Point Beach and restaurants are short walks away.

Location: Blowing Point.

Rooms: Deluxe and junior one-bedroom apartments with full kitchen, bath, dining and living room, plus two-bedroom, two-bath penthouse. All have water views, front and rear patios, ceiling fans, laundry facilities, cable TV and AC (extra fee).

Rates: EP.

Royal Palms

Features: Close to ferry and short walk to beach.

☎ 264-497-8284, fax 240-235-8247, www.pavillion-inn.com.

Royal Palms

This small apartment hotel offers spacious units overlooking the south coast of the island toward St. Martin. While inland, it is only a short distance from Rendez-vous Bay.

Location: South Hill.

Rooms: Six two-bedroom, two-bath units with living room, full kitchen, balcony or patio with dining area, daily housekeeping service, TV, AC, Internet access available.

Rates: EP.

Features: Freshwater pool, sundeck, landscaped gardens.

☎ 264-497-6448, fax 264-497-6484, www.royalpalms.ai.

Sydan's Apartments & Villas

This pleasant and highly regarded set of apartments has reasonable rates and is in a great location in Sandy Ground, right across the street from the beach.

Location: In Sandy Ground.

Rooms: 10 apartments with kitchens, living rooms, ceiling fans, TV; some rooms have AC.

Rates: EP.

Features: Central shaded courtyard, adjacent to Sandy Ground Beach, near restaurants and shopping.

☎ 264-497-3180, www.inns.ai/sydans.

Sydans

Private Villas

There are a large number of privately owned villas available for vacation rentals. Here are some of the agencies that handle villas; most offer websites where you can see what is available.

Anguilla Definitive Villas represents a range of luxury villas from two to 13 bedrooms in size. All of the available rental villas are shown on their website. ☎ 264-497-2300, fax 264-497-6105, www.anguilla-definitive-villas.com.

Island Dream Properties has an amazing array of one-of-a-kind luxury villas for rent all over the island, from Panarea in the West End, to Wesley House at Island Harbour and Bird of Paradise on Sandy Hill. ☎ 264-498-3200, fax 264-498-3201, www.islanddreamproperties.com.

Keene Villa Rentals helps you search for your perfect villa from among the 20-plus properties they manage on the island. See the website for details on each. They can also arrange car rentals, maid, chef and spa services, babysitting and a concierge service for activities. ☎ 264-497-2544, 248-237-4313 US, fax 264-497-3544, www.keenevillas.com.

Kokoon Villas has one of the most extensive lists of villas located all over the island, with a wide range of sizes and levels of luxury. They also emphasize renters' concierge services to arrange all your activities and personal services. ☎ 264-497-7888, fax 264-497-9888, www.kokoonvillas. com.

Day Spas

Anguilla Yoga Studio & Retreat Centre

Anguilla, more than any other island in the Leewards, stresses relaxation, wellness and health. As a result, the island is loaded with spas. You'll find hotel spas that are open to the public, private spas, yoga studios and wellness centers staffed by highly qualified therapists and alternative medicine practitioners.

Anguilla Yoga Studio and Retreat Centre, in South Hill, offers public yoga sessions led by Jeanne-Marie Derrick who has trained in yoga since 1983. Classes are small so that Derrick can give individual attention to students; private classes are available as well. She also leads yoga retreats at Sirena Hotel and Shoal Bay Villas.

☎ 264-497-6606, www.jeanne-marie.com.

Cap Juluca's spa services are billed as "an opportunity to experience healing and personal growth." Signature treatments include hot stone therapy, reflexology, Reiki, the Samvanhana or "Four Hands" therapy, and intriguing spa rituals with wraps, soaks and hydrotherapy. They also offer Shiatsu, Swedish, aromatherapy, Jamu and Lomi Lomi massages, plus body wraps and polishes, facials and other beauty services. ☎ 264-497-6666, fax 264-497-6617, www.capjuluca.com.

Guests at the **Venus Spa** at **CuisinArt Resort** can choose from a large menu of facials, massages, specialty treatments, body wraps and exfoliations, hydrotherapy and other beauty treatments. The luxurious spa facility, fitness center and yoga pavilion are housed in a separate, richly appointed 8,000-sq-ft three-story building. The resort offers a 10-day interactive retreat that emphasizes nutrition, exercise, body pampering and therapeutic guidance for stress and weight reduction. ☎ 264-498-2000, 800-943-3210 US, fax 264-498-2010, www.CuisinArtResort.com.

The Spa at Malliouhana is a beautiful new facility with more than 65 treatments, including massages, body treatments, facials and fitness programs, many of which draw upon Ayurvedic, European and Asian practices. Patrons have access to five indoor individual treatment rooms, one outdoor treatment area, three private spa suites with outdoor balconies, indoor and outdoor relaxation areas, an outdoor ocean-view Jacuzzi, steam and sauna rooms and fitness center. The spa is closed September and October. ☎ 264-497-6111, ext. 501/502, fax 264-497-6011, www.malliouhana.com.

The Spa at Malliouhana

The **OM Sweet OM Centre** in South Hill is owned by Françoise Le Meur, a Reiki master who holds Sivananda, Hatha and Yoga certifications. She is also trained in Oriental astrology. She conducts daily yoga classes in the Kripalu tradition and offers Barefoot Shiatsu, Swedish Esalen and Reiki massages. ☎ 264-497-4721/2922, www.web.ai/yoga.

The **Taino Wellness Centre** in South Hill is owned by Jill Walker, a Canadian registered massage therapist and acupuncturist who is also trained in aromatherapy, facial treatments, Trager, therapeutic touch, the Bowen Technique, body rolling and ear coning. Spa services include deep tissue massage, thermal palms, facials, manicures, pedicures, body treatments and acupuncture. There is a mobile service that provides private in-home sessions. ☎ 264-497-6066, www.tainoswellness.com.

Where to Eat

Dressing Up to Dine Out

Barrel Stay

This is a beach restaurant with atmosphere, so you don't need to dress fancy, but you'll feel you must to show proper homage to the outstanding French and Creole cuisine and the hospitality of owners Graham Belcher and Jill Shepherd. The Fish Soup, done like

French onion soup, is a favorite, and the desserts, especially the warm apple tarte tatin, are not to be missed. $$$$. Sandy Ground, on the beach. Open for dinner, closed Wednesdays. ☎ 264-497-2831.

RESTAURANT PRICE CHART	
$	Cheap eats, normally quick meals or take-out foods; US$8 or less per entrée.
$$	Good value, lots of West Indian cuisine; US$9-$14 for a plate of food.
$$$	A nice place with gourmet aspirations; US$15-$24 for a satisfying entrée.
$$$$	Positively elegant, usually requiring some dressing up; entrées range from US$25 to $50, depending on the island.

Blanchard's

Blanchard's

Bob and Melinda Blanchard created this well regarded, high-style restaurant and, along the way, changed their lives (see their book *Live What You Love*). The wine cellar is outstanding, as befits a regular winner of the Wine Spectator Award of Excellence, and the cuisine has received raves for its fusion of Caribbean, Asian, American and Mediterranean flavors. $$$$. Mead's Bay, near Malliouhana. Open for dinner only, closed Sundays. ☎ 264-497-6100, fax 264-497-6161, www.blanchardsrestaurant.com.

Covecastles

Executive Chef Dominique Thevenet of Lyons, France combines his classical training with an emphasis on organic and fresh ingredients. The garden setting adds to the romantic ambience. $$$$. Shoal Bay West. Open for dinner, closed Tuesdays. ☎ 264-497-6801, www.covecastles.com.

Deon's Overlook

The vistas from the plantation-style verandah dining area out over Sandy Ground Bay are breathtaking and the food here is just as impressive.

Chef Deon, who splits his time between Anguilla and Martha's Vineyard, offers a contemporary menu with Caribbean flair. Don't miss the garlic-encrusted snapper, and Deon's Decadent Chocolat Rum Cake. He also operates Deon At Your Villa Catering. $$$. South Hill. Open for breakfast, lunch and dinner, closed June through September. ☎ 264-497-4488.

View from Dean's

Hibernia

Raoul Rodriguez and Mary Pat O'Hanlon set an island standard when they opened this intimate, elegant restaurant in 1987. The chef trained in France, Laos, Thailand and Hong Kong, and the cuisine reflects this French/Asian fusion. Raoul and Mary Pat travel extensively to bring new ideas and tastes to the restaurant. The wine cellar is stocked with the best in French vintages. The setting includes a gallery specializing in Southeast Asian and Eastern European contemporary art. $$$$. Island Harbour. Open for lunch and dinner, closed for Sunday lunch and Mondays. ☎ 264-497-4290, www.hiberniarestaurant.com.

Koal Keel

Koal Keel

Set in one of Anguilla's oldest homes, this charming restaurant presents Anguillian cuisine in its most sophisticated interpretation, as well as a number of Tandoori specialties. The fish and seafood dishes are most popular and many include local ingredients such as tamarind, coconut, sweet potato and pumpkin. Another specialty is chicken roasted in a traditional rock oven, which requires ordering 24 hours in advance. Desserts have been described as works of art and are always outstanding. $$$$. The Valley. Open for dinner only, closed Mondays. ☎ 264-497-2930, fax 264-497-5379, www.koalkeel.com.

Malliouhana

Under the guidance of esteemed Parisian restaurateur Michel Rostang, Chef Alain Laurent brings a sophisticated Mediterranean-inspired cuisine to this luxury resort. The 25,000-bottle wine cellar is the largest in the Caribbean. The open-air setting with a view out over Mead's Bay is delightful. $$$$. Mead's Bay. Open for breakfast, lunch and dinner. ☎ 264-497-6111, www.malliouhana.com.

Pimm's

This dramatic restaurant sits on a coral outcrop just steps from the water with views of the Moorish architecture of Cap Juluca and the bay. The cuisine is described as "Eurasian/Caribe" and features exotic entrées mixing seafood, poultry and meat with unusual ingredients from the Caribbean and Middle East. $$$$. Maunday's Bay. Open for dinner seven nights a week. ☎ 264-497-6666, fax 264-497-6617, www.capjuluca.com.

Santorini's

This elegant restaurant at CuisinArt embodies the attention to detail and emphasis on quality synonymous with the CuisinArt brand. You can see what's cooking behind the kitchen's glass walls (they are big on teaching, you know), but you still won't be able to figure out the magic that produces the outstanding Mediterranean and Caribbean specialties using ingredients from the hotel's hydroponics farm and organic gardens. Don't miss the specials that come from the French rotisserie and the chef's tasting menu. $$$$. Rendezvous Bay. Open for dinner, closed Tuesdays. ☎ 264-498-2000, www.cuisinartresort.com.

Relaxing on the Water

George's

The beach bar and grill at Cap Juluca attracts a crowd for its tropical cuisine fusing Mediterranean and Caribbean flavors. Special nights include the Friday night beach barbecue and the Monday night Grand Marché Culinary Challenge, where dishes from India and the Far East are added. $$$. West End. Open for lunch and limited "sports bar" dinner. ☎ 264-497-6666, www.capjuluca.com.

Johnno's

Johnno's started out as a lowly beach shack, but it's now the hot spot on the island for live jazz. It also has a reputation for serving the best lobster on the island. The atmosphere is casual and lively, especially when the music is going. $$. Sandy Ground. Open for lunch and dinner, closed Mondays. ☎ 264-497-2728, www.johnnos.com.

Mango's Seaside Grill

Romantic atmosphere, great grilled lobster, crayfish and fish, extensive wine list, decadent desserts – Mango's is what every seaside restaurant should be. And you get good quality at reasonable prices. $$$. West End, on Barnes Bay. Open for dinner only, closed Tuesdays. ☎ 264-497-6479, www.mangos.ai.

Oliver's Seaside Grill

This beach restaurant cooks its West Indian and continental dishes in an authentic Anguillian rock oven. The rock oven-baked whole free-range chicken stuffed with gingered sweet potatoes requires reservations four hours in advance, but it's a dish well worth a little extra planning. $$$$. Long Bay, West End. Open for lunch every day and dinner every day except Monday. ☎ 264-497-8780, www.olivers.ai.

Oliver's

Roy's Bayside Grill

The English visitors come for the fish and chips, the Americans come for the grilled Angus beef, and they all come for Happy Hour at 5 pm, when drinks are half-priced. Plus, the sunsets are spectacular (what else is a good Happy Hour for?). $$. Sandy Ground, western coast. Open for lunch and dinner, closed for Saturday lunch. ☎ 264-498-0154.

Smokey's at the Cove.

Chef Smoke (aka Desmond Patrick) knows his way around the smoker, and most people come here for Smoke's excellent ribs and barbecued chicken. But the menu also includes West Indian favorites like jerk pork and curried goat. If you're not sure about venturing past the barbecue, try the combination appetizer for just a taste of the entrées. The atmosphere is casual during the day, but in the evening the fine china and linen come out. $$. Cove Bay, near Rendezvous Bay. Open for lunch and dinner every day. ☎ 264-497-6582.

Straw Hat

This restaurant is not at the water's edge, but over the water, on stilts. You may have seen it featured in *Bon Appetit*, *Gourmet Magazine*, *Caribbean Travel and Life*, or *Town and Country*. Chef Lee

Straw Hat

Masten not only works his magic on how the cuisine tastes, but how it looks – and the end result is impressive. $$$. The Forest, near the airport. Open for dinner only, closed Sundays. ☎ 264-497-8300, www.strawhat. com.

Sunsets Restaurant

Chef Shawn "Fresh" Hodge has a loyal following of both visitors and locals who come to Sunsets for Hodge's Anguillian-inspired continental favorites. A tip: don't overlook the soups, which are specialties of the house. Happy Hour runs from 4 to 6 pm, so you can gather to watch the sunset. They also have live music on Tuesdays and Fridays. $$. Sandy Ground. Open for lunch and dinner, closed Saturdays. ☎ 264-498-0177.

Uncle Ernie's

This unpretentious little beach shack is often referred to as "The Famous Uncle Ernie's" – a reputation that comes from having good beach-food basics like hamburgers, ribs, chicken and fish in a place where locals and visitors love to come and lime the day away. They offer live music on Sunday afternoons. $$. Shoal Bay West. Open for lunch and dinner every day. ☎ 264-497-3907.

Ethnic Foods & Favorites

Café Mediterraneo

Kemia

CuisinArt's open-air restaurant near the pool is good for midday meals, where you can choose from a menu that includes brick oven pizzas and salads picked from the restaurant's organic gardens. Dinner is casual and features a brasserie menu inspired by Spain, France, Italy, Morocco and Turkey. If you love lobster, plan to be there on Tuesday evenings for Lobster Night. $$. Rendezvous Bay. Open for breakfast, lunch and dinner every day. ☎ 264-498-2000, www.cuisinartresort. com.

Kemia

This Cap Juluca restaurant serves a menu of tapas (kemia means "small dishes" in Morrocan) reflecting the flavors of Peru, Spain, the Middle East, Northern Africa and Asia. The menu offers equally intriguing desserts. $$$. Maunday's Bay, West End. Open for dinner only. ☎ 264-497-6666, www.capjuluca.com.

Zen

It's difficult to find a Japanese restaurant in the Leewards, which makes Zen all the more special. The sushi and sashimi are fresh and exactly what you would expect from a high-quality restaurant. The menu also includes some French favorites. Take-out, delivery and villa service are also available. $$$. South Hill Plaza, on the Main Road at West End. Open for dinner every day. ☎ 264-497-6502, www.zenanguilla.com.

West Indian Cooking

English Rose

This local hangout has all the West Indian basics like baked chicken, jerk chicken and Creole snapper, plus entrées you'd expect at a pub. It's also part sports bar; the large screen TV is often tuned to the latest big cricket or soccer match. $$. The Valley. Open for lunch and dinner, closed Sundays. ☎ 264-497-5353.

Flavours

Kirk Hughes and his family offer local favorites in a breezy second-floor dining room in South Hill, overlooking Road Bay and Sandy Ground Harbour. Many menu items represent the best of West Indian cuisine, including Pepper Pot, Creole Conch, conch chowder and fish cakes. If you have people in your party that don't want to go native, there are a number of other savory entrées such as pastas, steak and sandwiches. $$$. Back Street in South Hill. Open for lunch and dinner, closed Sundays. ☎ 264-497-0629, www.flavoursrestaurant.com.

Gwen's Reggae Grill

This Shoal Bay favorite has the usual range of beach-bar food plus some local favorites. One of the best things to do after filling yourself with ribs or chicken is to stretch out for a nap in one of the comfy hammocks surrounding the dining area. $$. Shoal Bay East. Open daily for lunch only. ☎ 264-497-2120.

Sprocka's

Right across from the airport is this lively little joint, where Sprocka, an Anguillian musician who has

Gwen's

Anguilla

recorded several CDs and plays with various bands in the Caribbean, entertains while food is dished out from the Soul Kitchen. The dinner menu includes a lot of originals, such as mango gazpacho, shrimp with plantains, truffle fries, pumpkin gnocchi and Cajun barbecued shrimp. $$. Near Wallblake Airport. Open for dinner, closed Sundays and Mondays. ☎ 264-497-0882, www.sprocka.com.

Tasty's

When chef Dale Carty left Malliouhana after training under renowned French chef Michel Rostang, he took a lot of regular patrons with him. They love Carty's indigenous Anguillian cuisine touched with European influences, plus many entrées that can be considered "comfort food." Try breakfast here – it's a real Anguillian experience. $$. South Hill. Open for breakfast, lunch and dinner, closed Thursdays. ☎ 264-497-2737.

Quick Bites

Fat Cat Gourmet

This deli will pack picnic lunches for people on the go. They also offer salads, sandwiches, pâtés, cold meats and desserts so you can create a feast in your villa or hotel room. $$. Stoney Ground/The Valley. Open for lunch, closed Sundays. ☎ 264-497-2307.

Jocahu Caffe

This small deli offers gourmet panini sandwiches filled with whatever you like, along with iced coffees, lattes and other delights. $. On the Main Road, West End near the Galleria. ☎ 264-476-2222.

Le Cantina Pizzeria

For a quick bite while shopping, check out this pizza place in the Eldorado Mall. $. Eldorado Mall. Open for lunch, closed Sundays. ☎ 264-497-5282.

Shopping

With the multitude of upscale villas on the island, shopping in Anguilla rivals watersports as an attraction. The stores aren't just for tourists; they also cater to the well-heeled residents who shop to furnish their villas with furniture, art and accessories. For the visitor that means an abundance of beautiful imports and locally produced arts and crafts to choose from, in addition to the usual duty-free shopping.

Fine Art

Anguilla has many talented artists. You can see their work at galleries scattered around the island, including:

Cheddie's Carving Studio features the work of Cheddie Richardson. Cheddie transforms driftwood into incredible, lifelike animals and figures before your very eyes. Bedney's Plaza on the Main Road, West End. ☎ 264-497-6027, www.cheddieonline.com.

Christine's Art Gallery shows the works of contemporary French painter Loic Madec. Blowing Point Road. ☎ 264-497-8107, www.loicmadec.com.

Painting from Loblolly Gallery

Devonish Gallery features the sculptures and carvings of Courtney Devonish and bead jewelry made by his wife Carolle. Other local artists are represented here as well. Main Road, West End. ☎ 264-497-2949, www.devonishgallery.com.

Estate Hope Art Studio features handmade quilts and textiles. Crocus Hill, The Valley. ☎ 264-497-8733.

Loblolly Gallery offers original art from "Anguillians in Spirit" by artists in the US and Canada. Rose Cottage, on the road to Crocus Bay. ☎ 264-497-6006, www.loblollygallery.com.

Lynne Bernbaum Art Studio showcases the art of this American painter. George Hill Landing, just outside The Valley. ☎ 264-497-5211, www.lynnebernbaum.com.

From Lynne Bernbaum Art Studio

Pineapple Gallery offers Caribbean art, including Haitian works, and European and Caribbean antiques. South Hill Road, near Sandy Ground. ☎ 264-497-3609.

Savannah Gallery represents a wide variety of contemporary Caribbean artists in varied media. The Valley. ☎ 264-497-2263, www.savannahgallery.com.

Gifts, Clothing & More

There are three major areas of concentration for stores offering mementos, gifts, wine, cigars, clothing and more.

Bedney's Plaza, on the Main Road in The Cove, has Elio's Cigar and Wine Bar, a liquor store and deli.

World Art & Antiques

The Galleria area, also on the Main Road in the West End, has interesting places on both sides of the street. On the north side is **World Art & Antiques**, a large store filled with unusual furniture, home furnishings, art, textiles and more. Nearby are the **Devonish Art Gallery** and **Something Special**, duty-free shops offering golf wear, swimsuits, shirts, jewelry, hats and wraps, and gifts from other Caribbean islands. Across the road, a cluster of buildings houses **Cheddie Richardson's Carvings** studio and **Le Petit Gift Shop** (upstairs).

Then there is the **Eldorado Mall**, Anguilla's nod to American shopping habits, located on the Main Road in West End. This enclosed one-story air-conditioned building houses a number of individual stores. These run the gamut from shoes and accessories to household appliances and gadgets. There are also two restaurants, and more stores are being added all the time.

If you are looking for the traditional beachwear/t-shirts/local jewelry and souvenir store, drop into **Irie Life** at South Hill Village or at Sandy Ground beach next to Johnno's. The colorful shops offer Caribbean music CDs, island wear, swimwear, sandals and hats, along with their own unique t-shirts. ☎ 264-497-6526, 498-6526.

And if you're not shopped out yet, take the ferry over to St. Martin/Sint Maarten, where you can shop 'til you drop in the duty-free havens of Marigot and Philipsburg.

Nighlife

Although Anguilla markets itself as "Tranquility Wrapped in Blue," it has a surprising number of not so tranquil night spots where you can hear live music and have a great time.

Pumphouse

You can hear the music pumping out from this old rock-salt-factory-turned-bar as soon as you enter the Sandy Ground area. Rock, reggae and soca bands play every night except Sunday. The artifacts from the salt factory days decorate the walls and add atmosphere to the barn-like setting. Sandy Ground, at the waterfront. ☎ 264-497-5154

Dune Preserve

Reggae star Bankie Banks set about creating his own special place for music, and the result is a building partially created from salvaged driftwood. It may be one of the most unusual places you'll ever see. This place rocks on weekends when Bankie and his band play, and during a full moon they have a special beach bonfire celebration. During the week, a DJ brings in music for dancing until the wee hours. In late

At the Dune Preserve

March, the annual Moonsplash Festival brings Caribbean artists to the island to perform at Dune Preserve. Rendezvous Bay. ☎ 264-497-2660, www.dunepreserve.com.

Jazz'ezz

In addition to good food, this restaurant offers music from jazz to karaoke to string bands. At their Happy Hour on Wednesdays and Fridays, drinks are half-price for ladies and, on the last Sunday of the month, they have a great Sunday brunch with live entertainment. Stoney Ground. ☎ 264-498-5299.

Johnno's

You can dance out under the stars to live or DJ music seven nights a week at Johnno's. The crowd is a funky and eclectic mix of locals and visitors,

and the beach can't be beat. Sandy Ground beach. ☎ 264-497-2728, www.
johnnos.com.

Shoal Bay West

On Sunday afternoons Shoal Bay West is one long string of parties. The
restaurants on the beach all have their own bands that compete for the
attention of the beachgoers looking for a cool place to relax after a day on
the sand.

Sprocka's

Sprocka is a talented Anguillian native plays guitar, keyboard, saxophone
and trumpet. He also sings. You can catch his act at his restaurant Tuesdays, Fridays and Saturdays. He also occasionally performs at the hotels.
Near Wallblake Airport. ☎ 264-497-0882, www.sprocka.com.

The beaches of Anguilla

The Beaches of Anguilla

Anguilla's 30 spectacular beaches are some of the best in the Caribbean.
The sand is powdery white, the water is bright turquoise, and the snorkeling offshore is superb. As with most of the Leewards, all beaches are public.

Here are some of the most popular and appreciated beaches on the main
island. For a discussion of beaches on the smaller islands around
Anguilla, see the information provided earlier in this chapter.

Captain's Bay

At the northernmost end of the island you'll find this rugged beach with a wide stretch of sand bracketed by rock cliffs. It's not a beach for those who like to swim and snorkel because the undertow can be dangerous. However, it's a great choice if you like hiking and exploring; follow the dirt track to the eastern point of the island and you'll pass Abadam hole along the way.

Captain's Bay

Cove Bay

This beach on the southwest coast has some impressive sand dunes and is not heavily traveled, since the only facility here is Smokey's restaurant. The swimming is good, but the snorkeling is not. It's a good place for a romantic picnic and leisurely stroll.

Crocus Bay

Crocus Bay

This undeveloped beach (no restaurants or services) is midway down the northern coast, just outside the Valley. The water is shallow so swimming is good, and snorkeling is best along the cliff wall at the east end. From here you can hop a boat or swim to Little Bay, a tiny, secluded beach with great snorkeling. Turtles frequent this area, so you may see some when you are diving.

Forest Bay

This southern coast beach is well-known as the home of Straw Hat, the restaurant on stilts in the water. It's a good beach for swimming because the water is shallow and clear. The rocky bottom makes it good for shallow snorkeling, especially around the western side. The area around the restaurant has large coral formations and an abundant fish population. However,

Forest Bay

there are no facilities so you need to bring drinks, food and your own shade.

Limestone Bay

This small strand is sandwiched between rock formations on the Atlantic, so the currents are strong and there are no offshore reefs. What you do get is a beautiful beach with a view of Dog Island, and an area where turtles and iguanas like to play. It's a favorite with the locals for beach picnics, so bring a small grill and enjoy the natural beauty.

Meads Bay

Home to Malliouhana Resort, Carimar Beach Club and the Frangipani, this beautiful beach on the northern coast is good for sunbathing and swimming, but not so great for snorkeling. If you want to go *luxe*, you have access to the restaurants at the upscale resorts. Otherwise, you should bring a picnic lunch, because there are no typical beach shack-type eateries.

Rendezvous Bay

The calm, clear water and a small area of coral rocks for snorkeling make this southern coast beach a popular one for families. You can rent beach chairs and umbrellas at Anguilla Great House (which is where you get access to the beach), and have lunch at the Great House, Dune Preserve or Rendezvous Bay Hotel. This is also the point where you get the best view of St. Martin.

Sandy Ground

This is a bustling area on the northern coast, serving as the main port for ships and the beginning point for boat transfers to Sandy Island and Prickly Pear Cay. The swimming is good, but the port is too busy for snorkeling. Several restaurants are within easy access. The area is known for its night life and as the beginning point for the boat races.

Shoal Bay East

Clearly the most popular beach in Anguilla, this was voted one of the 10 best in the Caribbean because of the quality of the sand and water and the number of beach bars and activities along the strand. The reef just offshore is home to schools of colorful fish and plentiful coral, so the snorkeling is very good. Among the restaurants and bars here are Elodia's, Uncle Ernie's and Gwen's Reggae Grill, so you know you'll have access to great food. On Sundays the entire beach becomes a party, with live entertainment sponsored by the restaurants.

Shoal Bay West

At the other end of the island is this glamorous beach that shows up in all the stylish magazines because high-end properties Altamer and CoveCastles sit right on it. The swimming and sunbathing are excellent and you can find shells along the beach, but there are no reefs for snorkeling. For lunch the only restaurant available is Trattoria Tramonto.

Saint Martin/Sint Maarten

The Allure of the Island

This island is unique among the Leewards primarily because it is its own little UN. One side is a prefecture of France and one side is part of the Netherlands Antilles and the Kingdom of the Netherlands. Since the island is only 38 square miles, this very cozy state of affairs creates a unique cultural mix.

The duplicity is apparent in many ways – two acceptable forms of money (plus the US dollar), two separate phone systems, two Carnival celebrations, two tourism authorities and so on. But for the visitor, the dual system is virtually seamless. You don't need to show any documents as you cross from one country into another; no one stops you at the border, and in fact, most of the time you don't even know when you have crossed it. Often the only tip-off is the language displayed on the signs and

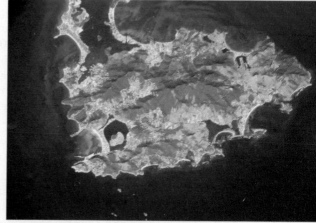

St. Martin from space

Club Orient Beach

menus. If it's French, it must be St. Martin. If it's English, it's Sint Maarten.

The Dutch side is very American in atmosphere. All-American institutions such as McDonalds, Pizza Hut and Burger King are among the gastronomic offerings. The casinos definitely remind you of Las Vegas, with all the neon and bright colors. The hotels are geared to Americans and are reminiscent of large resort hotels in America. Everything is transacted in US dollars, making the specification of the Dutch guilder as the 'official' money rather moot.

One more major difference from other Leewards is the density of population. In Antigua, almost 80,000 people live in 100 square miles, and there's a lot of open land between the villages and the major developments. In St. Martin (as I will refer to the island throughout this chapter), close to that same number of people (77,000) coexist in only 36 square miles. Tourist arrivals in St. Martin are almost triple those of Antigua, with about two million people visiting each year, as opposed to 700,000 in Antigua. This makes for a lot more people in a smaller space, and the increased density is apparent on the roads and beaches as well as in stores and restaurants.

That is not to say there aren't attractive areas in St. Martin. Why else would all those people travel here each year? **Orient Beach**, with its colorful umbrellas and lounges lined up in rows and the topless sunbathers languishing in the tropical breezes, is reminiscent of the French Riviera. **Anse Marcel**, with its collection of luxury hotels, is a beautiful harbor area with a tidy marina and a pretty beach. **Grand Case** is one of the gastronomic centers of the Caribbean, with more quality French restaurants per square mile than you'll find anywhere outside of Paris. The beaches around the southwestern edge of the island rival any found in the Leewards for powdery sand and gentle waves. And there is always plenty to do, as numerous companies offer all sorts of watersports and touring adventures.

So if you want an island where you have access to everything the Caribbean offers – including beautiful beaches, glitzy casinos, great restaurants and a wide variety of activities – this is your place.

Here's What to Look For According to the Type of Traveler You Are

The Perfect Cruise Passenger should check out the big self-contained resorts on the Dutch side, including the Wyndham Sapphire, Port de Plaisance Princess, Sonesta Maho Bay and the Westin Dawn Beach. They have everything you could desire – beach, activities, casino, spa and fine dining, all within easy reach. Their locations make it easy to get to the port-of-call duty-free shopping areas of Philipsburg and Marigot. As for day trips, there is a long list of day charter and boat tour providers that can take you anywhere around the island, to Anguilla or to other islands for a memorable visit.

The Boots-On Adventurer will not find a lot of challenges on this sybaritic island. Of course there are hiking trails up Pic Paradis and mountain biking throughout the hilly island. There is the Marine Park, where diving is excellent due to the extra protection provided by the reefs. But you will have to factor in a certain amount of ease and comfort, because there are not a lot of basic, stripped down eco-hotels or divers' dives. You may have to content yourself with pursuing the wild life at night on Orient Beach.

The Cultural Explorer will enjoy the duality – two languages, two Carnivals, and a lot of local color provided by the many nationalities that live and work here. Any of the fine restaurants in Marigot or Grand Case will give you real-life experience in what it is to be French and an appreciation of the finer things of life. Be sure to check out the French Market on the waterfront in Marigot, where you'll find a lot of locally made goods as well as *lolos* where you can sample West Indian cooking. Want to really feel European? Head to Orient Beach, and leave the bikini top at home while you work on a "strapless" tan.

The "I Like What I Like" Traveler will probably feel most comfortable choosing any of the lovely private villas where you can create your own little world. The island has a lot of American cultural icons to keep you comfortable, like McDonalds, Burger King, some good steakhouses, Las Vegas-style casinos, and shopping with American dollars. If you don't want to have difficulty communicating in another language, you should probably steer clear of many of the restaurants on the French side, although there are a lot more English speakers there than you would guess.

The Incurable Romantic will love some of the small, intimate inns on the French side, such as L'Esplanade, Le Petit Hotel, the Grand Case Beach Club, or La Plantation Hotel overlooking Orient Beach. And what could be more romantic than an elegant French dinner at one of the fantastic restaurants next to the beach in Grand Case? There are also a number of day spas where you can set up a day of pampering, followed by a day of shopping at the duty-free jewelry stores in Philipsburg.

The Family Social Director has an easy job keeping everyone happy in St. Martin. Pack up the clan and take them on a ferry to Anguilla to swim with the dolphins. Or trundle down to Orient Beach where everyone can choose their favorite water activity, be it parasailing, water skiing or snorkeling. Or line up a charter boat to take you all for a picnic and snorkeling on Tintamarre or Ilet Pinel. You could also take the family to the Zoo, or the Butterfly Farm, or Loterie Farm for a zip line adventure. The island has several movie theaters, a miniature golf course, and a water playground specifically designed for kids.

The Ultimate Shopper need go no further than Philipsburg, where two entire streets are lined with duty-free shops, boutiques and restaurants. Then there is Marigot, with its sleek West Indies Mall and colorful native French Market, as well as high-fashion boutiques in the Marina Royale and Plaza Caraïbes. Furniture, garden and home fashion stores are all over the island, where you can find unusual Caribbean décor items. And the selection of original art available is nothing short of amazing.

A Brief History

The commonly accepted story is that in 1493, Columbus sailed by St. Martin and named it for St. Martin of Tours, whose feast was being celebrated that day. Some historians dispute this, saying that he was looking at Nevis and that some of the names he bestowed are now different due to revisions in maps and history. Somewhere along the line, it all got straightened out, and the first designation of St. Martin with that name was in 1516, when the Reinel map of the Caribbean appeared.

Columbus

What Columbus failed to note on his acquisitive forays through the West Indies was that there were Arawak or Carib Indians who, by most estimations, had already been on St. Martin for thousands of years. Archeological evidence indicates the Arawaks populated the island as early as 200 BC. The agrarian-based Arawaks had a tough time co-existing with the warlike Caribs and eventually the Arawaks were subjugated by the more fierce Caribs. (The English word "cannibal" came from the Arawaks' word for the Caribs.) The Caribs dominated the island until the mid-17th century, when they were caught in the crossfire of Europeans fighting to gain control of the West Indies, and also succumbed to European diseases.

During the mid-16th century, the Spaniards were first to lay claim to the island, rounding up the Indians and putting them to work. Eventually, the Dutch began settling there, looking to harvest the salt that was plentiful around the many salt ponds. The Dutch became the dominant population until Spain sat up and took notice, recapturing the island in 1633. The banished Dutch residents moved on to Curaçao. With this second Spanish occupation came slavery, military forts and other colonizing evils.

Meanwhile, the Dutch were busy establishing colonies in Curacao, Saba, St. Eustatius, and eventually back in St. Martin. Both the French and the British were taking possession of various islands, and many passed from one crown to another during the 17th and 18th centuries. By 1648, the Spanish had given up their claim to St. Martin, leaving the Dutch and French colonists there on their own. The Dutch settled in the southern portion, around Great Bay, harvesting the bounty from the Great Salt Pond and shipping it to Europe. The French settled in the north around Grand Case and began growing tobacco. By 1648, the Treaty of Concordia officially divided the island into French and Dutch areas.

THE DIVIDING LINE

You may hear an interesting fable about how the border between the French and Dutch sides was drawn. It has to do with a walking race that was held, with a Frenchman and a Dutchman starting out from Oyster Pond on the eastern coast. The Frenchman headed north, the Dutchman south, and where they met after walking around the island would be where the line was drawn. Supposedly, the Frenchman fortified himself with wine, and the Dutchman carried a supply of gin. With gin being a more potent potable, the Dutchman had to stop more often to sleep off its effects, so the Frenchman got the larger portion of the route.

In reality, the line was a political decision influenced by the threat of a large French fleet sitting just offshore at the time the treaty was being negotiated. The French demanded many concessions in the drawing of the line and got a bigger slice of the island pie. In 1648, the treaty was signed on top of Mount Concordia. Because of the back-and-forth skirmishing between the two sides, the border changed 16 times, until the Treaty of Paris fixed the boundaries for good in 1815.

St. Martin

St. Martin/Sint Maarten

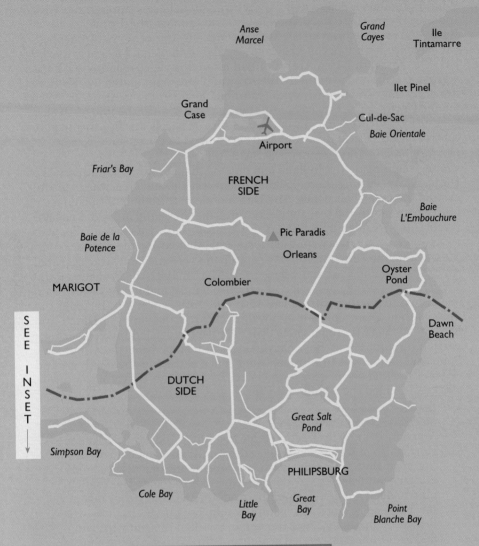

Anse Marcel

Grand Cayes

Ile Tintamarre

Ilet Pinel

Grand Case

Cul-de-Sac

Baie Orientale

Airport

Friar's Bay

FRENCH SIDE

Baie L'Embouchure

Baie de la Potence

Pic Paradis

Orleans

MARIGOT

Colombier

Oyster Pond

Dawn Beach

SEE INSET →

DUTCH SIDE

Great Salt Pond

Simpson Bay

PHILIPSBURG

Cole Bay

Little Bay

Great Bay

Point Blanche Bay

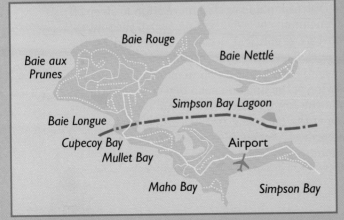

Baie Rouge

Baie Nettlé

Baie aux Prunes

Simpson Bay Lagoon

Baie Longue

Cupecoy Bay

Mullet Bay

Airport

Maho Bay

Simpson Bay

N

1 KM

1 MILE

© 2008 HUNTER PUBLISHING, INC

Other crops tested in St. Martin during this period were indigo and cotton. Cotton took precedence until the 1760s when sugar cane was introduced to the island. Paralleling the history of other Leeward Islands, St. Martin's population swelled when slaves were imported to work on the sugar cane plantations that sprung up all over the island. There was also an influx of English planters. The French were more aggressive at building the sugar industry on their side of the island, while the Dutch held on to their cotton fields for a while before adopting the cane completely. From 1775 to 1850, sugar ruled the economy of both sides of the island, following the West Indies arc that peaked and then waned when slavery was abolished.

St. Maarten/St. Martin Map Key

1. La Samanna, Cupecoy Beach Club, Ocean Club, Sapphire Beach Club
2. Summit Resort Hotel
3. Towers at Mullet Bay
4. Royal Beach, Mercure Simson Beach, Nettlé Bay Beach Club, Anchorage Margot Hotel, Le Flamboyant Resort
5. Royal Islander, Maho Beach Hotel & Casino
6. Caravanserai Hotel
7. Horny Toad Guesthouse, La Chatelaine, Mary's Boon Beach Plantation
8. Flamingo Beach Resort, La Vista, Pelican Resort & Casino
9. Atrium Resort, Royal Palm Beach Club, Turquoise Shell
10. Carl's Unique Inn
11. Sea Breeze Hotel
12. Belair Beach Hotel, Divi Little Bay Beach Resort
13. Fort Amsterdam
14. Zoo Sint Maarten
15. Blue Beach, Captain Oliver's
16. Butterfly Farm
17. Club Orient
18. Cap Caraïbes, Esmeralda Resort, Green Cay Village, La Plantation
19. Alizéa
20. Anchorage Little Key, Hotel Mont Vernon
21. Le Méridien L'Habitation, Hotel Privilège, La Résidence de Lonvilliers
22. Privilège Resort & Spa
23. Grand Case Beach Club, L'Esplanade Caraïbes
24. Pavillon Beach
25. Mount Vernon Plantation

- - - - Border

———— Paved Road

✈ Airports

·········· Unpaved Road

 Beaches

St. Martin

During the period of prosperity, there were a number of skirmishes between the Dutch and French to control the entire island. In 1801, a band of British sailors landed in the Great Bay area and took control, but were pushed out a year later. They returned in 1808 and, with the help of the Dutch, controlled both St. Martin and Guadeloupe until 1814. During these repeated invasions, the Dutch and the slaves maintained business as usual, while the French fled the island, only to return a few years later. Finally, in 1815 the Treaty of Paris set the governing structure and border division that remains to this day.

Another significant event was the abolition of slavery. The French abolished slavery in 1848, but the Dutch hung on for another 15 years before ending the practice. As was true throughout the Leewards, the abolition of slavery led to a dramatic economic decline, since large plantations were no longer tenable. Nothing could replace the lost wealth of sugar.

In 1939, the island was declared a duty-free port, which fueled the rise of the tourism industry. The Dutch jumped on this new industry right away and began developments to attract visitors. It wasn't until the 1970s that the French began to make their own towns and beaches attractive to foreigners. Today, more than two million visitors arrive annually to enjoy the natural beauty and continental sophistication of the island.

The Facts

Population: There are about 36,000 inhabitants in St. Martin, and 41,000 in Sint Maarten. The rich cultural mix includes descendants of the first French, Dutch and English inhabitants and of the slaves, as well as a large immigrant population from other Caribbean countries. Dutch Sint Maarten boasts of having 77 different nationalities in their space of 16 square miles.

Language: The official language of St. Martin is French, and the native languages of Sint Maarten are Dutch and English (although you rarely hear anyone speaking Dutch). Although the island caters largely to American tourists, you still encounter some French-only speakers among restaurant and hotel workers.

Main Cities: Marigot is the political and economic center of St. Martin, as well as a primary port. It is a beautiful little city, with top-notch restaurants and shopping areas bordering the sea to the west and on the northernmost tip of the Simpson Bay Lagoon to the east. The other major town is **Grand Case**, northeast of Marigot.

On the Dutch side, **Philipsburg**, located along Great Bay on the southern coast, is the capital city and major port. A newly built port along the southeastern edge welcomes large cruise ships, and the downtown area is a warren of duty-free shops, boutiques, casinos and restaurants

Philipsburg panorama

Government & Economy: This is where the duality of the island is most obvious. St. Martin has been an arrondissement of Guadeloupe, which is an overseas department of France. In 2003, the citizens of St. Martin and St. Barts, desiring more autonomy, began the process of seceding from Guadeloupe. The French legislature approved the request, and the new status became law in 2007. The island is dependent upon tourism as its major industry and revenue source.

Sint Maarten is part of the Netherlands Antilles, a parliamentary democracy represented by a governor who reports to the Queen of the Netherlands. Locally, the government is represented by a lieutenant governor, the executive council and the island council, which is the lawmaking body. On Dec. 15, 2008, Sint Maarten's status in the Kingdom of the Netherlands will change to that of a country within the Kingdom, and the Netherlands Antilles will cease to exist. Eighty-five percent of the employment on the Dutch side relates to the tourism industry. The government is currently investigating ways to balance the economy by diversifying into light manufacturing.

People & Culture: Being at the crossroads of the Caribbean, and having changed its colonizing country some 16 times during its history, the island is a melting pot of over 80 nationalities, including Spanish, French, Dutch and English. While English with a Caribbean lilt is the predominant lan-

View from Pic Paradis

guage, the official language is French on St. Martin, and Dutch on Sint Maarten. You will also hear a lot of Spanish, Creole and Papiamentu dialects spoken.

The primary cultural highlight of the year is **Carnival**, which is celebrated around the traditional pre-Lenten time by the French. The Dutch side holds Carnival after Easter, to coincide with the Queen's Birthday.

Geography: The 36-square-mile island is volcanic in origin; it has a number of peaks, the highest of which, at 1,391 feet, is **Pic Paradis**, located in the center of the island. There are also significant hills east and west of Philipsburg amenable to hiking and mountain biking. One of the major topographic features is the large **Simpson Bay Lagoon**, which occupies the western peninsula of the island and is bisected by the French-Dutch border. The island is dotted by salt ponds, the largest being the **Great Salt Pond** just to the north of Philipsburg.

There are 37 beaches surrounding the island on all sides, with reefs just offshore for snorkeling and diving. There are also a number of smaller offshore islands, with the most prominent being **Tintamarre** off the northeast coast. Others include **Ilet Pinel**, **Cayes Vertes**, **Coconut Grove** and **Rocher Creole**, all of which are uninhabited.

Climate: The weather is delightfully Caribbean with year-round highs in the 80-84°F range, and lows in the 70s at night. The hurricane season runs from July to October but, as with all the Leewards, the island has enjoyed quiet summers with no major storms for over a decade. The annual rainfall average is about 45 inches.

Flora & Fauna: The tropical vegetation of this island includes all that you'd expect: beautiful flamboyant trees draped in red

Flamboyant tree

Magnificent frigate bird

blossoms during the summer, tamarind trees with their unusual fruit, lots of palms in different varieties, and the ubiquitous sea grape bushes. The hotels and attractions take full advantage of the climate, landscaping their properties with bougainvillea, hibiscus and allamanda. Many varieties of flora can also be seen at the St. Martin Park.

Among the native animals you'll

St. Martin

find are mongoose, iguanas, geckos, sea turtles, and lots of birds, including brown pelicans, frigate birds, ruddy turnstones, black-bellied plovers and laughing gulls. Around the Great Salt Pond, snowy egrets, stilts and herons can be seen on a regular basis. Occasionally someone sights a monkey hanging around the resorts, but they are not as prevalent here as they are in Nevis. You will also encounter a number of domestic animals wandering along the streets, such as goats, cows, pigs and donkeys. Remember that they have the right of way and you will do a

Mongoose

lot less damage to your vehicle if you watch out for them.

The Nature Foundation was created in 1997 to preserve the natural beauty of the island, and has designated an extensive Marine Park area off the eastern coast to protect undersea life. The Foundation has also proposed legislation that would create a national park to protect the rich life found in the hills above Philipsburg.

Travel Information

When to Go

St. Martin boasts a warm and welcoming climate year-round, although the summer months are a bit more humid and hot. But many people like coming in the off-season because the rates are lower, the water is warmer, and there are not as many people clogging the streets. However, in true European fashion, many of the restaurants and some of the hotels on the French side close during August, September and October.

Getting There

With the large number of visitors from America, France and Canada traveling to St. Martin each year, the Princess Juliana Airport has become a major hub in the Caribbean. It is also the transit point for those traveling to St. Barts, Saba, Statia and Anguilla, offering flights and ferry connections to these islands. There are ports in Marigot and Philipsburg, where yachts and private charters can enter the countries.

> Note that American travelers are now required to have a passport to enter St. Martin as well as to return ticket to the US.

By Air

There are two airports, the large **Princess Juliana International Airport** (SXM), on the Dutch side at the southern rim of Simpson Bay Lagoon, and the small **Aéroport L'Espérance** (SFG) on the French side, just east of Grand Case.

Airlines Serving St. Maarten

American Airlines, with daily non-stop flights from Miami, New York (JFK) and San Juan on American and American Eagle jets. ☎ 800-433-7300, www.aa.com.

Continental Airlines flies non-stop six days a week from Newark. ☎ 800-231-0856, www.continental.com.

Delta Airlines has non-stop flights six times a week from Atlanta. ☎ 800-241-4141, www.delta.com.

Spirit Airlines, a low-cost airline, flies non-stop three times a week from Ft. Lauderdale. ☎ 800-772-7117, www.spiritair.com.

United Airlines has weekly non-stop service from Chicago and Washington (IAD). ☎ 800-538-2929, www.united.com.

US Airways flies daily non-stop from Charlotte, NC, and weekly flights from Philadelphia. ☎ 800-622-1015, www.usairways.com.

Airlines With Links to & from Other Islands

Air Antilles has flights between Pointe à Pitre, Guadeloupe and St. Martin/L'Espérance. ☎ 890-648-648 in Guadeloupe, www.airantilles.com.

Air Caraïbes flies daily to and from Guadeloupe and has several flights a week from San Juan to SXM and SFG airports. ☎ 877-772-1005 US, 590-590-27-71-90 St. Barts, www.aircaraibes.com.

Air St. Maarten offers private and shared charters from St. Martin to St. Barts using the airplanes of Windward Express. ☎ 599-581-9740, www.airsxm.eu.

Caribbean Airlines, formerly BWIA, has flights between St. Martin and Antigua, Barbados, Jamaica and Trinidad. ☎ 599-546-7660/7661 St. Martin, 800-744-2225 US, www.caribbean-airlines.com.

Heli St. Martin, a new helicopter service, offers flights from the Grand Case airport to St. Barts on a charter basis as well as private charters. ☎ 599-544-4100, 305-767-2531 US, www.helistmartin.com.

St. Bart's Commuter has daily flights from SFG in St. Martin and from SXM in Sint Maarten to St. Barts. ☎ 590-590-27-54-54, www.stbarthcommuter.com.

Take Air Dominica is a new airline based in Martinique with weekly flights between Dominica and St. Martin. ☎ 05960-596-421-608, www.takeairlines.com.

WinAir has two flights daily between Antigua and SXM, several daily flights to St. Barts. ☎ 866-466-0410 US, 599-545-4237 St. Martin, www.fly-winair.com.

Windward Express offers charter trips. ☎ 599-545-2001, www.windwardexpress.com.

By Sea

 Private charter yachts must report to the port authorities and immigration on arrival and departure at the clearing posts either in Philipsburg or Simpson Bay on the Dutch side or Marigot on the French side.

Cruise ships arrive at the new **Walthey Pier** at Point Blanche, just outside Philipsburg. The cruise pier includes Harbour Point Village, a collection of shops and restaurants for cruise visitors, and the John Craane Cruise Terminal for bus and taxi pickups and drop-offs.

 Customs: This is a duty-free island, so there are not a lot of restrictions on items brought into the country. Coming back into the US, you normally have an $800 exemption. This includes a maximum of 200 cigarettes, 100 cigars and one liter of alcohol.

CUBAN CIGARS ARE A NO-NO

You will see some shops carrying Cuban cigars, which you can enjoy while on the island (even though some around you may object). But you cannot take Cuban tobacco products into the US, regardless of where you purchased them, unless it was during an officially sanctioned trip to Cuba.

Special Events & Holidays

 Check the individual websites listed below for exact dates in the year you are traveling or see see www. st-martin.org or www.st-maarten. com/events.htm for an overall schedule.

January

New Year's Day, January 1 – Public holiday.

St. Martin Classic Yacht Regatta – Sponsored by the St. Martin-Sint Maarten Classic Yacht Regatta Foundation. ☎ 599-523-7671, www.classicregatta.com.

Carnival girl

February

St. Martin Carnival – Occurring just before Lent begins.

March

Annual Heineken Regatta – Sponsored by the St. Maarten Yacht Club. ☎ 599-544-2079, www.heinekenregatta.com.

Treaty of Concordia Day, March 23 – Commemorates the day the treaty was signed in 1648 to partition the island.

April

Good Friday – Public holiday.

Easter Sunday – Public holiday.

Easter Monday – Public holiday.

Unity Jump-Up Day – Beginning of Dutch side's Carnival, with celebrations on both sides.

Carnival dancers

St. Maarten Carnival – Occurring around Easter. See www.stmaartencarnival.com for exact dates and events.

Grand Carnival Parade & Queen's Birthday, April 30 – Public holiday.

May

Labor Day, May 1 – Public holiday.

Funny Festival – A week of stage performances by noted comedians. ☎ 590-590-87-78-67.

Quicksilver SXM Challenge – Two-day windsurfing/kitesurfing competition. See www.tropical-paradise.net/SXM-Windsurfing-Kitesurfing-Challenge.html for more information.

SMART, Annual St. Maarten/St. Martin Regional Annual Tradeshow – Sponsored by the St. Maarten Hospitality & Trade Association and Association des Hôteliers de St. Martin. ☎ 599-542-0108, www.shta.com.

St. Louis' Village Day, St. Martin – Family activities and local culinary specialties sponsored by the St. Louis Cultural Women's Association. ☎ 590-590-87-76-32.

Ecotourism Day at the Bellevue Estate – Activities and an arts & crafts show, with Captain Oliver's Carib Beer Regatta, organized by Captain Oliver's Yacht Club. Sponsored by the St. Martin Office of Tourism. ☎ 599-557-1990, www.ccregatta.com.

Nautical Fair – Two-day celebration of watersports, sponsored by the Sea Trades Association or METIMER. ☎ 590-590-51-94-25, www.metimer.org.

The Heineken Regatta (March)

St. Maarten Open Golf Tournament Championship – Sponsored by the St. Martin Golf Association. ☎ 599-545-2850, www.stmaartengolf.com.

International Museum Day – With an open house at the St. Martin Archeological Museum. ☎ 590-590-29-22-84.

Black Heritage Week, last week in May – Celebrates the abolition of slavery with entertainment, street fairs, ceremonies and traditional shows. Sponsored by Service Arts et Culture de la Mairie, ☎ 590-590-51-19-05.

June

Annual St. Martin Book Fair – Three days of literary and cultural interchanges between the Dutch and French sides sponsored by the Conscious Lyrics Foundation. ☎ 590-690-30-73-66.

Bill Fish Tournament – International deep sea fishing tournament based in Marigot, sponsored by Association Marlin Bleu. ☎ 590-590-87-05-60.

Soulinga Unity Cup Football Tournament – Matches for football clubs around the Caribbean. Sponsored by Association FC Marigot. ☎ 590-690-39-76-02.

Fête de la Musique – A weekend of musical entertainment in Marigot, sponsored by Service Arts et Culture. ☎ 590-590-51-19-05.

July

Emancipation Day, July 1 – Open house in the Museum in Marigot.

Annual St. Maarten Summerfest – Features noted Caribbean entertainers in venues on both sides. ☎ 599-545-3995, www.stmaartensummerfest.com.

I Love My Ram Contest – Judging of the best ram on the island in Colombier, sponsored by Chambre de Commerce et d'Industrie. ☎ 590-590-87-84-42.

Fête Nationale du 14 July (or Bastille Day) – Public holiday on French side, with sporting and cultural events and Courses de Canot Pays Boat Racing, with small island-made boats and local crews and those of Anguilla, competing along the Marigot waterfront and to Anguilla, sponsored by Commune Info. ☎ 590-590-87-17-76.

Eco-Tourism Day – Promotes eco-tourism and heritage awareness with musical entertainment, sporting events and craft exhibits in French Quarter. Sponsored by the Office de Tourisme of St. Martin. ☎ 590-590-87-57-21.

Grand Case Village Fest – One-day event with sporting and cultural activities and sailboat racing. Sponsored by Cultural Center of Grand Case. ☎ 590-590-87-88-75.

September

Moonlight Golf Tournament – Sponsored by the St. Martin Golf Association. ☎ 599-545-2850, www.stmaartengolf.com.

International Coastal Cleanup Day – Sponsored by Sint Maarten Pride Foundation. For more information, see sxmprivateeye.com/node/2557.

World Tourism Day – Sponsored by the Office of Tourism of St. Martin. ☎ 590-590-87-57-21.

October

Antillean Day, Oct. 22 – Public holiday.

Annual Fête de Cuisines – Cooking demonstrations, a food market in Philipsburg and activities at restaurants. Sponsored by Tourism Offices of St. Maarten and St. Martin and the St. Maarten Hospitality and Trade Association. ☎ 599-542-2337.

November

Caribbean Tourism Day – Official ceremonies organized by the Office of Tourism for both sides.

St. Martin's Day, Nov. 11 – Public holiday on both sides.

La Course de l'Alliance Race – Four days of sailing, parties and shows to celebrate the alliance of the Saint Martin, Sint Maarten, St. Barts and Anguilla yacht clubs. ☎ 590-590-51-11-11, www.coursedelalliance.com.

Concordia Trophy Golf Tournament – Sponsored by the St. Martin Golf Association. ☎ 599-545-2850, www.stmaartengolf.com.

December

Miss Caribbean Hibiscus Pageant – At the Casino Royale. ☎ 590-590-29-24-16.

St. Maarten Charter Yacht Exhibition – Features the world's finest luxury yachts, sponsored by the St. Maarten Marine Trades Association. www.charteryachtexhibition.com.

Annual Santa Scramble Golf Tournament – Sponsored by the St. Martin Golf Association. ☎ 599-545-2850, www.stmaartengolf.com.

Kingdom Day, December 15 – The day St. Maarten signed the accord with the Netherlands in 1954.

Santa Claus' Home – A privately held property open to the public for the month of December. Refreshments and entertainment offered; open every day from 6 to 11 pm Sponsored by the Good Friends Association. ☎ 590-590-29-05-54.

Christmas, December 25 – Public holiday.

Boxing Day, December 26 – Public holiday.

Orient Bay Midnight Dream Festival – With dinner, concerts and fireworks in Orient Bay Village to celebrate December 31. Sponsored by the "Music is Voice" Association. ☎ 590-689-14-23-64.

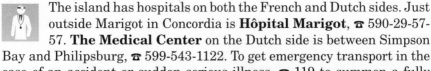
REOCCURRING EVENTS

Year-round events include **Go Local**, an evening of entertainment and dancing in Marigot on Wednesday and Sunday evenings, sponsored by the St. Martin Office of Tourism, ☎ 590-590-87-57-21, www.st-martin.org. **Harmony Nights** are regularly scheduled exhibitions of local music, art and handicrafts throughout Grand Case village, with streets turned into a pedestrian mall. Sponsored by Radio Calypso. ☎ 590-690-74-27-07.

Health

 The island has hospitals on both the French and Dutch sides. Just outside Marigot in Concordia is **Hôpital Marigot**, ☎ 590-29-57-57. **The Medical Center** on the Dutch side is between Simpson Bay and Philipsburg, ☎ 599-543-1122. To get emergency transport in the case of an accident or sudden serious illness, ☎ 119 to summon a fully equipped medi-van with EMTs. Other ambulance services are available by calling ☎ 599-541 3011 on the Dutch side, and either ☎ 590-87-86-25 (day) or 590-87-72-00 (night) on the French side.

Pets

 To bring an animal into St. Martin, you need to get certification from your veterinarian no more than one week before your arrival at SXM, stating that the animal has had all its appropriate rabies vaccinations and is in good health.

Crime

The island has seen an increase in thefts and burglaries over the last few years, so exercise caution in public places and in your accommodations. Don't leave purses or bags unattended, especially if they have your passport or valuables in them. Remember to lock your doors at night, always secure your vehicle, don't leave valuables in the trunk of your auto, and park in heavily traveled areas of parking lots.

Electricity

Again, the duality. On the French side, most villas and resorts are wired for 220 volt current, with the round, cylindrical plugs. You'll need a step-down converter to run computers, hair dryers and the like (although many hair dryers offer dual voltage). The Dutch side follows the American standard of 120 volts, using the same receptacles, so you'll be fine with your necessary appliances and battery chargers.

Tipping

Taxi drivers will expect a tip of US$1 or so, unless they take you on an extended tour. Airport porters should be tipped US$2 per bag.

SERVICE CHARGE IS A MYSTERY

The restaurant service charge is a point of much discussion on the island. Some restaurants automatically add it into the cost of food to cover personnel costs. Some visiting American tourists have noticed that it is sometimes added to their bill, but not to the bills of Europeans sitting near them. Do the restaurant owners know that Europeans will not stand for the extra charge, but that Americans will because they don't want to be rude? No one is clear on the true status, even though many feel it is illegal and that unscrupulous restaurateurs take advantage of Americans and harm the reputation of all the restaurants.

But one thing is clear – the tax doesn't get distributed to the wait staff directly. So, if your waiter did a good job, you should leave a tip. And be prepared to leave it in cash on the table, because many restaurants on the French side cannot accommodate additions to charge cards after the sale is entered.

Money Matters

As was mentioned earlier, acceptance of the American dollar is prevalent all over the island, although the official currency on the French side is the euro, and on the Dutch side, the guilder. There are many banks, ATMs and currency exchanges on both sides of the island. On the Dutch side most ATMs give out dollars, while on the French side you receive euros.

St. Martin

Weddings

Getting married in St. Martin/Sint Martin is no easy trick, although it sounds wonderfully romantic. For the French side, you need to be in residence on the island for at least one month, so many people opt to get married on the Dutch side, where the residency requirements are convoluted but much shorter. Foreign couples must be at least 21 years of age (and, if you are Dutch, you must be 23 years old). If you're not residing on the island, you must request permission to marry and receive a temporary tourist permit at least two to three months before your wedding date. Contact the Lt. Governor of the Island Territory of St. Maarten by mail at: **Lt Governor Franklyn Richards**, Government Administration Building, Clem Labega's Square, PO Box 943, Philipsburg, St Maarten, fax 599 542 4884. It will take at least two months to get a response, and then you need to be on the island two days before the ceremony. In addition, you need to register for marriage at the office of Civil Registry at least 10 days before the marriage – but fortunately this can be done by faxing their office at the following: **Chief Registrar**, Office of Civil Registry and Census Office, Soualiga Road, Philipsburg, St. Maarten, ☎ 599 542 2457, fax 599 542 4267.

Documents Required

- A certified or notarized birth certificate.
- In the event persons are not of Dutch nationality, a valid passport is required.
- Address of both parties.
- Duration of stay on St. Maarten.
- Unmarried persons must present a declaration of marital status not older than three months.
- If widow(er), a death certificate.
- If divorced, a divorce certificate or a final judgment decree; divorced persons may remarry in St Maarten but should provide a recent a valid divorce certificate or a final judgment decree.. Divorced women can only remarry after 306 days upon inscription into the registry of divorce at the office of Civil State.
- For minors (under 21 years of age), permission of the parents is required, plus names of parents, maiden name of mother, including place of birth and birth date, and professions of the bride, the groom and the parents.

You'll need to arrange for six witnesses if the marriage is performed outside of the Marriage Hall, or two witnesses if it is to be performed at Wedding Hall. Non-Dutch witnesses must present a valid passport or a birth certificate with a picture ID.

The cost for contracting foreign marriages is US$275.55 and includes civil ceremony, marriage books, stamps and certificates.

Original documents other than Dutch or English need to be translated into the Dutch language (i.e., a French or Spanish document must be translated into Dutch, not English). For translations, contact: **Cheryl LaBega**, Language translator, Government Administration Building, Clern LaBega's Square, Philipsburg, St Maarten. Please note that one to two weeks is required for translation. If you have any questions, contact the Registrar's office at the number listed above.

Wedding Planners

To help handle the the host of choices in location, caterers, photographers and all the other details of planning a wedding, you may want to use a local wedding planner who can guide you to some of the most scenic locations and the best caterers, as well as help with paperwork. Some on-island wedding planners include: **Weddings in St. Martin**, ☎ 599-557-5478, www.stmaarten-beachweddings.com; **Sint Maarten Marry-Me**, ☎ 599-542-2214, 305-768-0233 US, www.sintmaartenmarry-me.com; **Tropical Weddings**, ☎ 599-544-4143, www.sintmaarten-wedding.com; **Enchante Weddings**, ☎ 599-543-6900, www.enchanteweddings.com; **Sun and Fun Weddings**, ☎ 599-545-2133, 754-423-1017 US, www.sunandfunweddings.com.

Internet Access

WWW Most of the hotels on the Dutch side and many on the French side offer Internet connections either in your room or in the lobby. If you want to sign up for roaming Internet access at the growing number of WiFi hot spots, contact **Network IDL/Megatropic**, ☎ 599-544-3188, www.megatropic.com. They have hourly, weekly and monthly rates.

Communications

Many of the US cell phone companies now have affiliations in the Caribbean, so your phone may work here. The bad news is that the rates they charge for incoming or outgoing calls are exorbitant – so think about arranging for a temporary rental if you need a phone. The one exception to this is if you pre-register your cell phone with East Caribbean Cellular (www.eastcaribbeancellular.com). If you have a phone that can be switched to System B (consult your user's manual), you can use ECC's service by providing a credit card for billing the charges. Their rates are reasonable, and they have a two-tiered system for short stays and longer stays.

On the French side, you can use your GSM phone and arrange for local service that covers both sides of the island through **Amigo Reseau GSM**, which is affiliated with Dauphin Telecom, ☎ 590-590-29-00-77, www. dauphintelecom.fr.

Many people who don't want to adapt their cell phone to local usage rely upon **Sharon, the Queen of SXM** to provide a local cell phone on a weekly rental basis. She offers an incredible deal, with a minimal cost of US$15 to rent a phone, and you add as much time to the phone as you think you'll need. All incoming calls are free, and the rates for outgoing calls are much less expensive than what the US carriers charge. She'll assign the number in advance, so you can give it to family members before you leave home. See www.queenofsxm.com for more details.

Another service that rents out cell phones is **Pack Light Vacation Rentals**. They have similar rates and services to Sharon's, as well as rentals of other equipment that come in handy if you are staying in a villa. www.sxm-services.com/packlight

CALLING ST. MARTIN/SINT MAARTEN

For those not familiar with international calling, getting phone calls through this department of France can be challenging. Here's the way to do it:

■ **To call St. Martin from the US**, dial 011-590-590 + the six-digit unique phone number of the person/place you are trying to reach (this is why the numbers in this chapter always appear with the two 590 numbers). For cell phones, you replace the second 590 with 690.

■ **To call Sint Maarten from the US**, dial 011-599 + the seven digit phone number.

■ **To call the US from St. Martin and Sint Maarten**, dial 001 + area code + phone number. American technology makes this a lot easier.

OK, now it gets trickier:

■ **To call** *within* **the French side** from a local phone, dial 0590 + the six-digit phone number, or 0690 + the phone number for cell phones. **To call** *within* **the Dutch side**, just dial the seven-digit phone number.

■ **To call the Dutch side from the French side** you need to dial 00 + 599 + the seven-digit phone number. To **call the French side from the Dutch side**, you need to dial 00-590-590 + the six-digit phone number. Phew!

Media

 The major English-language newspaper is *The Daily Herald*, published in Philipsburg. It's filled with local news and has a weekly "Out and About" supplement with information on activities and events. You can find it in many places throughout the Dutch side, or check out the website at www.thedailyherald.com. News from both sides of the island appears at www.sxmnews.com.

Magazines include *Experience St. Martin* (which has an informative website at www.experiencestmaarten.com), *Nights, St. Martin Tourism, Saint-Martin Sint Maarten Nature* (on ecotourism), *St. Maarten Events*, and *Discover St. Martin / Sint Maarten*. These can be found at the Tourism Offices on both sides as well as at the airport and in hotels.

Radio stations include the Dutch-language Dolfijn FM 97.3, Island 91.9 FM and Laser 101.1 FM, as well as the French Radio Calypso, 102.1 FM, Tropixx 105.5 FM and Youth Radio 92.5 FM.

Sources of Information

 For more information, you can refer to the St. Martin website at www.st-martin.org, or the Sint Maarten website at www.st-maarten.com, or contact the offices below.

For St. Martin

In North America: **Saint Martin Tourist Office**, 675 Third Ave., Suite 1807, New York, NY 10017, ☎ 646-227-9440, fax 646-227-9448, nyoffice@st-martin.org.

In Europe: **Office de Tourisme de Saint Martin**, 30 Rue Saint Marc, 75002 Paris, France, ☎ 01-53-29-99-99, fax 01-42-96-15-16, bureauparis@st-martin.org.

In St. Martin: **Office de Tourisme, Accueil & Administration**, Rte de Sandy Ground, Marigot 97150 Saint Martin, ☎ 590-590-87-57-21, fax 590-590-87-56-43, info@st-martin.org.

For Sint Maarten

In the US: **St. Maarten Tourist Office**, 675 Third Avenue, Suite 1806, New York, NY 10017, ☎ 212-953-2084, fax 212-953-2145, toll free 800-786-2278 (1-800-STMAARTEN).

In Canada: **St. Maarten Tourist Office**, 2810 Matheson Blvd. E, Suite 200, Toronto, Ontario, L4W 4X7 Canada, ☎ 416-622-4300, fax 416-622-3431.

St. Martin

In St. Maarten: **St. Maarten Tourist Bureau**, Vineyard Office Park, WG Buncamper Rd. #33, St. Maarten N.A., ☎ 599-542-2337, fax 599-542-2734, info@st-maarten.com.

Getting Around

Since neither side of the island is British in heritage, you don't need to worry about driving on the wrong side of the road. On both sides, driving is on the right. The main roads loop the island, so if you get lost, you can always return to where you started just by following the loop. Roads are marked and recognizable, but traffic is always heavy. Intersections should be approached with caution. On a recent visit, the major intersection in Cole Bay, where the road from Philipsburg dead-ends into the road leading north to Marigot or south to Simpson Bay lagoon, was still a three-way stop with no stop signs or signal lights, and getting through it is always a shooting match. Another dangerous intersection is where the road to Pic Paradis comes off the main road into Marigot – turning into it is easy, going out is a terror because there is no clear view of oncoming traffic. Other places have slightly better traffic control, but you need to use a lot of caution and drive defensively.

Airport

The new **Princess Juliana International Airport (SXM)** terminal opened in 2006 to much fanfare and relief from those who travel to St. Martin regularly. It's more spacious, the walk to Immigration is much shorter, and there are a number of shops, food outlets, and on-site car rental agencies available.

The airport sits at the southern rim of the Simpson Bay Lagoon on the Dutch side. To get to Marigot or Grand Case, taxis will take you around the western rim, which has nice views of Mullet Bay and Cupecoy Beach – if you can see it through all the new condos and resorts being built. The trip to the hotels around Philipsburg is quicker, about 10 minutes going east from the airport.

The departure tax is US$30 per person over age two and often is included in the airfare.

Taxi Service

Taxis are ever-present at the airport, the cruise docks and the major hotels, as well as in downtown Marigot and Philipsburg. Dutch and French cabs service both sides of the island, but minimum fares and standard charges for luggage and late night fares differ.

Since the vehicles are unmetered, you should discuss the fare prior to starting off.

For late-night cab service on St. Maarten, call the taxi station at the airport, ☎ 599-545-4317. For taxis in Philipsburg, call %%599-542-2359. On the French side, you can arrange a ride through the Taxi Service & Information in Marigot, ☎ 590-590-87-56-54, or at the Grand Case airport, ☎ 590-590-87-53-03.

Some sample fares for two passengers (all in US dollars):

- SXM Airport to Grand Case – $25
- SXM Airport to Marigot – $15-20
- SXM Airport to Maho Bay hotels – $6
- SXM Airport to Philipsburg – $15
- SXM Airport to Orient Bay – $25
- Philipsburg to Marigot – $12
- Marigot to Grand Case – $15

Car Rentals

 A car rental is a good idea if you want to travel around and get to know both sides of the island. There are no border crossing formalities, and the roads are fairly easy to navigate, although crowded.

The car rental agencies require that drivers be at least 25 years old. Any driver's license is acceptable (you don't need to get a local one as in most of the other islands). Most of the major US rental agencies have offices in St. Martin, some near the airport and others around the island – and many have offices on both sides for customers' convenience. Most will arrange to deliver the car to your hotel.

There are almost 100 car rental agencies on the island, so this list is just representative of the major ones and some locally owned ones that I have heard good things about or used myself. Some of them also offer rentals on scooters and ATV quad vehicles.

Car Rental Agencies

Alpha Car Rental, ☎ 599-545-2885 Dutch side, 716-200-1282 US, www.alphacarrental.com.

Avis, ☎ 599-545-2847 Dutch side; 590-590-87-50-60 French side; 800-331-1212 US, www.avis.com.

Budget, ☎ 599-545-4030 Dutch side, 800-472-3325 US, www.budgetrentacar.com.

Competition Car Rental, ☎ 599-545-2103 or 599-557-5715 Dutch Side, www.competitioncarrental.com.

Golfe Car Rental, ☎ 590-590-51-94-81 French side, www.golfecarrental.com.

Hertz, ☎ 599-545-4541 or 599-54-54314 Dutch side, 800-654-3131 US, www.hertz.com.

Kenny's Car Rental, ☎ 599-545-3201 Dutch side, 800-686-1689 US, www.kennyscarrental.com.

Lucky's Car Rental/Hibiscus Car Rental, ☎ 590-590-52-24-76 French side, 599-526-3230 Dutch side, 800- 390-1681 or 800-390-1778 US, www. hlcars.com.

National, ☎ 599-545-5552 or 599-545-4415 Dutch side, 800/328-4567 US, www.nationalcar.com.

Panoramic Car Rental, ☎ 590-590-29-01-04 French side, 599-522-3675 Dutch side, www.panoramiccarrental.com.

Paradise Car Rental, ☎ 599-545-3737 or 599-545-2361, www.paradise-carrental.com.

SXM Travel Rent-A-Car, ☎ 599-547-6344 or 599-554-8961 Dutch side, www.sxmtravelrentacar.com.

Tropical-Tropicana Car Rental, ☎ 599-544-3470 Dutch side, 590-590-87-94-18 or 590-690-27-37-58 French side, www.tropical-tropicana.com.

Unity Car Rental, ☎ 599-557-1064 or 599-557-6760, 800-836-4529 US, 800-820-7918 24-hour phone.

Wally Car Rental, ☎ 590-690-35-71-96 or 590-690-35-08-15 French side, www.wallycars.com.

 Lose the Tourist ID: License plates on rental cars that identify the car as a rental let everyone know (and especially those up to no good) that you are a target. . . uh, I mean tourist. When renting a car on the Dutch side, ask for plates that do not start with an "R." French-side agencies do not use "R" plates, so you are okay there.

Scooter & Motorcycle Rentals

Want to rent a Harley and tool around the island in style? **SuperBikes** has the Harley you want, from Fatboys down to Softail Springers. ☎ 599-544-2704, www.h-dstmartin.com.

For scooters, the obvious choice is **St. Maarten Scooter Rental**, which offers both scooters and ATV quad vehicles, plus the necessary helmets and maps – and they'll deliver to your hotel. ☎ 866-826-2205, www. stmaartenscooterrental.com.

Another rental agency is **Aqua World-Go Scoot** at the La Palapa Marina in Simpson Bay. ☎ 599 545 4533, www.aquaworld-goscoot.com.

Or, if you want a quick rental, there are a number of scooter vendors located at the Walthey Port Complex that cater to cruise ship passengers.

Exploring

On Foot

St. Martin's hilly terrain provides good opportunities for hiking. In fact, there are more than 30 trails to choose from, many of which start at centrally located Pic Paradise, the highest point on the island. For a list of 17 recommended hikes, look for a copy of *Saint Martin Nature*, the eco-tourism magazine published by Spectra Editions in Marigot. You can choose hikes through historic areas such as old sugar mills and plantations, past Arawak petroglyphs, or beaches and other idyllic spots not accessible by motor vehicles.

The **St. Maarten Museum** offers two publications for sale that describe the various trails; the museum also sponsors a monthly hiking tour. Check the local papers or call or stop by the museum in Philipsburg to get more information. ☎ 599-542-4917.

Among the people and organizations that offer hiking tours, guides or more information are:

Decouvrez Les Caraïbes à Velo (French tours), ☎ 590-590-87-05-11, frog.leg1@wanadoo.fr.

Dutch Hiking Club, ☎ 599-542-4917.

Trisport, ☎ 599-545-4384, www.trisportsxm.com.

Nicolas Watripon, ☎ 590-590-51-98-20, wawanico@wanadoo.fr.

Musée de Marigot, ☎ 590-590-29-22-84.

On Wheels

St. Martin offers plenty of opportunities for bikers, whether you bike for pure pleasure or extreme sport. There are also challenges available for aficionados of off-road vehicles. Agencies that can help get you started include:

Car or Jeep

Almost all of the car rental agencies offer 4WD vehicles and "jeeps," as the small SUVs are called. Some agencies, such as **Panoramic**, **St. Maarten's Scooter Rentals** and **Lucky's**, also have ATV quad vehicles, which are ideal for exploring the trails of Pic Paradis. **St. Martin Quad Express** offers three-hour tours using ATV quads. ☎ 599-556-6762 or 590-690-56-20-36.

Bicycling & Mountain Biking

St. Martin is ideal for bicycle riding. The rolling hills of the north and the flatlands of the south provide routes for riders of all skill levels. Among the favorite routes for regular biking are the loop from Port de Plaisance resort to Marigot, which goes past three of the island's beaches. Another loop is Bellevue, which has a rigorous leg going uphill to Pic Paradis, and then an easier glide down through the Colombier Valley to Friar's Bay beach. A third route goes from Oyster Pond to Le Galion beach, tracking along the ocean's edge for beautiful vistas.

Trisport (mentioned above) has bike rentals and serves as the informal headquarters for many of the biking/triathlon/running events on the island. They offer a detailed schedule on their website, www.trisportsxm. com. **Decouvrez Les Caraïbes à Velo** (see above) provides guided bicycle tours as well as walking tours.

Scenic & Historic Tours

It's a small island, but there's a lot to see. If you're a first-timer or even if you have visited before, chances are you haven't seen all the various interesting spots like Loterie Farm, Mont Vernon Plantation, Hope Estate, the Butterfly Farm and the famous beaches. Hire a taxi, or check with the tourism offices to see the latest list of recommended tour guides (they change frequently).

Butterfly Farm resident

On Water

Scuba Diving

With more than 50 dive sites, many of them in a protected Marine Park, you have a multitude of choices about where and when to dive. Many of the sites are not coral reefs, but rather reefs formed from artificial materials or created by lava flows from eons ago. The underwater sights are beautiful, and many people call St. Martin the most under-appreciated dive destination in the Caribbean.

The Nature Foundation St. Martin is a major force in protection of the reefs. It is establishing a mooring program in the Marine Park to prevent damage to the most popular reefs and a reef ball program to set up artificial reefs. For more information, see www.naturefoundationsxm.org.

Dive sites vary from 30-foot depths suitable for beginners to deep wreck dives with maximum depths of 120 feet for the more experienced. Shallow reefs include Little Bay on the east side and Creole Rock and Frenchman's Reef on the west side. There are a total of 11 wrecks for diving. Among those off the eastern coast are the

Caribbean reef sharks

Carib and the *Teigland* cargo ship, and the famous *Proselyte*, a British frigate that sank in 1801. Off the western coast is the *Fu Sheng* wreck, a fishing vessel sitting 120 feet down, an ideal deep dive for advanced divers.

In addition, St. Martin has become a base of operations for those who want to explore the waters around Saba, St. Eustatius and Anguilla. Many of the dive operators offer tours and packages to these islands and will equip you for the trip.

Dive Operators

Blue Ocean offers PADI certification, dives and trips to outer islands. Baie Nettle, ☎ 590-590-87-89-73, www.blueocean.ws.

Dive Adventures is a division of AquaMania, and offers PADI certification, dive trips, Nitrox dives, advanced open water dives and trips to dive sites in Saba. Simpson Bay, ☎ 599-544-2640, www.stmaarten-activities.com.

Dive Safaris provides PADI certification courses, dive trips, resort dives, Nitrox dives, Discover Scuba dives and Shark Awareness dives. It operates out of The Scuba Shop in Simpson Bay. ☎ 599-545-2401, or Philipsburg, ☎ 599-542-9001, www.divestmaarten.com.

Neptune Dive Center has daily exploration dives, courses, scuba diving sessions or snorkeling trips to the beautiful surrounding islands. Orient Beach, ☎ 590-690-50-98-51, www.neptune-dive.com.

Ocean Explorers Dive Center's legendary diver LeRoy French leads the dives; he also sells videos of his travels all over the world. Simpson Bay, ☎ 599-544-5252, www.stmaartendiving.com.

Scuba Fun Caraïbes offers PADI certification courses, diving and snorkeling trips, night dives and equipment rental. ☎ 590-50-87-36-13 Anse Marcel, ☎ 599-557-0505 Philipsburg, www.scubafun.com.

Dive Equipment Sales, Rental & Service

Visit **The Scuba Shop** at La Palapa Marina, Simpson Bay, ☎ 599-545-3213, or **Captain Oliver's Marina**, Oyster Pond, 590-590-87-48-01, www.thescubashop.net.

Snorkeling

With so many bays and reefs just offshore, St. Martin is a snorkeling paradise. Most of the dive shops will rent equipment. They offer tours, primarily to the outer islands of Tintamarre and Ile Pinel. Among the most interesting beaches for snorkeling are Friar's Bay and Dawn Beach.

For a real treat, you may want to try power snorkeling, which uses the mini-submersible water scoots and a fresh air supply float that follows you around so you can go down to about six meters without scuba equipment. **Blue Bubbles Watersports** offers the equipment at their location in Oyster Bay. ☎ 599-554-2502, www.bluebubblesxm.com.

If the idea of going off to discover snorkeling places on your own appeals to you, get a **Rhino Safari** inflatable boat for each person in your party, and then head off. These small, one-passenger boats are easily maneuverable. Rhino Safari provides instructions as well as a guide to take groups around to various sites. ☎ 599-544-3150 or 590-690-2-RHINO.

Watersports

Most of the hotels on the beaches offer watersports programs, including access to snorkeling gear, Sunfish sail boats and other non-motorized gear. For those not staying in a hotel, head to Orient Beach, the watersports capital of the island. There are numerous vendors offering everything from Hobie Cats and surfboards to jet skis.

On the Dutch side, you can rent wave runners, go water skiing and generally pursue your watersports fantasies at Kim Sha Beach, where **Westport Watersports** provides equipment and guides. ☎ 599-544-2557 or 599-522-6499, westport@stmaarten.com.

On Simpson Bay at Pelican Marina, **AquaMania** offers rentals of wave runners as well as guided tours using these fun machines. ☎ 599-544 2640, www.stmaarten-activities.com.

Another well-known watersports supplier is **Blue Bubbles Watersports**, with locations at Oyster Pond Greathouse Marina, Bel Air Beach Resort and Oyster Bay Beach Resort. The type of equipment they offer varies at each location. ☎ 599-554-2502, www.bluebubblessxm.com.

Surfing

Surfer *(Stan Shebs)*

Although surfing is not a sport you think of when you imagine the Caribbean, there are sufficient waves during certain times of the year to merit attempts at riding the waves. Winter waves reach the north and west coasts of the island from November through March and the east coast sees real breakers when tropical storm systems move through from July to November.

Among the prime surfing spots are Guana Bay, Le Galion, Orient Bay, Cole Bay and Mullet Bay. Suppliers offering board rentals are **Windy Reef**, ☎ 590-590-87-08-37, and **Tropical Wave**, ☎ 590-590-87-37-25. The **Soul Seeker Surf Shop** on Cole Bay also has boards and information on the best sites. ☎ 599-581-7082, www.soulseekersurf.com.

Windsurfing & Kitesurfing

The Atlantic side of the island is where most of the windsurfing action takes place. Orient Bay, while frequently choppy, has the best geographic location facing the ocean. You'll find flat water as well as swells and chops, especially between Green Cay and Pinel Island. Le Galion Beach is also a favorite for beginners and intermediate surfers.

Windsurfing

One of the most active windsurfing and kitesurfing groups is **Club Nathalie Simon** at Orient Beach. They rent out windsurfing and kitesurfing equipment, also running competitions and offering instructions. ☎ 590-590-29-41-57, www.cnsorientbay.com.

Windsurf Equipment Providers

Bikini Beach, ☎ 590-590-27-07-48

Club Orient Watersports, ☎ 590-590-87-33-85

Kakao Beach, ☎ 590-590-27-49-94

Kontiki Watersports, ☎ 590-590-87-46-89

Le Galion Watersports (Tropical Wave), ☎ 590-590-87-37-25

Wind Adventures, ☎ 590-590-29-41-57

Windy Reef, ☎ 590-590-87-08-37

Parasailing

Orient Beach is also the location of most of the parasailing activities on St. Martin. **Sun Smile Parasail**, next to Pedro's at the southern end of the beach, can set you up with instructions and all you need to soar above the mere mortals on the beach. ☎ 590-690-71-47-80, www.sunsmileparasail.com.

On the Dutch side, Kim Sha Beach is where most of the parasailing takes place, with **Westport Watersports** providing equipment, instructions, and rides. ☎ 599-544-2557 or 599-522-6499, westport@stmaarten.com. In addition, you can parasail Simpson Beach with **AquaMania**, based at the Pelican Marina. ☎ 599-544 2640, www.stmaarten-activities.com.

Water Tours

With all the visitors that flood St. Martin, and the natural beauty offered by the beaches and landscape, it's no wonder there are a multitude of boat owners offering tours, charters and little bit of everything else under the sun. You definitely have a choice of things to do on the island.

One of the more unusual tours involves a semi-submarine – or specifically the *Seaworld Explorer*. Described as a "cruising, underwater observatory," the vessel is designed so that it remains above sea level, but the hull is surrounded with windows and sits five feet below the surface. So if you don't like snorkeling or diving, here's your chance to view the fascinating world under the sea while sitting in air-conditioned, dry comfort. A knowledgeable guide narrates as you watch schools of yellow tails, barracuda and all sorts of tropical fish float by. The ship departs from Grand Case and tours last about 1¼ hours. ☎ 599-542-4078, www.atlantisadventures.com.

Bluebeard Charters offers a day-long tour to Prickly Pear Cay on the 60-foot catamaran *Heineken*. The tour includes drinks and lunch at Alan's

Beach Bar and Restaurant, along with all the snorkeling and sunning you desire. ☎ 599-557-5935, bluebeard_charters@yahoo.com.

Another day trip in demand is the one aboard the *Lambada*, a sleek catamaran with a crew that loves to party. It's offered by **AquaMania Adventures** and sets out from the Pelican Marina in Simpson Bay. ☎ 599 544 2640, www.stmaarten-activities.com.

AquaMania Adventures

Eagle Tours offers island tours on the 76-ft *Golden Eagle* catamaran. The Explorer Cruise stops for shopping in Marigot. Their Friday Farewell Party, with a full-day sail around the island, is considered by many frequent visitors one of the "must do" activities on the water. ☎ 599-543-0068, www.sailingsxm.com.

Turtle Tours uses 11-ft and 16-ft Boston Whalers as well as their Captain's Yacht to conduct tours around the Simpson Bay lagoon and around the coastlines. They have their own mooring setup at Creole Rock for snorkeling and can customize tours to your itinerary. ☎ 599-526-4662, www.turtletours-sxm.com.

Scoobi-Too

If your love of boat transportation tends more toward self-propelling kayaks, get in touch with **Trisports**. They offer a Discover Explorer Island Tour, a Snorkel Kayak Adventure, and a Sunset Kayak Tour, as well as kayak rentals for do-it-yourself tours. ☎ 599-545-4384, www. trisportsxm.com.

Tours offered on the 75-ft *Scoobi-Too* catamaran include a half-day Snorkeling and Sunset Cruise, a cruise to Prickly Pear Cay, trips to St. Barts and Anguilla and a day-long trip visiting Tintamarre and Anguilla. ☎ 590-590-52-02-53, www. scoobidoo.com.

You may have done pub crawls on land where the ground starts to feel like you're on a rocking boat, but in St. Maarten, you can do the **Lagoon**

Pub Crawl on the 40-ft *Celine* catamaran, and you won't have to worry about your sea legs. You'll visit some of the best restaurants on the Simpson Bay Lagoon (and there are many). They also offer a Sunset Cruise with or without dinner at the SkipJack Restaurant. www. sailstmaarten.com.

The 57-ft *Swaliga II* catamaran tour combines a stop for shopping in St. Barts with snorkeling opportunities, either on the way back from St. Barts or on the reefs off Anguilla. Trips depart from Dock Maarten, just outside Philipsburg. ☎ 599-542-3667, www.swaliga2.com.

ONE-STOP TOUR AND CHARTER PLANNING

Because of the vast array of activities options in St. Martin, some enterprising operators have set up one-stop booking sites where you can arrange everything from a fishing adventure to a sunset cruise, parasailing or picnicking on Tintamarre. Among the activities-reserving websites are:

■ **www.atlantisadventures.com** is an international site booking activities for Hawaii and Guam as well as a number of Caribbean islands. They also operate the *Seaworld Explorer* boats in many locations.

■ **www.saint-martin-activities.com** offers choices ranging from bar-crawl cruises and deep-sea fishing to horseback riding, parasailing and mountain bike rentals.

■ **www.stmaarten-activities.com**, the website of AquaMania, offers diving and snorkeling tours, kids' activities, sunset and dinner cruises, shopping and sightseeing tours, America's Cup Yacht racing and much more.

■ **www.stmaarten-excursions.com** is the website of St. Maarten Shore Trips & Excursions, which bills itself as a "boutique" online activities store. They have the full range of activities, including water tours, sailing adventures, big game fishing, snorkeling and scuba trips and more.

■ **www.sxmtravelguide.com** is a classy looking site sponsored by the Hotel Rental Group. You can book your hotel here as well as all the activities. It's great for those who want to plan out every minute of the trip in advance.

■ **www.viator.com** is a large international concierge service that offers a Philipsburg boardwalk tour, a pirates tour, daytrips to Anguilla, St. Barts, Saba and other islands, a Calypso dinner cruise and all sorts of other interesting adventures.

Deep-Sea Fishing

The waters around St. Martin are teeming with sport fish, including dorado, wahoo, sailfish and tuna. The Billfish Tournament held each June attracts dedicated fishermen from all over the world. So if you want to spend at least a little time in pursuit of big-water game, arrange for a deep-sea charter.

Deep-Sea Fishing Operators

Lee Halley, a fisherman who eventually opened up his own restaurant in St. Maarten (Lee's Roadside Grill), now takes people out to share his knowledge of the seas around the island. His boat, *Baby Blue's*, is equipped with all you need for landing the big fish. ☎ 599-544-4233, www.leesfish.com.

Rudy's Deep Sea Fishing trips benefit from the fishing expertise of Captain Rudy Sierens, who has 21 years of experience in St. Martin's waters. ☎ 599-545-2177, www.rudysdeepseafishing.com.

Taylor Made Charters and experienced Captain Dougie will take you out on a 28-foot Bertram Sportfisher to some of the best fishing spots. ☎ 599-552-7539, www.stmartinstmaarten.com/TaylorMade.

Boat Charters

Have that independent spirit and prefer your own tour, stopping where you want rather than where the group wants? Then you need a boat charter to make your vacation dreams come true. There are many to choose from in St. Martin.

Offshore Sunsations Cigarette

If you want to hit the open waters and get to one of the offshore islands as fast as possible, do it in real style with **Offshore Sunsations'** two go-fast boats, the 38-ft Top Gun Cigarette or the 42-ft Chris Craft motor yacht. You can plan a trip to Tintamarre, Scilly Cay, Sandy Island or a host of other places, and have the boat all to yourself. ☎ 599-552-6026, 330-431-8722 US, www.offshoresunsations.com.

Aquaworld Boat Rentals offers vessels that are a little more manageable, including 18-ft Century boats or inflatable fiberglass-hull boats. You have a choice of being the captain or having one provided. ☎ 599-545-4533, www.aquaworld-goscoot.com.

Reve Marine has an extensive collection of vessels available for bareboat or crewed charters out of Marigot. Among the ones available without a crew are a six-passenger semi-rigid inflatable, a six-passenger Robalo open bow, an eight-passenger Boston Whaler and a six-passenger Angler for fishing. The available skippered yachts range from a 31-ft Sunseeker to a 50-ft Sea Ray motor yacht. They also have several boats for deep-sea fishing trips. ☎ 590-590-87-91-74, www.revemarine.com.

Another company with a selection of different motor and sailing yachts to charter is **Luxe Caraïbes**, based at Charter Plaisance Marina. Among their vessels are Sunseeker Super Yacht 50 and V46 Princess motor boats, or a Lagoon 410, a Nautitech 475 and an 84-ft catamaran. They are available for full- and half-day trips or sunset tours. ☎ 590-590-29-51-93, www.luxecaraibes.com.

Stargazer Yacht Charters has four catamarans ranging from 38 to 40 feet available for bareboat or crewed charters. Or you can become a member of the Stargazer Cruise Club and reserve several weeks of a charter over five years' time. ☎ 599-523-6552 or 590-690-88-58-06, www.stargazer-charter-maritime.com.

Sea Line Charters offers a 42-ft Sea Ray motor yacht for private charters, day-trips and special occasions. The boat is based at Bobby's Marina, Philipsburg. ☎ 599-543-6262, www.sxm-activities.com/sealine.

Sailing

 The waters are bright turquoise, the winds are perfect to inflate sails, the weather is warm – the Caribbean is a sailor's fondest dream. It comes as no surprise that someone would take advantage of all this by basing their sailing yachts in St. Martin and making them available for people to enjoy.

If you ever dreamed of being a crew member on an America's Cup vessel, racing through the waters while you pull your weight to win the Cup, now's your chance to shine. The **12-Metre Challenge** offers a chance to crew on one of five racing vessels that have competed in the famed worldwide race and now participate in regattas around the island. They run four regattas a day, giving you plenty of opportunities to be a part of the excitement. ☎ 599-542-0045, www.12metre.com.

What's more fitting for a pirate's cruise than a Tall Ship? Your entire family may enjoy a day with the ***Lord Sheffield* Tall Ship Adventures**. The ship, a 72-ft two-masted Brigantine, sails from Dock Maarten under billowing canvases to a beach on the leeward side for lunch and snorkeling – and plank-walking of course. Along the way the crew is happy to show you how the sails work and let you inspect the cannons or even take a turn at the helm. The ship is also available for private charters and weddings. ☎ 599-552-0875, www.lordsheffield.com.

As you cut through the waves on the 65-ft Morgan Catalina schooner operated by **Captain Morgan Charters**, you'll feel as if you've left the world behind. The boat sails out of Simpson Bay, skirts the western edge of the island up to Creole Rock for some snorkeling, then anchors in a secret tranquil spot for chilling out before the trip back. If you have a large group, you can charter the entire boat and design your own itinerary. ☎ 599-526-2467, www.captainmorgandaycharters.com.

If you have a group and want to sail the bounding main in a smaller boat, take a look at ***Random Wind***, a 54-ft traditional sailing clipper that can accommodate 18-22 people for day tours, private charters and private sunset cruises. Also available are two power boats, a rebuilt 26-ft Navy launch named *At Random*, and a speedboat named *Random Ly*. ☎ 599-557-5742, www.randomwind.com

Lord Sheffield Tall Ship Adventures

Horizon Yacht Charters has boats available for charter in St. Martin as well as in Antigua, the British Virgins and the Grenadines. Available vessels for bareboat charters range from a Bavaria 40 to a Bahia 46 catamaran, and you can also get a fully crewed Asante Jenneau 49. They will map out a seven- or 10-day itinerary for sailing around St. Martin or one that takes you from St. Martin to Antigua. ☎ 268-562-4725 in Antigua, 866-439-1089 US toll free, www.horizonyachtcharters.com.

Alizes Tropique offers *Bikini*, a Jeantot/Alliaura Marine 465 catamaran for crewed charters throughout the West Indies. They carry along a sea kayak, water skiing and fishing equipment, so you have plenty to do while you island hop or tour your favorite spots. ☎ 590-590-29-65-45, www.alizes-tropique.com.

Looking for a way to practice your sailing skills on a smaller boat? **Lagoon Sail Boat Rentals** offers Sunfast 20 boats that can be taken around Simpson Bay Lagoon. They also host races on Saturday afternoons for those who want to test their skills in actual competition. ☎ 599-557-0714, www.lagoonsailboatrental.com.

Anyway Marine offers sailing catamarans ranging from a Lagoon 380 to a Fountaine Pajot Marquise 56 for day-sails or week-long private crewed charters. ☎ 590-590-87-91-41, www.anywaymarine.com.

On Horseback

 Ride along the island's miles of white sand beaches and scenic trails, dip into the surf to cool off, or head up a mountain trail.

Riding Stables

Lucky Stables in Cole Bay offers one- and two-hour trail rides, one- and two-hour sunset rides, and a unique Champagne Night Ride with a campfire and marshmallow toasting. ☎ 599-544-5255.

A NEW BREED OF HORSES IN ST. MAARTEN

When Roderick and Alexandra Halley returned to their home in the Cay Bay valley after hurricane Luis struck in 1995, they found their horses from Lucky Stables had survived after being released into the wild for their protection. They decided to let them flourish in this wild state until they reached the age of three, at which time they are taken back into the stables to be broken and trained for riding. The horses are now identified as a breed of wild mustangs known as Antillianos, and the Halleys are seeking to have the breed officially recognized. Many people come to the stables and the Cay Bay area to see the wild mustangs.

Bayside Riding Stables at Le Galion Beach near the Butterfly Farm also has beach rides, a champagne ride for two, and a sunset or a full-moon beach ride (how romantic!), ☎ 590-590-87-36-64, www. baysideridingclub.com.

Eco-Travel

The biggest eco-attraction on the island is actually offshore – the **Sint Maarten Marine Park**, which surrounds the island on the Dutch side from Oyster Pond to Cupecoy Bay. It encompasses the coastal waters and beaches and extends down 200 feet. The

best way to enjoy it, of course, is to get in the water. A snorkel or dive here gives you a window into an incredible array of marine life that is now protected, thanks to the Nature Foundation Sint Maarten. To find out more about the Park and the Foundation's preservation activities, see www.naturefoundationsxm.com.

Playing & Watching Sports

Golf

While it can't boast the lush layout and perfectly manicured greens of Anguilla's Temenos Golf Course or Nevis' Four Seasons course, the **Mullet Bay Golf Course** is adequate for 18 holes of action to keep up your skills. The course, which used to be part of the Mullet Bay Resort until a hurricane took it out in 1995, is still maintained by the resort

Mullet Bay's #9 green

and is frequently used by the St. Maarten Golf Association. They offer numerous tournaments, plus monthly Medal Play. ☎ 599-545-3069 or 599-545-2801, stmaartengolf.com.

Families will enjoy the the fun at **Sputter's Miniature Golf**. The 18-hole course is located in Simpson Bay opposite Three Palms Plaza. You play through miniature models of historical buildings and monuments from the island. The course is open from 3 to 10 pm every day, so you don't need to play in the hot sun. ☎ 599-557-1437, www.sputtersminiaturegolf.com.

Tennis

Most of the tennis action takes place on the more than 70 courts at hotels across the island. Using hotel courts means access to a pro and a pro shop for balls, clothing, equipment and repairs, plus lights for night play when the temperatures are a little cooler. There are public courts at the **Alberic Richards Stadium** in Marigot and the **Taoul Illidge Sports Complex** on the Dutch side. **Michael Sprott**, St. Maarten's leading tennis pro, offers clinics and lessons at several properties. ☎ 599-542-6281.

St. Martin

Skydiving

 Tandem-skydiving will give you a brand new perspective on the island. You get a five-minute pre-jump briefing and then follow your guide, an experienced skydiver from **Caribbean Sky Dream** (☎ 590-590-51-02-57), on a breathtaking, 30-second, free fall of about 12,500 feet before the parachute opens and you float safely to the ground.

Bowling

Bowling alleys are a real rarity in the Leewards, but there is one on the Dutch side. **Crown Pin Bowling Alley** on Illidge Road has reasonable prices for use of the lanes. It's a good rainy afternoon activity. ☎ 599-543-0203.

Triathlon/Runs

If you don't want to take a break from your training while on vacation, you can join in numerous triathlons, runs and other types of foot races that occur frequently on the island. The Trisports website has a complete listing of events sponsored by various groups, including Avenir Sportif, Roadrunners, FIAC and Bottom Braquette. ☎ 599-545-4384, www.trisportsxm.com.

Rollerblading

In 1999, Marigot built the **Galisbay Gravity Park**, a unique facility for rollerblading, skateboarding and street hockey, so your kids and teens may want to bring their skates.

Family Fun

KID FRIENDLY St. Martin is a great place for families and offers a good mix of activities on water and on land. If the kids tire of the beach and pool, take them to **The Butterfly Farm** on Le Galion Beach Road. The butterflies move freely around the large mesh-enclosed Butterfly Sphere, so don't be surprised if one takes a ride on your shoul-

Denizen of The Butterfly Farm

der. Landscaped gardens, a waterfall and a koi pond create a serene atmosphere within the Sphere. Expert guides are on hand to answer questions. They advise wearing your brightest colors or a citrus-based perfume, which will attract the creatures to you. Get there early in the morning to see newborn butterflies emerging from their chrysalis. Open 9:30 am to 3:30 pm daily. ☎ 590-590-87-31-21, www.thebutterflyfarm.com.

Squirrel monkeys in St. Maarten Park

Up near the top of Pic Paradis is the **Loterie Farm Fly Zone**, a structure of cables that allows you to soar high up in the branches of 200-year-old mango and mahogany trees. Participants are fitted with harnesses and given a safety briefing before taking off on a 1½-hour traverse course with speedy zip-line runs. For those less than four feet tall, they offer the Ti'Tarzan course of suspended bridges, swinging ropes and other activities. The only requirement is that you wear closed-toe shoes that will stay on your feet even when you are suspended. ☎ 590-590-87-86-16, loteriefarm.com.

St. Maarten Park is a delightful small zoo, with over 500 species of mammals, birds, reptiles, amphibians and invertebrates collected and displayed amid a tropical garden. The park is considered a regional center for animal conservation and works with international agencies on species protection for the highly endangered golden lion tamarind monkeys and other animals. The zoo also has the largest playground on the island, as well as a snack shop and souvenir store. For those who can stay up late, they

Cotton top tamarin (St. Maarten Park)

offer a guided Night Safari Tour one evening a week. The park is open from 9 am to 5 pm daily. ☎ 599-543-2030, www.stmaartenpark.com/english/home.htm.

The **Playstation** at Pelican Marina offers hours of water fun for kids. A catamaran has been converted into a barge-like floating structure with Tarzan and other swings, a water trampoline and two slides. There's easy access on and off the float so kids can get in the water on paddle boats. It's open daily from 9:30 am to 4:30 pm, and children under 12 must be accompanied by an adult. You can just show up at the Marina's Watersports Office, or contact AquaMania for more information. ☎ 599-544-2640, www.stmaarten-activities.com.

AquaMania also offers a **Calypso Tour** designed especially for children. It departs once a day at 3 pm for a 1½-hour trip. The boat cruises around Simpson Lagoon, the kids get to help steer the boat, and, stroke of genius, are given water balloons to lob at a target wreck in the water. There are games with prizes, and drinks are provided, but there is no swimming on this trip. There is some shade, but you need to have the kids coated in sun block and wearing hats. ☎ 599-544-2640, www.stmaarten-activities.com.

Swim with the Dolphins in Anguilla

While St. Martin does not have a dolphin park, you can take a day-trip to Anguilla to swim with these amazing mammals. The **Dolphin Discovery** at Mead's Bay houses two large tanks where you can get so close you may get a kiss on the cheek. Older children and adults can ride the gentle water creatures, all the while learning about their special talents and needs. The only exclusion is that pregnant women are not allowed in the water with the animals, for safety reasons. ☎ 264-497-7946, 800-293-9698 US and Canada, www.dolphindiscovery.com.

Movie Theaters

It's a rainy afternoon and the kids are driving you nuts. Take them to a movie for a few hours of uninterrupted family calm.

Philipsburg

WG Boncamper Rd

Juancho Yrausquin Blvd.

To Dawn Beach, Orleans

Emmaplein **Kanalsteeg**

Back St. **Front St.** **Simartin Museum**

7

Bobby's Marina

Walter Nisbeth Rd.

EC Richardson St.

CA Cannegieter St.

DC Steeg

Old Street

Hospital

6

Tourist Information

Police

Pastoriesteeg

5

P

Wilhelmina

4

Groene

Government Administration Building

Captain Hodge Pier

St. Jansteeg

3

Post Office

Hotelsteeg

Schoolsteeg

Smidsteeg

Front St.

2

Walter Nisbeth (Pondfill) Rd.

Back St. **Drukker Water**

Visserssteeg

N

HUNTER PUBLISHING

Great Salt Pond

Kruythoff

Begroeide

Manzanilla **Sisal**

Great Bay

Kerkhofstraat

Bega Street

Philet St. **Armenhuis-steeg**

Long Wall Road

To Maho & Airport

1

To Fort Amsterdam

1. Great Bay Beach Hotel & Casino
2. St. Maarten Sea Palace
3. Sea View Hotel
4. Court House; Wathey Square
5. Horizon View Beach Hotel
6. Holland House Beach Hotel
7. Passangrahan Royal Guest House

400 METERS

© 2008 HUNTER PUBLISHING, INC.

The **Caribbean Cinemas Megaplex** at Cole Bay is a typical mammoth multi-screen theater, with seven screens and a wide choice of first-run releases, so you can make everyone happy at the same time. Check their website for current films and screening times. ☎ 599-544-4777, www. caribbeancinemas.com.

For an evening out without the kids in tow, check the **Philipsburg Theatres**. This is a movie-lover's dream house where you can relax in comfortable lounge chairs and sofas as you watch classic films. The Foyer Café offers not only the usual snacks, but also wine, champagne and liquor – in fact, you can call ahead and reserve a bottle as well as your seats. The theater is regularly open on Wednesday evenings and hosts a number of special theme nights, such as Indian, Spanish or Dutch nights, where refreshments include samplings of the theme country's cuisine. ☎ 599 543-0001, www.philipsburgtheatres.com.

On the French side, the **MJC Sandy Ground** offers French films with English subtitles, along with film festivals, and even a cartoon festival for children. ☎ 590-590-87-76-02.

Seeing the Sights

Sampling the Culture

The French, Dutch, Amerindian, and African cultures represented on St. Martin are what set it apart from the rest of the Leewards. Sometimes the islands seems more European than West Indian, especially on the French side (and at the topless Orient Beach), but the musical heritage is definitely Caribbean, and the ever-present sounds of calypso, soca, zouk, steel bands and reggae keep the island on beat.

Carnival

And then there is **Carnaval** – celebrated twice for double the revelry and spectacle. The French do it in the Mardi Gras fashion, with parades through the street before Lent. The Dutch follow more of the Caribbean traditions, holding it after Easter and coinciding with their celebration for the Queen's birthday. If you are on the island at either time, you'll see how music, food and clothing are intimately intertwined with the islanders' culture and heritage.

Marigot

To Hotel le Grand St. Martin,
Grand Case, Airport

Rue de Galisbay

Rue Fichaut

Rue de Hollande

Rue Paul Mingau

Rue de la République

Marigot Bay
(Baie de Marigot)

Rue Felix Eboue

Rue Maurasse

Rue de L'Hotel
de Ville

Rue de Palais Justice

Marigot Waterfront

Boulevard de France

Rue de la Liberté

Rue Charles de Gaulle

Rue St. James

Rue de Hollande

Rue de President Kennedy

Marina Port
La Royale

Simpson Bay
Lagoon

To St. James,
Bellevue,
Philipsburg

To Sandy
Ground

1. West Indies Mall
2. Fort St. Louis; Marina
3. Pier; Port
4. Gendarmerie
5. Marketplace (Marché)
6. City Hall (Mairie)
7. Police
8. Library; Banana Market
9. Post Office
10. Hotel La Résidence
11. Hotel Royale Louisiana
12. Hotel Marina Royale
13. Musée de Saint Martin
14. Cemetery
15. Hotel Beach Plaza

P Parking

100 METERS

© 2008 HUNTER PUBLISHING, INC.

For a quick dip into the culture that is modern-day St. Martin, visit the **French Market** along the waterfront in Marigot. This colorful collection of more than 100 stalls is the biggest handicraft market in the Caribbean. It showcases local artisans' works, ranging from jewelry and textile works to pottery, paintings and woodcarving. At one end of the complex is **Les Lolos**, a collection of traditional Creole restaurants where you can sample the dishes that make this region unique.

Loterie Farm (Jessica Payne)

One of the mainstays of the St. Martin culture is agriculture. The history of the island is a history of salt, sugar and those foodstuffs that were for many years the 'gold' that nations sought to own. While there are no more cane fields or salt factories, you can still see some agricultural remnants such as **Loterie Farm** near Pic Paradis (☎ 590-590-87-86-16, www.loteriefarm.com), an old plantation that is slowly being recreated with the cultivation of mango, banana and other fruit trees. Or visit the **Carib Isle Plantation** on Route de Colombier (☎ 590-590-52-93-92), a working watermelon plantation where you can learn about the history of the fruit, along with many delicious recipes.

While most visitors encounter the boat industry here while planning sea excursions or wandering through the marinas to look at the mega-yachts, boating and boatmaking are full of cultural traditions. Colorful hand-made vessels reflect the pride of individual villages as they race around the island in frequent regatta and on public holidays. Take a seat at one of the seaside French restaurants and watch crews prepare the open-hulled, single-masted boats for a local regatta.

The culture of St. Martin is one of hospitality and warmth in the European tradition, flavored with the color and passion of the Caribbean.

Make sure you get out of your hotel to see the countryside, meet some of the people, and enjoy all that this interesting island has to offer.

Reliving History

Many travelers like to get a sense of the history of the place they are visiting, and St. Martin makes that history entertaining in several ways. If you're shopping in Marigot, take an hour out of your shopping time to see the display of Arawak relics at the **Marigot Museum** (☎ 590-590-29-22-84). Be sure and check to see if one of the talks on the pre-colonial period is scheduled. Or take a walk up to **Ft. Louis**, a

Fort Louis

defensive battery built in 1789 on the hill to the north of the harbor. It was designed to protect the port from pirates, privateers and invading armies. In Philipsburg you can also visit the remains of military battlements at **Fort Amsterdam** and **Fort William**.

The site of the sugar mill at **Plantation Mont Vernon**, just outside of Grand Case, is now a demonstration garden depicting how local products were historically processed and prepared for export. As you wander along the paths and listen to the audio guide, you learn how salt, tobacco, indigo, cotton, sugarcane and rum were integral parts of the island's economy and history. ☎ 590-590-29-50-62, www.plantationmontvernon.com.

Where to Stay

Luxe Hotels

French Side

$$$$$ –These are the most expensive accommodations on the island, ranging from US$460 to $950 a night for a double beach-front junior suite or equivalent lodging. All are either BP or EP rates.

Esmeralda Resort

This mid-sized resort on Orient Beach has a small-resort feel since the rooms are situated in villas scattered around the property and its lush gardens. There are no more than four rooms to a villa (which can be interconnected), and each villa has its own pool. The property has a beach bar at Coco Beach, and beach chairs are available near the bar for guests, so you won't have to fight the crowds at the adjacent Orient Beach for chairs and service. The resort provides a Privilege Card that allows you to charge your restaurant or bar tab at any of the five Orient Bay restaurants. If you want to be where the watersports action is, this is an ideal hotel for you. The hotel is closed annually from the end of August to the end of September.

Esmeralda Resort

Location: Orient Beach, on the eastern side of the island.

Rooms: 65 in 18 villas, including superior, deluxe and oceanfront rooms and superior and deluxe suites. Deluxe suites can be joined with deluxe rooms to create a two-, thee- or four-bedroom suite for families or groups. All rooms have kitchenettes, private terraces, satellite TV and AC.

Rates: EP.

Features: Restaurant, beach bar, two tennis

courts with lights, 18 pools, watersports, beach chairs and umbrellas, concierge service, WiFi service in lobby.

☎ 590-590-87-36-36, 800-622-7836 US, 01-45-61-56-00 France, fax 590-590-87-35-18, www.esmeralda-resort.com.

THE DOLLAR-A-DAY PROGRAM BENEFITS EVERYONE

If you are staying in a St. Maarten hotel, you may see a $1 charge added to your bill for every day of your stay. This is a voluntary contribution to the St. Maarten "Dollar-A-Day" fund, which goes to tourism development and programs for local youth. A large part of the fund's investment is in education, including scholarships for tuition at the University of St. Maarten as well as seminars and professional enhancement workshops. In addition, the fund contributes to environmental clean-up programs and other activities to protect natural resources.

The program is sponsored by the St. Maarten Hospitality & Trade Association. For more information, see the association's website at www.shta.com.

Le Domaine de Lonvilliers

This elegant resort is removed from the hustle and bustle of the rest of the island by virtue of its location on Anse Marcel, which has its own marina, shops and restaurants. The buildings are clustered around a main promenade that leads down to the beach, a white sand beauty with VIP cabanas and lounges with thick cushions. The comfortable rooms are done in bright Caribbean colors and colonial décor. A gym and tennis/squash facility are located nearby for those who want to stay active,

Le Domaine de Lonvilliers

and the restaurant on-site consistently receives high marks. Be aware however, that Radisson is renovating the resort adjacent to this property, and work is expected to continue through 2008.

Location: Anse Marcel, in the northwestern part of the island.

Rooms: 112 rooms and 18 suites, all with private balconies, coffee/tea service, designer toiletries and welcome gift, TV, complimentary WiFi in room, robes and slippers. Suites have sofa beds and separate shower.

Rates: BP.

Features: Restaurant, bar, two pools (one for children), beach with cabanas, spa services on beach, complementary buffet breakfast.

☎ 590-590-52-35-35, fax 590-590-29-10-81, www.hotel-le-domaine.com.

Villa at La Plantation

La Plantation Hotel

Up on the hill above Orient Bay sits this stylish yet homey resort where you'll feel like a long-treasured returning guest even on your first visit. The colonial-style villas are set amid tropical gardens, and the rooms are colorfully decorated with bright colors and hand-done stencils and murals. Each villa has one master suite and studios on each side, which can be combined or rented separately. The restaurant, Café Plantation, is highly recommended and has a very romantic setting around the pool, overlooking the sparkling lights of Orient Beach at night. The hotel is closed annually from September 1 to October 15.

Location: On the hill above Orient Bay, on the eastern side of the island.

Rooms: 17 suites and 34 studios, all with ceiling fans, safes, TV, beds with mosquito netting, AC and Internet access in room (fee). Suites have a full-sized kitchen and separate living room, while studios have kitchenettes.

Rates: BP.

Features: Restaurant, bar, pool, small gym, small boutique, beach chairs and towels, access to tennis courts and a pro (fee), Orient Bay Card for charge privileges at beach restaurants, concierge services, Internet access in lobby.

☎ 590-590-29-58-00, fax 590-590-29-58-08, www.la-plantation.com.

St. Martin

Terrace at La Samanna Hotel

La Samanna Hotel

Take a look at "The Best" lists in any magazine dealing with Caribbean resorts, and you'll find this resort listed among the top 10. As part of the Orient-Express Hotel collection, the hotel has an air of refined relaxation, with luxury appointments and stellar personal service. Of course, it all comes at a price, and this is one of the most expensive hotels in the Caribbean. The rooms underwent significant renovations in 2006 to update the décor and furnishings. The suites are the most lavish, with oversized bathrooms, marble floors and separate living, kitchen and patio areas – some even have private plunge pools on roof terraces. The Elysées Spa has a long list of luxury treatments and massage services using Physiodermie and St. Barth products. In 2006, the hotel started a luxury villa project, adding very expensive, very large villas, which will be privately owned. Two of them will eventually be included in the hotel stock of available rooms. The hotel closes for the months of September and October every year.

Location: On the western tip of the island at Baie Longue.

Rooms: 81, including ocean-view rooms, deluxe and premium one-bedroom suites, two-bedroom suites, three-bedroom villas, and five specialty suites. All have private terraces, ceiling fans, AC, safes, luxury bath amenities, bathrobes, slippers, satellite TV, VCRs, and mini-bars.

Rates: BP.

Features: Two restaurants, champagne bar, beach bar, fitness center, spa, Pilates studio, two pools, three tennis courts, beach, cabanas (fee), watersports, business center.

☎ 590-590-87-64-00, 800-854-2252 US, fax 590-590-87-87-86, www. lasamanna.com.

Dutch Side

Princess Resort & Casino, Port de Plaisance

This complete resort on its own island in Simpson Lagoon is a favorite with boat people, since they can moor the boats in the marina right outside the main entrance; it's also popular with people who are looking for one-stop activity shopping. The rooms are large and accommodating, with

Port de Plaisance

full kitchens and views overlooking either the marina or the gardens. One of the main attractions is the Princess Casino, which has 650 slots and 20 gaming tables. Dining rooms offering various cuisines surround the casino.

Location: At the eastern edge of Simpson Lagoon.

Rooms: 88, including junior, one- and two-bedroom suites, all with kitchens, cable TV, safes, AC and DSL Internet access.

Rates: EP.

Features: Three restaurants, two bars, casino, pool with waterfall, health center, fitness center, seven tennis courts, spa, WiFi in lobby, and marina.

☎ 599-544-5222, fax 599-544-2315, www.princessresortandcasino.com.

Sonesto Maho Beach

If you like big resorts with lots of rooms, restaurants, shops, entertainment and activities right outside your door, this is your place. The Maho is like a little city unto itself. The high-rise Sky Tower has 400 rooms and the low-rise Ocean Terrace has 137 newly renovated luxury rooms. A casino, several restaurants, night club, disco, spa, fitness center, and shopping mall are just adjacent. The rooms on the top three floors have been renovated and designated as "premier." The beach is on the leeward side so the waves are calm and a lot of people spend time in the water playing various sports.

Location: Maho Bay, on the southern side of the island.

Rooms: 537, including Supersaver doubles and kings, Pool-Ocean View doubles and kings, Island View-Garden doubles and kings, Premier Island View doubles and kings, Premier Ocean View dou-

Sonesta Maho Beach

bles and kings, and junior suites. All have cable TV, AC, tiled floors, and data ports with Internet access (fee).

Rates: EP, with AI and other packages available.

Features: Three restaurants, several bars, pool, Good Life Spa, fitness facility, four tennis courts, casino, nightclub, disco, and shopping mall.

☎ 599-545-2115, 800-223-0757 US, fax 599-545-3180, www.mahobeach. com.

Westin Dawn Beach

Westin Dawn Beach

This is the newest addition to the hotel scene on the island, and the finishing touches were still being put on it in early 2007. It is a large, glitzy resort true to the Westin style, with their trademarked Heavenly Beds, Heavenly Baths, Westin Kids Club and other features. There is a casino, spa, fitness room, restaurants, pool, beach, business center and pretty much anything else you desire, all in one location convenient to Philipsburg and Orient Beach. And it's on Dawn Beach, known to be one of the best on the island.

Location: Dawn Beach, on the eastern side of the island.

Rooms: 317, with 311 rooms and six suites, including three Presidential suites and three Parlor suites. All include refreshment centers, coffee/tea service, ceiling fans, oversized baths, balconies, TV, AC and Internet access (fee).

Rates: EP.

Features: Two oceanfront restaurants, pool café, two bars,

Pool at Westin Dawn Beach

room service, casino, spa, fitness center, business center, large infinity edge pool, Westin Kids Club, watersports, dive shop, concierge.

☎ 599-543-6700, 800-937-8461 US, fax 599-543-6004, www.starwoodhotels.com/westin.

Luxury with Limits
French Side

$$$$ – These properties are more moderate but still luxurious hotels that offer a range of amenities and beachfront living. Rates range from US$350 to $400 per night for a double beach-front junior suite or equivalent lodging. All are either BP or EP rates.

Alamanda Resort

Alamanda Resort

While not immediately on Orient Beach, this hotel is as close as you can get. The Kakao Beach restaurant – one of the Five Stars of Orient Beach – is here and provides complimentary beach chairs and umbrellas to the Alamanda's guests. The rooms are done in British colonial/West Indies style with rattan furniture and colorful accents for a real island feel. The hotel is closed from the end of August to the end of September every year.

Location: Just off Orient Beach, eastern side of the island.

Rooms: 42, including singles, junior suites and two-bedroom duplexes. The choices are between ground floor/pool or beach front rooms and first floor/ocean view rooms. Many of the rooms are interconnected and can be rented as two-bedroom accommodations. All have kitchenettes, ceiling fans, satellite TV and AC.

Rates: EP.

Features: Two restaurants (with several others adjacent), pool, beach, two tennis courts, easy access to watersport rentals.

☎ 590-590-52-87-40, fax 590-590-52-87-41, www.alamanda-resort.com.

Hotel Beach Plaza

Hotel Beach Plaza

Location is the big plus for this modern hotel just outside Marigot and right on the beach. The views of Marigot Bay are beautiful, and the rooms are comfortable, if not overly luxurious. The lobby is an open three-story atrium with a unique glass floor and fountains. The soft white sand beach has shade huts, and you can snorkel right in front of the hotel.

Location: Just outside Marigot on the road to the southern part of the island.

Rooms: 144, including six suites; all have mini-fridges, safes, private balconies, TV with satellite cable, WiFi access (fee) and AC.

Rates: BP, with meal plans available.

Features: Restaurant, two bars, pool, beach with watersports, pier with sundeck, meeting rooms.

☎ 590-590-87-87-00, fax 590-590-87-18-87, www.hotelbeachplazasxm. com.

Hotel L'Esplanade

This charming European-style hotel sits on the hill above Grand Case. All accommodations have great views of the bay and its sunsets. The service is warm and accommodating, and the rooms are done with a lot of dark wood paneling and heavy furniture for a cozy ambiance. The staff will

L'Esplanade

deliver a delightful continental breakfast with freshly baked croissants, but you will want to take the path down the hill to Grand Case for all your other meals so you can sample the incredible restaurants lining the beach and main street there. In 2008 they will be adding eight more units above the current hotel – called The Villas at L'Esplanade.

Location: Grand Case, western side of the island.

Rooms: 24, including deluxe studios, deluxe lofts, oversized lofts and one-bedroom suites. All have full European kitchens, dining areas, ceiling fans, luxury bath amenities, terraces, cable TV, CD player w/sound system, Internet access and AC. Some studios and lofts have open-air showers.

Rates: EP, with BP available.

Features: Pool with swim-up bar, Internet in room, access to Grand Case Beach.

☎ 590-590-87-06-55, fax 590-590-87-29-15, www.lesplanade.com.

Marquis Resort

Situated high on the hill above Anse Marcel, the Marquis is a small luxury boutique hotel with easy access to one of the largest fitness complexes on the island. The fully-equipped gym, four tennis courts and two squash courts are available to Marquis guests free of charge. The hotel also offers free transportation down to the beach and charge privileges at the beach bar and

Marquis Resort terrace

the restaurants at the marina. This hotel is closed annually from the end of August to the first week in October.

Location: Above Anse Marcel, on the northeast side of the island.

Rooms: 17, with superior and deluxe rooms and suites. All have private terraces with a view to the sea, minibars, ceiling fans, AC, satellite TV, CD and DVD players, safes, and WiFi access at no fee.

Rates: BP.

Features: Bar, pool, fitness facility, shuttle to beach, beach chairs, airport transfers (included in rates), spa treatments, concierge service.

☎ 590-590-29-42-30, fax 590-590-87-46-33, www.hotel-marquis.com.

Le Petit Hotel

Le Petit Hotel

This intimate Mediterranean-style beauty, the sister hotel to L'Esplanade, is close to all that Grand Case offers and has a great beach just steps away (literally, for the beachfront studios). The rooms are furnished with dark Balinese furniture, the walls are stark white, and beds are piled with quality white linens and down pillows. As is true for the Petriluzzi's other hotels, Le Petit has earned many accolades from guests and the media for its warm and personal service.

Location: Grand Case, on the western side of the island.

Rooms: 10, including oversized beach-front studios, deluxe second- and third-floor studios and one-bedroom suites. All have king-sized "Celestial Beds," kitchenettes, sitting areas, dining areas, large terraces, safes, ceiling fans, AC, cable TV with DVD player, CD player and sound system, WiFi Internet access, bathrobes and luxury French bath amenities.

Rates: BP.

Features: Beach, near Grand Case.

☎ 590-590-29-09-65, fax 590-590-87-09-19, www.lepetithotel.com.

Princess Heights Hotel

This addition to the St. Martin luxury hotel scene has been receiving rave reviews from the media and guests. It's across from Dawn Beach, up on the hill for dramatic ocean views. Each one- or two-bedroom suite is done in a unique style, and all have rich appointments, such as marble floors, whirlpool baths, granite kitchen counters and large, comfortable rooms.

Princess Heights

As a family-run hotel, the standards for service are very high and it shows.

Location: Dawn Beach area, eastern side of the island.

Rooms: 15, including one- and two-bedroom suites. All have full kitchens, extensive balconies, living/dining rooms, safes, ceiling fans, central AC, whirlpool tubs and cable TV.

Rates: EP.

Features: Grocery-stocking service.

☎ 599-543-6906, 800-441-7227 US, fax 599-543-6007, www.princessheights.com.

Dutch Side

Belair Beach Hotel

This all-suite hotel is on Little Bay Beach, right outside Philipsburg, so you have views to the harbour and the incoming cruise ships as well as Saba, Statia and St. Kitts. The suites are furnished in Caribbean modern – white furniture, colorful textiles – and are very functional. They have a beach café, and you are centrally located near all the restaurants of Philipsburg.

Belair Beach Hotel

Location: Little Bay Beach, southern part of the island.

Rooms: 72 one- and two-bedroom suites, all with ocean views. All suites have living/dining areas, private terraces, full kitchens, safes, ceiling fans, AC, and satellite TV/VCR. The two-bedroom suites also have a sofa bed in the living room.

Rates: EP.

Features: Beach restaurant, pool, tennis court, beach, watersports, on-site store, car rental desk, activities desk, Laundromat, video rental and book exchange.

☎ 599-542-3366, fax 599-542-6017, www.belairbeach.com.

Great Bay Beach Resort & Casino

This large hotel just on the edge of Philipsburg is a favorite of older visitors, outbound cruise passengers and groups, because all the conveniences – including a casino – are right there. The beach is not soft sand, but rather broken-up coral, so it can be a little rough for walking, and it's facing the busy harbour so the water isn't always clear. But the resort underwent a large-scale renovation in 2005 and 2006 as part of its addition

Great Bay Beach Resort

to the Sonesta chain, so the rooms are attractive and comfortable.

Location: Great Bay, on the southern part of the island.

Rooms: 210 rooms and 52 newly renovated suites. Room choices are ocean-view and mountain-view standard and superior rooms, or one- and two-bedroom suites. All have balconies, safes (fee), satellite TV and AC.

Rates: EP, with AI available.

Features: Two restaurants, two bars, Golden Casino, pool, outdoor whirl-pool, tennis court, Vitality Oasis Health Club and Spa, gift shop, activities center.

☎ 599-542-2446, fax 599-542-3859, www.sonesta.com/greatbay.

Reasonable, Comfortable Hotels

$$$ – These are the value accommodations, ranging from US$300 to $350 a night for a double beach-front junior suite or equivalent lodging. All are either BP or EP rates.

French Side

Cap Caraïbes

Terrace at Cap Caraïbes

This all-suite hotel on Orient Beach is great for those who love being in the middle of the action. The beach is the central headquarters for much of the watersports, sun tanning and limin' on the island. Sold initially as condos, many of the suites are now available for vacation rentals. The units are furnished in bamboo and teak and many face the sea. Dining tables on the balconies give you a front-row seat for people-watching on the beach below. Guests can use complimentary beach chairs at the La Playa or Waikiki restaurants.

Location: Orient Bay, eastern side of the island.

Rooms: 35 one-bedroom suites, with a choice of deluxe ocean-view, superior ocean-view and superior garden-view price levels. All have kitchens, sitting areas, safes, TV, AC and dual voltage outlets.

Rates: EP.

Features: Restaurant, beach with watersports and chairs, children's playground, tennis court, volleyball courts, charge privileges at beach restaurants, Internet access (fee).

☎ 590-590-52-94-94, fax 590-590-52-95-00, www.cap-caraibes.com.

Club Orient

This infamous naturist (nudist) resort on Orient Beach was rated the best clothing-optional resort in the Caribbean by Caribbean Travel & Life magazine. The resort is relatively new, and has a nice layout of chalets, suites and studios along the beach and scattered throughout the property. All are done in a pleasant, uncluttered style. There is also a three-bedroom villa with a plunge pool available for families or groups, plus a Wellness Center and two restaurants.

Location: Orient Beach, on the eastern side of the island.

Rooms: 137, including chalets, deluxe mini-suites, mini-suites, studios, and the three-bedroom villa. All have either a sleeper sofa or day beds for additional guests, full kitchens, sitting areas with desks, outdoor eating area, beach lounges, ceiling fans, AC, dual voltage outlets and Internet access.

Club Orient

Rates: EP.

Features: Two restaurants, bar, beach with watersports, lounges and umbrellas, Wellness Center (spa), fitness center, tennis court and general store

☎ 590-590-87-33-85, 800-690-0199 US, fax 590-590-87-33-76, www. cluborient.com.

Le Flamboyant Resort

Le Flamboyant

This large hotel sits on the narrow strip of land between the Simpson Lagoon and Baie Nettle, facing the lagoon and the beach. The three-story buildings are clustered together, so you may get a view of nothing but another room across the way, although garden- and lagoon-view rooms are available. There is a beach on the lagoon for watersports and a daily shuttle to Baie Rouge, where the water is clearer, for swimming. This is one of the few hotels on the island with an all inclusive option, which includes all meals and drinks and non-motorized watersports, as well as beach, casino and shopping shuttles. The hotel is closed annually from early September to mid-October.

Location: Simpson Lagoon at Baie Nettle.

Rooms: 271 in 23 buildings, with standard garden-view and deluxe lagoon-view rooms and suites, and standard garden-view and deluxe lagoon-view two-bedroom duplexes. All have terraces with kitchenettes and dining area, safes, satellite TV and AC.

Rates: AI or EP.

Features: Two restaurants, bar, two pools, Jacuzzi, volleyball, fitness room, lighted tennis court, table tennis, non-motorized watersports, boutique, activities desk, car rental desk, massage center, Internet in lobby.

☎ 590-590-87-60-00, 800-221-5333 US, fax 590-590-87-60-57, www.le-flamboyant.com.

Grand Case Beach Club

Terrace at Cap Caraïbes

This lovely beachfront hotel sits at the northern end of Grand Case village, a quaint town of wonderful restaurants and shops. The rooms, even the studios, are large, and the duplex and loft units look out to the water. The pool sits out on a peninsula with the Sunset Café, where guests and non-guests can enjoy a good meal at water's edge.

Location: Grand Case, on the western side of the island.

Rooms: 67, including ocean- and garden-view studios, ocean-view studios with lofts, ocean- and garden-view one-bedroom units and ocean-view two-bedroom duplexes. All have kitchens, balconies or terraces, safes, satellite TV, CD player and AC.

Rates: BP.

Features: Restaurant, two beaches with watersports, lighted tennis court, pool and art gallery.

☎ 590-590-87-51-87, 800-344-3016 US, fax 590-590-87-59-93, www.grandcasebeachclub.com.

L'Hoste Hotel

This is another Orient Beach favorite, located just off the beach behind La Playa Restaurant so guests have immediate access to the watersports and tanning activities. All accommodations are junior suites and vary by the type of furnishings (i.e. , Bamboo Suites have all bamboo and rattan furniture), and the type of view. Guests have charging privileges at all five Orient Beach restaurants in addition to the two restaurants on-site. Guests can start with the continental breakfast poolside, and then wander down to La Playa to set up their beach chairs and umbrellas.

Pool at L'Hoste Hotel

Location: Orient Beach, on the eastern side of the island.

Rooms: 57 one-bedroom suites, including garden-view, Bamboo and deluxe categories. All have kitchenettes, sitting areas, private balconies, safes, ceiling fans, AC, cable TVs and VCR.

Rates: BP.

Features: Two restaurants (and access to four more), pool, fitness room, library and activities desk.

☎ 590-590-87-42-08, 888-843-4779 US, fax 590-590-87-39-96, www. hostehotel.com.

Dutch Side

Atrium

Atrium

This high-rise on Simpson Bay is primarily a timeshare resort that also makes rooms available for vacationers not in the timeshare pool. The accommodations are comfortable and attractive in a generic hotel room kind of way, and include kitchens, living and dining areas. The beach is white powdery sand and the water right in front of the hotel is good for swimming; the other side of the hotel faces the Simpson Lagoon.

Location: Simpson Bay, near the bridge, on the southern coast.

Rooms: 87 studios, one-bedroom and two-bedroom suites. All have full kitchens, AC, cable TV, balconies.

Rates: EP.

Features: Restaurant, beach with lounges and umbrellas, pool, activities desk, laundry facilities.

☎ 599-544-2126, fax 599-544-2128, www.atrium-resort.com.

Caravanserai Beach Resort

This sprawling resort near the airport has recently undergone renovation and is expanding, with the addition of 46 new units. Its real advantage is the location, central to all the restaurants and nightlife of Simpson Bay and near Philipsburg. It is also self-contained, with four restaurants, four pools, a beach, tennis courts and a casino.

Location: Burgeaux Bay, near the airport, on the southern coast.

Rooms: 116 rooms and one-bedroom suites. All rooms have balconies, safes, cable TV, AC and fax machines. The standard rooms have coffeemakers; the suites have full kitchens.

Rates: EP.

Features: Four restaurants, four pools, beach, tennis complex, seaside boardwalk, boutique, Dunes Casino and tour desk.

Caravanserai

☎ 866-786-2278, www.caravanserai-beachresort.com.

Divi Little Bay Beach Resort

This large self-contained resort is situated on a peninsula that reaches out into Little Bay, adjacent to Great Bay and Philipsburg.

Divi Little Bay Beach Resort

Everything you need in a Caribbean vacation is right here – pools, tennis, fitness, shopping, restaurants and watersports.

Location: On Little Bay, southern coast of the island.

Rooms: 235, including beachfront rooms and hillside one- and two-bedroom suites. All have balconies, AC, satellite TV; suites have kitchens, dining and sitting areas.

Rates: EP with meal plans available.

Features: Three restaurants, three pools, beach, watersports, lighted tennis courts, fitness room, activities center and shopping area.

☎ 599-542-2333, 800-367-3484 US, fax 599-542-4336, www.divilittlebay. com.

Flamingo Beach Resort

This Sunterra resort sits on the point at Pelican Key, surrounded on three sides by water. Primarily a timeshare resort, it makes rooms available for walk-in vacationers (those not in the timeshare program). Rooms are done in bright colors and are large enough to comfortably accommodate king-size beds.

Flamingo Beach Resort

Location: Simpson Bay/ Pelican Key, on the southern coast.

Rooms: 240, including garden-view, Saba-view or beachfront studios; hillside, garden, ocean or beachfront one-bedroom units, and hillside or ocean two-bedroom units. All have kitchens, balconies, ceiling fans, AC, satellite TVs with DVD/VCR players and safes.

Rates: EP.

Features: Restaurant, bar, pool, beach, tennis court, watersports and activities desk, mini-market, gift shop and launderette.

☎ 599-544-3900, US 800-424-1943, fax 599-544-3727, www.flamingo-beach-resort.com.

Holland House

This urban hotel is a favorite of Caribbean nationals, business travelers, and vacationers who want to be near all the shops and restaurants of

Holland House

Philipsburg. It has a beach on Great Bay, looking out toward the Walthey Pier where the cruise ships dock, and is conveniently located near the Boardwalk. Service is reputed to be excellent, and the rooms are basic comfortable hotel style.

Location: Philipsburg, on the eastern edge near the cruise ship docks.

Rooms: 54, including standard, street-view and beach-view rooms, junior suites and a one-bedroom penthouse. All have balconies, mini-fridges, ceiling fans, AC, satellite TVs and modem Internet access.

Rates: EP.

Features: Restaurant, open-air bar, beach, ocean-front lounge deck, concierge, business services, gift shop, laundry and shops.

☎ 599-542-2572, 800-223-9815 US, fax 599-542-4673, www.hhbh.com.

La Vista Resort/La Vista Beach Resort

Tucked into the hillside overlooking Pelican Key, this small resort has a variety of different rooms and cottages stepping up the hill. The La Vista Beach Resort is a building with beachfront studio and two-bedroom suites. While the beach referred to here is really a rocky strand, it's

La Vista Resort

the accommodations and the personal service that keep guests coming back. The beachside pool is nice, but expect to walk down to Pelican Resort for a soft-sand beach and watersports activities.

Location: Pelican Key, southern coast of the island.

Rooms: In La Vista Resort there are 32, including junior suites, deluxe suites, penthouse, one-bedroom cottages, sleeps-four deluxe room, one-bedroom deluxe and one-bedroom penthouse. La Vista Beach Resort offers 18 studios and two-bedroom suites. All units have kitchenettes, safes, cable TVs and AC.

Rates: EP.

Features: Restaurant, two pools, sundry shop, laundry.

☎ 599-544-3005, fax 599-544-3010, www.lavistaresort.com.

Mary's Boon Beach Hotel

This popular historic hotel shows up on many of the major travel magazines' lists of the best hotels – although you have to wonder if the reviewers are deaf because the hotel sits right by the runway for the airport. On the plus side, the rooms front Simpson Bay beach, the service is warm and family-oriented, and the

Mary's Boon

suites are beautifully decorated. You have a choice of location and view, but the prime accommodations are the ones right on the beach. One nice touch is that meals are served family-style, so you and your fellow travelers can share experiences.

Location: Simpson Bay Beach, near Philipsburg.

Rooms: 26, including studios and one- and two-bedroom suites, with various locations and views. All have kitchens or kitchenettes, AC and cable TV.

Rates: EP.

Features: Dining room, honor bar, pool with swim-up bar, beach, Jacuzzi.

☎ 599-545-7000, fax 599-545-3403, www.marysboon.com.

Oyster Bay Beach

This popular large resort is situated on a point, with Oyster Bay on one side and Dawn Beach on the other, giving guests plenty of water views. The location is so well-liked by timeshare participants and vacationers that the resort is adding a new 18-residence Lighthouse structure as well as 40 additional timeshare units over the next few years. One of the major draws, other than Dawn Beach, is the sprawling infinity-edge pool that

Oyster Bay Beach

runs along the ocean. It garnered an award from *Trip Advisor* for the Best Pool in the Caribbean.

Location: Dawn Beach at Oyster Point, on the eastern side of the island.

Rooms: 178, including superior rooms, studios, junior suites, deluxe lofts and one- and two-bedroom units. Choices are oceanfront, marina front or beachfront. All have kitchenettes or mini-fridges, dining areas, ceiling fans, AC, safes, private balconies, satellite TVs with VCR, CD player.

Rates: EP.

Features: Restaurant, bar, pool, whirlpool, beach with chairs and umbrellas, fitness facility, laundry, gift shop, jewelry store, activities desk.

☎ 599-543-6040, 866-978-0212 US, fax 599-543-6695, www.obbc.com.

Pelican Resort

This is one of the largest hotels on the island. It has 342 rooms and is a self-contained resort with pretty much everything you would want – including a casino, marina, spa and shopping arcade. The beach is on Simpson Bay and a great place from which to watch mega yachts and other boats heading toward the

The beach at Pelican Resort

drawbridge and into the lagoon marinas. It is also a timeshare resort that makes units available to non-members when available.

Location: Simpson Bay, southern coast of the island.

Rooms: 342, including studios and one- , two- and three-bedroom suites, with ocean or hillside views. All have kitchenettes, dining areas, sitting areas with sofa bed, patios, safes, satellite TVs and AC.

Rates: EP.

Features: Two restaurants, two bars, five pools and children's pool, beach, large watersports center, four lighted tennis courts, children's playground, casino, marina, dive shop, L'Aqualigne Spa, shopping arcade and guest laundry.

☎ 599-544-2503, fax 599-544-2133, www.pelicanresort.com.

Royal Palm Beach Club

This is another of the Sunterra timeshare resorts on the island, located at Simpson Bay near the bridge leading into the Lagoon. The six-story building is shaped like a wide V spanning the powdery white sand beach, so views out to the sea are beautiful. The rooms are done in white wicker furniture with pastel textiles for an airy feel.

Location: Simpson Bay, on the southern coast of the island.

Royal Palm Beach Club

Rooms: 140, including one- , two- and three-bedroom suites. All have kitchenettes, dining areas, sitting areas with sofa beds, balconies, ceiling fans, AC, satellite TVs with VCR/DVD player

Rates: EP.

Features: Restaurant, bar, pool, beach with watersports, fitness center, gift shop/grocery and beauty salon.

☎ 599-544-3711, 800-438-2929 US, fax 599-544-5965, www. royalpalmbeachresort.com.

Wyndham Sapphire

This high-rise beauty is on Cupecoy Beach, facing out to the Caribbean and backing up to Simpson Bay Lagoon. In addition to rooms in the tall building, there are villas right on the beach with dramatic views out to the sea. All rooms facing the ocean have private Jacuzzis on the balconies, and the villas and penthouse suites have their own pools. The beach is

Wyndham Sapphire

rocky in places, but generally has some good stretches and is a prime spot for swimming, snorkeling and watersports.

Location: Cupecoy Beach, southern coast of the island.

Rooms: 180, including one- and two-bedroom suites, penthouses and villas. All have kitchenettes or full kitchens, marble baths, sitting areas, dining areas, safes, AC, satellite TVs with VCRs, high-speed Internet access.

Rates: EP.

Features: Restaurant, health club, two pools, beach with watersports, hair salon and day spa, business center, video arcade, stores, activities desk, car rental desk.

☎ 599-545-2179, 877-231-8767 US, fax 599-545-2178, www.wyndham. com.

Good Value Hotels

$$ – These are generally simple, no-frills hotels, with rates ranging from $220 to $300 per night.

French Side

Captain Oliver's Hotel

This resort is distinguished by the fact that it spans the French-Dutch border, and much of the activity here is based around the marina. The property has a unique glass-sided pool, a mini-zoo, an aquarium, and a restaurant with a glass floor so you can see the fish swimming below. If you are into boating, everything is here, including yacht charter and brokerage, a dive shop, a sports bar and even water taxis to the beach. The rooms are basic, nicely furnished junior suites.

Location: Oyster Pond, eastern side of the island.

Rooms: 50 junior suites, with a choice of marina or ocean view. All have minibars, room service, safes, balconies, AC and satellite TVs.

Rates: EP, with packages including meals offered.

Features: Restaurant, two bars, pool, marina, dive shop, stores, minizoo, shuttles to the beach, activities desk, cyber café.

Aerial View of Captain Oliver's

☎ 590-590-87-40-26, fax 590-590-87-40-84, www.captainolivers.com.

Mercure Simson Beach

The Mercure Simson Beach

This hotel sits on the thin stretch of land between Baie Nettle and the Lagoon, facing the Lagoon. The property is done in West Indian style, and it's very convenient to Marigot, the golf course, and the Maho Bay area.

Location: Simpson Bay Lagoon, on the western peninsula of the island.

Rooms: 168, including superior rooms and superior duplexes with choice of lagoon, garden or pool views. All have kitchenettes, balconies with dining area, safes, AC, satellite TVs and WiFi Internet.

Rates: EP.

Features: Restaurant, snack bar, two pools, beach with watersports, beach volleyball, tennis court, table tennis, water polo, billiards.

☎ 590-590-87-54-54, fax 590-590-87-92-11, www.mercure.com.

St. Tropez Hotel Caraïbes

St. Tropez Hotel Caraïbes

This hotel in Orient Bay is a good value; it's near the great beach, shares some amenities with Hoste Hotel, and has comfortable, European-style rooms.

Location: Orient Bay, on the eastern side of the island.

Rooms: 28, including garden, superior and deluxe. All have kitchenettes, balconies, cable TVs and AC.

Rates: EP.

Features: Pool (shared with Hoste Hotel).

☎ 590-590-87-42-01, fax 590-590-87-41-69, www.st-tropez-caraibes.com.

Dutch Side

L'Espérance

If you are traveling on a tight budget, this is a good hotel to consider. While it's not near the beach in Cay Hill, it is centrally located so that you can get to most attractions and beaches within a 10-minute drive. The rooms are clean, comfortable and simply done, with king-sized four-poster beds and white rattan furniture.

Location: Cay Hill, just outside Philipsburg.

L'Espérance

Rooms: 22 one- and two-bedroom suites, with kitchenettes, sitting areas, balconies, safes, AC, cable TVs.

Rates: EP.

Features: Pool.

☎ 599-542-5355, fax 599-542-4088, www.lesperancehotel.com.

Summit Resort

While not a beachside resort, this hotel has a panoramic view over the Simpson Bay Lagoon and out to Marigot. The suites are located in cottages scattered around the landscaped hillside property and are done in dark woods and bright textiles. It's in a great location for reaching any part of the island.

Location: Simpson Bay Lagoon, on the western peninsula of the island.

Rooms: 50, including standard and deluxe with choice of garden or lagoon views. All have balconies, safes, dining areas, sofa beds in sitting area, AC, cable TVs and high-speed Internet access (Ethernet). The deluxe rooms have kitchenettes and the standard ones have mini-fridges and coffeemakers.

Summit Resort

Rates: EP.

Features: Restaurant, bar, pool, activities desk, WiFi in lobby.

☎ 599-545-2150, 718-671-1160 US, fax 599-545-2615, www. thesummitresort.com.

Villas, Villa Resorts & Condos

St. Martin, on both sides, is a villa renter's paradise. There are hundreds to choose from – far more than can be described in this limited space. Choices include beautiful homes in the exclusive gated Terres Basses area on the western peninsula, elegant contemporary high-rise condominiums with multi-bedroom units like AquaMarina or The Cliff at Cupecoy, and great villas on the beach at Beachside Villas in Simpson Bay. Many are stand-alone homes, others are in resorts with common amenities like pools and beach areas.

You can spend hours Googling "villas St. Martin" and examining each page you pull up. But the easiest way to identify your perfect vacation villa is to check out the websites of the rental agencies that represent the villa owners. Most of these have photos and descriptions of the residences, so you can get a good idea of whether your dream fits the reality.

St. Martin Villa Rental Agencies

www.caribbeandays.com – This site offers villas all around the Caribbean. Their list of St. Martin rentals is extensive and you can search by size. The descriptions are very detailed and a number of photos are included for each villa.

www.gobeach.com – Again, a number of islands appear on the website, and over 150 villas are featured in St. Martin. The photos are large enough to show you details.

www.islandhideaways.com – This site represents 90 villas throughout St. Martin and other Caribbean locations. They are sorted by size, have lots of photos, and include reviews from people who have stayed there.

www.islandpropertiesonline.com – They specialize in villas for St. Martin and St. Barts only, and the lists are not as extensive as on some of the other sites. They also feature comments from guests, which are always fun to read ("A joy, a gift, a grace, a blessing, a feast for the senses!" says one).

www.jennifersvacationvillas.com – Jennifer, an ex-New Yorker who resides in St. Martin, is a specialist on the island. She has an extensive listing of villas and a neat map where you can click on what area you want to be in and then a list of available villas for that area appears.

www.pierres-caraibes.com – This is another local St. Martin agency, and the site gives you the option of searching by size or by location, allowing you to create a list of your favorites so you can compare them in an organized way. The photos of the luxury villas are gorgeous, making you want to sign up as soon as you view them. They also publish a DVD and a guidebook with photos of the villas and information on the island.

www.stmartin.com – This is the website of St. Martin Rentals & Management, a local firm. It lists a number of villas, and you can search by location, size or price range.

www.sunsea.com – Sunsea is a locally owned business that offers villa rentals and sales, as well as direct bookings for hotels, guest houses and accommodations in St. Barts and Anguilla.

www.sxmtravelguide.com – This general-purpose site is run by the Hotel Rental Group, and you can search their listings by location or size.

www.unusualvillarentals.com – All the villas around the world represented on this site can't be that unusual, but there are some pretty interesting, and expensive, ones. Check out Little Jazz Bird – not so little in price, but a great home sitting right on Baie Rouge beach, complete with a private tennis court.

www.wimco.com – This large international villa management company represents 70 luxury villas in St. Martin. They can handle other trip arrangements as well, such as car rentals and air reservations.

Small Inns/Guest Houses

These represent real value accommodations for the budget-minded. For double accommodations, usually with either a queen or king-sized bed, you can expect to pay US$100-$130 per night in low season, and $145-$200 in high season. Some include breakfast in the rate, sweetening the deal.

French Side

Colombus Hotel

This small gem is on Oyster Pond, within walking distance to Dawn Beach. The rooms are fairly good-sized, and include kitchens.

Location: Oyster Pond, on the eastern side of the island.

Rooms: 10, including one- and two-bedroom suites. All have kitchens, sitting and dining areas, AC in bedrooms, safes and satellite TVs.

View of Oyster Pond Marina from Colombus Hotel

Rates: BP.

Features: Restaurant, pool, free airport transfers for stays of one week or longer.

☎ 590-590-87-42-52, fax 590-590-87-39-85, www.colombus-hotel.com.

Villa Hôtelière Soleil de Minuit

The five loft suites of this small hotel overlooking Oyster Pond are comfortable and airy, and the views out to the marina are great. One suite has a private Jacuzzi.

Location: Above Oyster Pond, on the eastern side of the island.

Rooms: Five one-bedroom suites, with king beds in loft, private terraces, sitting areas with sofa beds, kitchens, AC, TVs.

Rates: BP.

☎ 590-590-87-34-66, fax 590-590-87-33-70, http://perso.orange.fr/soleil. de.minuit.

The Dove's Nest

View from The Dove's Nest

This four-unit guest house on the hill above Petit Plage, just north of Grand Case, is a newcomer to the French hotel scene. The owners' goal was to set up a serene retreat convenient to all the great restaurants, beaches and activities on the island, and they have reached their goal.

Location: Petit Plage, on the north-western coast of the island.

Rooms: Four, including a one-bedroom suite and three two-bedroom suites. All have large kitchens, sitting areas, AC in the bedrooms and satellite TVs. The one-bedroom units and one of the two-bedroom units have balconies with sea views.

Rates: EP.

Features: Beach, two passes for boat rides to Ile Pinel, welcome pack of beverages.

☎ 590-590-29-52-36, fax 590-590-52-39-26, www.info-res.com/dovesnest.

Dutch Side

Pasanggrahan Royal Guest House

This stately royal residence turned guest house is the oldest inn on the island, and routinely receives great reviews from travel publications. With 28 rooms, it's rather large for a guest house, but it maintains its intimate feel through the use of period furniture and stately gardens. It's right on Front Street in Philipsburg, so you have ready access to shopping and restaurants.

Location: Downtown Philipsburg.

Rooms: 28, including the Queen's Room, specialty, deluxe and standard rooms, based on location in the east or west wings. All have antique

Pasanggrahan

furniture, mosquito netting on beds, ceiling fans, AC, safes, balconies, refrigerators and cable TVs.

Rates: EP.

Features: Restaurant, bar, beach with lounges, watersports, social hours, gift shop, on-site car rental.

☎ 599-542-3588, fax 599-542-2885, www.pasanhotel.com.

The Horny Toad Guest House

The Horny Toad

The name sets you up for the quaint and unique qualities of this eight-unit hotel. The main building was a former governor's house, and each room is decorated in distinctive style. The Horny Toad sits right on Simpson Bay beach, so you are never far from water. Host Betty Vaughn and her staff have garnered a great reputation for the gracious hospitality extended here.

Location: Simpson Bay, on the south coast of the island.

Rooms: Eight, each with king-sized bed, kitchen, sitting and dining area. Some units are air-conditioned.

Rates: EP.

Features: Beach, barbecue pavilion with two gas grills, provisions program.

☎ 599-545-4323, 800-417-9361 US, fax 599-545-3316, www.thtgh.com.

The Royal Turtle Inn

Two years ago, owners Dwayne and Joann converted a residence on Simpson Bay Lagoon into an eight-room inn to deliver four-star service at a two-star price. Some rooms have views of the Lagoon and others of the pool on the property. All have romantic king or queen four-poster beds with mosquito netting. They are done in bright and inviting Caribbean colors.

Location: Simpson Bay Lagoon, on the south coast of the island.

Rooms: Eight, each with four-poster beds, refrigerator, coffee maker, AC and cable TVs.

Rates: BP.

Features: Restaurant adjacent, pool, nearby dock.

☎ 599-545-2563, www.theroyalturtle.com.

Day Spas

Following the international trend, many of the hotels are adding toney new spas that offer luxurious pampering. Right now, St. Martin has a number of spas to rejuvenate your body and soothe your soul; by the time this book is published, the list may be much longer.

Using the Physiodermie line of luxury skin products, **The Good Life Spa** is one of the premier day spas on the island. In the Sonesta Maho Bay Resort, this spa offers a range of massages including wellness massages to transform not only your body but your mind. The massage rooms are designed to follow the five elements of creation – earth, fire, water, air and ether. Treatments include wraps and body scrubs and a unique steam treatment in their Thalatherm Steamdome, as well as facials, hand and foot care, and cellulite treatments. They also offer packages combining various treatments. ☎ 599-545-2540, www.thegoodlifespa.com.

At **Indulgence by the Sea**, at the Divi Resort, you can get that all important relief from sun-stressed skin while relaxing in cool comfort. Among their special treatments is The Sun-Kissed Body Booster, where your skin temperature is taken down a few degrees by a cooling body wash, then lubricated with lavender hydrating gel and aromatherapy oil. Add a Swedish massage, and your body will be thanking you. Other services include massages for one or two, facials, body treatments and beauty services. ☎ 599-542-2333, www.spastmaarten.com.

Massage at the Elysée Spa

As you would expect from the most discriminating resort on the island, La Samanna has an outstanding luxury spa, **The Elysées Spa**. The massage menu includes some unusual choices, such as the Energetic Chinese Massage with Moxa, the Massage of Seven Chakras, Korean Massage and Four Hands Massage, as well as Shiatsu, Swedish, Reflexology and other massages. Body treatments include wraps and polishes, sunburn rescue and a bust treatment regimen. They also have options such as the Elegance package that includes body wrap and polish, massage, facial, and manicure, for a half-day of delightful pampering. ☎ 590-590-87-65-69 Ext. 6569, www.lasamanna.com.

L'Aqualigne, the spa at the Pelican Resort, offers a complete beauty clinic with eight treatment rooms, sauna, steam room and ice-plunge therapy pool. Lead cosmetologist Marc Van Thielen has developed his own signature methods for exfoliations, including laser light treatments. Check out the Smile and Shine package, where they offer four face-makeover technologies, including teeth whitening, glycolic acid peel, high-definition mask and hair styling. Among the other services are massages, facials, anti-cellulite and anti-wrinkle skin treatments, along with the usual range of beauty services. ☎ 599-544-2426, www.pelicanresort.com/services.htm.

The Vitality Oasis Spa at Great Bay Beach Resort offers "therapies, treatments and teachings to enhance the art of vital living," according to its brochure. Among the signature treatments are wellness massages and services in bodywork to relax, decongest, detox and release stress for holistic healing. Among the more interesting offerings are reflexology, gua sha detox skin brushing, and disease reading consultations where patrons learn ways to rebalance their bodies. ☎ 599-542-2446, www. greatbaybeachresort.com.

While not a spa in the strict sense, another beauty outlet is **Hairlusions by Marie-Antionette** and **Body by Bonny Louise**, a salon emphasizing services for the hair, body, hands and feet. They use the Carole Franck line of treatments, which are said to be especially good for mature skin, and the Biolite system for cellulite control. The salons are at the Wyndham Sapphire Beach Club (☎ 599-545-2179 ext. 583), the Holland House Beach Club (☎ 599-542-2572 ext. 406), and on Airport Boulevard (☎ 599-545-4090). Plans were underway to open an Express Spa and Salon at the new airport terminal in 2007. marie_antoinette@caribserve. net.

Where to Eat

St. Martin – particularly on the French side – is considered the culinary capital of the Caribbean, with more quality French restaurants per square mile than you find anywhere except in France. There are three things to note: First, depending on the current exchange rate between the euro and dollar, many of the French side restaurants offer a €1 to US$1 if you pay in cash. This represents about a 20% savings, since the normal rate is €1 to US$1.20; second, the French-side restaurants are not equipped to add a tip on credit card transactions, so you have to leave it in cash; and three, many restaurants, especially on the French side, close in September and part of October for their annual vacation. It's also a good idea to make reservations wherever you decide to dine, especially in high season.

With all that said, it is difficult to list the best of the best, because everyone has an opinion on their favorites – and there are hundreds to choose from. If you want to see reviews from people who have recently visited the island, go to www.gobeach.com/restrant.htm.

As a start, here's a list of suggestions, based on my own and return visitor reviews. But you should really try as many as you can and decide for yourself.

RESTAURANT PRICE CHART	
$	Cheap eats, normally quick meals or take-out foods; US$8 or less per entrée.
$$	Good value, lots of West Indian cuisine; US$9-$14 for a plate of food.
$$$	A nice place with gourmet aspirations; US$15-$24 for a satisfying entrée.
$$$$	Positively elegant, usually requiring some dressing up; entrées range from US$25 to $50, depending on the island.

Dressing Up to Dine Out
French Side

La Vie en Rose

This Marigot favorite has been the "Grande Dame" of St. Martin restaurants for 26 years, and continues to offer intimate, romantic ambience along with some of the best French cuisine on the island. It's on the second floor of an old home on the waterfront in Marigot, with lovely views of the harbor. $$$$. Open for lunch and dinner daily. ☎ 590-590-87-54-42, fax 590-590-87-82-63, www.lavieenrosestmartin.com.

Le Bistrot Nú

It's a little hard to find this restaurant, tucked away in a well-lit alley across from the soccer stadium in Marigot, but it's well worth the search. The menu is French brasserie style with some inventive creations. $$$. Allée de l'Ancienne Geôle in Marigot. Open for dinner weekdays only. ☎ 590-590-87-97-09.

Le Gaïac

A great restaurant in a shopping mall? Only in St. Martin, at the West Indies Mall. It's out on the terrace, so you can watch the sunset while dining on incredible French dishes. Many frequent St. Martin visitors cite this as the best on the island. $$$$. Marigot waterfront. Open for dinner only, closed on Sundays. Closed from the first of September to mid-October. ☎ 590-590-51-97-66, www.le-west-indies.com.

Le Pressoir

When anyone talks about the best French restaurants, this one is bound to be mentioned. It's in a traditional Creole house in Grand Case, and the romantic atmosphere matches the quality of the cuisine. $$$. Grand Case. Open for dinner only, closed Sundays. ☎ 590-590-87-76-62.

Le Pressoir

Le Santal

For celebrity sighting, head to this gem in Sandy Ground,

Le Santal

with views out to Anguilla. As befits one of the best five-star restaurants on the island, the menu offers some amazing combinations of classic French elements and Caribbean tastes. $$$$. Sandy Ground. Open for dinner every day. ☎ 590-590-87-53-48, www.restaurant-lesantal.com.

Le Tastevin

This bright and colorful restaurant looking out over Grand Case Bay gets rave reviews from most patrons, and reports of uneven service from others. The draw here is fresh seafood and unusual culinary combinations in a romantic setting. $$$$. Grand Case. Open for lunch and dinner, closed Sundays. Closed from September to October. ☎ 590-590-87-55-45.

 Grand Case Tuesdays Demand Reservations: If you are visiting the island while the Tuesday night Harmony Nights street fair is going on in Grand Case, and you want to eat at one of the indoor, sit-down restaurants, be sure to make reservations ahead of time. These establishments fill up quickly, and you may lose out on a delightful dining experience.

The Restaurant, La Sammana

The Restaurant proves it's not just the hotel that excels in personalized service and high quality. The Restaurant offers an opulent, open-air dining room where you look out over the sea while enjoying dishes that are a fusion of French, Creole and Caribbean classics. $$$$. Baie Longue. Open for dinner only. ☎ 590-590-87-64-00, fax 590-590-87-87-86, www.lasamanna.com.

Sol e Luna

Having been voted the Most Romantic Restaurant on the island by the readers of *The Daily Herald*, you expect a lot from this restaurant – and it delivers. It's in a beautiful home in the Mont Vernon area that has been converted to a lovely place serving Provençal cuisine. $$$$. Open for dinner only. Closed from mid-September to the end of October. ☎ 590-590-29-08-56, www.solelunarestaurant.com.

Spiga

This nouvelle Italian dining experience is not to be missed. Homemade pastas, excellent seafood, and beef dishes keep the faithful coming back for more. It's at the northern (and quiet) end of Grand Case. $$$. Open for dinner daily. Closed annually from mid-October to early November. ☎ 590-590-52-47-83, www.spiga-sxm.com.

Dutch Side

Le Baccara at the Princess Casino

This is the perfect place for a complete, multi-sensual evening. Located at the Princess Casino, there's a nightly floor show featuring Brazilian dancers, easy access to the gambling floor, and the French cuisine is first-rate. The interior room away from the casino floor provides a more intimate atmosphere. $$$$. Simpson Bay. Open for dinner nightly. ☎ 599-544-2224, www. sxm-simpsonbay.com/east/baccara.

Le Baccara

Le Pressoir

Saratoga Restaurant

If you get tired of all the French food and just want a solid American meal in a nice restaurant, this is the place to go. You can sit on the deck overlooking the Simpson Bay Yacht Club or inside in the mahogany-lined dining room. The wine list is outstanding, and the choice of aged Scotches is probably the best on the island. $$$$. Simpson Bay Lagoon. Open for dinner only, closed on Sundays. ☎ 599-544-2421.

Temptations

Chef Dino Jagtiani has a lot of fun putting together his menus. He takes a bit of this and a bit of that and ends up with entrées like tandoori, osso buco, sashimi, pad thai and good old beef tenderloin. Located at the Atlantis Casino, the softly lit, romantic dining room was designed by hot restaurant designer Craig Span to be welcoming and relaxing. $$$$. Mullet Bay area. Open for dinner nightly. ☎ 599-545-2254, www.nouveaucaribbean.com.

Relaxing on the Water
French Side

Restaurant du Soleil

French cuisine with tropical flavors is featured at this Grand Case favorite. The dining rooms are bright and airy, overlooking the water with views to Creole Rock. They offer a €1=$1 rate when the exchange rate is good. $$$. Grand Case, beach side. Open for lunch and dinner every day. ☎ 590-590-87-92-32, www.restaurantdusoleil.com.

La California

This Grand Case restaurant sits right on the beach, so you can enjoy watching the water activities while you dine on excellent French cuisine. And it's all here – lobster, fish, pasta, pizzas, crêpes, salads and more. A delightful place to spend an afternoon watching all the beachgoers and sailors. $$$. Grand Case, beach side. Open for lunch and dinner every day. Closed from late August to late October. ☎ 590-590-87-55-57, fax 590-590-87-99-54, www.california-st-martin.com.

Sunset Café

This popular restaurant literally hangs over the beach at the north end of Grand Case. It's one of the best places to watch the sunset and then stay for a romantic meal out on the terrace watching the waves that are lit at night. $$. On the beach at Grand Case Beach Club. Open for breakfast, lunch and dinner every day. ☎ 590-590-87-51-87, esk@sxm-info.com, www.sunset-cafe.com.

Layla's

This hard-to-find but worthwhile restaurant is on Nettle Bay, providing access to the beach. The French seafood entrées are highly regarded and the view out to the sea is beautiful. $$. ☎ 590-590-51-00-93. On Nettle Bay, next to Hotel Royal Beach. Open for lunch only.

Five Stars of Orient Beach

The Five Stars of Orient Beach is the constellation of five distinctly different restaurants that line Orient Beach, the popular beach on the island. The Five Stars mark their territory with uniquely colored umbrellas and beach chairs for rent. They include:

Kontiki. This one is more high-style, with a menu that includes grilled lobster, steak and rack of lamb entrées. The Sunday night party is famous, but can get a little over the top. They also put on special events featuring live music, fashion shows and theme parties. $$$. Open for breakfast, lunch and dinner. ☎ 590-590-87-43-27, fax 590-590-29-40-29, www.kontikibeachsxm.com.

Coco Beach. The atmosphere is lively, and the food is what you'd expect at a Caribbean beach bar – salads, hamburgers, fajitas and grilled fish Creole-style, plus one surprise – a sushi bar. $$. Open for breakfast, lunch and early dinner (open for late dinner in high season only). ☎ 590-590-87-34-62, www.cocobeachsxm.com.

Waikiki. Here you'll find a great mix of Asian, Creole, Italian and French entrées, appetizers and desserts. $$$. Open for lunch and early dinner. ☎ 590-590-87-43-19, www.waikikibeachsxm.com.

Kakao. The French Polynesian style and family-friendly menu of hamburgers, pizzas and the like make Kakao a very popular spot. $$. Open for breakfast, lunch and dinner. ☎ 590-590-87-43-26.

Bikini. Here you'll find tapas, salads, seafood and even Thai entrées. They recently added a juice bar with freshly squeezed juices, and also offer a snack bar for those who prefer to spend their time on the beach. $$. Open for breakfast, lunch and dinner. ☎ 590-590-87-43-25, fax 590-590-87-46-99, www.bikinibeach.net.

Dutch Side

Halsey's Restaurant

This relatively new restaurant has been getting great reviews for its innovative cuisine melding the best of Caribbean and traditional American tastes. The view out over the Lagoon is also nice, and the place has a real five-star feel. Happy hour in the lounge features wine and cheese tastings, a

Halsey's

St. Martin

sushi bar and various types of martinis. $$$. Simpson Bay. Open for dinner only. Closed from the middle to the end of September. ☎ 599-544-2882, www.halseysrestaurant.com.

Mr. Busby's Beach Bar/Daniel's by the Sea

A bustling beach bar by day that morphs into a romantic Italian restaurant at night. Mr. Busby's is prized for its all-American breakfasts that make IHOP look pitiful, as well as lunch that includes salads, sandwiches and grilled favorites, including lobster. $$. Dawn Beach. Open for breakfast, lunch and dinner every day. ☎ 599-543-6828, www.dawnbeachsxm.com/busby-index.shtml.

Sunset Beach Bar

Everyone who visits St. Maarten has to stop here at least once to enjoy this classic beach bar on beautiful Maho Bay. An added attraction are the jets that fly right overhead as they approach for landing at SXM. In high season the restaurant has great American breakfasts; they start firing up the BBQ about 11 am and the burgers, ribs, hot dogs and seared tuna keep coming until midnight. The live entertainment starts at noon and goes into the wee hours. $$. At the entrance to the Caravanserai Resort. Open for breakfast (high season only), lunch and dinner every day. ☎ 599-545-3998, www.sunsetbeachbar.com.

Turtle Pier Restaurant

This popular restaurant located over the waters of Simpson Bay Lagoon offers a wide selection of Caribbean, Creole and American favorites. For a real experience, choose your own lobster from their special pool, which local fishermen replenish every day. $$$. Simpson

Halsey's

Bay. Open for breakfast, lunch and dinner daily. ☎ 599-545-2562, www.turtlepier.com.

French Cuisine

Needless to say, these are all on the French side.

Bistrot Caraïbes

Brothers Thibault and Amaury Meziere welcome you to this delightful French restaurant where the menu has a slight Creole influence and a lot of quality French entrées. $$$. Grand Case. Open for dinner every day. ☎ 590-590-29-08-29, www.bistrotcaraibes.com.

Bistrot Caraïbes

L'Alabama

Another long-time staple on the Grand Case dining scene, this ultimate French restaurant has a loyal following. Be sure to pay attention to the specials, which change quite often. The dining room is lovely, with bright blue linens and beautiful flowers. $$$. Grand Case. Open for dinner only, closed Mondays in low season. ☎ 590-590-87-81-66, www.lalabama.com.

L'Auberge Gourmande

This restaurant was the third to open in Grand Case many years ago, and has maintained its reputation through the years. The service is great, the atmosphere inviting, and it's an all-round good choice. $$$$. Grand Case. Open for dinner only. ☎ 590-590-87-73-37, www.laubergegourmande.com.

L'Hibiscus

Located out of the main Grand Case restaurant row, this charming restaurant receives high marks for warm, intimate service and the creative menu featuring French dishes served with Caribbean flair. The three-course lobster menu is a favorite. $$$. Grand Case. Open for dinner only every day. ☎ 590-590-29-17-91, www.hibiscus-restaurant.com.

La Petite Auberge des Isles

This Marina Royale favorite is known for its quality French cuisine and reasonable prices. The *prix fixe* menu is a real value. $$. Marina Royale, Marigot. Open for lunch and dinner, closed Sundays. ☎ 590-590-87-56-31.

Le Chanteclair

Many return to this place for Chef Cécile Briaud-Richard's incredible way with French cuisine. The foie gras dishes, and especially the appetizer sampler, are memorable, as is the chef's "Innomable" dessert (think pastry, chocolate and ice cream). $$$$. Marina Royale, Marigot. Open for dinner only. ☎ 590-590-87-94-60.

Le Taitu

Take a trip out to Mont Vernon for this delightful open-air restaurant featuring Creole and French favorites. They also have a children's menu. $$. Open for lunch and dinner daily. ☎ 590-590-87-43-23, www.letaitu.com.

Le St. Germain

Often called the best family restaurant in Marigot, this Marina Royale favorite features the atmosphere of a Parisian brasserie – light and fun. They offer a children's menu that includes toys to play with – a godsend for parents. $$. Marina Royale, Marigot. Open for breakfast (high season only), lunch and dinner daily. ☎ 590-590-87-92-87, fax 590-590-87-45-01, www.stgermainrestaurant.com.

Le Ti Provencal

Herve Sageot, the chef and owner of this beachfront Grand Case restaurant, was named the Taste of St. Maarten Chef of the Year in 2005. He turns out consistently great dishes, especially seafood, in a relaxed French bistro atmosphere. $$$. Open for lunch and dinner. ☎ 590-590-87-05-65.

Ethnic Foods & Favorites
French Side

Il Nettuno

One of the best, if not the best, Italian restaurant on the island, this Grand Case institution is very popular. One of the specialties is sea bass baked in rock salt for two, but the pastas and other seafood items are also great. $$$$. Grand Case, beach side. Open for lunch and dinner in high season, dinner only in low, and closed from the beginning of September until mid-October. ☎ 590-590-87-77-38.

Mai's Vietnamese Restaurant

The scene of this beauty is a 100-year-old Marigot residence, where the terrace and dining room have been converted into a lovely, serene dining area. The cuisine is reminiscent of French Indochina, with a blend of Vietnamese and French flavors. $$$. Rue de Holland, Marigot. Open for dinner only, closed Tuesdays. ☎ 590-590-77-18-94, www.stmaarten. org/Restaurants/Mais. html.

Mai's

Dutch Side

La Gondola

This Italian restaurant in the Atlantis Casino complex is prized for its homemade touch, including sausages made by the owner's father, and the use of fresh ingredients. Owner David Foini made pasta to sell to individuals and restaurants before opening his own signature restaurant. The pasta is outstanding. $$$. Cupecoy Beach area. Open for dinner daily. ☎ 599-545-3938, lagondola@stmaarten.com.

Tabba Khady

It's tough to identify the ethnicity of this relative newcomer, since the menu features flavors from Thailand, Israel, India, Vietnam, Morocco, Italy, Tunisia, Senegal, Mexico, the Caribbean and France. Whew! All the entrées sound fascinating, and owners William Rattinger and Philippe Milovidoff pull it off with style. $$$. Oyster Pond. Open for dinner only. ☎ 599-586-3434, www.tabba-khady.com.

Shiv Sagar

This was the first Indian restaurant on the island, and remains the best according to many. The menu contains traditional curries and kebabs, and has a Tandoori oven for the usual favorites. It's convenient to all the

Dutch side hotels. $$. Front Street in Philipsburg. Open for lunch and dinner daily. ☎ 599-542-2299.

Wajang Doll

This restaurant reflects the Indonesian influences on the island, which came from the country's history as a Dutch colony. If you haven't had this cuisine, this is a must stop. $$$. Front Street in Philipsburg. Open for lunch and dinner. ☎ 599-542-2687.

Los Gauchos

It's not common to find Argentinian cuisine in the Caribbean, so many value the addition of this place to the St. Maarten restaurant scene. If you love steaks, or any beef dish for that matter, this is your place. Give the Argentine wines a taste, too. $$$. Pelican Resort Club Marina. Open for dinner only. ☎ 599-542-4084

For Americanophiles

Cheri's Café

This open-air restaurant in the Maho Bay shopping complex is know as much for its bar as for the restaurant. And then there's the live music and dancing every night, which are really the main attractions. It's an American place, with burgers, steaks, salads, seafood, pasta, and the usual bar/café appetizers. Try the guavaberry coladas here, as well as other specialty drinks. $$. Maho Bay Plaza. Open for lunch, dinner and dancing every day. ☎ 599-545-3361, cheriscafe@megatropic.com.

Jimbo's Rock & Blue Café

There's something uniquely American about this restaurant with a pool and swim-up bar. The burgers are outstanding and "gourmet Mexican" specialties from the mesquite grill bring out the spice. You'll also love the fishbowl Margaritas. $$$. Simpson Bay Lagoon Marina. Open for lunch and dinner every day. ☎ 599-544-3600, www.jimboscafe.com.

West Indian Cooking

Arawak

This ultimate *lolo* is in a permanent structure on one of the most prominent corners in Marigot and offers authentic West Indian BBQ dishes, including lobster and prawns. $. ☎ 590-590-87-99-67.

Lee's Roadside Grill

Captain Leonel Halley of fishing charter fame decided to open a restaurant serving local dishes and seafood, some of which comes directly from his boat. You'll find delicious fresh lobster and seafood as well as beef and chicken done local-style. $$. Simpson Bay. Open for lunch and dinner every day. ☎ 599-544-4233, www.leesfish.com.

Mark's Place

This interesting Creole restaurant offers the usual favorites of conch stew, goat stew, christophene and other dishes that everyone should taste before leaving the island. $$. Philipsburg, in the Grand Marché supermarket parking lot. ☎ 599-543-2625.

Sports Bars

Ric's Place American Café & Sports Bar

This popular bar and grill has a bit of everything to keep gamers happy, including big screen TVs, live music, air hockey, darts and arcade machines. The patio overlooks the Lagoon, and the food is basic hamburgers and Tex-Mex. Breakfasts are American, with omelets, burritos and eggs. $$. Airport Road in Simpson Bay. Open for breakfast, lunch and dinner every day. ☎ 599-545-3630, www.ricsplace-sxm.com.

> **Quick Bites:** While the Dutch side has a number of American fast-food restaurants such as Burger King, McDonalds, Pizza Hut and Subway, the more interesting alternatives are the native lolos, the roadside stands where locals grill fish, lobster and chicken and serve them with traditional sides.

Shopping

St. Martin is one of the most popular duty-free centers in the Caribbean. Even Caribbean residents travel here for the great prices on European goods. The array of jewelry, electronics, cameras, fine china, liquors, watches and perfumes is incredible, and it's tons of fun to browse as well as shop. There are some real bargains to be had.

In Marigot

This lovely French Caribbean city is often likened to the French Riviera with a dash of the West Indies thrown in for color. Most of the shopping activity centers around the two marinas, the Waterfront/Ft. Louis and Marina Port du Royale.

French Market

On the waterfront you'll find the colorful **French Market** vendors' mall where you can pick up souvenirs and made-in-St. Martin goods. For high-style shopping, head to the **West Indies Mall** – you can't miss it if you are standing anywhere near the water's edge. It's a massive new building at the north end of the port, with several floors of shopping in air-conditioned comfort. Among the 22 stores are **Diamond Creations**, **Lacoste**, **Lancel**, **Vic-**

Marigot Harbour

tory/Escada, **Vanity First** and **Lipstick**. The building also houses some restaurants, and a luxe set of washrooms where you have to pay to enter.

The waterfront for **Marina Royale** is the Simpson Bay Lagoon, which stretches into the Marigot environs on the northern tip. Around the rectangular-shaped marina are stores and restaurants, each of which gives you an authentic Marigot experience. Among the shops are luxury shoe stores, women's ready-to-wear, and La Casa del Habano, a cigar store with a selection of Cuban cigars. This is also a great place to have lunch, since 11 restaurants line the waterfront.

Across from the Marina on the corner of Rue du Pres. Kennedy and Rue du General de Gaulle is **Plaza Caraïbes**, the headquarters for luxury brands on the island. Here you'll find **Cartier**, **Hermes**, **Longchamp** and **Passions Jewelers** in a pleasant setting of West Indian style houses.

In Philipsburg

Duty-free shopping Dutch-style extends down both sides of **Front Street** and onto **Back Street**, both of which have undergone significant renovations to make them more appealing to visitors (you know, palm trees, wooden façades and the whole bit). Now it's a charming city, with a permanent craft market in the center and a boardwalk along the beach lined with restaurants and bars.

Surviving Philipsburg Shopping

There are two important things to know about shopping in downtown Philipsburg if you want to have an enjoyable experience.

First, this is a major port for cruise ships and a favorite shopping spot for their passengers, who literally flood the streets. Before you make plans to head into town, check the port schedule at travelcal.traveltalkonline.com/sxm.cgi to see how many ships are in port that day. You could spare yourself a lot of agitation by picking a day with a low cruise ship quotient.

Second, the merchants in the electronics duty-free shops expect some haggling and deal-making. If you are looking at a camera, for example, don't just settle on the first model and the first price. If you act like you are heading to the door to another store, you may be informed that the owner of the present store also owns several of the others, and that you'll get the same deal. But if you still hesitate, they are likely to throw in extras like lenses, cases, memory cards and more to sweeten the deal. Have fun with it, and know that you'll get some pretty good deals this way.

St. Martin

Among the most noted stores are **Boolchand Jewelers**, **DK Gems**, **Shiva's Gold & Gems**, **Shoppers Haven** and **Colombian Emeralds** for designer jewelry, loose gems, and watches. There are also a number of electronics stores and clothing boutiques, so it's very easy to spend a lot. All the prices are in US dollars. Some of the stores close

Old Street, Philipsburg

during lunch, and this is a great time to check out some of the restaurants. One of my personal favorites is **Vanille & Chocolat** on the Boardwalk near Holland House, a heavenly crêperie that serves tea in dainty porcelain cups and scoops of handmade sorbets drenched with fresh fruit sauce in huge brandy snifters.

Guavaberry Emporium

Another "don't miss" store is the **Guavaberry Emporium** on Front Street. World-famous Guavaberry Liqueur is the pride of the island, and is available in most liquor stores on the island. However, here at the Emporium you see the full selection of products, including other artisan-flavored rums, gourmet food items, logo wear and perfumes. They also give out samples of Guavaberry Coladas and tastes of the flavored rums.

If you are looking to update your wardrobe with some hot new swimsuits or resort wear, wander off the main drag to **Rima Beach World** on Pondfill Road (parallel to Back Street near the salt pond). If you want a St. Martin remembrance you won't see in other ports, get a handbag from **Patricia's Caribbean Floral Baskets by Alta** (www.patriciasfloralbasketsbyalta.com). These beautiful flower-laden bags, very distinctive and tropical, are available at three stores – at the Palapa

Marina, the Solar Splash Market, and Harbour Point Village (at the cruise ship dock).

In Maho Bay

Another shopping hot spot is the area around the Sonesta Maho Bay and Casino Royale. The **Marketplace** includes 40 upscale duty-free boutiques and souvenir shops. Many stay open until late, to take advantage of the impulse buyers who have done well at the casino.

Galleries Around the Island

With so many beautiful vistas and inspirational scenes, the island has become a haven for artists working in a variety of media. Among the best-known are painter Roland Richardson, realist painter Ken Danby, abstract painter Francis Eck, watercolor master Antoine Chapon, ceramic artist Marie Moine and native portrait painter Ruby Bute. All have galleries around the island, usually attached to their studios so you can get a glimpse into their worlds. A complete listing of the galleries appears in the *Nights St. Martin* magazine, available at the airport, the tourist authorities and in many hotel rooms.

Nighlife

This is one island where having a good time is very easy to do. Between the glittery casinos, the clubs and the beach bars, there is a party going on somewhere in St. Martin all year round.

Casinos

The Dutch side is where all the gambling goes on, by law and custom. Some are large, Las Vegas-style pleasure palaces with shows and restaurants; others are smaller and welcome those who just want to gamble.

Dutch Side Casinos

Atlantis World

This large complex in Cupecoy offers 27,000 sq ft of gaming action and a sports book area as well as its own Gourmet Village with eight restaurants. Open 24 hours every day. ☎ 599-545-4601, www.atlantisworld.com.

Beach Plaza Casino

Cruise passengers frequent this downtown Philipsburg casino that offers 150 slots and other games in an 1,800 sq-ft building. Open 9 am to 1 am every day. ☎ 599-543-2031, www.beachplazasxm.com.

Casino Royale

The largest casino on the island, this glitzy palace at the Sonesto Maho Bay Resort offers 250 slots, table games, and a high roller area for high stakes play as well as live entertainment. Open 24 hours. ☎ 599-545-2590, www.sonesta.com/stmaarten.

Coliseum Casino

The ancient Roman theme is very Vegas-like. It offers three floors of gaming including a private gaming room with blackjack, rou-

Casino Royale

lette and stud poker. Open 9 am to 1 am every day. It's on Front Street in Philipsburg. ☎ 599-543-2101.

Diamond Casino

This is another Front Street casino, offering 250 slots and table games including Caribbean poker and mini-Baccarat. Open 11 am to 3 am every day. ☎ 599-543-2583, www.diamondcasinosxm.com.

Dolphin Casino

Relocated from the Caravanserai Resort to the Sunset Building in Simpson Bay, this casino offers high-style gaming including live table games, video games, slots and a VIP room for high-stakes blackjack and Baccarat. Open 1 pm to 4 am every day. ☎ 599-544-3411, www.stmaarten.org/casinos/dolphin.

Dunes Casino

This is the newest casino, added to the Caranvanserai Resort in 2007. ☎ 866-STMAARTEN.

Golden Casino

Hosted by the Great Bay Beach Resort, this casino was substantially renovated in 2006 to brighten the atmosphere. It offers 10 gaming tables plus 84 slots with attractive payouts. ☎ 599-543-2523, www.sonesta.com/greatbay.

Hollywood Casino

The upbeat celebrity theme at this Pelican Resort casino is an attraction, as are the 100 slot machines, sports book with nine screens, and 20 table games. There's a late-night buffet for night owl gamers. Open 1 pm to 4 am every day. ☎ 599-544-4463, www.hollywoodcasino-stmaarten.com.

Jump-Up Casino

Situated near the cruise ship pier, this Philipsburg casino with a Carnival theme attracts the cruise crowd. Live entertainment on the weekends. Open 10 am to 6 am every day. ☎ 599-542-0862, www.jumpupcasino.com.

Paradise Plaza Casino

This casino is noted for its large sports book operation with 20 viewing screens. They also have 250 slots in their location on Airport Road in Simpson Bay. Open 11 am to 3 am every day. ☎ 59-544-4721, www.paradisecasinosxm.com.

Princess Casino

In the Port de Plaisance marina complex, this is a luxurious 12,000-sq-ft casino with 20 table games, private high-roller rooms and tons of slots, as well as restaurants and live floor shows. Open 2 pm to 4 am every day. ☎ 599-544-4311, www.princessportdeplaisance.com/casino.

Rouge et Noir

This downtown Philipsburg casino is small and futuristic in design, with slots, video keno and video poker as well as table games and bingo. Open Monday-Saturday 9 am to 4 am, Sunday 11 am to 4 am. ☎ 599-542-2952, www.casinorougeetnoir.com.

Clubs

What's a vacation without music and dancing? From the racy to the sublime, both sides of St. Martin keep you entertained in style. This listing is not all-inclusive by any means, since there are many clubs, and they seem to appear and disappear with some frequency. To find out exactly what's going on while you are on the island, check out the schedules at www.k-pasa.com or www.sxmvibes.com.

AXUM Jazz Café

Live jazz, blues and reggae are on tap at this downtown Philipsburg club. Open mic nights, theater performances and poetry readings are offered on some nights, and the space is decorated with local works of art. Open Tuesdays through Sundays. ☎ 599-542-0547.

Club One

This private dance club on the French side gathers crowds after 10 pm on the weekends, shaking the night away to Top 40 music. Located in Marigot. ☎ 590-590-27-13-11.

Golden Eyes

Along with the casinos come adult clubs with topless dancers. This club near the bridge in Simpson Bay Village has theme nights and welcomes couples as well as bachelor and bachelorette parties. ☎ 599-545-4601, www.goldeneyesclub.com.

The Platinum Room

This stylish club, in the Maho Bay shopping complex, is open every night from 10:30 pm with topless dancing and other very adult activities. ☎ 599-557-0055, www.theplatinumroom.com.

Sopranos Piano Bar

Live performances by guest pianists from around the world are the highlight at this elegant club, located in the Maho Bay area. They also have a dance floor and the pianist honors all requests, so make it a special evening. www.sopranospianobar.com/stmaarten.

Opal Ultra Lounge

Passion Club

A little off the beaten path at Cul-de-Sac, this club is popular with the dance crowd. The featured music is mainly Caribbean, and they host Ladies Nights on Wednesdays and Latin Night on Sundays. ☎ 599-524-0476, www.passionclubsxm.com.

Opal Ultra Lounge

This elegant new club in the Westin Dawn Beach has a trendy South Beach feel. They have hookah pipes, DJ music with a dance floor, and Bar Chefs who come to the tables to prepare cocktails using unusual fresh ingredients and herbs. ☎ 599-543-6700, www.myspace.com/opalstmaarten.

Bliss

With a beautiful ocean view from the dance floor and the best party atmosphere on the island, Bliss always draws a crowd. They import DJs from Europe to keep the mood lively. There's a pool with private cabanas and a VIP area near the stage. In the Caravanserai Resort complex in Simpson Bay. ☎ 599-545-3996, www.theblissexperience.com.

Q Club

This large, classy club within the Casino Royale complex offers nightly DJ music, a frenetic light system, and two dance floors with an elevated VIP area. Theme nights are regularly offered, so check local listings to see what might be going on. ☎ 599-545-2632, www. qclubdisco.com.

International Cabaret Cubana

At the Q Club

This comedy club at the Maho Beach Resort is open Wednesday through Sunday beginning at 10 pm for laughs and good times. ☎ 599-545-2115 ext. 4830.

Beach Bars

With all the entertainment options, you can't forget the beach bars. Many have evening entertainment on a regular basis, and some get downright rowdy. Frequent visitors have their favorites, so you have to go out and explore, then pick your spot for when you return.

Bikini. Sundown Beach Party on Sundays beginning at 4 pm on Orient Beach. ☎ 590-590-87-43-25, www.bikinibeach.net.

Boo Boo Jams. Rocking parties Friday and Sunday nights on Orient Beach with DJ music. ☎ 590-590-87-03-13, www.booboojam.com.

Kontiki. Sunday Beach Party on Orient Beach from 10 pm. ☎ 590-590-87-43-27, www.kontikibeachsxm.com.

Bamboo Bernie's. Kuta Beach. Young crowd, DJ music every night, Wednesday Ladies Night, Movies on the Beach on Thursdays. ☎ 599-545-3622, www.bamboobernies.net.

Sunset Beach Bar. Stage with live music. ☎ 599-545-3998.

For something completely different on the water, try **The Pub Crawl** around Simpson Lagoon on Wednesday nights. The Celine catamaran picks participants up at SkipJack's near the Bridge and then sails with stops at Peg Leg Pub, Shrimpy's and then back to SkipJack. You spend about an hour in each restaurant. ☎ 599-545-3961, www.sxm-activities. com/lagoonpubcrawl.

The Beaches of St. Martin/ Sint Maarten

 The island is blessed with 37 beautiful white sand beaches that ring the entire island. By far the most famous is Orient Beach on the French side, which everyone likens to the French Riviera. The southern shore beaches of Simpson, Maho and Cupecoy bays are also very popular with those who love white, powdery sand, clear water and the convenience of bars, restaurants and watersports activities nearby.

 Note: Since the island is very closely connected to Europe through heritage, history and expatriate population, the people tend to follow the European model of topless or clothing-optional beaches. You will find this on most of the beaches around the island – to your unending delight if you want an all-over tan, or to your chagrin if you have children whom you would rather not expose to this particular anatomical lesson.

Let's take a tour around the island, starting at the western end in the French zone.

On the French Side

Long Bay/Baie Longue

The site of the La Samanna hotel, this extension of Cupecoy is named for what it is, the longest stretch of beach on the island. There are no watersports, restaurants or vendors, so you can enjoy this less-populated beach in its uncluttered state, complete with some spectacular sunsets. The water is calm most of the time, and there is some undersea life for snorkeling but no coral reef right offshore.

Plum Beach/Baie aux Prunes

At the westernmost tip of the island, this beach is calm and deserted most of the time, since there are no vendors. Just offshore are some coral reefs, so snorkeling is good but you have to watch where you walk into the water. Surfers like the waves farther out in the bay.

Baie Rouge

Rouge Bay/Baie Rouge

Bordered by Bird Cliffs on the west and Devil's Hole on the east, this beautiful beach is not as crowded as the eastern side beaches. There are some food vendors at the entrance near the parking lot and there is a vendor providing beach chairs and umbrellas, but otherwise the beach is unpopulated and serene. As you snorkel toward the eastern end you'll find an underwater cave to explore.

Nettle Bay/Baie Nettle

This is a busy beach, lined with hotels, apartments, shops and restaurants. It's also the site of many watersports activities, including wakeboarding, waterskiing and kitesurfing. You can gain access near Ma Ti Beach or Layla's Beach Bar, which provide food, drinks and services. The view is toward Anguilla and Marigot Bay.

Friar's Bay

This small, family-oriented beach is protected from swells to provide a calm swimming area for little ones and some interesting seashell collecting.

Friar's Bay

There are three beach bars for refreshments and services, but otherwise this beach is fairly quiet.

Grand Case

Grand Case

This nice stretch of soft white sand sits in front of the numerous restaurants that make Grand Case the gourmet capital. If you are on the beach and don't want to dress up to go into the restaurants, you can visit the lolos along the beach where you'll find great local food. The view from the northeastern end faces beautiful sunsets. The *Seaworld Explorer* departs from this area for tours to Creole Rock.

Anse Marcel

St. Martin

Anse Marcel

The northernmost port of Port de Lonvilliers is host to this beach, which edges upon two luxury hotels, one of which is still under construction. The beach is not large, but the sand is good, the swimming is pleasant and there is plenty of shade along the edges. Restaurants and services are available at the marina.

Orient Beach

The Godzilla of all St. Martin beaches, this one reminds you of St. Tropez with the multitude of colored beach umbrellas and lounges lined up in orderly rows, the topless female sunbathers trying to look all chic and nonchalant, and the many restaurants and watersports outlets plying their trade there. Most of the time someone will be trying to parasail over the coastline or whip around in jet skis while music blares from the bars, making this a busy, noisy place. But it's all in good fun and the activity draws crowds any day of the week.

Le Galion Beach.

This gem of a beach near the Butterfly Farm is popular with families and locals. The coral reef protecting it creates an area on the northern end where there are calm, crystal-clear waters perfect for young children or those who don't like rough surf. The surf is rough enough to attract kite and windsurfers along the end where the Le Galion Hotel was. There is a beach bar and watersports concession here where you can rent chairs, umbrellas and watersport equipment.

On the Dutch Side

Oyster Pond/Dawn Beach

Oyster Pond

This area sits on the border between the two sides, on the Atlantic coast. The marina at Captain Oliver's provides a haven for boats from the rough Atlantic waters, and you can walk or take a water taxi from there to the sheltered area of Dawn Beach. This is one of the best beaches for snorkeling on the island, because the reef comes up close to the shore, but the rough surf can be challenging for children or non-swimmers. Also, true to its name, it's a great place to watch the sun rise.

Guana Bay

This is another beach where you'll have to bring your supplies because there is not much in the way of services – or people using the beach for that matter. With the Atlantic surf being rough, this is a popular place for surfers and body surfers. It's a little difficult to find and very windswept so you won't see big crowds here.

Great Bay Beach

This beach is much like Grand Case – it's busy because it's right in an urban area, paralleling all the shops and restaurants of Front Street in Philipsburg. The view is out toward the harbor and the cruise ship docks, and near the end in front of the Great Bay Beach Resort the sand is mostly broken shells and tough to walk on. But along the boardwalk you find some nice tanning areas, and the access to food and drinks is outstanding.

Kim Sha Beach

This busy beach lies at the end of Simpson Bay and outside the lagoon, making it a popular launching point for scuba boats and motorized watersports. Some areas of the beach are man-made as a result of hurricane damage. At the eastern end you'll find good sunset views and two beach bars to make the day perfect.

Simpson Bay Beach

In spite of it being in a heavily populated area, this beach is relatively quiet and unpopulated except for the people staying in the villas along the shore or at Mary's Boon Plantation or the Royal Palm. One of the drawbacks is the amount of airplane noise since the beach ends right at the airport runway area.

Maho Beach

By nature of its proximity to some large resorts, this is a bustling beach. The proximity to the airport here is an attraction, with thrill seekers standing along the beach to enjoy the vibrations as the low-flying jets pass overhead. The beach is lined with rocks and the water can be rough. On the other hand, you can enjoy an exotic drink at the Sunset Beach Bar or visit the restaurants of the resorts along the edges.

Mullet Bay Beach

This long beach has rolling waves, making it popular with surfers. There can be a rip tide and the water is rough, so never swim alone here. Just offshore are rocks that make for interesting snorkeling. The line of palms at the back of the sand are a picture-perfect Caribbean backdrop (as well as shade). A few lolos at the end

Baie Rouge

of the beach provide sustenance, and on clear days you have nice views of Saba.

Cupecoy Beach

Cupecoy Beach

This small, clothing-optional beach on the southern coast has become a gathering point for naturists, especially at the far western end. With dramatic sandstone cliffs as a backdrop, the narrow coral sand beach is good for those who enjoy a little rough surf and beautiful scenery. While there are no bars or restaurants directly on the beach, there are many in the area. This is also a hotbed of condo construction, so the drive in can be trying at times.

Tintamarre

On the Offshore Islands

Pinel

A five-minute water taxi ride gets you to this tropical isle. The water is calm and crystal clear and the beach gets sun late into the day, so swimming and sunbathing on the clothing-optional beach is outstanding. While there is no running water on the island, there are two beach bars where you can get a filling lunch and drinks, as well as beach lounges and umbrellas.

Pinel Island

Tintamarre

This 80-acre island off the eastern coast of St. Martin is paradise for snorklers and beach goers, but you can only get here on one of the catamarans or boats that offers island tours, which is just as well because there are no services, no water, and no restaurants. The tours with lunch are a perfect way to spend the day here. Another highlight are the mud baths, where you can coat yourself in muddy sand, let it dry and then wash off in the sea for an all-over skin treatment that rivals those in the best spas.

Green Cay

The smallest of the three islands, it is deserted and uninhabited – perfect for romantic interludes and tanning. Again, you'll need to be on a boat charter or tour in order to get the drinks, food and services you need.

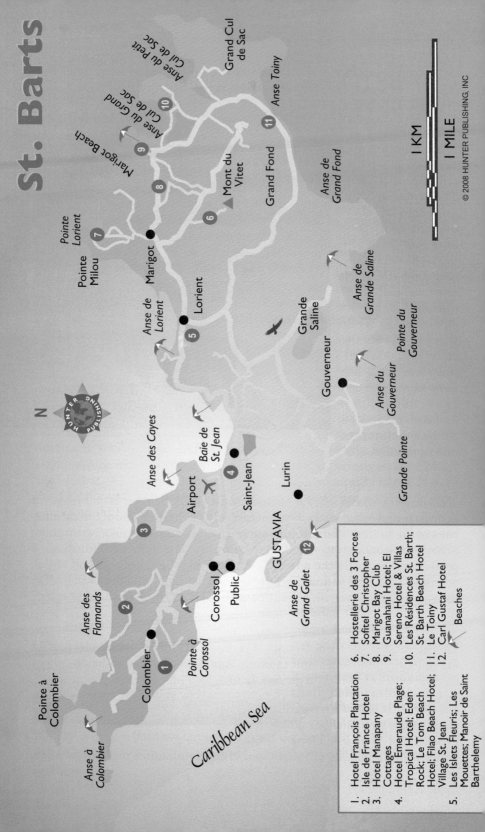

St. Barts

Caribbean Sea

N

Pointe à Colombier

Anse à Colombier

Anse des Flamands

Pointe à Corossol

Colombier

Corossol

Public

GUSTAVIA

Anse de Grand Galet

Airport

Anse des Cayes

Baie de St. Jean

Saint-Jean

Lurin

Grande Pointe

Gouverneur

Grande Saline

Anse du Gouverneur

Pointe du Gouverneur

Anse de Grande Saline

Pointe Milou

Pointe Lorient

Anse de Lorient

Lorient

Marigot

Marigot Beach

Anse du Grand Cul de Sac

Anse du Petit Cul de Sac

Grand Cul de Sac

Mont du Vitet

Grand Fond

Anse de Grand Fond

Anse Toiny

1. Hotel François Plantation
2. Isle de France Hotel
3. Hotel Manapany Cottages
4. Hotel Emeraude Plage; Tropical Hotel; Eden Rock; Le Tom Beach Hotel; Filao Beach Hotel; Village St. Jean
5. Les Islets Fleuris; Les Mouettes; Manoir de Saint Barthelemy
6. Hostellerie des 3 Forces
7. Sofitel Christopher
8. Marigot Bay Club
9. Guanahani Hotel; El Sereno Hotel & Villas
10. Les Résidences St. Barth; St. Barth Beach Hotel
11. Le Toiny
12. Carl Gustaf Hotel

↖ Beaches

I KM

I MILE

© 2008 HUNTER PUBLISHING, INC

St. Barthelemy
The Allure of the Island

Whenever you hear about St. Barts, it's usually in connection with which celebrities are partying there. It's definitely known as the island of the stars. Why is that?

Well, it may be because of the island's pristine beauty. And while it's small, only eight square miles, there are a lot of hills, inlets, coves, beaches and tropical landscape packed into that space. Driving around the island, wherever you go, the villages are neat, houses are

well-tended, roads are good (although narrow and winding), and even the cemeteries are beautiful.

Then there are the hotels and villas. The hotels have been carefully planned to be small and precious, with an emphasis on exquisite service and a guarantee of privacy. The luxurious private villas outnumber the available hotel rooms and overlook the sparkling turquoise sea. The villas are self-contained residences with wait staff, pools, Jacuzzis, and home theaters – ideal for hiding from crowds of admirers and paparazzi.

But wait, there are also the restaurants. The French heritage shines through loud and clear, and the fusion of French and Creole cuisines is offered in gorgeous settings. Even the plentiful beach restaurants turn the typical barbecue and burger fare into gourmet experiences. But the choices also include American favorites. After all, this is St. Barts and the watchword is: You want it? You got it.

With its long history as a duty-free port, you know there are some bargains to be had. The shops in Gustavia and St. Jean offer couture clothing, accessories, jewelry and more. It's Parisian shopping in paradise. And no doubt a big part of the allure comes from what the island doesn't have – flashy casinos, high-rise hotels and crowded beaches. The real draw of St.

Barts, whether you are rich or poor, is the chance to enjoy the ambience and character of France in a tropical setting. The island is part of Guadeloupe, a department of France, the official language is French, the electrical current is 220 and the official form of money is the euro. There is a distinctly European feel to the entire island that combines with island nuances for a unique cross-cultural experience.

What to Look for According to the Type of Traveler You Are

The Perfect Cruise Passenger will enjoy the port of Gustavia, where you can wander through lovely streets snapping up duty-free bargains and designer clothing. If you are thinking of seeking an "authentic" experience in a limited amount of time, visit the clothing-optional beaches at Saline or Shell Beach near Gustavia. And if you love high-quality traditional French cuisine, you can't find a better place outside of France itself.

The Boots-On Adventurer will have to settle for an afternoon of diving, windsurfing, horseback riding in the countryside, or trips to Saba and St. Eustatius. Adventure here costs money and it's ultimately for well-heeled folks looking to veg out in a setting where celebrities are no big thing and prices are high.

The Cultural Explorer will find some interesting activities but should remember that St. Barts is more French and American than West Indian. There are celebrations throughout the year commemorating the island's French and Swedish heritage. Carnaval**Carnival? and festivals held in the summer by some of the villages will give you an idea of local cuisine, crafts, music and art.

The "I Like What I Like" Traveler can settle into any of the numerous villas that dot the hillsides and feel quite at home. It's difficult to find an American steak house, but you can get a good burger at Le Select and JoJo Burgers in Gustavia. For those on strict diets, you can always hire one of the many private chefs to stock your villa with exactly what you want and cook meals to your liking.

The Incurable Romantic only needs to visit one of the many seaside restaurants to get in the mood. The small, intimate hotels like Les Ondines are perfect for a honeymoon, and the lovely Le Toiny hotel caters to those who want to be left alone in paradise. The numerous outstanding spas offer enough massages and body treatments to bring out the sybarite in anyone.

The Family Social Director will love this island where families rule, the crime rate is very low, and the beaches are kid-friendly, except for Saline where they may get an unexpected anatomy lesson. The villas are big and accommodating for large groups. Many have their own pool and Jacuzzi. Watersports like windsurfing and jet skiing are readily available. The Marine Reserve provides opportunities for snorkeling and, if the kids don't relish that, they can ride in a submarine to see the undersea world. If they get too bored, load everyone onto the ferry to St. Martin and visit the St. Martin Park Zoo or the above-ground rope rides at Pic Paradis.

The Ultimate Shopper finds nirvana in St. Barts. Check out the section below on the delights of Gustavia and St. Jean's, where designer boutiques line the *rues* and luxury reigns. The duty-free shopping is also good, and you'll find a lot of locally made clothing and accessories, as well as the wonderful Le Ligne St. Barth body care and spa products.

A Brief History

This is another island that Columbus got to name merely by seeing it. He named it after his brother Bartolomeo. But he saw no real value in this little rock with no fresh water, so the Spanish never colonized it. The first settlers were French colonists who arrived in 1648 from nearby St. Kitts. Because of the dry weather and lack of fresh water, this first settlement was unsuccessful and in 1651, when the island was sold to the Knights of Malta, only a few settlers remained.

In 1656, those nasty Caribs arrived and slaughtered what colonists were still there. The practice of displaying the heads of the victims on poles at L'Orient Beach sufficed to scare off resettlement. After about a hundred years, the Caribs had disappeared and settlers from Normandy and Brittany returned to the island. They welcomed French buccaneers who came with their gold and plunder to trade. Gradually, many seamen stayed on land and became tradesmen, shopkeepers, fishermen and farmers.

The most critical determinants in the history of the island were the dry climate and rocky soil. The cash crops like sugar and tobacco that supported the other Leeward Islands during the 18th and 19th centuries could not be grown here, so the plantation system never took root. Therefore, there was no large importation of slaves, and the population remained basically European.

The lack of a sugar crop also meant the island was of little value to countries like France that needed the revenue from sugar colonies. The island remained a French possession (with one brief military takeover by Britain in 1758) until 1784, when Louis XVI traded it to King Gustaf III of Sweden in exchange for duty-free trading rights in the port of Gothenburg. During this period, the Swedes invested in the island and the port thrived as a busy free-trade zone and supply center for the French, Spanish and British ships in the Caribbean.

St. Barts

In 1801, the British seized the island, but the Swedes regained control after two years. When slavery was abolished in 1847, St. Barts saw a huge decline in trade as revenue from the islands dependent on slave labor declined. A devastating hurricane hit in 1852, followed by a fire, and most residents left the island. Sweden sold the island back to France in 1878. As part of the sale, the Swedes stipulated that the island would remain duty-free and the residents would never pay taxes.

In 1946, the island was lumped together with St. Martin and Guadeloupe and given legal status as a Department of France, with all privileges and responsibilities attached, including French citizenship for all residents. However, the mother country was not offering a lot of economic help and the island developed a special relationship with the US Virgin Islands, where many St. Barts residents went to work because of the number of jobs available. They built communities and assimilated with the population, sending home their earnings and introducing the St. Barts' population to American ways. This close tie resulted in the many American customs and mannerisms you encounter when you are there.

Eventually, the French and Americans discovered the tourism potential of the island. The population has steadily grown as St. Barts has attracted those looking for a measure of independence from France and a beautiful island refuge.

The Facts

Population: 7,000, comprised mainly of "St. Barths People," as the natives call themselves, plus émigrés from France, Portugal and the US.

Language: The official language is French, but many residents are fluent in English and other European languages. You'd be surprised how many service people do not know English, so you may find a French phrase book extremely helpful.

Main City: The primary city and main port is Gustavia, on the southwestern side of the island.

Government & Economy: St. Barts is a dependency of Guadeloupe, which in turn is an Overseas Department and Region of France. Residents participate in French elections. The island government includes a mayor, elected every seven years, and a town constable. France stations a security force of six policemen and 13 gendarmes here for two-year tours of duty.

St. Barts' longstanding desire for independence from Guadeloupe got some leverage in 2006 when the French government initiated a legislative framework aimed toward independence – so by the time you read this book, the governmental structure may be dramatically different.

People & Culture: The endemic population takes their allegiance to France very seriously, but also honors its Swedish heritage. The islands are somewhat reserved and hold to social standards established long ago – basing business arrangements on a handshake or a person's word, taking personal responsibility for their property and conduct, disliking a lot of government interference, and holding family as a very important part of life. They are also fiercely protective of their beautiful island, and actively discourage large-scale development or anything that would disturb its idyllic small-town feel.

Geography: St. Barts is a small island of a little more than eight square miles, located 125 miles east of Puerto Rico and 15 miles southeast of St. Martin. It is composed of hills and valleys that vary in topography, density, architecture and plant life. The 14 beaches are white-sand strands of varying sizes and shapes and many are protected by offshore reefs. Several of the reefs are included in a Marine Reserve where diving is regulated.

Climate: The weather, as you would expect, is pleasantly warm and breezy year-round. It rarely rains, which is good for the tourists but not so great for the plants and residents. Water desalinization plants provide the necessary water. Since it is a Caribbean isle, it follows the same hurricane season calendar as the rest of the islands and has been enjoying a relatively calm period for the last eight-10 years.

Flora & Fauna: Because it is an arid island, you would expect the landscape to be filled with cactus and brush. However, there is a marked diversity of plant life and a few species of animals fare well on the island – but there is none of the rainforest commonly seen on the other Leeward Islands. Trees include the fragrant frangipani and gorgeous flamboyant as well as palms, sea grape and lignum vitae. In irrigated areas there is a profusion of flowers, including oleander, hibiscus, bougainvillea, Mexican creeper and plumbago, as well as cactus and succulents in dry areas. One of the highlights is the Englishman's head cactus, a low, round, spiky plant sprouting a red top that blooms into a flower.

Among the animal life are mongoose, iguanas, sea turtles and a vibrant sea bird population including brown pelicans, herons and frigate birds.

Travel Information

When to Go

 This is a great vacation island anytime since temperatures average between 79°F and 82°F year-round and the climate is arid, delivering nearly 300 days of sun a year. Rates are lower in summer, providing a chance to visit some of the luxury hotels at rates most budgets can afford. Summer is also a good time to learn about the culture since many of the villages hold their festivals during July and August.

Getting There

The landing strip at the airport near St. Jean is quite short, so planes larger than 20 seats cannot land. There are no direct long-distance flights, and visitors arrive primarily by smaller planes from St. Martin and Guadeloupe, or by ferry from St. Martin. The airport has no capacity for night landings, so you need to make sure your connecting flight arrives before sunset.

St. Barts Airport

 Be advised that you will need a passport to get into St. Barts and St. Martin, as well as for return to the US.

By Air

 The opening of a new terminal at St. Martin's Princess Juliana Airport in 2006 has simplified travel to St. Barts. From the new terminal, you can easily transfer to smaller airlines serving St. Barts, including **Air Caraïbes**, **St. Barth's Commuter** and **Winair**; the flight takes about 10 minutes.

Airlines Serving St. Maarten

American Airlines has several daily non-stop flights from Miami, New York (JFK) and San Juan. ☎ 800-433-7300, www.aa.com.

Continental Airlines flies non-stop six days a week from Newark. ☎ 800-231-0856, www.continental.com.

Delta Airlines offers non-stop flights six times a week from Atlanta, and once a week from Miami. ☎ 800-241-4141.

United Airlines has weekend non-stop service from Philadelphia and Washington (IAD). ☎ 800-538-2929, www.united.com.

US Airways flies daily non-stop from Charlotte, and once weekly from Philadelphia. ☎ 800-622-1015, www.usairways.com.

Airlines Offering Links to St. Barts

Air Caraïbes has daily flights from Guadeloupe and several flights a week from San Juan to St. Bart via St. Maarten. ☎ 877-772-1005 US, 590-590-27-71-90 St. Barts, www.aircaraibes.com.

Air St. Maarten, calling itself a "virtual airline," organizes private and shared charters from St. Martin to St. Barts using the airplanes of Windward Express. ☎ 599-581-9740, www.airsxm.eu.

Heli St. Martin offers flights by helicoptor from the Grand Case airport to St. Barts on a charter basis. It's said to be very pricey, but for those who can afford it, this is another alternative. ☎ 599-544-4100, US 305-767-2531, www.helistmartin.com.

St. Barth's Commuter has daily flights from L'Espérance Airport in St. Martin and from Princess Juliana Airport in Sint Maarten. ☎ 590-590-27-54-54, www.stbarthcommuter.com.

WinAir offers several flights a day from St. Maarten's Princess Juliana Airport. ☎ 866-466-0410 US, 599-545-4237 St. Maarten, www.fly-winair.com.

Windward Express has charter trips. ☎ 599-545-2001, www.windwardexpress.com.

By Sea

 High-speed catamarans provide daily ferry service between St. Barts and St. Martin/Sint Maarten. The trips average 40 minutes from Oyster Pond on the Dutch side, to 75 minutes from Marigot on the French side. If you don't have good sea legs, you should probably fly. The eastward voyage (to St. Barts) can be rough on days when the waves are high, although ferry operators attempt to smooth out the ride with offers of ginger ale and other drinks while you are onboard.

Among the ferry operators is the **MV *Voyager***, which runs from Marigot and Oyster Pond to Gustavia on a regular schedule. Reservations are highly recommended and are required in high season. ☎ 590-590-87-10-68, www.voyager-st-barths.com.

The **Rapid Explorer** also provides scheduled ferry service between St. Barts and St. Martin aboard four air-conditioned hydrofoil catamarans. The boats depart from the Chesterfield Marina in Pointe Blanche, St. Maarten, a short taxi ride from the airport. ☎ 590-590-27-60-33, www.sbonline.com/Rapid_Explorer.htm.

St. Martin-based charter operators that also offer airport shuttles via motor yacht, based on your timetable include:

Marine Service, based in Gustavia, runs a 41-ft high-speed cruiser between St. Maarten and St. Barts. ☎ 590-590-27-70-34.

Master Ski Pilou offers 24/7 airport shuttles aboard their 40- to 55-ft motor yachts. ☎ 590-590-27-91-79, www.st-barths.com/master-ski-pilou.

Ocean Must Boat Rental Center is based in Gustavia and has various powerboats available for the trip. ☎ 590-590-27-62-05, www.oceanmust. com.

Yannis Marine, based in Gustavia, offers luxury-fitted sport cruisers of varying sizes. ☎ 590-590-29-89-12, www.yannismarine.com.

TRAVELING 'IN TRANSIT' TO SAVE TIME

When traveling from St. Maarten to St. Barts, you can use the Transit Gate to save a bit of time. Because you are "in transit" to another island, you eliminate a stop at Immigration and do not have to pay the Transit Tax, which means fewer lines to stand in.

The Transit Gate is near the Transfer Information Desk in the new terminal. You should have a boarding pass in hand and you must have checked your luggage through to St. Barts, although carry-on/hand luggage is allowed.

Customs

 As a duty-free port, the customs regulations are very relaxed. Items for personal use such as tobacco, cameras and film are allowed without regulation or tax, unless they are in excessive quantities.

Special Events & Holidays

 Many of the special events throughout the year in St. Barts are centered on religious or national holidays. In addition, the island hosts two major international festivals, one for music and dance in January, and one for film (although St. Barts does not have a movie theater) in April. For more information on these events, see the St. Barts' Tourism website at www.st-barths.com.

January

New Year's Day, January 1 – Public holiday.

Three Kings Day or *Galette des Rois*, January 8 – Epiphany cake served at all fêtes.

St. Barth Music Festival – Jazz, chamber, classical music and dance at various venues around Gustavia and L'Orient. www. stbartsmusicfestival.org.

February

Carnaval School Parade – In the streets of Gustavia.

Carnaval – Beginning of Mardi Gras; costumed parade concluding with the burning of Vaval (King of Carnaval) at Shell Beach. Most businesses are closed.

March

International Women Day – Commemorated by the Lyceum Club, City Hall.

St Barth's Bucket – A three-day invitational mega-yacht regatta.

April

Easter weekend – Religious and public holiday.

Caribbean Film Festival – A gathering of Caribbean films and filmmakers, sponsored by AJOE/L'Orient. www.stbarthff.org.

May

Labor Day, May 1 – Public holiday.

Annual archery competition proposed by Les France Archers.

Armistice Day, May 8 – Public holiday.

Theatre Festival of St. Barthelemy – A week-long festival at three venues on the island, organized by SB Artists. ☎ 0690-55-20-09, sbartists@ wanadoo.fr

Ascension, May 17 – Religious and public holiday.

Pentecost – Religious holiday.

June

Mother's Day – Family celebrations.

Father's Day – Family celebrations.

July

Fête de l'Anse des Cayes et Anse des Lézards – Music, sport, show and ball.

Fishing Contest – Organized by Ocean Must. www.oceanmust.com.

Bastille Day, July 14 – Public holiday.

St. Barths Volleyball Cup – A series of matches beginning mid-July.

Fête des Quartiers du Nord – Contests, regattas, dance and comedy performances, and fireworks in Colombier.

August

Boubous Music Festival – Two-week festival that brings in ethnic and African musical artists to perform at the Hôtel Christopher, Pointe Milou. www.boubous-festival.com.

Fête des Quartiers du Vent – Regatta, music, and fireworks in L'Orient.

St. Barts

Pitea Day, August 14 – Religious and public holiday. Commemorates the special relationship between St. Barts and Pitea, Sweden, with fishing tournaments, games, regatta, and barbecue on the beach.

Assumption Day, August 15 – Religious holiday.

Festival of Gustavia – Regattas, marathon, dance, fishing tournament and fireworks at Quai du General de Gaulle.

Festival of St. Barthelemy, August 24 – Patron Saint Feast Day. Church and official ceremonies, regattas, public ball, fireworks in Gustavia.

St-Louis Festiva – Fishing contests, regattas, dances and fireworks in Corossol.

Seniors Day – Special entertainment for older citizens.

November

All Saints Day, Nov. 1 – Religious and public holiday.

Armistice Day, Nov. 11 – Public holiday commemorating the end of World War I.

Swedish Marathon or *Gustavialoppet*, mid-November – Traditional annual race of three km for children and 12 km for runners from all over the world.

December

Christmas, December 25 – Religious and public holiday.

New Year's Eve Regatta-Race, December 31 – Organized for fun around Saint-Barth.

New Year's Eve, December 31 – Celebration with live music from 9 pm at Quai General de Gaulle in Gustavia, fireworks at midnight and parties in some restaurants.

Health

The island has a small hospital, **Hopital de Bruyn**, in Gustavia, ☎ 590-590-27-60-35, and a medical laboratory. There are a number of general physicians and specialists in cardiology, ENT, OB/GYN, pediatrics and rheumatology, as well as a number of dentists. Pharmacies around the island where you can purchase over-the-counter remedies include those in the La Savane Commercial Center in St. Jean, at the airport and in Gustavia. For medical emergencies or more extensive services, you may need to travel to San Juan, Miami or Guadeloupe. There are two medical evacuation services, Medicall (☎ 590-590-29-04-04) and SCII (☎ 590-590-52-02-71).

Pets

 If you bring along a pet, it must be accompanied by your animal's rabies vaccination record and by a health certificate from your veterinarian dated no more than five days prior to arrival. There is one veterinary clinic on the island.

Crime

Because of the small population and the closeness of the communities, the crime rate on St. Barts is very low. However, you should take the normal precautions of locking up jewelry, cash or valuables when you are not in your hotel room or villa.

Electricity

 The island is on the European standard of 220 volts for most outlets. You will need to bring a voltage converter and adapter plugs, although many hotels have dual-voltage outlets in bathrooms for shavers and will provide converters for guests. If you plan to use a laptop, you will need a heavy-duty (at least 100 watts) converter and if you plan to connect by phone modem, a modular telephone adapter. These can be found at most travel stores or online at Magellans.com or TravelSmith. com.

Tipping

Restaurateurs follow the French model of including a service charge in the bill. However, since this money is shared among all the servers, it is customary to leave an additional 5-10% at the table for your server. Leave your tip in cash, because many of the establishments are unable to add a tip to the credit card bill.

Money Matters

The official currency of the island is the euro (€), which is currently set at an exchange rate of €1 to US$1.30 and all prices shown in menus or stores are in euros. American dollars are accepted in most places at the current exchange rate. When the rate is low (around €1 to US$1.20), some aggressive marketers will advertise a more equitable exchange rate by putting a sign out front that reads: 1€ = $1. This means you get a 20% reduction in what you would otherwise pay.

St. Barts

To get cash (in euros only), there are ATM machines at the **Banque Francaise Commercial** (BFC), rue du Général-de-Gaulle and the **Banque Nationale de Paris**, rue du Bord-de-Mer in Gustavia.

Weddings

While many people enjoy getting married at one of the beautiful seaside hotels or a hillside villa, they have to comply with French laws, including a requirement that one of the couple must have resided on the island for at least one month prior to getting married. Among the documents required are original birth certificates (or copy with raised seal); certificates of good conduct (including certification of "single status"); residency cards (to prove the one-month requirement); and medical certificates (including blood tests) issued within three months of marriage. Any documents originating in English must be translated to French. A Bulletin de Mariage and Livret de Famille are then delivered at the ceremony.

Internet Access

Many of the hotels and villas on St. Barts have WiFi Internet access, with more being added every day. If you don't plan to carry a computer, you can get access to one at **Centre Alizes** in Gustavia, ☎ 590-590-29-89-89, or in the Internet café at **Terrazza** in St. Jean, ☎ 590-590-27-70-67. To arrange for short-term service while staying in a villa, contact **Power Antilles**, ☎ 590-50-87-97-92, www.powerantilles.com.

You can also take advantage of the many WiFi zones springing up all over the island. There is free access at **Maya's To Go** in St. Jean and **Le Repaire** in Gustavia, as well as at other restaurants and cafés.

Communications

You can use your digital cellular phone on St. Barts by pre-registering with **East Caribbean Cellular** for service billed to a credit card ((☎ 599-542-2100, www.eastcaribbeancellular.com) or with **Saint Martin Mobiles** (☎ 590-590-87-16-16, www.stmartinmobiles.com). Both offer online enrollment or enrollment by fax. Or you can wait until you are in St. Martin, dial 0 on your cell phone and an operator will then register you. However, some St. Barts locals report that this service only works when you are in an area where you have a clear sightline to St. Martin.

Another way to get cellular service if you have a GSM phone is to go to **France Telecom**'s office in St. Jean to have the SIM card replaced with a local one. This will give you a local number and a certain amount of time you can use.

DIALING TO & FROM ST. BARTS

For those not familiar with international calling, getting phone calls through this department of France can be challenging. Here's the way to do it:

■ **To call St. Barts from the US**, dial 011-590-590+the six-digit unique phone number of the person/place you are trying to reach (this is why the numbers in this chapter always appear with the two 590 numbers). For cell phones, you replace the second 590 with 690.

■ **To call the US from St. Barts**, dial 001+area code+ phone number. This is a lot easier.

■ **To call within the French system** (St. Barts and St. Martin) from a local phone, dial 0590+the six-digit phone number, or 0690+the phone number for cell phones.

It helps to carry a calling card while on vacation in order to charge the fees, especially if you are staying in a villa. For better rates, you can purchase a prepaid phone card when you arrive. The cards have clear instructions and are available at the supermarket Match and the gas station near the airport.

Media

Publications include the weekly *Journal de St. Barth*, a French-language paper which is summarized in an English-language version called *St. Barth's Weekly*, published during the winter months only. You can see the latest issue at www.st-barths.com/jsb. The island also offers numerous publications to let visitors know what is available on the island. They include *Discover, Tropical Saint-Barth, VIP Guide to St. Barth* and, for restaurant listings, *Ti Gourmet*. All are available at the airport and the Tourist Authority offices.

Sources of Information

In St. Barts

Office du Tourisme/St. Barthélemy Tourist Office, B.P. 113, Gustavia 97098, St. Barthélemy, F.W.I., ☎ 590-590-27-87-27, fax 590-590-27-74-47.

In the US

French Government Tourist Office (Maison de la France-New York), 444 Madison Ave., 16th floor, New York NY 10022, ☎ 212-838-7800, fax 212-838-7855; **French Government Tourist Office (Maison de la France-Chicago)**, 676 N. Michigan Ave., Chicago, IL 60611-2819, ☎ 312-751-7800, fax 312-337-6339; **French Government Tourist Office (Maison de la France-Beverly Hills)**, 9454 Wilshire Blvd., Ste. 715, Beverly Hills, CA 90212-2967, ☎ 310-271-6665, fax 310-276-2835; **French Government Embassy,** 4101 Reservoir Road NW, Washington DC 20007, ☎ 202-944-6000

In Canada

French Government Tourist Office (Maison de la France), 30 St. Patrick St., Suite 700, Toronto, Ont., M5T 3A3,, ☎ 416-593-6427, fax 416-979-7587.

Getting Around

Since the island is basically an extension of France, you don't need to worry about driving on the left – although reading road signs in French presents its own challenge. St. Barts is correctly known as a playground for celebrities from North America, but you will encounter many service people who do not understand English.

The island is shaped like a V, with many roads forming loops that lead to other loops that lead to roads that dead-end in villages or beaches. But St. Barts is only eight square miles, so you acclimate quickly and by the end of a day you should know your way around. No destination is more than 20 minutes away, and the roads either have incredible vistas or quaint roadside views.

Airport

The airport is small, with a short runway that ends at the sea. The landing is one of the most exciting in the Caribbean. You come in over some hills and take a sharp vertical dive before abruptly straightening out to land just before, it seems, you run into the sea. Once you are through kissing the ground, it is easy to find transportation to your hotel or villa. Taxis are always waiting out front, and the car rental agencies are well marked.

FREEDOM FROM WORRYING ABOUT THE DETAILS

There are a number of private concierge/VIP travel companies on the island that cater to those who don't want to hassle with details like arranging airport transfers, car rentals, boat charters and other activities. Some of those companies are:

St. Barth Services, based at the airport, will meet you at the airport, or at any other area airport, such as San Juan, Antigua or St. Martin, to make sure you get to your final destination in comfort and style. They are agents for WinAir, Caraïbe and Inter Island Express airlines and can arrange private boat charters, parties, spa visits and other activities. They'll even set up cell phone rental for you. ☎ 590-590-27-56-26, www.stbarth-services.com.

Premium IV can take care of all your travel arrangements, including your initial flights to St. Martin or Antigua, airport transfers, and car rentals. They will also stock your villa with food, find a babysitter, organize spa outings, plan adventure activities, and even arrange parties and weddings. ☎ 590-590-29-00-07, www.premiumiv.com.

Taxi Service

As in most of the Leeward Islands, the taxi drivers are some of the best tour guides available. They know their way around and delight in showing visitors their island. If you need to make special arrangements, there are taxi stands at the airport (☎ 590-590-27-75-81) or in Gustavia (☎ 590-590-27-66-31).

Car Rentals

This is the preferred mode of travel for almost everyone who visits St. Barts, because it is the best way to explore this tiny island. You can rent pretty much any type of vehicle through a number of agencies; most provide drop-off or pickup at your hotel at no extra cost. Remember that the roads are narrow and twisting, so vehicles like Hummers or large SUVs are virtually nonexistent on the island. There are only two gas stations on the island, and both are closed on Sundays so plan ahead for weekend excursions.

CAR RENTAL AGENCIES

Avis	☎ 800-831-2847
Barth'loc Rentals	☎ 590-590-27-52-81
Budget	☎ 590-590-29-62-40
Caraïbes Welcome Center	☎ 590-590-27-82-54
Europcar	☎ 590-590-27-74-34

St. Barts

Gumbs Rental	☎ 590-590-27-75-32
Hertz	☎ 800-654-3131
Island Car Rental	☎ 590-590-27-60-61
Maurice Rental	☎ 590-590-27-73-22
Soleil Caraibe	☎ 590-590-27-67-18
Star Location Car Rental	☎ 590-690-42-28-42
Top Loc	☎ 590-590-29-02-02, www.top-loc.com
Tropic'all Rent	☎ 590-590-27-64-76
Turbe Car Rental	☎ 590-590-27-60-70

Scooter Rentals

With the narrow and snakey roads, scooters are a popular mode of transportation, especially for young people. But give the scooter (and its rider) wide berth; they tend to make for a rather unpredictable combination. If you have it in your head that you want to really look hip and European and that renting a scooter is the way to do that, enjoy yourself – but be aware that you need a special license and must wear a helmet. The scooter agencies are clustered around the airport and many also rent motorbikes, mopeds and mountain bikes.

SCOOTER RENTAL AGENCIES	
Barth'loc Rental	☎ 590-590-27-52-81
Chez Beranger	☎ 590-590-27-89-00
Ets Dennis Dufau	☎ 590-590-27-54-83
Fredo Moto	☎ 590-590-27-67-89
Meca Moto	☎ 590-590-29-72-28
Tropic'all Rent	☎ 590-590-27-64-76

Exploring

On Foot

Hiking the hilly terrain on St. Barts is a favorite activity for visitors. There are no guided tours, but the Office du Tourisme in Gustavia has maps of the most used routes. Be aware that some lands are private and the owners will ask you to leave, so stick to the obvious trails.

Anse de Colombier

The best-known and easiest path is from **Petite Anse** to **Anse de Colombier**, where the beach is only accessible by hiking or boating in and the snorkeling is said to be fantastic. The trail, an old goat path, starts at the end of the paved road from Flamands. There is another trail starting from a parking lot at the end of a paved road west of the village of Colombier, but it is steep and rocky and will challenge all but the best hikers.

Another route with great vistas goes up **Morne du Vitet**, the highest point on the island (992 feet). You can drive to the top and then hike through the forest. **Toiny Point** at the southeastern end of the island takes you through an interesting array of native vegetation. The path ends at steep cliffs overlooking Anse à Toiny, where surfers enjoy the rugged beach.

At the end of **Le Chemin Douanier**, a 10-minute hike from the beach at Grand Fond, is **The Washing Machine**, a large natural tidal basin. The sea flows into the basin, creating a swirling motion that ends in breakers prized by local surfers. Past the basin, the trail goes up Morne Rouge to high ground overlooking the sea to the south.

On Wheels

Car or Jeep

Many taxi drivers offer tours of the island. (You can request an English-speaking one to get the most from the tour.) There are no set itineraries or rates, so negotiate the route and cost with your driver before setting out.

For off-road trekking, many car rental agencies offer Mini Mokes, which are at home on sand or other terrain.

St. Barts

On Water

Scuba Diving

Thanks to a designated Marine Reserve that prohibits fishing, and tough laws about anchoring on reefs, the underwater habitat around St. Barts is great for diving. In the Reserve, there are 22 dive sites with reefs, caves and canyons ranging from 20 to 90 feet in depth. Other popular sites are around the outer islands of Ile de Forchue, Le Tortue, Ilets Coco, Le Baril de Boeuf and Pain de Sucre, and at L'Ange Rouge off the Colombier Bay area. You'll see varieties of coral, angelfish, barracudas, sponges, sea turtles, lobsters, groupers, morays and even a dolphin or two.

Most dive spots are no more than five to 20 minutes from Gustavia, so you'll spend more time in the water than getting to it. The leeward sites are better for divers without a lot of experience; the windward dives tend to be in rougher waters and the terrain is more rugged.

Rules of the Marine Reserve

Since St. Barth created the **Marine Reserve** in 1996, the variety and quantity of marine life around the island has increased immeasurably. This means diving and snorkeling in the 2,000 acres of protected park areas around the island are more enjoyable than ever before. For a map of the entire reserve area, see www.reserve-naturelle-stbarthelemy.com.

Activities banned in the reserve include underwater hunting with spears or harpoons, the use of motorized equipment (jet skis, etc.), water skiing, trash disposal, collecting of coral or plants, collecting of shells and shellfish, such as lobster and conch (dead or alive), and anchoring, except in certain designated zones. Floats are provided for boats to tie-up.

Divers in the parks are asked to donate €1 per dive for maintenance of the reserve. Divers can purchase an unlimited year-long pass for €15 at the Marine Reserve office on the dock in Gustavia. If you are diving on your own, you are asked to stop by the Marine Reserve office to pay these fees; otherwise the dive operators collect them.

Dive Operators

Plongées Caraïbes offers dive instructions, equipment and a choice of dive tours on the 48-ft catamaran *Blue Cat*, the largest dive boat on St.

Barts. Dive packages of five and 10 dives are available, and they also offer snorkeling tours. ☎ 590-590-27-55-94, www.plongee-caraibes.com.

Ouanalao Dive is on Grand Cul de Sac beach. It offers three daily dive trips, all equipment rentals and a PADI diving school for certifications. They also offer snorkeling tours. ☎ 590-690-63-74-34, www.st-barths.com/ouanalao-dive.

Ile Fourchue

Splash Diving Center in Gustavia offers instruction and dive tours using certified instructors. ☎ 590-690-56-90-24.

St-Barth Plongée offers tours on a 28-ft flat-hull diving boat. In addition to the standard instructions and certifications, you can take a night dive (three or more divers) or a shark-feeding dive. From January to June, a "Song of the Whales" tour offers the chance to view humpbacks traveling through the area. ☎ 590-590-27-54-44, www.st-barthplongee.fr.

West Indies Dive is at the Yacht Club Pier in Gustavia. They offer three dive tours each day on a 31-ft Ocean Master boat that can accommodate up to eight divers per trip. The dives are primarily in the leeward areas, although they will travel to the outer islands. ☎ 590-690-59-82-14, www. westindiesdive.com.

VIEW THE UNDERWATER WORLD IN A SUBMARINE

Don't like diving and can't get the hang of snorkeling gear? You can still view the incredible beauty underwater by taking a trip on the **Yellow Submarine**. This semi-submersible craft sits on the water and has a seating area surrounded by panoramic windows six feet below decks. You have a great view of reefs, wrecks and an array of marine life, while sitting as dry and comfortable as a landlubber.

The trip, about one hour in length, goes from Gustavia's pier through the Marine Park and around Gros Ilets toward Les Petits Saints and back. Along the way, the crew provides narration to make sure you see all the best sights. Once a week they also offer a night tour, where special lights illuminate the nocturnal happenings in this rich underwater world. For reservations, see the website at www.yellow-submarine.fr or email contact@yellow-submarine.fr, ☎ 590-590-52-40-51.

Snorkeling

Because the island is ringed with reefs, you can get to some prime snorkeling areas just offshore at L'Orient and Colombier beaches and Petit de Anse. Many dive and boat charter operators also offer snorkeling tours. Among the prime offshore sites are **Forchue Island** and the **Marine Reserve**, where you can see a great deal

Purple and yellow gorgonians

without going deep. A popular tour is offered by **Marine Service** on a 41-ft sailing catamaran. ☎ 590-590-27-70-34, www.st-barth.com/marine.service.

Surfing & Windsurfing

Facing the Atlantic on the east and north, the island offers surfers many places for whipping across the waves. For body surfers, the favorite beaches are Anse des Cayes, Saline, Flamands, and of course the interesting Washing Machine near Anse du Grand Ford. Board surfers prefer the rough waves near Pointe a Toiny as well as the northern beaches of Pointe Milou, Anse de L'Orient, Baie de Saint Jean, Anse de Cayes and Anse des Lezards. For more on surf conditions, contact **Reefer's Surf Club**. ☎ 590-590-27-67-63. To rent or buy equipment, stop by **Totem Surf Shop** in Gustavia. They also have skateboards and kitesurfing equipment. ☎ 590-590-27-83-72, totemsurfshop@hotmail.com.

Windsurfing has really taken off on the island, and there are now a few companies providing equipment and lessons. These include **Saint-Barth Waterplay**, ☎ 590-690-61-38-40, and **Windwave Power**, ☎ 590-590-27-82-57. Taking full advantage of windy conditions, both companies also rent out small catamarans and Sunfish for playing in the water while learning how to sail.

Jet Skiing & Water Skiing

Again, the waters around St. Barts are perfect for pursuing these sports – but you need to be aware that use of motorized equipment is prohibited within 300 yards of shore to keep the noise levels down and the beaches peaceful. There are several operators who will take you out beyond the restricted area where you can play to your hearts content. These include **Master Ski Pilou**, **Marine Service** and **Yannis Marine**, all listed below.

Deep-Sea Fishing

St. Barts has a teeming fish population offshore and sport fishing for tuna, bonito, dorado, marlin, wahoo and barracuda is popular in all seasons. The waters north of L'Orient, Flamands and Corossol are prime fishing areas, and there are several boat charter operators offering half-day and full-day excursions. Among these are **Master Ski Pilou**, **Marine Service**, **Ocean Must** and **Yannis Marine**, all listed below.

Boat Charters

When your plane rounds the top of the hill to start its descent into Gustavia, you will see an amazing array of motor and sailing yachts in the harbor. The harbor can accommodate up to 40 yachts, and St. Barts is known as a major international sailing stopover, as it is halfway between the yachting centers of Antigua and St. Thomas. If you can't find a boat to charter here, you are not talking to the right people.

Charter Operators

Côte Mer has a 47-ft Lagoon catamaran available for snorkeling, half- and full-day charters and sunset cruises. ☎ 590-590-27-91-79, www.cote-mer.com.

Marine Service, based in Gustavia, offers charters, deep-sea fishing excursions and other boating-related services. ☎ 590-590-27-70-34, www.st-barths.com/marine.service.

Master Ski Pilou is a one-stop company for all boating needs, from sunset cruises and day charters on motor or sailing yachts, to scuba tours, deep-sea fishing, and jet ski rentals. ☎ 590-590-27-91-79, www.st-barths.com/master-ski-pilou.

Ocean Must is a complete boating company offering fishing excursions, boat charters, water skiing and water tours. Among their fleet is the *Nina of St. Barth*, an 80-ft Maxi catamaran used for day charters and sailing

Gustavia Harbour

excursions. Ocean Must also operates its own dive shop, Le Bulle, and offers dive excursions. ☎ 590-590-27-62-25, www.oceanmust.com.

Top-Loc will rent you everything from a car to a boat. The boats include the 45-ft *Wayayi Privilège* catamaran and the 23-ft open *Koum Koum* motor boat, available for half-day and full-day charters and sunset cruises. ☎ 590-590-29-02-02, www.toplocstbarth.com.

Yannis Marine has a number of boats in its fleet, from the 31-ft Contender fishing boat to a sleek 58-ft Predator motor yacht, available for day charters, deep-sea fishing, sunset cruises and island tours. They also rent jet skis and have a catamaran available for snorkeling and diving tours. ☎ 590-590-29-89-12, www.yannismarine.com.

Take a Walk on the Wild Side - The Outer Islands

For an afternoon completely away from civilization, have one of the charter operators take you to **Ile Forchue**, an uninhabited nature preserve island off the western coast of St. Barts. The views from the top of the hills are beautiful, and the terrain is rocky and dry with no trees. Take water, beach umbrellas, hats and some kind of sustenance, since your only encounters will be with wild goats.

The waters offshore are part of the Marine Reserve, so if you snorkel you'll see an amazing array of sea life. This is also true at the other out-islands of **Ile Fregate**, **Ile Toc Vers** and **Ile Coco**, although they are on the windward side and may be a little rough to get to.

Gustavia

La Pointe

Museum

Mairie

Rue Duquesne

Rue Chanzy

Fort Oscar

Rue Jean Bart

Rue Sur la Colline

Rue Jeanne d'Arc

Rue Schoelcher

Hospital

Rue de la France

Rue Rio Oscar II

Rue du Général de Gaulle

Rue de la République

PARKING

Tourism Office

Rade de Gustavia

Rue Thiers

Rue Gambetta

Rue du Centenaire

Rue Coubret

Rue des Normands

Post Office

Rue Père de Bruyn

Rue Victor Hugo

Rue de l'Eglise

Fort Karl

Anse de Grand Galet

Hotel Carl Gustaf

Shell Beach

To Plage du Gouverneur

N

NOT TO SCALE

Sailing

Boats with sails are a major occupation in St. Barts, as evidenced by the frequent regattas and related events. If you want to start your children's addiction to the sport while young, enroll them in the sailing school sponsored by the St. Barth Yacht Club in Gustavia. ☎ 590-590-27-70-41 or 590-590-59-03-58.

Included in the fleet available for the smaller set are "optimists" – a soapbox with a sail – and 14-ft Lasers. The school organizes regattas all year-round for any category, and on those days, the sea-side and all the viewpoints are crammed with local people.

Sailboats can also be chartered through **St. Barth Caraïbes Yachting**, ☎ 590-590-27-52-06, or **Nautica FWI**, ☎ 590-590-27-56-50, www.nauticafwi.com.

On Horseback

If you have a fantasy of galloping through the surf on a deserted stretch of beach, St. Barts is happy to oblige. **St. Barth Equitation at Ranch des Flamands**, ☎ 590-590-27-13-87, can outfit you with a gentle horse, a solid saddle, and a guide to take you through the countryside above Anse des Flamands and down to the beach.

Playing & Watching Sports

Golf

With all the hills and winding roads, St. Barts' topography does not lend itself to the creation of a golf course. But that's what neighbors are for, and great courses are just an airplane ride away. **The Temenos St. Regis Course** on Anguilla, **The Four Seasons Golf Course** on Nevis, **The Royal St. Kitts Golf Club** in St. Kitts, the **Carambola Golf Course** in St. Croix or the **Mahogany Run Course** in St. Thomas are all available to golf enthusiasts willing to spend a day off-island.

Entrepreneurial golf pro Emmanuel Dussart has come up with a complete **Fly & Golf** package, where for one fee you and two other golfers fly with him to St. Kitts, Nevis or Anguilla for a day of play. The package includes taxes, taxis, pro fees and transportation, and then at your destination you pay for the greens' fees and club rental, plus food and drinks. It's a fairly expensive trip, but if you just have to play golf, it's an easy and enjoyable way to go. ☎ 590-690-30-58-73, www.flygolf.net.

If you just want to work on your swing, St. Barts now has an **aqua driving range** at Grand Cul de Sac. It's open most afternoons, and you can get a bucket of balls and clubs for just a few euros. ☎ 590-690-37-46-45.

Tennis

 Tennis is popular in St. Barts, with adults' and children's clubs hosting tournaments and welcoming visitors. Resorts with courts include Hotel Guanahani, Hotel Manapany and Hotel St. Barth Isle de France. In addition, there are some tennis clubs that welcome visitors, including:

- **Tennis Club du Flamboyant** in Grand Cul de Sac, ☎ 590-590-27-69-82.
- **AJOE Tennis Club** in Orient, ☎ 590-590-27-67-63.
- **ASCCO** in Colombier, ☎ 590-590-27-61-07.

For instructions or racket repair, contact one of the on-island tennis pros such as Patrick Sellez, ☎ 590-690-35-58-86, www.st-barths.com/patrick-sellez; Tennis Olivier, ☎ 590-690-43-31-33; or Yves Lacoste, ☎ 590-690-75-15-23.

Seeing the Sights

Sampling the Culture

As you read the history of St. Barts, you realize that it is unique among the Leewards in cultural development. Rather than celebrating the plantation culture, here you get more identification with France, and to some extent Sweden. This produces some interesting events during the year, including a Carnaval

Corossol beach

St. Barts

based on Mardi Gras and the many village fêtes that take place during the summer. There is also the Swedish Marathon in November and the celebration of Pitea Day (in honor of the friendship with Pitea, Sweden) in August.

One area where you can step back into St. Barts' past is **Corossol**, a fishing village on the western coast. It is sometimes called the "straw village" because women from old established families there still weave hats and crafts from palm fronds, and sell them to the public. Some of the older women still speak an old Norman dialect and dress in traditional clothes, including starched white bonnets called "quichenottes." It's also a great place to walk along the beach and see all the colorful fishing boats lined up.

The **InterOceans Museum** in Corossol offers another interesting view into St. Barts' culture. Ingres Magras spent his life collecting shells from all over the world – more than 9,000 in all – and they are displayed here. It's a way to identify those you've been picking up on the beach, as well as to see beautiful ones gathered from other places. ☎ 590-590-27-62-97.

Reliving History

While there are not a lot of historic buildings or markers on St. Barts, there is one museum on the island that testifies to the past. It's **Wallhouse Museum** in Gustavia, housed in a recently restored building from the Swedish period of the island's history. The collection includes artifacts from past inhabitants, and the museum is working to preserve important sociological and ethnographic information about the past for future generations. ☎ 590-590-29-71-55.

Street in Gustavia

Where to Stay

Luxe Hotels

> ## Off-Season Closures
>
> For a majority of the hotels on St. Barts, off-season is early summer, and way-off-season is when local residents take their vacations. So a majority of hotels – as well as some restaurants and stores – close for the period from mid-August until about mid-October. If you are planning a vacation for the fall, be sure to check with your target hotels early in your planning so you won't be disappointed.

$$$$$ – St. Barts is expensive, with more luxury hotels at upper-bracket rates than any other island in the Leewards. Expect high-season rates in this category to range from US$800 to $2,000 per night, and in low season US$550 to $625.

Eden Rock

 This was the first hotel built here and it sets the tone for the entire island. It offers a *luxe* collection of unique suites and rooms piled upon a rock out in the sea. Rooms can be selected "on the rock" or on the beach, and all have different décor and layouts. Try for the Heavenly Suites, with great views to the ocean, or the Premium

Eden Rock

Suites, with ocean-view terraces. Each has little special touches, such as a suite done up like a captain's cabin, or the Frigate Suite with brass portholes for windows. The two restaurants, On the Rocks and the Sand Bar, are outstanding, but pricey.

Location: Baie de Ste. Jean, northern coast.

Rooms: 19 in all, starting with the Diamond Suites in the penthouse, Heavenly Suites, Premium Suites, Classic Rock Suites, Beach rooms and cottages. The property has five privately-owned villas available for rental plus a three-bedroom Beach House. Some rooms have private plunge pools or Jacuzzis. All have balconies or patios, luxury baths, TVs and AC. Rates include breakfast buffet, use of all watersports equipment, airport transfers and taxes.

Rates: EP.

Features: Two restaurants, beach, saltwater pool, library with CDs, on-site spa, gym, boutique and art gallery.

☎ 590-590-29-79-99, US 877-563-7105, fax 590-590-27-88-37, www.edenrockhotel.com.

Hotel Carl Gustaf

Hotel Carl Gustav

Up above the Gustavia harbor sits this venerable hotel, often cited as one of the best in the Caribbean. It offers 14 beautifully furnished suites with private plunge pools, views out to the harbor and the sunset, and a highly regarded restaurant. A short walk down Rue des Normands takes you to Shell Beach, and at your doorstep are all the great shops and restaurants of Gustavia. Despite its "urban" location, you feel as if you're in your own private garden, being taken care of by a staff that really cares.

Location: Eastern end of Gustavia.

Rooms: 12 one- and two-bedroom suites with plunge pools, one Best View suite with Jacuzzi and one Sports Suite. All have kitchenettes, computers with Internet access, luxury baths, TVs with VCRs and DVD players, ceiling fans and AC. Rates include continental breakfast, airport transfers and welcome champagne.

Rates: EP.

Features: Restaurant, 24-hour room service, bar, fitness room, sauna, access to spa services and charter of the hotel's 52-ft motor yacht.

☎ 590-590-29-79-00, fax 590-590-27-82-37, www.hotelcarlgustaf.com.

Hotel Guanahani & Spa

This beautiful resort sits on the peninsula forming one end of Grand Cul de Sac in the northeast corner of the island. The guest cottages are strategically placed around the property to guarantee privacy for the 71 cottage rooms. Room choices are either as doubles or suites, 14 have private plunge pools. Three of the suites are designed for families, with two or three bedrooms, and there are specific areas near the beach for children's activities. The Guanahani Spa is one of the largest on the island, with a full range of body and facial treatments, massages, hydrotherapy and beauty services. The entire estate is awash in color from the gardens and the exteriors of the cottages, to the rooms and the orchids placed in them. The hotel lives up to its Five Star Diamond Award as one of the best in the world.

Guanahani pool

Location: Grand Cul de Sac.

Rooms: 71 total, with garden-view, ocean cove and ocean bay rooms; ocean and garden one-bedroom suites; ocean and garden one- and two-bedroom pool suites; two three-bedroom pool suites, one with garden view and "La Villa" with a romantic private pool; plus a wellness suite adjoining the spa. All have TVs with DVD players. Rates include full American breakfast, airport transfers and service charges.

Rates: BP.

Features: Two restaurants, lounge, beach bar, beach with watersports (kayaks, windsurfers and snorkeling gear at no additional cost), two tennis courts, fitness center, spa, concierge, boutique, Internet access in lobby.

☎ 590-590-27-66-60, 800-216-3774 US, fax 590-590-27-70-70, www.leguanahani.com.

Le Sereno

The last few years have been significant for this Grand Cul de Sac resort. New owners brought in renowned interior designer Christian Liaigre to completely change the look and feel of the property. Liaigre has introduced a cool, sophisticated sensibility through the use of dark woods, bright white luxury linens and comfortable furniture. The 37 suites are

St. Barts

Le Sereno

set into lush gardens and have ocean views. Many of the rooms open onto the beach. They are equipped with the latest high-tech gadgets, including WiFi Internet connections, flat screen TVs, DVD players and stereo equipment. The pool area is equally sophisticated. Looking almost too perfect to actually use, the double-wide and single lounges lining the pool are padded with thick, soft cushions. Four-bedroom villas are being added to the property to attract more families and large groups.

Location: Grand Cul de Sac beach.

Rooms: 37 rooms, including 21 beach suites, 13 terrace suites, two sea-view villas and one Fisherman's Villa with a private pool. All have air conditioning, TVs, WiFi Internet, DVD players and stereo systems.

Rates: EP.

Features: Restaurant, lounge, 24-hour room service, pool, beach club with attendants, access to all non-motorized watersports, fitness center with trainers, spa, private airport transfers.

☎ 590-590-29-83-00, fax 590-590-27-75-47, www.lesereno.com.

Le Toiny

Le Toiny

This is the place celebrities go when they don't want to be seen by anyone, but want to be pampered in true West Indian style. On the hill overlooking Anse Toiny, this unique, small hotel offers comfortable suites in the colonial style with hardwood floors, furniture and white walls. Each suite has a minibar and small kitchenette, as well as a patio leading out to beautiful views of the sea and a private pool. They also have a two- to three-bedroom villa suite where the master suite is adjoined by two bungalows, with all three sharing a pool. It's refined luxury in a quiet setting, perfect for getting away from it all.

Location: Anse Toiny, at the southeastern end of the island.

Rooms: 15 villa suites with pools and kitchenettes; one can be combined with two bedroom bungalows to make a larger family suite. All have air conditioning, plasma screen TV, DVD player, Bang & Olufsen stereo, WiFi Internet access, fax, minibar, microwave, hot plate and icemaker. Rates include continental breakfast and airport transfers.

Rates: CP.

Features: Restaurant, bar, Ligne St. Barth spa treatments, chauffeur, concierge, international newspapers, 24-hour room service, DVD library. ☎ 590-590-27-88-88, fax 590-590-27-89-30, www.hotelletoiny.dom.

St. Barth Isle de France

St. Barth Isle de France

Everywhere you look on this property, you see cool white contrasted with bright colors – the white of the reception area is set off by the turquoise sea of Flamands Beach; the white floors, walls and bed linens of the suites are accessorized with bright red bouquets of flowers and luxurious pillows and throws. From the beach, the buildings march up the hill, providing incredible views to the sea or the lush tropical gardens of the estate. The main building has nine air-conditioned rooms, and the other accommodations are in bungalows and villas facing the ocean or nestled into the gardens. The best room is the ocean-side suite with two bedrooms and a sizeable living area that includes a deck with a hot tub.

Location: Flamands Beach, northwestern end of the island.

Pool at St. Barth Isle de France

St. Barts

Rooms: 36 in all, including three beach rooms, three garden rooms, three beach junior suites, 13 garden bungalows, a Tropical Villa, two two-bedroom villas, a Hillside Bungalow, the Fisherman's Cottage and the two-bedroom oceanside suite. All have mini-fridges, coffee/tea service, minibars, satellite TVs with DVD players and AC. Rates include continental breakfast.

Rates: BP, with many packages available.

Features: Restaurant, two pools, beach with watersports, two tennis courts, extensive spa, fitness center, yoga classes, weekly fashion show.

☎ 590-590-27-61-81, fax 590-590-27-56-33, www.isle-de-france.com.

Taiwana

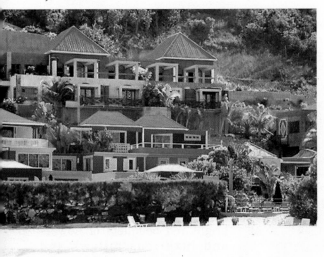

Taiwana

This hotel underwent major renovations in 2006. The number of rooms went down and the quality went up. It's one of the most expensive hotels on the island, so you can expect a very high level of service. The property is stunning, with water gardens popping up between buildings, bungalows done in intense earth tones, and views out to Flamands Bay. Each suite is unique in style and furnishings, and some have private plunge pools. By the time this book is published the dust should have settled and the restaurant should be up and running – but call ahead to make sure.

Location: Flamands Beach, northwest corner of the island.

Rooms: 13 suites and two rooms, some with sitting areas, large balconies and plunge pools.

Rates: EP.

Features: Restaurant, pool, beach with watersports.

☎ 590-590-27-65-01, fax 590-590-27-94-07, www.hoteltaiwana.com.

Tom Beach

If you have heard anything about Ti St. Barth, the wild nightclub that sets a standard for good times, you'll understand the ambiance at Tom Beach, since it's owned by the same people. Carole Gruson and Thierry de Badereau have created a light, playful atmosphere here with bright colors

Tom Beach

and non-intrusive but attentive service. Consider trying one of the two beachfront rooms, with terraces that allow you to walk right out to the sea.

Location: Baie de St. Jean, center part of the island.

Rooms: 10 with private terraces, king-sized, canopied beds, minibar, TVs with VCRs, and AC. Rates include continental breakfast and airport transfers.

Rates: CP, with packages available.

Features: Restaurant, pool, beach with watersports.

☎ 590-590-27-53-13, fax 590-590-27-53-15, www.tombeach.com.

Luxury With Limits

$$$$ – When you look at prices on St. Barth, you realize they are astronomical. The hotels in this range come with rates running from US$700 to $800 in high season, and US$370 to $600 in low.

Hotel Emeraude Plage

Baie de Saint Jean and its beautiful beach are the setting for this small luxury hotel near the airport. But don't worry about planes disturbing your serenity – only a few small planes use the runway, and there are no nighttime landings or takeoffs, so you can enjoy the sounds of the waves in peace. The hotel features suites and cottages with either full kitchens or kitchenettes and is ideal for those not wanting to rely upon restaurants for every meal. Club Eau de Mer, the beach bar on-site, offers breakfast, lunch and sunset cocktails. Its central location is ideal for shopping in Gustavia, dining anywhere, and tak-

Emeraude Plage

St. Barts

ing advantage of all that St. Barts offers.

Location: Baie de St. Jean, center of the island.

Rooms: 14 in all, with a two-bedroom villa, a two-bedroom ocean-view suite and the two-bedroom Stone House, plus eight one-bedroom studios, cottages and suites with various views. All include private terraces with kitchens or kitchenettes, TV, ceiling fan, and AC.

Rates: EP.

Features: Beach bar, beach with watersports, daily maid service, laundry service, concierge, Internet access in lobby.

☎ 590-590-27-64-78, fax 590-590-27-83-08, www.emeraudeplage.com.

Francois Plantation

Francois Plantation

In 2005, this lovely hotel at the top of a hill in Colombier was acquired by English-man Robert Eden, who also owns a vineyard in France. He made renovations to the hotel and to the restaurant, so that today visitors have a beautiful retreat featuring lush gardens, panoramic views to the sea, and first-class dining. The cottages and villa are furnished with reproduction mahogany furniture, the baths are white marble and the floors are dark hardwood, giving an overall historic and luxurious ambiance. The restaurant is a favorite of epicures all over the island, and Eden's Chateau de Combebelle wines are featured.

Location: Colombier, at the northwest tip of the island.

Rooms: 12 one-bedroom cottages with garden or ocean views (some can be adjoined), plus a one-bedroom villa with private pool and kitchen. All have queen-sized beds, private terraces, minibars, CD player, TV, ceiling fans and AC.

Rates: CP, with car rental included from Nov. 1-Dec. 19 and Apr. 18-Aug. 31.

Features: Restaurant, pool, airport transfers.

☎ 590-590-29-80-22, fax 590-590-27-61-26, www.francois-plantation.com.

Le Manapany

The Manapany has undergone a transformation, making it even more luxurious than it was. They've eliminated the kitchenettes, enlarged the rooms, and updated furnishings and linens with high-quality touches. The new beachfront junior suites are gorgeous  and feature king-size four poster beds, terra cotta floors, a Villeroy and Bosch bathtub, and showers with Art Deco glass bricks and marble tiles. Two of the suites have a private solarium with Jacuzzi. The hotel overlooks beautiful Anse des Cayes, one of the best and least traveled beaches.

Location: Anse des Cayes, on the north/central portion of the island.

Rooms: 44 rooms and suites, including hillside superior rooms, oceanview and beach-front suites or junior suites. Two of the junior suites and full suites have private solariums and Jacuzzis. All rooms have ceiling fans, TVs and AC.

Rates: EP, with BP, MAP, FAP and packages available.

Features: Restaurant, pool, tennis court, spa, fitness room, beach with watersports.

☎ 590-590-27-66-55, fax 590-590-27-75-28, www.lemanapany.com.

Reasonable & Comfortable Hotels

$$$ – All things being relative, the rates at these properties are a little more reasonable. They range from US$470 to $700 in high season, and US$280 to $400 in low.

Hotel Baie des Anges

This small, pretty hotel done in bright blue clapboard with white trim on Flamands Beach shares the island's best beach with its tonier neighbors St. Barth Isle de France and Taiwana. You get comfortable accommodations at lower rates and owner Annie Turbe-Ange works hard to make her guests feel at home.

Location: Flamands Beach, northwest corner of the island.

Rooms: 10 studio rooms on two levels, with a choice of sea-view, sea-front and sea-front deluxe. All have kitchenettes, TVs and AC.

Rates: EP.

Features: Restaurant, pool, beach.

☎ 590-590-27-63-61, fax 590-590-27-83-44, www.hotelbaiedesanges.com.

Hotel Christopher

This long-standing St. Barts favorite sits on a hillside of Point Milou. It overlooks the Atlantic; the beaches of L'Orient and Marigot are just minutes away. The rooms are simply furnished, the bathrooms clean and bright, and the private terraces scattered with teak furniture. The free-form infinity pool is the largest on the island, and includes a shallow children's area. Since it is not beach-side, the hotel offers concierge services and shuttles to Gustavia, St. Jean, the beaches and other parts of the island.

Location: Pointe Milou, northeast side of the island.

Rooms: 41, including classic oceanfront, superior ocean-view and deluxe ocean-view rooms and two family suites. All have private terraces, minibars, TVs, phones with answering machines, satellite TV, WiFi Internet, ceiling fans and AC. Rates include breakfast and airport transfers.

Rates: CP.

Features: Two restaurants, pool, shuttle to beaches and villages, concierge services.

☎ 590-590-27-63-63, US 866-287-8017, fax 590-590-27-92-92, www. hotelchristopherstbarth.com.

La Banane

Bungalow at La Banane

This small, intimate hotel sits inland, equidistant from the beaches at St. Jean and L'Orient. The nine West Indian bungalows are surrounded by shady and lush gardens and are furnished with contemporary, minimalist furniture and accents. Bathrooms feature access to a garden or patio, for an au naturel bathing experience.

Location: Near L'Orient, center part of the island.

Rooms: Nine bungalows, with minibars, TVs with DVD players, CD players, ceiling fans and AC.

Rates: EP.

Features: Bar, two pools, reading room/library.

☎ 590-590-52-03-00, fax 590-590-27-68-44, www.labanane.com.

Le Village St. Jean

This homey hotel run by the Charneau family looks down on the village of St. Jean, and is just a short walk uphill from the beach. The views out to Baie de St. Jean are outstanding and are best seen from the deluxe ocean-view cottages. The accommodations range from hotel rooms to one- and two-bedroom cottages with kitchenettes, all done in bright colors and true West Indian style. The property is beautifully landscaped around the pool and Jacuzzi.

Terrace at Le Village St. Jean

Location: St. Jean, central part of the island.

Rooms: Six single and double rooms (no kitchenettes); 20 standard and deluxe one- and two-bedroom cottages with garden or ocean view. All have AC and each is individually decorated. The hotel rooms include continental breakfast.

Rates: EP/CP.

Features: Restaurant, pool.

☎ 590-590-27-61-39, fax 590-590-27-77-96, www.villagestjeanhotel.com.

Les Ilets de la Plage

St. Barts' best beach, Plage de St. Jean, is the site of this small, all-cottage hotel. Four of the bright West Indian-style cottages sit right on the beach, and the others are situated in a tropical garden just a few steps from the beach. If you love to sunbathe, this is the place for you. It is centrally located so you can reach any place on the island within a few minutes.

Location: Plage de St. Jean, central part of the island.

Les Ilets de la Plage

Rooms: 11 cottages (four one-bedrooms on the beach and seven one- to three-bedrooms in the garden). All have teak furnishings, patios, kitchens, CD players, ceiling fans; AC in the bedrooms.

Rates: EP.

Features: Beach with lounges and watersports. ☎ 590-590-27 88 57, fax 590-590-27-88-58, www.st-barths.com/ilets-de-la-plage.

Les Ondines

This relative newcomer to the St. Barts hotel scene is a delightful one, with breezy, open suites, contemporary styling, luxury tile baths, and a warm, welcoming staff. A delicious continental breakfast of fresh croissants and breads, jams and beverages can be brought to your room each morning for a great start to the day. The soft sand beach of Grand Cul de Sac is just steps away.

Location: Grand Cul de Sac, on the eastern edge of the island.

Rooms: Six one- and two-bedroom suites with kitchens and living rooms. All have TVs, CD players and Internet connections; AC in the bedrooms. The larger suites have dishwashers and washing machines.

Rates: EP.

Features: Pool, beach, Internet access in lobby, breakfast in room on request (fee).

Beach at Les Ondines

☎ 590-590-27-69-64, fax 590-590-52-24-41, www.st-barths.com/les-ondines.

Résidence Les Lataniers

The old Hotel Yuana has been transformed into this small gem, which offers six junior suites with kitchenettes, perfect if you're trying to stay within a budget. All the hillside suites face Anse des Cayes and are just a short ride away from the beach.

Location: In the hills above Anse des Cayes, on the northwestern coast.

Rooms: Six junior suites and a one-bedroom classic suite with a Jacuzzi. All suites have kitchenettes, TVs with VCRs, ceiling fans, a convertible sofa and AC.

Pool at Résidences Les Lataniers

Rates: EP.

Features: Private balconies with views to the sea.

☎ 590-590-27-80-84, fax 590-590-27-78-45, www.st-barths.com/leslataniers.

Good Value Hotels

$$ – These smaller hotels represent good value, with a range from US$160 to $320 per night in high season, and US$100 to $215 in low.

Hostellerie de Trois Forces

As you wind your way up the hill to Vitet, you wonder why anyone would put a hotel way up here. But Hubert and Ginette Delamotte are not traditional hoteliers in any sense. Hubert, an outgoing and playful guy, is a classically trained chef and wine expert *and* a well-known astrologer and proponent of holistic health methods. His seven cottages, simply furnished, painted in bright colors and named after signs of the Zodiac, have accommodated the likes of Meryl Streep and Ram Dass.

Location: Near the top of Morne du Vitet, in the eastern part of the island.

Rooms: Seven cottages, some with kitchenettes. All have AC, and each is uniquely decorated. Rates include breakfast.

Rates: BP.

Features: Restaurant, pool, library, access to holistic health seminars held at the hotel, astrological readings by Hubert.

☎ 590-590-27-61-25, fax 590-590-27-81-38, www.3forces.net.

Hotel Le P'tit Morne

This hotel up in the hills of Colombier is a great place to stay, with beautiful views, for a very low price (considering where you are). The 14 rooms include kitchens and balconies looking out to the sea.

Location: Colombier, northwestern end of the island.

Rooms: 14, including standard, superior and deluxe. All have kitchens, one or two balconies (depending on category), satellite TV, AC.

Rates: EP.

Features: Pool, views to the ocean, daily housekeeping services.

☎ 590-590-52-95-50, fax 590-590-27-84-63, www.timorne.com.

Sunset Hotel

This is a perfect choice if you want to be in the center of activity in Gustavia but can't pay the Gustaf's prices. You get a view of the harbor, everything is right outside your doors, and the newly renovated rooms are comfortable.

Location: Rue de la République in Gustavia.

Rooms: 10 single and double standard or superior rooms. All have minibars, TVs and AC.

Rates: EP.

Features: Continental breakfast for small fee, weekly rates available.

☎ 590-590-27-77-21, fax 590-590-27-81-59, www.st-barths.com/sunset-hotel.

Tropical Hotel

This pretty little hotel sits above St. Jean, giving you a convenient location, although you'll need to walk down the hill to the beach. The rooms are airy with four-poster, canopied beds and breakfast is served every morning. The views to the sea available in some units are suitably tropical and gorgeous.

Location: Above St. Jean, in the central part of the island.

Rooms: 21 double rooms with choice of garden or sea views. All have terraces, minifridges, TVs and AC. Rate includes breakfast.

Rates: EP, with some packages available.

Features: Central location.

☎ 590-590-27-64-87, fax 590-590-27-81-74, www.tropical-hotel.com.

Small Inns/Cottages

These charming alternatives to hotels are a natural choice for those who like having the convenience of a cottage with a kitchen, and don't mind the absence of the beach. The nightly rates are comparable or slightly lower than the $$ category hotels above, running about $160-$200 per night in low season, and $200-$265 in high. The exception is La Paillote, which has cottages at $280 in low and $490 in high season.

Hotel Les Mouettes is one of the few in this category that is right on the beach, this one at L'Orient near a busy intersection. The seven units, of which six are in duplex buildings, are air-conditioned and nicely furnished. Kitchenettes and balconies are standard. ☎ 590-27-77-91, fax 590-590-27-68-19, www.st-barths.com/hotel-les-mouettes.

Beach at Les Mouettes

Ker Roc'h glaz Cottages are two West Indian-style cottages atop a ridge in Colombier, with great views of the Atlantic and Caribbean. Each has a kitchen, a covered terrace dining area and deck, a grill and an outdoor Jacuzzi. ☎ 590-590-52-93-02.

La Bohème's five cottages offer comfortable accommodations in the historic village of Corassol. You have a choice of a small, large or super cottage for two people, or a suite cottage for four. All have kitchenettes, gardens and air conditioning, and the larger units have a Jacuzzi. ☎ 590-590-27-76-48, fax 590-590-29-86-88.

La Paillote offers blindingly white cottages near the beach in Grand Cul de Sac. The rooms are open and furnished in a contemporary, minimalist style. Accommodations include suites, one-bedroom cottages and a two-bedroom villa. ☎ 590-590-27-57-95, www.lapaillote-st-barth.com.

Le Manoir de Marie

Le Manoir de Marie makes you feel like you've stepped back in time, with the Norman-style manor dictating the style of the eight cottages surrounding it. Some cottages have kitchens and private gardens, all have air conditioning, minibars and TV. The complex is located in L'Orient, and is surrounded by lush tropical gardens. ☎ 590-590-27-79-27, fax 590-590-27-65-75, www. lemanoirstbarth.com .

Les Islets Fleuris is a collection of eight studio cottages nestled around a pool in the L'Orient area of the island. Each has a kitchenette and terrace, and one has a separate living room. The sea-view cottages are air-conditioned, and weekly rates include a rental car. ☎ 590-590-27-64-22, fax 590-590-27-69-72, www.islets-fleuris.com.

Résidence du Bois de l'Angelique's bright white and blue bungalows overlook the lagoon at Grand Cul de Sac. Each features a kitchenette and is equipped with TV, ceiling fans and AC. There is a central pool for the complex. ☎ 590-590-27-92-82, fax 590-590-27-96-69, www.st-barths.com/bois-de-angelique.

Salines Garden offers five impressive cottages, each decorated in a style reflecting the owners' travels throughout the world – i.e., Waikiki, Cap Ferrat, and Padang Padang. The property is near Salines Beach and overlooks Grande Saline salt pond. Three units have kitchenettes, and all

Salines Garden

are air-conditioned and have private terraces. The property also has a pool and pool bar that serves as a gathering place for the guests. ☎ 590-590-51-04-44, fax 590-590-27-64-65.

Private Villas

The villas in St. Barts greatly outnumber the hotels and are the preferred accommodations for most visitors. They offer a beautiful home away from home, so you can pretend that you actually are living the life on a beautiful tropical island. The best way to find your dream spot is by contacting one of the agencies that represents the owners. Among the agencies are:

French Caribbean International represents villas in St. Barts, St. Martin, Guadeloupe and Martinique. The website answers FAQs to help you make a decision about what type of villa to rent, and what to expect. ☎ 800-322-2223 US and Canada, 805-967-9850 International, www.frenchcaribbean.com.

ICI et LA Villas represents a range of villas from one to seven bedrooms in size. They will also arrange for housekeepers, car rentals, phone and Internet services and guide you to some of the best activities on the island. ☎ 590-590-27-78-78, fax 590-590-27-78-28, www.icietlavillas.com.

Sibarth is affiliated with West Indies Management Company (WIMCO), the largest villa representative in the Caribbean. They handle over 200 rental properties, including some of the largest and most prestigious on the island, and offer a long list of services, including provisioning, concierge services and transportation. ☎ 590-590-29-88-90, fax 590-590-27-60-52, www.sibarth.com.

St. Barth Properties is affiliated with Sotheby's, which tells you a lot about the level of villas they represent. One of their agents, Peg Walsh, has been recognized by *CondéNast Traveler* as one of the best in villa rental service. They manage over 100 villas, ranging from one to 12 bedrooms in size. ☎ 800-421-3396 or 508-528-7727, fax 508-528-7789, www.stbarth.com.

St. Barth Villas in Paradise (VIP) offers a selection from the more modest to high-class, meaning you may find something within your price range. Their website shows their current offerings and the descriptions are quite detailed. ☎ 590-590-27-94-86, fax 590-590-27-56-52, www.st-barth-vip.com.

Day Spas

Beauté des Iles, in L'Orient, offers a full range of treatments for women and men, including massages, body scrubs, electro stimulation, facials and manicures, all using quality French products. ☎ 590-590-27-90-67, fax 590-590-52-44-13, galletsbh@wanadoo.fr.

Spa Guanahani

Espace Beauté provides massages, beauty treatments and beauty services in a bright Caribbean cottage in Grand Cul de Sac. Try one of their tempting scrubs, either with sand (which is said to render your skin as soft as a baby's bottom), or with papaya, coconut oil, pink clay, Caribbean sea water or camphor and eucalyptus. These are great for skin that has seen a little too much sun. ☎ 590-590-27-66-23, www.saint-barths.com/espacebeaute.

Set in the gardens of the luxury hotel of the same name, **Spa Guanahani** offers body scrubs, wraps and facials treatments using Clarins products, as well as massages using methods from around the world. The outdoor massage pavilion is otherworldly. ☎ 590-590-52-90-36, www.spaguanahani.com.

Institut Venus Beauty Spa, in downtown Gustavia, offers a full menu of services, including massages (Shiatsu, deep tissue, Swedish and Thai), body treatments, manicures and pedicures, facials and waxes. ☎ 590-590-27-59-46, www.saint-barths.com/venusbeautyspa.

Little Spa brings spa treatments to your villa, hotel or yacht or you can go to their facility in St. Jean. Services include massages, facials, manicures and pedicures, body wraps, spray tanning, epilations and more. ☎ 590-590-29-19-57.

Done in the same elegant, restful and contemporary style as the adjoining hotel, the **Spa at St. Barth Isle de France** is a delight for the senses. They use the techniques and products of Molton Brown and the massages fuse different techniques, e.g., the Shiatswe massage. Also available are body wraps, facials and unique hand and foot treatments. ☎ 590-590-27-61-81, fax 590-590-27-86-83, www.isle-de-france.com.

The homegrown beauty products developed by **Ligne St. Barth** are showcased at the **St. Barth Spa**. The magical elixirs produced from flowers, fruits and spices grown on the island are used to create unique and nourishing body treatments and massages. Five different spa menus highlight different areas of the body and particular products. They do "house calls" at Le Sereno and La Toiny hotels and many of the exclusive villa properties. You can purchase their products at boutiques on the island and around the world. ☎ 590-590-27-82-63, fax 590-590-27-70-93, www.lignestbarth.com.

Where to Eat

St. Barth and St. Martin are the two islands where food rules. People who live and visit here appreciate the best in life, and that includes meals. The incredible number of outstanding restaurants feature classic French cooking, "cuisine gastronomique" (a mix of French and Creole tastes), and a generous sampling of cuisines from around the world. The following list hits the highlights but by no means is all-inclusive. To find your own special place, pick up a copy of *Ti Gourmet*, the little book that captures the world of St. Barts gastronomy.

RESTAURANT PRICE CHART	
$	Cheap eats, normally quick meals or take-out foods; US$8 or less per entrée.
$$	Good value, lots of West Indian cuisine; US$9-$14 for a plate of food.
$$$	A nice place with gourmet aspirations; US$15-$24 for a satisfying entrée.
$$$$	Positively elegant, usually requiring some dressing up; entrées range from US$25 to $50, depending on the island.

Dressing Up to Dine Out

Le Bartolomeo

The piano playing in the background adds to the relaxing atmosphere at this open-air restaurant at the Guanahani. The entrées are consistently outstanding and reflect a fusion of French and Caribbean tastes. The foie gras and chocolate soufflé are said to be the best. $$$$. Guanahani Hotel in Grand Cul de Sac. Open daily for dinner. ☎ 590-590-27-66-60, www.leguanahani.com.

Francois Plantation

Michelin Star Chef Frank Renimel directs the innovative Mediterranean-inspired cuisine at this lovely plantation house high in the hills at Colombier. New owner Robert Eden offers cooking classes and tastings of the wines he produces in his French vineyard, among others. $$$$. Colombier. Open for dinner every evening except Monday. ☎ 590-590-29-80-22, www.francois-plantation.com.

Taino

Chef Phillippe Bossi runs the kitchen at this restaurant overlooking the Atlantic Ocean. The room is furnished in dark wicker and wood and the menu has some delightful surprises as well as seafood, meat and poultry, homemade pastas and foie gras. $$$$. Hotel Christopher, near Point Milou. Open for breakfast, lunch and dinner every day. ☎ 590-590-27-63-63, www.hotelchristopherstbarth.com.

Le Gaiac

This elegant restaurant overlooks Anse Toiny and the dramatically lit pool of Le Toiny. Chef Maxime Deschamps offers French cuisine with Caribbean influences, and the list of seafood entrées outnumbers all the rest. The Sunday brunch is an island favorite. $$$$. Le Toiny hotel, on the southeastern end of the island. Open for breakfast, lunch and dinner daily, closed Mondays in summer. ☎ 590-590-27-88-88, www.letoiny.com.

Le Gaiac

The Rock

This beautiful restaurant with brightly colored banquettes, dark woods, and a view of the sea is at Eden Rock. Cuisine gastronomique here is taken to new levels with exciting combinations of flavors. $$$$. On the beach at St. Jean. Open for dinner. ☎ 590-590-29-79-99, www. edenrockhotel.com.

The Wall House

Consistently on the list of the best of St. Barts, this Gustavia restaurant offers amazing French cuisine in an atmosphere that inspires romance. Among the choices are grilled and rotisseried favorites like lobster, steak, rack of lamb and duck. Dishes can be ordered à la carte, or you can select from their daily prix fixe menu, which is a real value. $$$. On the far side of the harbor in Gustavia. Open for lunch and dinner, seven days a week. ☎ 590-590-27-71-83, www.wall-house-stbarth.com.

Zanzibarth

Despite a name that conjures up visions of earth tones, this sleek restaurant is draped in white and crystals. Its minimalist décor, French-Belgian and Italian dishes, attract an international crowd. The bar is also very popular, especially on weekends. $$$$. Route de Saline in St. Jean. Open for dinner every day. ☎ 590-590-27-53-00.

Relaxing on the Water

Do Brazil

Owners Boubou and Yannick Noah add celebrity and interest to this Shell Beach restaurant, making it a must for lunch. The cuisine is heavily influenced by Thai flavors, and the setting is wonderful. Also be sure to check out the drink menu for some of the most unusual offerings on the island. $$$. Shell Beach, near Gustavia. Open for breakfast, lunch and dinner. ☎ 590-590-29-06-40, www.dobrazil.com.

La Gloriette

On the beautiful beach of Grand Cul de Sac is this open-air delight, offering traditional French and Creole cuisines. Seafood is done in unique ways and desserts include cooling sorbets and ice creams as well as coconut and apple tarts. They are known for their seafood salad and the after-dinner flavored rums. $$$. Grand Cul de Sac. ☎ 590-590-27-75-66.

La Plage

This is said to be the only restaurant on St. Barts where you can have your meal right on the beach with the sand beneath your feet. As with the rest of Tom Beach, the emphasis here is on having fun, doing something crazy, and enjoying life. Don't miss the lobster, the specialty of the house. $$$$. Baie de St. Jean. Open for breakfast, lunch and dinner, closed Mondays for dinner. ☎ 590-590-27-53-13, www.tombeach.com.

La Plage

La Vela

This restaurant lays claims to one of the best waterfront locations in Gustavia, the eastern end overlooking all the yachts. The cuisine is Southern Italian with freshly made pastas. $$$. Rue Samuel Fahlberg in Gustavia. Open for lunch and dinner, closed Sundays. ☎ 590-590-27-51-51.

Le Case de Isles

The luxe setting of the hotel St. Barth Isle de France is highlighted in this lovely beach restaurant. Stay for a long lunch, where one of the favorites is the cheese plate with salad, enough for a full meal. Other specialties include fresh salads, homemade soups and sandwiches. Dinner offerings include grilled fish and chicken as well as steaks, duck and rack of lamb. $$$$. Anse des Flamands. Open for lunch and dinner every day. ☎ 590-590-27-61-81, www.isle-de-france.com.

L'Esprit Salines

The fish and seafood entrées at this sophisticated and lively restaurant are consistently outstanding, as is the ambiance, aided in no small part by its setting on beautiful Saline Beach. $$$. Open for lunch and dinner, closed Tuesdays. ☎ 590-590-52-46-10, lesprit3@wanadoo.fr.

La Langouiste

La Langouste

This delightful café tucked into a small hotel on Ange des Flamands is made even more charming by the hospitality of owner Anne Ange. The impressively sized-lobsters, plucked from the restaurant's tank, are prepared as they should be – simply and with flavor. $$$. Flamands Beach. Open for lunch and dinner. ☎ 590-590-27-63-61. www.hotelbaiedesanges.com.

Le Rivage

Seafood reigns at this lovely place on the deck at Grand Cul de Sac. Choose a lobster from the tank, or enjoy a salad or panini sandwich. The rhum vanilla flows freely here, and it's a delightful place for lunch. $$. Open for lunch and dinner every day. ☎ 590-590-27-82-42, gaveve@ wanadoo.fr.

Nikki Beach

This is the hip place to be on St. Barts, especially at night when the stars come out at St. Jean. The restaurant has evolved into a party place and a trend-setting company that now has locations around the world. The cuisine is a global festival of tastes, emphasizing the chic and new. While you eat, you can gaze out at Eden Rock, brightly lit and shimmering in the sea, or take a

Nikki Beach

break and relax in one of the large canopied beds lining the beach area. $$$$. St. Jean, on the beach. Open for lunch and dinner every day. ☎ 590-590-27-64-64, www.nikkibeach.com.

Ethnic Foods & Favorites

Bête à Z'ailes or BAZ

This is one of the few places on the island to get sushi and sashimi, and it's done well here. The place is also known as an entertainment hot spot with live music in the evenings. $$$. Gustavia. Open for lunch and dinner every day. ☎ 590-590-29-74-09, www.st-barths.com/baz.

K'Fe Massai

Don't let the African décor fool you. The menu here is heavily French, with some unexpected additions. The prix fixe menu has some real values, and the reviews are consistently good. $$$. On the main road in St. Jean. ☎ 590-590-29-76-78, pinpin@wanadoo.fr.

K'Fe Massai

La Mandala

The cuisine is Thai with sashimi and curries, and the setting is exotic with lots of plants, Far Eastern art and unusual furnishings. It's a great place to enjoy the sunset overlooking Gustavia. $$$. On the hill above Gustavia. Open for dinner every evening. ☎ 590-590-27-96-96, www.lamandala.com.

Le Repaire des Rebelles

This restaurant doesn't fall into any easy category, but offers great seafood and chicken in unusual combinations, like the shrimp prepared with ginger and vanilla. It's a relaxed place where you can also stop for ice cream, juices or a drink. $$. Rue de la République, Gustavia. Open daily for breakfast, lunch and dinner. ☎ 590-590-27-72-48, ceric3@wanadoo.fr.

Le Sapotellier

This restaurant is often cited as having the most authentic French cuisine and the most romantic atmosphere on the island. The atmosphere in the dining room with its old stone walls is welcoming, and the garden setting is lovely. $$$. Rue du Centenaire, Gustavia. Open for dinner, closed Mondays off-season. ☎ 590-590-27-60-28.

Le Wok

One of the few Asian restaurants on the island, Le Wok reflects a pan-Asian sensibility, with dishes from Vietnam, China and Thailand. The combination platters give you a good sampling of their specialties, and the entrées offer some fusion tastes. They also do carry-out. $$$. L'Orient. Open for dinner only, closed Mondays. ☎ 590-590-27-52-52, www.lewok-saintbarth.com.

Terrazza

Refined Italian cuisine in a relaxed atmosphere is the hallmark of this restaurant overlooking Baie de St. Jean. There are daily specials and a prix fixe menu, and while you are waiting for your meal you can check the Internet or the latest sports scores on plasma screens. $$$. On the hill above St. Jean. Open daily for dinner. Internet café open 7 am to midnight. ☎ 590-590-27-70-67, www.st-barths.com/terrazza.

Terrazza

Creole Cooking

Au Port

One of the oldest restaurants on the island, Au Port owes its longevity to good food served in generous portions and good service where the customer is always well treated. Try the pumpkin soup or, if you are adventurous, the goat or calamari stew. If you are timid, order from the great menu of seafood and more traditional favorites. $$$$. Rue Sadi-Carnot, in the heart of Gustavia. Open for dinner only. ☎ 590-590-27-62-36.

La Route des Bucaniers

Owned by Creole chef and authority Francis Delage, this interesting Gustavia bistro shows how Creole cooking is done right. Among the standouts are the avocado salad and a seafood mélange in a red bean sauce. $$$. Rue de Bord de Mer, Gustavia. Open for lunch and dinner daily. ☎ 590-590-27-73-00.

Maya's

This has been one of the most popular restaurants on the island for many years. Martinique native Maya Gurley makes sure the food is simple and well prepared, with a combination of French and West Indian cuisine. $$$$. On the ocean's edge at Public. Open for dinner, closed Sunday. ☎ 590-590-27-75-73, mayasrestaurant@wanadoo.fr.

Wishing Well/Chez Rolande

For as true a West Indian experience as can be found in St. Barts, visit this small restaurant and try some of the unique favorites like Creole black sausage, codfish fritters and goat stew. $$. Flamands. Open daily for lunch and dinner, closed on Sunday evening and all day Monday. ☎ 590-590-27-51-42.

Quick Bites

Cocoloba

Choose from paninis, burgers, and salads for a quick meal outdoors on the Grand Cul de Sac beach. Another specialty at Cocoloba is barbecue, served Saturdays and Sundays. $$. Open for lunch every day but Monday. Bar service available from 10 am to 10:30 pm every day but Monday. ☎ 590-590-27-75-66.

JoJo Burger

When all that fancy cuisine gets to be too much, visit this little joint for a great burger at a good price. $. L'Orient. ☎ 590-590-27-50-33.

La Cantina

A stop at this popular meeting place in Gustavia for lunch, a drink or ice cream is a great antidote to shopper's fatigue. They also serve a continental breakfast. It overlooks the harbor and also serves a continental breakfast. $$. Rue du Bord de Mer, Gustavia. Open for breakfast and lunch, plus bar and ice cream bar service until late. ☎ 590-590-27-55-66.

Le Bouchon

All day long, every day of the week, you can get something to eat here, from pizzas to salads, burgers and sandwiches. Eat-in or take-out available. $$. L'Orient. Open for breakfast, lunch and dinner every day. ☎ 590-590-27-79-39, lebouchondesaintbarth.com.

Le Crêperie

This is a good place to stop for breakfast, lunch or dinner and try one of the savory and sweet crêpes. The bright, air-conditioned dining room makes it a perfect place for a break from shopping, and the service is excellent. The ice cream bar features home-made ice cream and sherbets. $$. Rue du Roi Oscar II, Gustavia. Open for breakfast, lunch and dinner every day. ☎ 590-590-27-84-07.

Delis & Take-Out

Caviar Island

If you have a sudden urge for caviar or other exotic foods, head to this high-end deli and open air café in Gustavia. It lives up to its billing as the place for "fancy food and drink of rare and unusual quality," with an amazing array of comestibles. Le Carre d'Or, Gustavia. ☎ 590-590-52-46-11.

Kiki-E Mo

This Italian deli offers pizzas, pastas, antipasto, and panini sandwiches plus a grocery section where you can add wines, cookies and other Italian products to your basket. They also offer catering and private chef services. On Route de St. Jean, ☎ 590-590-27-90-65, www.st-barth.com/kiki-e-mo.

Maya's To Go

On the go and want great food to take along? Call this place, and they will be happy to pack up a picnic for a hike, a complete gourmet dinner to take back to the villa, or a snack for the plane ride. They do catering as well. Les Galeries du Commerce, St. Jean. ☎ 590-590-29-83-70. mayastogo@wanadoo.fr.

Private Chef Services

Bertrand Dantec Private Caterers

Also known as **Food Lovers**, this private catering service delivers French, Creole, vegetarian and Provençal meals and will stock your kitchen prior to your arrival. ☎ 590-590-52-46-06, foodlover56@hotmail.com.

Chez Vous

This private chef service brings Chef Emmanuel Maurin to your villa or yacht. ☎ 590-690-53-22-26, chezvouscatering@wanadoo.fr.

David Cocktail

For a party or special event on a yacht or in a villa, this private catering service will provide the best in French cuisine. In addition, they will provision your villa with 48 hours advance notice and provide daily delivery of croissants and baked goods. ☎ 590-690-38-97-80, www.stbarth-catering.com.

Pasta Fred

This private catering service will customize menus and meals in a range of cuisines from French and Italian to Creole and Asian. Not available from September 1 to October 15. ☎ 590-690-75-15-22, pastafred2000@yahoo.fr.

St. Barth Chef Service

Meals can be prepared by Bernard Javelle, known as one of the best French chefs on the island, which is saying a lot. Choose from sample menus, create your own or order a welcome basket to dive into when you arrive. ☎ 590-690-59-13-33, www.stbarthchefservice.com.

Shopping

St. Barts offers the best shopping in all of the Leewards. It has an array of designer boutiques along with duty-free shops and a number of local enterprises.

Most Olympic-caliber shoppers start their marathons on the beautiful tree-lined streets and in the colonial-style buildings of **Gustavia**. Take a stroll down Rue de La République past duty-free jewelry and designer shops like **Bulgari, Cartier, Dior, Hermes** and **Louis Vuitton**. The ready-to-wear boutiques along this route are also outstanding, and include such names as **Bahia, Calypso, Forman, Geisha Vampire, Lolita Jaca** and **Giorgio Armani**. Swimwear, perfume, and leather goods stores fill in the gaps along the way. A visit to the mini-mall, **Le Carré d'Or**, is recommended, and a few shops, art galleries and local craft stores are scattered along Rue Charles de Gaulle.

Another lively shopping area is St. Jean's, which takes the concept of a strip mall to new heights. **La Villa Creole** is a hotbed of clothing, swimwear, leather goods and perfumes. **Centre Vaval** houses a number of shops with ready-to-wear lines. You can also find home decoration and

St. Barts

accessories here. **La Savane**, near the airport, has shops for children's wear, sunglasses, and furniture, a pharmacy, a liquor store, and a store for CDs and DVDs. The Match Supermarché here displays its array of produce and gourmet goods with typical French panache

MID-DAY BREAKS ARE TAKEN SERIOUSLY

When planning your shopping trip, be aware that most shops follow the French model of taking a midday break. They are closed for an hour or two starting at noon. It's a good chance to indulge in a little dolce vita and have a long, leisurely lunch.

Among the other supermarkets on the island are **La Superette** at the airport, **KiKi et Mo** in St. Jean **and JoJo's Supermarché** in L'Orient. For wine, be sure and visit **La Cave** in Marigot. It has 300 varieties of French wines and is said to be the largest wine cellar in the Caribbean.

If you want to make sure you go home with some items that originated on the island, look for **La Ligne St. Barth** beauty and spa products in the pharmacies and gift stores (www.lignestbarth.com). Also look for the clothing lines of **L'Avion** (www.lavionstbarth.com) and **Sabina Zest** (www.sabinazest.com), both of which call the island home. A sure bet to find authentic St. Barth goods are the **Made in St. Barth** stores in Gustavia and St. Jean.

Nighlife

When people talk about nightlife in St. Barth, you have to remember that it is a place where villas outnumber hotels so families outnumber singles. As a result, the nightlife isn't wild with casinos and discos as it is in St. Martin. The atmosphere is much more laid back.

The best-known of all night spots is **Ti St. Barth** at Pointe Milou (☎ 590-590-27-97-71). It be a wild scene at times and it also has theme nights, such as Marrakesh Evening (with belly dancing), Pirate's Night, Ti Brother Night, Night of the Angels and Crazy Weekend, as well as fashion shows.

Casa Nikki, brought to you by the same people who run Nikki Beach, is a private

Le Ti St. Barth

club in Gustavia where the music goes on until late and there are special nights, such as Bling Bling Please and Studio 54 (☎ 590-590-27-99-88). **Le Yacht Club**, owned by Carole Gruson and Thierry de Badereau, who also own Ti St. Barth and La Plage, shows films and offers live entertainment, including late-night pole dancing, at its harbor-side location in Gustavia (☎ 590-590-27-86-39). **La Feelings** is out in the village of Lurin, and features live music and dancing that start around 10 pm (☎ 590-590-27-88-67).

Restaurants with separate bars that often feature live entertainment in the evenings include **Nikki Beach**, **La Plage**, **BAZ**, **K'Fe Massai**, **Do Brazil** and **Ti St. Barth**.

During the day, one of the favored hangouts for sailors and sportsmen is **Le Select** in downtown Gustavia. This bar was supposedly the inspiration for Jimmy Buffett's song "Cheeseburgers in Paradise." It's a good place to get a Corona and burger and fries in a pleasant outdoor setting.

The Beaches of St. Barts

St. Barts has 14 beaches (or *anses* in French) with great sand, bright turquoise waters and a host of services from beachside restaurants to windsurfing schools. All are open to the public, although the strands in front of the more exclusive hotels will seem unwelcoming to all but hotel guests.

Since it is so closely tied to Europe in sensibility, you can expect to see a lot of topless bathers. If you have young ones in tow, you may want to steer away from Anse de Grande Saline or Anse du Gouverneur, where nude sunbathing is the norm.

Anse de Cayes

This beach on the northern side of the island is favored by surfers because of the high winds and good waves.

Anse de Colombier

Many love this beach simply because it is difficult to get to, making the journey more rewarding. It lies at the

Anse de Colombier (Don Wiss)

St. Barts

far western end of the island, and can be reached using hiking trails from Flamands (a nice walk on an old goat path) or from west of the village of Colombier (a steep and rocky trail). From the trails you can see St. Martin and the yachts anchored in the bay below. There are no trees or facilities, so you need to pack water, food, umbrellas and snorkeling gear.

Anse des Flamands

Another of the leeward beaches, this one has beautiful palms for shade and enough wave action for a little body surfing, so it's popular with families. There are plenty of hotels and restaurants along the beach to take care of any needs. The island you'll see offshore is Ile Chevreaux.

Anse des Flamands, left, and La Petite Anse, right (Don Wiss)

Anse de Grande Saline

While it gets its reputation from the nude sunbathers, this is a beautiful beach that many habitual visitors love. The long strand is without restaurants or activities, so it's a nice place to get away from the crowds and enjoy the water.

Anse du Gouverneur

This beach on the leeward side is loved by those who value calm water, great sand, and no company. Snorkeling is good at the cliffs on either end. Toward one end, people do nude sunbathing, but there aren't as many as on Saline. There are no facilities, so bring a picnic basket as well as some shade.

Anse Toiny

This beach is on the wild western end of the north coast, so it's rough and surrounded by steep cliffs. Swimming is not recommended because of the currents and waves, but you can watch the surfers, who love the area and the wind.

Anse du Grand Cul-de-Sac

All the hotels and resorts surrounding this beach make it a popular one. Since it is on the windward eastern coast, the windsurfing is good, and the snorkeling around the offshore reef is excellent. There are many places to get a good lunch and enjoy yourself.

Anse du Grand Cul-de-Sac (Don Wiss)

Anse de L'Orient

The main part of this beach is protected by an offshore reef, so the swimming is good and the beach is beautiful. Surfers gather at the less protected far eastern end, and facilities are available at the village just a short walk from the beach. Island families often spend Sunday afternoons here.

St. Jean Beach

St. Jean Beach

This is where the beautiful people go, to be watched and pampered. The beach is split in two by the Eden Rock Hotel, and along the shore are many restaurants and watersports huts. It gets quite crowded during high season because of its celebrity, calm waters and central location on the northern coast.

Shell Beach

This small beach near Gustavia is popular for the many shells to be found there. People arriving on small cruise ships usually head here since it is so close to the docks. Among the facilities is the popular Do Brazil restaurant.

The Washing Machine

This natural pool can be reached by hiking through the hills above Grand Ford. The swirling water caused by sea flows creates breakers that the surfers love, so you'll see lots of them here. Plan to bring all you need because, again, there are no facilities.

Saba, with the airport at left (Tommy Mogren)

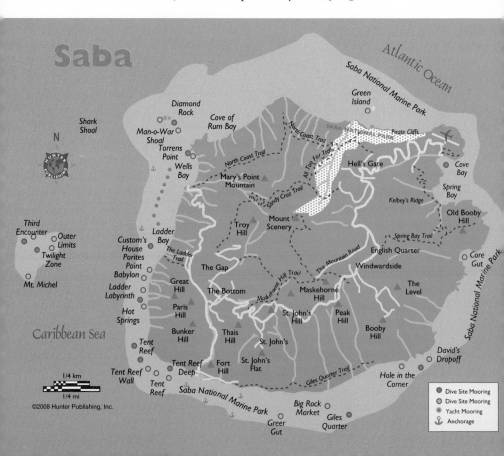

Saba

Atlantic Ocean

Saba National Marine Park

Caribbean Sea

1/4 km
1/4 mi

©2008 Hunter Publishing, Inc.

Shark Shoal

N

HUNTER PUBLISHING

Diamond Rock
Man-o-War Shoal
Torrens Point
Wells Bay
Cove of Rum Bay

Green Island
Pirate Cliffs
Cove Bay
Spring Bay
Old Booby Hill
Hell's Gate
Kelbey's Ridge
Spring Bay Trail
English Quarter
Windwardside
Core Gut

North Coast Trail
All Too For Trail
Sandy Cruz Trail
North Coast Trail

Mary's Point Mountain

Third Encounter
Outer Limits
Twilight Zone
Mt. Michel

Custom's House
Porites Point
Babylon
Ladder Labyrinth
Hot Springs

Ladder Bay
The Ladder Trail

Troy Hill
Mount Scenery

The Gap
The Bottom

Great Hill
Paris Hill
Bunker Hill
Tent Reef
Tent Reef Wall
Tent Reef Deep
Tent Reef

Thais Hill
Fort Hill

St. John's Flat
St. John's

St. John's Hill
Maskehorne Hill
Peak Hill
Booby Hill

Maskehorne Hill Trail
The Mountain Road

The Level
David's Dropoff
Hole in the Corner

Giles Quarter Trail

Saba National Marine Park

Saba National Marine Park

Big Rock Market
Greer Gut
Giles Quarter

● Dive Site Mooring
○ Dive Site Mooring
⚓ Yacht Mooring
⚓ Anchorage

Saba

The Allure of the Island

his island is an anomaly in the Leewards. Beautiful beaches? None. Colorful duty-free ports to shop in? None. Glitzy casinos, nightclubs and beach bars? None. Sprawling luxury villas? None. Golf courses? None. Popular family attractions? None.

So why on earth would you go to Saba? Because you want to see what the Caribbean was like before out-of-control development of huge hotels and high-priced villas blanketed the landscape. Saba is called "The Unspoiled Queen" of the Caribbean. The name is not lightly bestowed, but it is solidly earned by this adventurers' paradise.

The ancient volcanoes that formed the peak of Mt. Scenery and its outlying hills created a rocky cliff coastline and jagged topography that made settlement and road building difficult on Saba. But it also gave Saba a varied ecosystem that ranges from dry evergreen forests and thickets to tropical rainforests and even a rare cloud forest. And it caused the island to be surrounded by waters rich in marine life that flourishes in the underwater canyons and the Saba Bank Atoll.

All this means that Saba offers hikers and nature lovers an enlightening, diverse place to explore, and for dive enthusiasts it has some of the most pristine deep-dive opportunities in the world. Perhaps that's why the readers of *Travel + Leisure* voted it the "Best Caribbean Island" in 2006.

Here's What to Look for According to the Type of Traveler You Are

The Perfect Cruise Passenger won't have a lot of interest in staying on little Saba. There aren't any large hotels with everything in one place, no casinos, very limited duty-free shopping, and no beaches. But it's a great place for a day-trip to discover the beautiful countryside with its quaint villages, to take a hike into rainforests, or to find a special gift of Saban lace.

The **Boots-On Adventurer** comes to Saba to climb the mountain, hike the trails, and dive in the Marine Park. It's one of the few pristine marine environments left in the world, and the deep-dive opportunities are exciting. The wilderness is accessible through numerous trails and you can immerse yourself in natural beauty for days. Favorite lodgings including Scout's Place, Ecolodge Rendezvous and El Momo Cottages. The latter two are studies in ecology and getting back to nature, while Scout's is part of the Saba Divers' complex.

The **Cultural Explorer** should plan a trip to Saba to visit the hillside villages and take time to talk with the locals. Meet the ladies who create the unique Saban lace or watch glass being blown into art at the Jo Bean Art Glass Studio. And of course, as with the other islands, Saba has an annual Carnival to celebrate the local culture. If you can't visit in the summer for Carnival, spend some time in any of the Saban bars or small restaurants, where locals gather to gossip and meet the visitors. Hotels that offer the best chance of local atmosphere are Juliana's, El Momo Cottages and Ecolodge Rendezvous.

The **"I Like What I Like" Traveler** won't find a lot to do on Saba unless hiking or diving are among the acceptable activities. There are some private villas that can be set up to your liking, and many of the restaurants offer the basic "meat and potatoes" cuisine. For familiar dining atmospheres, check out In Two Deep for a New England pub setting, or drop into Swinging Doors bar to share jokes with owner Eddie Hassell, a naturalized American (**? Is he Saban?) who makes his beliefs (**political or what?) known to all.

The **Incurable Romantic** can get away from it all by staying up in the clouds at Willards of Saba or in luxury at the Queen's Garden Resort. Honeymooners love this island because they can go for days and see no one but each other. Those who are into pampering themselves have access to a day spa, massage and Reiki practitioners and other wellness resources. The Rainforest Restaurant offers a romantic candlelit setting, and Willards has the most elegant dining experience on the island.

The **Family Social Director** can find villas to accommodate all the family, but may have to stretch to find activities if some of the group doesn't dive or hike. Sabans are warm and welcoming, and you get a great feeling of security on the island since crime is low and everyone seems to look out for each other. If you take the group on a hike in the rainforest, a guide is highly recommended so that everyone is kept safe and on the right paths. Most of the restaurants offer American standards such as hamburgers, steaks and French fries, so even the pickiest eater will find something to like.

The Ultimate Shopper may want to limit the visit to a day-trip from St. Martin or, if you're staying on Saba, take a day-trip to St. Martin. You can cover all the available shopping opportunities in six hours or less. If you are confined to Saba, look for Saban lace and a locally made rum called Saban Spice, only available on the island. Other treasures include art glass from Jo Bean's studio and artwork from local artists. But if you don't hike, dive or snorkel, the rest of this island may bore you because it is, after all, basically five square miles of forests and hills.

A Brief History

Saba was sighted by Christopher Columbus in 1493, but he passed it by because of the island's inhospitable coastlines. When a shipwrecked crew landed there in 1632, they found some remains of Carib occupation, as well as a rocky coastline and interior that was difficult to traverse. They were happy to be rescued. Nonetheless, this first landing launched a history of colonization.

In 1635, some plucky Frenchmen finally decided to venture there from St. Martin to claim the island for Louis XIII of France. In 1640, the Dutch West Indies Company, always on the alert for colonization opportunities, sent people to the island from St. Eustatius to establish a settlement near Tent Bay, the only area where safe ship landings could be made. King Charles I of England saw it as a great place to exile troublesome Irish rebels, and the wild buccaneer Sir Henry Morgan launched one of the few successful invasions of the place, sending the Dutch settlers to St. Maarten, and making the island a popular hideout for pirates and other undesirables. During the Napoleonic Era, the island was in British hands, and then the Netherlands took final possession in 1816.

During the 17th and 18th centuries, sugar and rum emerged as the major industries. Because of the lack of a large population to help with the plantations, the owners often worked side-by-side with the slaves. In 1863, Saba became the first Leeward island to abolish slavery. At that time there were just over 1,000 white inhabitants and 700 freed slaves on the island. The population peaked in 1915 at 2,500, but never reached that point again.

As crops declined, many Saban men took to the sea and became fishermen or emigrated to work in the oil refineries of Aruba and Curacao. Between 1920 and 1930, Saba became known as the "island of women" because the population was comprised mostly of the fairer sex. One of the women was sent to Venezuela to study and learn lace making, which she brought back to the island. The women adopted it and made the craft their own, creating Saban lace as a major export of the island.

Saba

In 1963, a landing strip was built on the northeastern tip, the only flat area of the island. It is the shortest commercial runway in the world. Then in 1972, a pier was finally built at Fort Bay, enabling ferry service from St. Martin. Now the island is known mostly for tourism, as experienced divers make their way there to explore the Saba Bank and other deep dive areas surrounding the island, and climbers venture up to Mt. Scenery's peak.

The Facts

Population: 1,500 inhabitants.

Language: While Dutch is the official language, the primary language spoken and used in the schools is English.

Main City: The Bottom serves as the main town and seat of government. Other settlements include Windwardside, Upper Hell's Gate and Lower Hell's Gate.

Government & Economy: As part of the Netherlands Antilles, Saba had status within the Kingdom of the Netherlands as an autonomous region. Internal affairs of the island group were administered by a central government in Curacao. In 2006, Curaçao and Sint Maarten managed to convince the monarchy to consider disbanding the Antilles as a political entity so that they could each determine their own governmental affairs. On December 15, 2008 the Antilles will cease to exist, and Saba and St. Eustatius will become a direct part of the Netherlands as special munici-palities, governed by their own mayors, aldermen and municipal council. While the citizens retain their right to vote in Netherlands elections, it is not clear yet whether all the laws of the kingdom will apply in these "Kingdom Islands." For example, they will not be forced to use the euro as currency, and existing laws that make prostitution and same-sex mar-riages legal in the Netherlands may not be applied to the islands.

People & Culture: Inhabitants come from all over the world, and include a small number of native families who are proud of Dutch, Scot-tish, Irish and African heritage. In addition, there is a large group of expa-triates and immigrants, many of whom came to the island to teach or learn at Saba University School of Medicine.

Geography: This tiny island, only five square miles in area, consists of a large, dormant volcano called Mt. Scenery and a number of smaller volca-nic peaks. Mt. Scenery is 2,828 feet high, the highest point in the King-dom of the Netherlands. The topography of the mountain is primarily woodland forest and rainforest with an area of mountain cloud forest where clouds and mist help create a unique tropical ecosystem rich in dis-tinctive species.

The rest of the island is basically high hills and deep valleys, meeting the sea at steep cliffs and rocks – your basic precipitous terrain with some small valley areas for cultivation. Unlike all of its Leeward neighbors, the island has no beaches. There is one road, a twisting, turning route through the hills and around Mt. Scenery aptly called "The Road," which connects the settlements and the port at Fort Bay.

The village of Windwardside on Saba

Then there is the Saba Bank Atoll, the largest actively growing atoll in the Caribbean and the third-largest in the world. One-third of the atoll lies within Saba's territorial waters. It is a pristine ecosystem that provides fishermen with teeming life and divers with a vast area to explore. In 2006, an exploration team of researchers discovered more species of fish than previously known in the region as well as vast beds of seaweed and new types of algae. However, the atoll lies in the major shipping lanes for supertankers delivering oil to the transshipment depot in St. Eustatius. While awaiting orders to enter Statia, the ships drop anchor in the atoll, destroying large areas of coral reefs. Conservationists are actively campaigning to have the area declared a no-anchor zone.

Climate: The delightful climate offers 80°F temperatures year-round, with evening temps a bit cooler. In winter, women may want to wear a light wrap. As you go up in altitude, the temperatures drop slightly, so if you are hiking you'll welcome the cooler atmosphere of the forests. The island receives about 40 inches of rain a year, so expect a shower or two during your stay unless you're visiting during the dry season months of December through July.

Flora & Fauna: Historically, the island was covered in mango and mahogany trees. However, a particularly disastrous hurricane in the 1960s took out many of the mahogany trees and now they are at risk of going extinct.

The island is a wonder of biodiversity, due to the various climate zones up and down the mountain. In the highest regions you'll find the Elfin Forest, a montane cloud forest with mosses, ferns, bromeliads and orchids. Lower down are wild plantains, redwood, sea grape and mountain fuchsia trees, as well as cactus. The flatter elevations are covered in grassy meadows. There are also a number of fruit tree species, including avocado and sour lemon.

Check Out the Virtual Herbarium

If you are really into plants, you'll want to see the new Saba Virtual Herbarium at sweetgum.nybg.org/saba. Created by the New York Botanical Garden, it presents a package of photos and descriptions of hundreds of plants compiled by photographer Carol Gracie and researchers who have been visiting the island for years.

The site was created as part of the NYBG's ongoing study of Saba and part of its larger commitment to study of the West Indies that began back when the Botanical Garden was founded in the 1890s. The study, funded by Conservation International, aims to catalog every plant on the island and then make the information available to researchers and the general public.

Black-eyed susan

Flowers found on the island include wild orchids and heliconia in the rainforests, and hibiscus, oleander and wild begonias in other areas. The national flower is the black-eyed susan, a non-native species brought to the island by Dutch colonists.

Among the animals you'll encounter are a species of Anoles lizards found only on Saba. You'll also see racer snakes, iguanas and tree frogs. The island is also home to 60 species of birds, notably sea birds, including frigate birds, terns, tropic birds, boobies, doves, hawks, hummingbirds, thrashers and bananaquits. *A Guide to the Birds of Saba*, published by local bird enthusiast Martha "Mandy" Walsh-McGehee, is a good introduction to birding here. You should be able to find it on the island.

The **Saba Conservation Foundation** (SCF) was established in 1987 to protect and preserve its beauty. SCF founders wisely foresaw that the strength of the island's economy would be closely tied to the sustainability of Saba's rich unspoiled resources. Among the Founda-

Bananaquits (Leon Bojarczuk)

tion's current projects are creation of the Saba National Park, an area reaching from the mountain down to the northern coast and encompassing all the vegetation zones that exist on the island; the Saba Marine Park, which surrounds the island; and the Elfin Forest Reserve, an area of cloud forest at the top of Mt. Scenery. The SCF also operates the Hyperbaric Facility for divers. ☎ 599-416-3295, fax 599-416-3435, www.sabapark.org

Travel Information

When to Go

The climate of Saba is hospitably tropical year-round, although it joins the other Leewards in occasionally being affected by hurricanes during the June to October period.

Getting There

With only a tiny landing strip and a single port city, you can imagine how restricted the choices of transportation are.

By Air

The only air provider to the island is **WinAir**, with several daily flights from SXM in St. Maarten to **Juancho E. Yrausquin Airport** (SAB), and two daily flights between Saba and St. Eustatia (EUX).

GETTING THROUGH SXM THE EASY WAY

If you are going to Saba via air, you'll be transiting through the new and much improved Princess Juliana Airport Terminal in St. Maarten. After you clear Immigration, you'll pick up your baggage, and then report to the WinAir desk, which is right near the baggage retrieval area. If your connections are tight, have one person stand in the WinAir line while others get the bags, since the WinAir line can be long.

Then head to the departures lounge, which is up a flight of stairs with a blue railing on your right as you leave WinAir (or you can take the elevator if it is working). You'll clear security before entering the lounge, which has places to get drinks and food.

Carefully listen for flight announcements, because WinAir has a reputation for not announcing the Saba flight and occasionally leaving earlier than scheduled. So don't wander far from the gate and keep alert. If you miss the flight or it is cancelled due to cross-winds on Saba, you have an alternative. The *Dawn II* ferry, which leaves from Great Bay, has a 5 pm departure on Saturdays, Thursdays and Tuesdays. Allow about one hour to get to their dock in Philipsburg, and be sure to call ahead to make your reservations (see phone number below). If you are there on other days, or cannot make this departure, you'll need to overnight in St. Maarten. See if you can get a reservation on the next day's flight to Saba and, if not, call either *Dawn II* or *The Edge* (contact info below) to get a seat on the morning ferries.

By Sea

Two ferry services operate from Sint Maarten to the island. The trip takes approximately 75-90 minutes each way.

The *Dawn II* runs between Dock Maarten and Fort Bay on Tuesdays, Thursdays and Saturdays. ☎ 599-416-3671, www.sabactransport.com.

The Edge operates from Simpson Bay/Pelican Marina on Wednesday through Sunday. ☎ 599-544-2640, www.stmaarten-activities.com.

Customs

 Since Saba is a free port, there are no customs inspections or duties. To get back into the US you'll have to have your passport and you need to adhere to the US Customs regulations, where you normally have an $800 exemption including a maximum of 200 cigarettes, 100 cigars and one liter of alcohol.

Special Events & Holidays

 As with all the Leewards, the big event of the year is Carnival, which is held the last week in July.

January

New Year's Day, January 1 – Public holiday.

April

Good Friday – Public holiday.

Easter – Public holiday.

Easter Monday – Public holiday.

Coronation Day & Queen's Birthday, April 30 – Ceremonies commemorating the coronation and birthday of Queen Beatrix of the Netherlands.

May

Labor Day, May 1 – Public holiday.

Ascension Thursday, May 17 – Public holiday.

Saba Summer "Carnival" Festival, last week in July – A grand celebration including parades, music, food and dance. www.sabatourism.com.

October

Sea & Learn, entire month of October – This month-long celebration of the island's natural resources brings in scientists and naturalists from around the globe for presentations and field projects open to all. ☎ 599-416-2246, www.seaandlearn.org.

Antillean Day, October 21 – Public holiday

December

Saba Day & Weekend, first weekend in December – Island-wide festivities including barbecues, sporting events, concerts and dance contests. www.sabatourism.com.

Christmas Day, December 25 – Public holiday.

Boxing Day, December 26 – Public holiday.

Saba

Health

While small, the island has good medical coverage. The **Saba University School of Medicine** has a full contingent of professors and doctors, and the island maintains the **A.M. Edwards Medical Center** (☎ 599-416-3239/416-3288).

Due to the number of divers that travel here each year, the Saba Conservation Foundation hosts the **Saba Marine Park Hyperbaric Facility** for the Caribbean region. It has a four-person recompression chamber, and is staffed by specially trained volunteers. Many of the volunteers are students in the medical school's Hyperbaric Medicine Masters Degree Program. ☎ 599-416-3295, www.sabapark.org.

Pets

Animals are admitted temporarily to the island as long as they are accompanied by a health certificate dated no more than 10 days before the visit and a record of inoculations, including proof of a rabies shot administered no more than 30 days prior to the visit.

Crime

With only 1,500 people on the island, everyone pretty much knows everybody's business so it's difficult for evil-doers to hide. The crime rate is very low.

Electricity

The entire island is on 110 volt current.

Tipping

A service fee of 10 to 15% is normally added to your bill at the restaurants. However, don't forget to tip the taxi drivers and guides.

Money Matters

The official currency is still the Dutch guilder, but US dollars and credit cards are accepted pretty much everywhere. The three banks on the island are the **Royal Bank of Trinidad**

and **Tobago** and **First Caribbean International Bank**, both in Windwardside, and **Windward Island Bank** in The Bottom. They will exchange money or provide cash advances on VISA and MasterCard. There are ATMs at the banks, the airport and other locations on the island where you can get cash if you have a Cirrus or Plus system card or VISA or MasterCard. Some merchants are reluctant to accept travelers' checks because the banks, burned by some fraudulent checks, now require them to obtain detailed address and identification information from the bearer of the check.

Weddings

As in St. Maarten, the requirements to get married on Saba are lengthy. Here's a quick recap of what you need to do.

First, you need to set a date and register your intent to be married on the island by sending an email at least two months in advance to the Civil Registrar (nelliepeterson_4@hotmail.com), accompanied by a letter requesting permission from the Lt. Governor of Saba to marry (mailing address: Government Offices, The Bottom, Saba, Netherlands Antilles).

Then, at least a month before your marriage date, you need to file a Notification of Marriage by submitting the following documents, dated the same year as the year you are being married in, to the Civil Registrar (mailing address: Nellie Peterson, Civil Registrar of Saba, Census Office, The Bottom, Saba):

- Original or certified copies of birth certificates, mentioning the names of the parents.
- Whether parents are living or deceased.
- Maiden names of mothers.
- An original proof, not older than six months, of single status.
- If previously married, an original document of dissolution of the marriage or divorce decree.
- Copies of passports for both parties.
- Written request to the Lt. Governor if you want to be married somewhere other than the Court Room of the Government Building in The Bottom.

You will also need to secure witnesses who are residents of the Netherlands Antilles; you need two if you are married in the Court Room and six if you are married elsewhere. Copies of each witness' Dutch identification card or a copy of their passport must be submitted with the above documents.

If you have questions, contact Ms. Peterson at the Census office ☎ 599-416-3497/3311/3312 or fax 599-416-3582.

Internet Access

WWW The instant access revolution is even reaching remote places like Saba, and hotels are installing wireless capabilities at a quick pace. So if you are planning on taking your laptop with you (although you are on vacation), check with your hotel to see if they have WiFi. If not, **Island Communications Services**, an Internet café, is located in Windwardside.

Communications

 Most of the hotels don't have phones in the rooms, but you can direct dial anywhere from the front desk, although it will be costly. There are three public pay phones on the island, at Sea Saba, Juliana's and Scout's Place. They only accept locally sold phone cards or guilders. New international pay phones that accept credit cards or collect calls are springing up in all areas of the island.

Cell phones are provided by **East Caribbean Cellular** (www. eastcaribbeancellular.com) and CellularOne (www.carib-vacation.com/islands/sxm/cellularone.html), and they can arrange for international service on your own cell phone. **CellularOne**, based in St. Maarten, also rents cell phones on a daily or weekly basis, or you can rent a local "Chippie" cell phone for a very low rate.

Media

The local news actually appears in a non-local newspaper, the *St. Maarten Herald*, which has a Saban correspondent. You can view the latest articles on www.seasaba/news.

Sources of Information

i For any further information, check the official Saba Tourism website at www.sabatourism.com, or contact Saba Tourist Office, PO Box 527, Windwardside, Saba, Dutch Caribbean, ☎ 599-416-2231/2322, fax 599-416-2350, iluvsaba@unspoiledqueen.com or holmglenn@hotmail.com.

Getting Around

Airport

The **Yrausquin Airport** underwent renovations and a rededication in 2003, but it is still not a major terminal with services for travelers. You can, however, find taxis right outside to take you to your hotel or lodgings.

Taxi Service

Taxis can be found easily at the airport or around the island. Most drivers are quite knowledgeable about the various hotels and restaurants as well as where to go for hiking and diving arrangements. Talk to them – and be sure to tip.

Car Rentals

The Road has 10 miles of paved surfaces that seem like hundreds of miles when you have to navigate the endless twists and sharp turns. Since the island is only five square miles, most people rely upon taxis for short hauls if the roads are steep, or on shoe leather if they aren't. There are no major international car rental chains represented on the island, but there are a few local firms if you are inclined to be independent and gutsy.

Car Rental Companies

Caja's Car Rental Kennedy 599-416-2388
Johnson's Rent A Car 599-416-2269
Kenny's Rental 599-416-2388
Scout's 599-416-2205

Exploring

On Foot

Saba is a hiker's paradise, especially for those who love testing their quads by tackling steep hills. Also, the steep cliffs and outcrops are a rock climber's dream.

Hiking

Pretty much anywhere you go on this tiny, hilly island is a real hike. However, if you want to explore or get away from it all, there are trails leading to rainforests, tide pools, historic ruins and lush secret gardens. One trail up Mt. Scenery is via a staircase of about 1,000 steps, great if your legs are used to Step workouts. The trails are maintained by the Saba Conservation Foundation and the Tourist Office. Information on them is available at both organizations' offices. The SCF has an informative map that shows 12 of the most accessible trails, including The Ladder, Mt. Scenery Stairway, Sulphur Mine Track and All Too Far Trail.

You'll need a guide for some of the more obscure trails. Check with the Foundation (The Bottom, ☎ 599-416-2630) or the Tourist Office (Windwardside, ☎ 599-416-2231/2322) for recommenda-

The path up Mt. Scenery

tions. One of the most recommended guides is "Crocodile James," who provides lots of authentic information about history, culture, flora and fauna along the way.

Climbing

On this volcanic island, outcroppings and boulders are within easy access from the many groomed hiking trails and in some cases can be found near hotel properties. Two strong climbing advocates and devotees are diving instructors Stuart Gow and Laura Shepherd, who have climbed many of the rocks in their time. They have compiled a guidebook with maps and safety outlines, now available from the Saba Conservation Foundation.

On Water

Saba's reputation as a stellar diving destination stems from the incredible diversity and color of the Saba Marine Park and the Saba Bank Atoll. The park, which was created originally to protect a pristine habitat rather than to restore a damaged one, has 25 unique dive sites and is zoned for various activities including snorkeling and fishing.

Scuba Diving

Seasoned divers from all over the world travel to Saba to dive the pinnacles, sharp volcanic mountain peaks that start at a depth of 80 feet, and go down to the abyss in many places. These unusual formations attract many types of sea life and reward divers with some incredible experiences.

But the Marine Park also offers beginning divers and those looking to improve their skills many opportunities. In all, the dive sites range from a depth of 35 to 120 feet, with the leeward sites being most accessible (they are not as subject to the vagaries of weather as the windward sites). Most of the dive sites are within 120 feet of shore, and since Saba is so small, it takes only five to 10 minutes to get to the sites, giving you lots more time in the water than on it. All divers must be accompanied by a Saban-approved dive operator who knows the various areas and

Diamond Rock (Clark Anderson/Aquaimages)

restrictions. For each dive, you will be contributing $3 to the park's conservation efforts.

Dive Operators

Nassau grouper (Clark Anderson/Aquaimages)

Saba Deep Scuba Diving Center departs for trips from its dive center in Fort Bay Harbour three times a day. They offer packages with the hotels on the island and have their own restaurant, In Too Deep, a hangout for a lot of the divers. ☎ 599-416-3347, 866-416-3347 US, fax 599-416-3397, www.sabadeep.com.

Saba Divers & Scout's Place is all-inclusive, with a dive center, hotel, restaurant and bar, along with two dive boats. They were the first on Saba to offer Nitrox32 for free, supplying it as they would regular compressed air. They also offer Nitrox certification as well as a full range of PADI

Great barracuda & jacks (Clark Anderson / Aquaimages)

courses. The hotel is described in the *Where to Stay* section below. ☎ 599-416-2740/2205/2213, 866-656-7222 US, fax 599-416-2741, www.sabadivers.com. **Sea Saba Advanced Dive Center** in Windwardside has two 38-ft dive boats, with Nitrox dives and certification as well as a full range of PADI courses. They also offer packages in conjunction with most of the hotels on the island, where you get accommodations, airport transfers, dives and equipment. The Sea Saba website is a great resource, with details on dive sites as well as other activities on Saba. ☎ 599-416-2246, fax 599-416-2362, www.seasaba.com.

Snorkeling

Hawksbill turtle (Clark Anderson / Aquaimages)

While diving is the main attraction, Saba also has some good snorkeling sites just offshore. The most popular site that can be reached without a boat is at the end of Well's Bay road where a sandy beach sometimes appears, depending on what the weather is doing. Other hikes that end in snorkeling opportunities, if the waves are right, are at the end of The Ladder in the Tent Bay area and in Cove Bay. The best way to enjoy the Marine Park is by boat and all the dive operators offer snorkeling along with their diving.

Kayaking

 Sea Saba carries sea kayaks along on its boats. You can try kayaking for the first time in a learning environment; the more experienced boaters can take one out for some snorkeling away from the crowds.

Water Tours

 The only real organized boat tour around the island is offered by the **Saba Conservation Foundation**. The Foundation's boat accommodates up to 10 people and operates 1½-hour tours on Tuesdays and Thursdays, weather permitting. During the tour you learn about the history of the island, the sea bird population, the Marine Park, coral reefs, and flora and fauna. For more information, contact SCF, ☎ 599-416-3295, fax 599-416-3435, www.sabapark.org.

Saba's only port (Clark Anderson / Aquaimages)

Boat Charters

Most people interested in chartering boats to explore the areas around Saba rely upon the large fleets available in St. Martin. See the St. Martin chapter for a listing of these companies.

Playing & Watching Sports

Tennis

 The island has one court, located at the **Willard's of Saba** resort. It's in a beautiful setting up on a cliff, so you look out on beautiful ocean views while you play. If you've forgotten your racket, one can be rented. ☎ 599-416-2498, www.willardsofsaba.com.

Triathlon

Imagine a triathlon on the island known for its steep, rocky roads. Well, leave it to the daring people of Saba to host one. The event is growing in size and attracting entrants from afar. The triathlon takes place in early December and coincides with Saba Day weekend activities. For more information, contact the Tourism Office.

Sampling the Culture

The Bottom

Because of its small size and native ownership of all the hotels, you are immersed in Saban culture from the time you step foot on the island. Take a hike around, and you'll see examples of the lovely, but strangely uniform, Saban architecture, where all buildings have red roofs, white siding and green trim. Visit the restaurants' bars, and invariably you'll strike up a conversation with a native who will regale you with tales of the island. Or take the formal route and visit during Carnival, held in the third week of July, when Sabans celebrate all that is unique and wonderful about their island.

You'll also want to wander through the towns of The Bottom and Windwardside. The Bottom has some charming cobblestone streets lined with the unique Saban architecture. The homes have true Dutch doors that open halfway, so neighbors can chat through the doorway. Windwardside is more of a commercial village, with many shops and restaurants, but it still has alleyways and byways reflecting the history and charm of the island.

Reliving History

Reminders of Saban history are everywhere, from the churches built in the 18th and 19th centuries, to the remnants of Carib and Dutch settlements you can see on various hikes. Check with the SCF Trail Shop in Windwardside for the trails most likely to yield some history. One of particular note is the trail to Spring Bay, where a freshwater well, once a point of contention between Dutch settlers and Caribs, has been restored.

The newest hiking trail created by the SCF takes you on a walk around Windwardside leading to the Harry L. Johnson Museum. The Historic Village Walking Tour starts from the Trail Shop, goes up steps into the rainforest and then to a restored Saban cottage, to a museum showcasing period furniture, and to a gallery with Arawak and Carib artifacts. Then you travel down Park Lane past typical Saban cottages to the Windwardside Anglican Church, built in 1877, and then to Lambee Place where you can view the historical tribute to Josephus Lambert Hassell, famed creator of The Road.

Where to Stay

Comfortable Hotels & Small Inns

$$$ – These are the posh hotels of Saba, but are considerably less than what you'd expect for top-level hotels on other islands. For a deluxe double, you'll pay $250-$350 a night in low season, $340-$400 in high.

In Saba, nothing is large. This includes the hotels, which are comfortable and homey places where the owners come to greet you and you get to know the other guests. Since there are only eight of them, they are presented here in alphabetical order.

Queen's Garden Resort

This is one of the island's two luxury hotels. The suites are furnished with antiques, dramatic four-poster beds and artwork. The resort sits at a 1,200-ft elevation and has beautiful views out to the sea. Cool breezes keep the rooms comfortable. Many of the suites have private

Queen's Garden Resort

Jacuzzis that capitalize on the view, perfect for a romantic getaway.

Location: Troy Hill.

Rooms: 12 one-bedroom (deluxe and superior) and two-bedroom royal suites, plus a villa that sleeps six. All have kitchens, separate dining and living room areas, balconies, ceiling fans and cable TV. Some royal suites have decks with Jacuzzis, and some suites have Internet access.

Rates: EP.

Features: Restaurant, bar, pool.

☎ 599-416 3494, fax 599-416-3495, www.queensaba.com.

Willard's of Saba

Willard's of Saba

As the highest hotel in the Kingdom of the Netherlands, at 2,000 feet above sea level, this well-respected hotel (sister to the Willard's Hotel in Washington, DC) offers lovely vistas and superior service. Check out the "In the Sky" room, the highest room in the Kingdom and an incredible aerie where you can watch clouds go by right outside your window.

Location: Booby Hill

Rooms: Seven in all, including Garden Room, Sunset Room, Lower Cliffside, Upper Cliffside, Eagle's Nest and In the Sky rooms. All have cedar ceilings, ceiling fans and balconies. Other amenities vary by room. Some have cable TV.

Rates: EP, with honeymoon and dive packages available.

Features: Restaurant, bar, pool, hot tub, tennis court, exercise room.

☎ 599-416-2498, US 800-504-9861, fax 599-416-2482, www. willardsofsaba.com.

Good Value Hotels

$$ – The middle level in terms of cost gives you a delightful room in Saba and you can choose from several hotels with great ocean views. You'll pay $100-$125 in low season, and $120-$135 in high.

The Cottage Club

The heart of this hotel is the antique-filled plantation house that serves as the reception and lobby area. Rooms are in 10 gingerbread cottages stacked down the hillside. Each has its own kitchen and balcony with ocean views.

Location: Windwardside.

Rooms: Nine with queen-sized beds plus one with a king bed. All have kitchen, dining area, balcony and cable TV.

Rates: EP; honeymoon and dive packages available.

Features: Pool, central location, daily maid service, Internet café in lobby area.

☎ 599-416-2486, fax 599-416-2476, www.cottage-club.com.

The Gate House

One of the larger hotels on the island, the Gate House stands on a ridge with spectacular views to the Caribbean. The accommodations include rooms, a cottage and a luxury villa, all surrounded by tropical plants and trees. The owners make a sincere effort to accommodate all your needs, and are willing to arrange whatever activities you want to pursue.

Location: Hell's Gate.

Rooms: Five rooms in the hotel plus a private villa that sleeps eight and a honeymoon cottage for two. Rooms have private

The Gate House

baths and balconies or patios. Villa has a full kitchen, dining area, living room, four bedrooms, three baths, cable TVs and balconies, and shares a pool with the cottage. The cottage has a kitchenette, dining area and private patio.

Rates: BP, with diving and honeymoon packages.

Features: Pool, award-winning restaurant, WiFi in main hotel.

☎ 599-416-2416, fax 599-416-2550, www.sabagatehouse.com.

Juliana's

Located in Windwardside and near the restaurants, shops and spas, this genteel and peaceful hotel offers a high level of personal service. Rooms are available in the main hotel as well as in two cottages and an apartment adjoining the property. Many say that once they settle into the hammocks on their patios here, it's hard to leave – even to enjoy the attractions in Saba.

Orchid Cottage at Juliana's

Location: Windwardside.

Rooms: Nine rooms in the hotel (garden- or ocean-view), plus two cottages and an apartment. All rooms have ceiling fans, mini-bars, coffee/tea service and cable TV. The two-bedroom cottages have ceiling fans, kitchens, living/dining areas, private balconies, cable TVs and AC in some bedrooms. The one-bedroom apartment has ceiling fans, kitchen, living/dining area, large deck, cable TV, AC in bedroom,

Rates: EP, with dive packages available.

Features: Restaurant, pool, two decks with Jacuzzis, recreation room with library, board games and honor bar, WiFi and Internet access in lobby.

☎ 599-416-2269, 888 289 5708 US, fax 599-416-2389, www.julianas-hotel. com.

Scout's Place Hotel

This little gem of a hotel sits in the heart of Windwardside and is often filled with divers, not surprising considering that Saba Divers runs the hotel and offers room/dive packages. This is the original hotel building and it's done in the white-clapboard, red-roofed Saban style, with nice views. The bedrooms were recently renovated and feature four-poster beds and private balconies.

Scout's Place Hotel

Location: Windwardside.

Rooms: Five regular, five deluxe and three cottage rooms. All have refrigerators, fans, double or twin beds, cable TVs and Internet access.

Rates: EP, with dive packages available.

Features: Restaurant, bar, pool, entertainment, dive shop and boutique.

☎ 599-416-2740/2205/2213, 866-656-7222 US, fax 599-416-2741, www. scoutsplace.com.

No-Frills Hotels

$ – The two hotels in this price range are the "eco-hotels," with simple settings in the rainforest. You will experience some unusual amenities and get plenty of exercise walking up and down the hills. Expect to pay $80-$90 a night in low season, and $100 in high.

Ecolodge Rendez-Vous

This family-run eco-resort is located in a rainforest area, so it's surrounded by lush vegetation and away from the more urban (all things being relative) areas. There are no radios, TVs or telephones in the rooms and no vehicular access. The resort was built with eco-friendly and recycled materials; lighting and hot water are powered by solar collectors; the water supply comes from cisterns that collect rainwater; the faucets are water-frugal; the toilets are composting and an organic vegetable garden supplies the resort's restaurant. Each cottage is decorated in a different nature theme, featuring artwork from island artist Heleen Cornet. Staying here is definitely an experience.

Rainforest at Ecolodge Rendez-Vous

Location: In the forest outside of Windwardside.

Rooms: 12 cottages, each different in layout and amenities. Some have queen beds, kitchenettes, private hot tubs, views of ocean or forest, balconies and other special features.

Rates: EP.

Features: Restaurant, sweat lodge, cold and hot water tubs.

☎ 599-416-5507/ 3348, 877-257-0524 US, fax 599-416-3299, www.ecolodge-saba.com.

El Momo Cottages

This is another eco-hotel, offering quiet and peaceful accommodations in one-room cottages graced with artwork. Walking from here to other points in Saba can be challenging – you climb 150 steps to get up to the hotel – but it's a great workout if you're fit. From the hillside you have great ocean views, and from

Pool at El Momo Cottages

October through March, you can see the sunset.

Location: Booby Hill, near Windwardside.

Rooms: Six cottages with private or shared bathrooms. Some larger units have kitchens. All have balconies and views to the ocean.

Rates: EP.

and tableware at **Saba Lace Boutique** in Hell's Gate, **Artisan Foundation** in The Bottom, and at **Heritage Shoppe, Peggy's Boutique** and **Helen's Notions & Fabrics** in Windwardside.

Another local product of some renown is hand-blown glass. **Jo Bean's Art Glass Studio** is said to be the only flame-working glass studio in the Caribbean. After watching the artisans at work you may decide to sign up for one of the workshops offered by the studio. ☎ 599-416-2490, www.jobeanglass.com.

Lizard pendant, JoBean

And yes, tiny Saba actually has a shopping mall. It's **Lambee Plaza** in Windwardside, where you can find shops offering souvenirs, clothing and art. One of the must-see shops is **The Peanut Gallery**, offering works from Saban as well as other Caribbean artists. Owner Judy Stewart makes some of the pottery as well as the placemats. The store also offers wood carvings, ceramics and, delight of delights, made-in-Saba banjos. ☎ 599-416-2509.

Pendant from JoBean

Nighlife

The nightlife on Saba is much quieter than what you find on the other islands. The definition of a Saban good time is gathering at the bars at **In Two Deep** or **Scout's Place** to lime with the divers, who are usually heard talking about the day's underwater thrills.

Or stop in at the **Tropics Café** in Windwardside for one of the theme nights. On Fridays, the café hosts Saba's only outdoor movie theater, where you can order a burger and watch a movie poolside. Saturdays are Caribbean Nights, with steel pan music, and Tuesdays are Dive Buddy Buffet nights. And any night, you can take a dip in the pool or lounge in the hot tub, drink in hand.

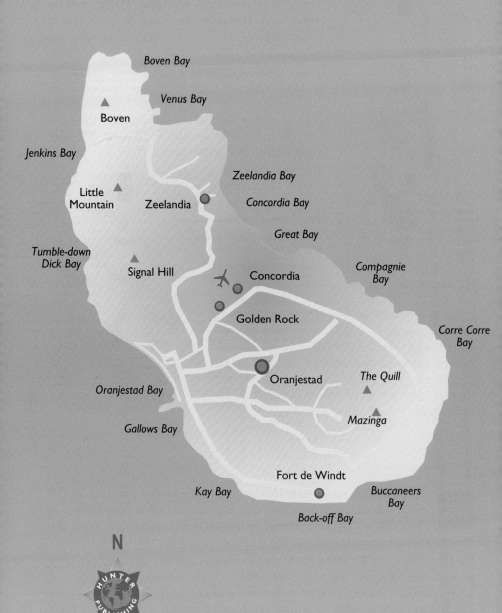

Statia

Boven Bay

Venus Bay

▲ Boven

Jenkins Bay

Little
Mountain ▲

Zeelandia

Zeelandia Bay

Concordia Bay

Great Bay

Tumble-down
Dick Bay

▲ Signal Hill

Concordia

Compagnie
Bay

Golden Rock

Corre Corre
Bay

The Quill
▲

Oranjestad Bay

Oranjestad

Gallows Bay

Mazinga ▲

Fort de Windt

Kay Bay

Buccaneers
Bay

Back-off Bay

N

HUNTER
PUBLISHING

2KM

©2008 Hunter Publishing, Inc.

St. Eustatius
The Allure of the Island

L ike Saba, Sint Eustatius (here-after Statia) is a reminder of what the Caribbean was like before the islands were overrun with tourists and mega-resorts. The small island has a population of only 2,000 residents and a bounty of natural beauty on land and sea. But see it now. Statia reported a 25% jump in visitors in 2006 and its secrets are slowly being uncovered by modern day adventurers and day-trip-pers from St. Kitts and St. Martin.

St. Eustatius from space

The major topographic feature on Statia is **The Quill**, a 1,968-ft dormant volcano with an interior crater that forms a terrarium for the lush rainforest within. The island's volcanic history spawned fantastic beauty above and below sea level, where lava blocks and flows created interesting shapes for coral to glom onto. The dive environment today is rich in sea life studiously protected by the St. Eustatius National Park (STENAPA) system.

Another attraction of this dot in the Caribbean is its history as a lively trading port. It was also the first foreign entity to formally recognize the United States as a country during the Revolutionary War. Because there has not been rampant development, many of the historical buildings and artifacts have remained intact and, fortunately, the powers-that-be recognize the value in preserving and protecting the island's past. The buildings and artifacts provide a look at life in the Colonial period, and ongoing archeological digs are still uncovering the island's valued history.

One of the major corporate influences is **Statia Terminal**, a petroleum distribution depot that attracts large tankers to the adjacent waters. The facility is on the western side of The Mountains area, and uses a pier at Tumble Down Dick Bay for shipments.

While there is much to enjoy in the way of diving, snorkeling and visiting historic ruins, don't look for shopping and nightlife. There's not much shopping to speak of, and it's fairly quiet in the evenings, although there are some good restaurants, due mainly to the fact that oilmen do like fine dining. So be prepared to spend evening hours enjoying the quiet of your small, family-run hotel, reading, and getting to know the locals, who are very warm and hospitable.

Here's What to Look For According to the Type of Traveler You Are

The Perfect Cruise Passenger should probably bypass Statia, unless you like to dive or hike. There is little to offer in the way of shopping, nightlife, or unadventurous activities.

The Boots-On Adventurer will be right at home on Statia, where diving, hiking and water adventures abound. An extensive national park system, including an offshore Marine Park, provides a number of activities, and the hotels seem to revolve around the diving community. If you love archeology, put on your Indiana Jones hat and take part in digs with the St. Eustatius Center for Archeological Research.

The Cultural Explorer will find a place that time forgot – especially when it comes to development trends seen elsewhere in the Caribbean. The small hotels and restaurants provide perfect settings for getting to know the locals, and special events such as Carnival showcase all there is to love about the Statian culture.

It's also a place that reveres its history; it has carefully renovated old buildings and structures to keep its colonial past alive.

The "I Like What I Like" Traveler probably should choose to go to elsewhere, unless you want a place to simply sit back and relax, talk to the locals and the divers, and enjoy what the Caribbean used to be like.

The Incurable Romantic will find a lot to love in the beautifully restored historical center of the island. You'll enjoy quiet picnics in one of the many parks, romantic walks through gardens, and starlit strolls on nearly deserted beaches. The Old Gin House offers cozy accommodations in a beautiful historic setting, and the restaurants, while few, are delightful.

The Family Social Director will feel comfortable on Statia, since there is very little crime and everyone looks out for everyone else. Younger children may find the historical buildings and treks up into the rainforest interesting, but this is really an island for older kids who love to snorkel and dive. It's definitely a G-rated island, family-friendly and welcoming, without a casino or strip joint in sight.

The Ultimate Shopper will be lost on this island, and should stick to St. Martin as a destination since you will probably end up there anyway. There is virtually no shopping, although there is a lot of sitting back and taking it easy – a concept Type A shoppers can't quite grasp.

A Brief History

 Statia's history departs significantly from that of its neighbors in the Leewards, especially when discussing the colonial and sugar plantation eras.

The prehistoric beginnings of the island trace the path of the groups migrating from South America through the Antilles, starting around 500 BC and continuing through 1400 AD. When the first Europeans visited

18th-century view of St. Eustatius harbour

the island in the early 17th century, all these indigenous groups had disappeared. However, they left a rich trove of historical objects in the area around Golden Rock that the St. Eustatius Center for Archeological Research (SECAR) is now exploring and documenting for posterity.

As with most of the Leewards, Christopher Columbus was the first European to discover Statia. Between 1493, when Columbus landed, and 1636, the island changed hands at least 22 times as the French, English, Dutch and Spanish battled for ownership of the Leewards and their potential revenues. After the Dutch took final control in 1636, the island's unique history began taking shape.

Unlike the neighboring islands, Statia was not a hospitable place for crops like tobacco and sugar, since there was not enough fresh water to sustain plantations. The enterprising Dutch realized that the island's real strength lay in its location between all the other bountiful islands. They established Statia, along with Curacao and St. Maarten, as a neutral trading hub where African slaves, raw materials from the New World and finished products from the Old World could be distributed. By the late 18th century, Statia, with its leeward port and proximity to major sea lanes, was one of the busiest ports in the Caribbean and had a population of over 20,000.

Statia's economy at that time was based on the slave trade and the legal and illegal trade of sugar and raw materials from the surrounding islands. The island's merchants also made substantial profits by providing arms to the fledgling American colonies, although by doing so they invited the wrath of Great Britain. The British persuaded the Dutch West India Company to ban the arms trade, but the traders simply ignored the ban. As the only link between Europe and the colonies, Statia prospered to such a degree that it acquired the nickname, the Golden Rock.

On November 16, 1776, the American ship *Andrew Doria* sailed into the harbour of Statia and fired a 13-gun salute to indicate the declaration of American independence. The cannons at Fort Oranje replied with an 11-gun salute, making Statia the first foreign entity to officially recognize the United States of America.

CELEBRATING THE AMERICAN CONNECTION

Statians are so proud of their historical connection to the US that each November they host Statia-America Week. The first night of the celebration features a Gospel Show, followed by calypso, reggae, band-o-rama, soca and international music nights. The week ends with a day-long celebration on November 16, including a flag raising ceremony to mark the First Salute to the American Flag.

Visitors enjoy being here during the celebration because it's like a mini-carnival that showcases Caribbean music and culture while also honoring the links between the two countries. For a complete schedule of events, see the Statia Tourist Office website at www.statiatourism.com.

When the slave trade declined and sugar lost its importance in the Caribbean, the economy of the island declined precipitously. By the early 1800s Statia's standing as a major port had all but disappeared. The British and French controlled the island between 1801 and 1816, imposing taxes and regulations that drove the small island to its knees. The Dutch reclaimed it in 1816, settling in as the island became a quiet place, tending to its own business.

In the 1960s and 1970s, the Statians began realizing the tourism potential of their historic island. They began creating the structures to preserve and protect

Cannon at Fort Orange (Galen Frysinger)

its heritage and make it known to the world. Out of this came the St. Eustatius Historical Foundation and its subsidiary SECAR, which are now responsible for showcasing the island's history through museums, archeology projects and renovations. The island's offerings to tourists are much richer because of their efforts.

The Facts

Population: The island now is home to just under 3,000 people.

Language: While Dutch is the official language, English is spoken throughout the island and is taught in the schools. Some islanders are also fluent in Spanish, owing to the influx of people from other Caribbean nations.

Main City: The seat of government, principal port and main city is Oranjestad, named after the Netherlands' Royal House of Oranje. The town is made up of two parts, Upper Town and Lower Town. Other towns include Concordia, Golden Rock, Zeelandia and Fort de Windt.

Government & Economy: Like Saba, Statia was a part of the Netherlands Antilles and had status within the Kingdom of the Netherlands as an autonomous region. Internal affairs of the island group were administered by a central government in Curaçao. However, in 2006 Curaçao and Sint Maarten managed to convince the monarchy to consider disbanding the Antilles as a political entity so that they could each determine their own governmental affairs. On December 15, 2008 the Antilles will cease to exist, and Saba and St. Eustatius will become a direct part of the Netherlands as special municipalities, governed by their own mayors, alder-

Statia

men and municipal council. While the citizens retain their right to vote in Netherlands elections, it is not clear yet whether all the laws of the kingdom will apply in these "Kingdom Islands."

People & Culture: The natives are descendants of the European settlers and African slaves. As with all the Caribbean islands, there has been an influx of foreign visitors who have decided to make the island their residence, and now more than 20 nationalities are represented.

Geography: This small island, five miles long and two miles wide, totals 11.2 square miles. The dominant feature is The Quill, a 2,000-ft-high extinct volcano in the southeastern end of the island.

Saban anolis lizard (Joseph Burgess)

Climate: Statia is delightfully tropical year-round, with maximum temperatures in the 80s during the day at the 70s at night.

Flora & Fauna: With a tropical climate and topography ranging from flatlands to mountain rainforests, many varied species enjoy life on Statia. **St. Eustatius National Park** (STENAPA), a non-profit organization, protects the island's valued natural resources through a number of programs (☎ 599-318-2884, www.statiapark.org). The island also has a number of protected parks, including Marine Park, Quill-Boven National Park, and the Mariam C. Schmidt Botanical Gardens.

The Dutch Caribbean is home to more than 35 globally endangered or vulnerable species, including trees, snakes, sea turtles, birds, whales and fish. In the parks created since STENAPA was formed in 1997, animals such as the red-bellied racer snake, the Saban anolis lizard, the Lesser Antillean iguana, three species of sea turtles, the queen conch and other

Lesser Antillean iguana

valuable and threatened species are being sheltered and supported.

Bird species, both land and sea-based, are astonishingly numerous. You'll find everything from brown pelicans and frigate birds to zenaida doves, grey kingbirds and the Lesser Antillean bullfinch. One of the best places to view the birds is the **Jean Gemmill Bird Observation Trail** at the Botanical Gardens.

Tropical flora range from fruit trees such as the mango, papaya and guava, to endemic mahogany trees, palms and the delicate species of the elfin rainforest. Those who love tropical flowers should not pass up a visit to the Botanical Gardens where you can wander through acres of educational plantings.

BOTANICAL GARDENS UNLIKE ANY OTHER

The **Miriam C. Schmidt Botanical Gardens** is not only a place for preservation and protection of the island's flora and fauna, but also a respite from the world where visitors can find peace and relaxation among the flowered paths and lookout points.

Since its beginning in 1998, the park has established a five-phased plan for development of the gardens. The first phase is complete and includes the Main House, powered by solar collectors and rainwater, the Pavilion with hammocks and picnic tables, the Jean Gemmill Bird Trail, the Palm Garden, the Lookout Garden, with views to St. Kitts, the Sensory Garden and the Shade House. Future phases will add a children's garden, a fruit garden, pre- and post-Columbian gardens, and an island flora garden featuring endemic species.

One of the favorite spots is the Sensory Garden, an experiential outdoor classroom where children and adults can learn about plants that appeal to all the senses. Pavilions representing each of the senses (sight, smell, sound, taste and touch) are paired with plants and trees as demonstrations of the flora's multifaceted allure.

The gardens are open from sunrise to sunset, and guided tours are available. Further information and guides are available at the National Park Visitors Centre at Gallows Bay or online at www.statiapark.org.

Statia

Travel Information

When to Go

 With its moderate tropical temperatures, Statia is a year-round delight. The months of heaviest rainfall are April, June and September, and of course the island is subject to hurricanes during the season from June through October. The last major hurricane to hit the island was in 1998.

Getting There

When you inquire about getting there, you quickly realize that in terms of access you are dealing with one of the more remote Caribbean islands. You can only reach Statia by air (unless you charter your own boat from St. Maarten), and the only airline that flies to Statia is WinAir.

By Air

 WinAir makes the 20-minute flight from St. Maarten five times a day. You can make reservations through them directly at ☎ 599-545-4237, 545-4230 or 545-4210, www.fly-winair.com. There are also WinAir flights from Saba and St. Kitts on an ever-changing schedule. The two travel agencies on the island can make changes and reconfirm your trip back to St. Maarten.

By Sea

 The number of arrivals at Statia by sea has increased significantly over the past few years as more bare-boat and crewed charters put the island on their itinerary. There is one anchorage at Orange Baai. From there you have to check in with the Statia Port Authority in Oranjestad, and pay dues for the Statia Marine Park.

Customs

The island is a duty-free port, so you will not have to deal with customs.

Special Events & Holidays

 As described previously, the island celebrates its history with the United States during a special day in November, and has a summer Carnival, as do most of the Leewards.

January

New Year's Day, January 1 – Public holiday.

April

Good Friday – Public holiday.

Easter Sunday – Public holiday.

Easter Monday – Public holiday. Island-wide beach picnics, music, food and drinks.

Queen's Birthday, April 30 – Public holiday, with celebrations around the island, including cultural events, sports and picnics.

May

Labour Day, May 1 – Public holiday.

Ascension Day, May 17 – Public holiday.

July

Emancipation Day, July 1 – Public holiday celebrating the abolition of slavery.

Carnival, mid-July – Week-long celebration at Carnival Village, with beauty and calypso competitions, showcases, food and music.

Carnival Monday, last Monday in July – Public holiday.

Antillean Day, October 21 – Public holiday with cultural festivities, speeches, sports and music.

November

Golden Rock Regatta, November 9-16.

Statia-America Day, November 16 – Public holiday commemorating the first salute to the American flag by a foreign power. Kicks off a week of cultural activities and visits from foreign dignitaries.

December

Christmas Day, December 25 – Public holiday.

Boxing Day, December 26 – Public holiday.

Health

 The small **Queen Beatrix Hospital** is the main health care facility on the island, and offers the services of two doctors who are on call 24 hours, seven days a week. ☎ 599-318-2371/2211.

Statia

The island also offers divers two **hyperbaric chambers** for decompression, staffed by the able technicians trained at the University of St. Eustatius Medical School's Undersea and Hyperbaric Medicine Program.

Crime

 With such a small population and low number of tourist visits, crime is not a big problem on Statia.

Electricity

 Voltage throughout the island is 110, so all American appliances will work here without a transformer. This time, Europeans have to bring the converters.

Tipping

 The hotels add a 15% service charge in the restaurants, in lieu of gratuities. As always, cab drivers and tour guides will appreciate gratuities.

Money Matters

 Most credit cards and US currency are accepted on the island. Banks include **First Caribbean International Bank** and **PostSpaarbank**. The **Windward Island Bank** has an ATM in Mazinga Square.

Weddings

 To get married on Statia you must be at least 18, and file a raft of paperwork with the lieutenant governor of St. Eustatius at least 14 days prior to the ceremony. The notarized documents you will need include:

- A birth certificate. These documents should be provided with an "Apostille" stamp.
- In the event persons are not of Dutch nationality, copies of valid passports.
- Addresses of both parties.
- Duration of stay on St. Eustatius.

- Unmarried persons must present a declaration of marital status not older than three months.
- If widow(er), a death certificate.
- If divorced, a divorce certificate or a final judgment decree.
- For minors, permission of the parents is required.
- Names of parents, maiden names of mothers including place of birth and birth date.
- Professions of the bride, the groom and the parents.
- The names of six witnesses if the marriage is performed outside of the Marriage Hall. Non-Dutch witnesses must present a valid passport or a birth certificate with a picture ID.

Original documents other than Dutch or English need to be translated into the Dutch language (i.e., a French or Spanish document must be translated into Dutch, not English).

The cost for contracting foreign marriages is US$275.55 and includes civil ceremony, marriage books, stamps and certificates. For more information, contact the Lieutenant Governor's office at lt.governor@statiagovernment.com.

Internet Access

The local phone company, **Eutel**, provides DSL service to its customers, and some of the hotels are now signing on in order to offer Internet access for their guests. Check with your hotel to see what they have. There is also public access available from the Public Library in Oranjestad and at Computers & More, ☎ 599-318-2596, e-mail mbvi@goldenrock.net.

Communications

Eutel also provides public pay phones with calling cards as well as GSM cellular service. You can purchase a local SIM card and prepaid minutes, if you want to use your own phone.

Media

The island's news is disseminated by two local radio stations, and occasionally stories about Statia appear in *Amigoe*, a Dutch Antilles newspaper based in Curaçao, and in the *Daily Herald* in St. Maarten.

Sources of Information

i For detailed information on Statia, see the official tourism website at www.statiatourism.com or call the number below. You can also contact the **St. Eustatius Tourism Development Foundation** at Fort Oranje, Oranjestad, St. Eustatius, Netherlands Antilles, Dutch Caribbean, ☎ 599-318-2433, fax 599-318-2433, euxtour@goldenrocknet.com.

Getting Around

Airport

The small **Franklin Delano Roosevelt Airport** (EUX) is located inland, near the town of Concordia. The 4,200-ft runway can accommodate small planes and jets, but no large jets. There are minimal services at the airport, but a Tourist Information Desk is available for questions.

Taxi Service

There are several capable taxi operators that will pick you up at the airport as well as provide tours around the island. The dispatcher at the airport can call you a cab or you can arrange for one through your hotel. The rates (no meters) are set in advance, so confirm the fare before you set out. A complete tour of the island will take two to three hours and cost around US$80.

Car Rentals

Since the island is so small, you won't spend a lot of time in a car. But if you like having one available so you can visit one of the beaches or historical sites on your own, you can arrange a rental at the Tourist Information Desk at the airport or through your hotel.

Car Rental Companies

ARC Car Rental	599-318-2595
Brown's Car Rental	599-318-2266
Rainbow Car Rental	599-318-2811
Richardson Jeep Rental	599-318-2149
Schmidt Car Rental	599-318-2788
Trep Car Rental	599-318-2626
Walter's Car Rental	599-318-2719

Exploring

On Foot

Whether you want to wander on your own or take an organized walking tour, Statia offers many opportunities for the walking enthusiast. The island is small but hilly, with numerous footpaths to explore. Trails lead up The Quill, part of the St. Eustatius National Parks (STENAPA).

Walking Tours

The **St. Eustatius Historical Foundation** offers two-hour walking tours of Oranjestad. The tour begins at the Museum and then passes by the old Catholic Church, Fort Oranje, the Government Guesthouse, the Dutch Reformed Church and the Honen Dalim Synagogue. ☎ 599-318-2288, www.steustatiushistory.org.

Other interesting walks are offered at the **Botanical Gardens** (see above), where you can stroll through the bird observation area and various gardens.

Quill volcano (Shenwalee)

Hiking

The premier hiking trails are part of the **The Quill National Park**, which wraps around the extinct volcano that is the highest point on the island. The slopes up to the crater are mostly woodlands and semi-evergreen forests, contrasting with the crater and crater rim, which are evergreen forests. The five main trails range in difficulty from rambling walks on the Round the Mountain Trail to more rigorous climbs to the rim and lush interior of the crater. Two of the trails in the Botanical Gardens have paths leading to the Round the Mountain Trail, which takes about five hours to complete.

Other trails can be found at **Boven National Park**. This area is comprised of five hills in the Northern Hills of St. Eustatius, including the Boven, Venus, Gilboa Hill, Signal Hill and Bergje. The trails start from the end of the road at Zeelandia. They are not as well maintained as the Quill trails because of some disputes over land ownership. But many hikers say the effort is worth it for the beautiful panoramas and views of old buildings and plantations.

There is an entrance fee for the Quill trails, payable at the **National Parks Office** in Gallows Bay, which is also where you can pick up a detailed map of the area and arrange for guided tours. ☎ 599-318-2884, www.statiapark.org.

On Water

In addition to the land trails, STENAPA maintains the Statia Marine Park, established in 1996. The park surrounds the island and extends from the high water park (**mark?) to 100 feet from shore. The reserves contained in the park feature pristine coral reefs where sea life abounds, leading to the area's popularity with divers and snorkelers. Since these are no-anchor areas, STENAPA has created 42 mooring buoys. STENAPA enforces strict guidelines on diving, snorkeling and yacht mooring (see details at www.statiapark.org). Also, expect to pay fees for any activities in this protected park.

Scuba Diving

The secret about the fantastic diving around Statia has gotten out to the diving community, and the island has become a destination for dive charters and organized trips. The 36 prime sites in the Park offer a variety of wrecks, historic sites and volcanic formations, and an incredible diversity of marine life. One of the highlights is the artificial reef created by the scuttling of the 327-foot *Charles Brown* cable-laying ship, which now offers one of the longest dive sites in the Caribbean. The STENAPA website has a detailed map of the sites.

The rules of the park require that all divers must be accompanied by a certified dive operator. Your diving guide will arrange for payment of the dive fees as well as guide you to the best sites for your interests and skill level. Be advised that most of the dive shops close during the month of September, traditionally the slowest month for visitors.

Dive Operators

Dive Statia has two boats, a dive catamaran and a 36-ft Bonner dive and fishing boat, as well as eight underwater Seadoo scooters. They offer Nitrox dives, night dives, PADI courses and a Discover Scuba Diving course for beginners, operating a full-service dive shop in Lowertown as well. ☎ 599-318-2435, US 866-614-3491, fax 599-318-2539, www. divestatia.com.

Golden Rock Dive Center offers a 38-ft catamaran and 32-ft dive boat for a variety of dive tours. Golden Rock, a PADI National Geographic Dive Center, operates out of the Old Gin House Hotel, where they have a well stocked dive shop. The Center also has PADI classes, equipment rentals, including underwater photography equipment, and  overnight equipment storage. ☎ 599-318-2964, US 800-311-6658, www. goldenrocknet.com.

Scubaqua has a dive shop next to the Blue Bead Restaurant. They offer environmentally sensitive dives with free Nitrox tank fills for certified divers, as well as certification. They have four multilingual PADI dive instructors and four dive masters, so there is always someone available to take you out to the best dive sites. ☎ 599-318-5440, fax 599-318-2160, www.scubaqua.com.

Kayaking

 If you want to explore the shoreline or remote beaches in a more solitary fashion, take advantage of Dive Statia's six Malibu Two XL ocean kayaks. You can rent one by the hour, half-day or day. They also run guided trips and snorkeling trips. ☎ 599-318-2435, US 866-614-3491, fax 599-318-2539, www.divestatia.com.

Snorkeling

A number of the colorful coral reefs are available to snorkelers, including the historic ruins of Oranje Bay, Crooks Castle Beach, and three sites accessible by boat. The dive operators can take you out to Blind Shoal, Twelve Guns and Inner Jenkins Bay, with depths up to 19 feet, where you can see a variety of sea life including turtles and rays. Snorkelers, like divers, are required to get a dive pass, since they will be using the facilities of the Marine Park.

Boat Charters

Most boat charters are booked from St. Martin (see the chapter on St. Marin for more details). In addition, Dive Statia has a 36-ft Bonner powerboat equipped for deep sea fishing and day charters. ☎ 599-318-2435, US 866-614-3491, fax 599-318-2539, www.divestatia.com.

Playing & Watching Sports

Tennis

Statia maintains tennis courts at the Community Center on Rosemary Laan in Upper Town (☎ 599-318-2249). Court fees are US$3 per hour. You supply your own rackets and balls, and there is a changing room on-site.

Seeing the Sights

Sampling the Culture

As you wander the island, you'll find the Statian culture as welcoming as it is irresistible. Many liken the island to the old Caribbean, where islanders warmly welcomed visitors and were always eager to talk about their island and their lives. It's still that way in Statia, and it's still quite possible to walk around without being part of a horde of tourists. From a physical standpoint, many of the old colonial-era buildings remain intact, and throughout the towns, especially in Oranjestad, you get a good picture of what life was like in Statia.

Special events such as **Carnival**, **Antillean Day** and **Statia-American Day** also impart the sense of history and culture that still flourishes here. Plan a visit during these times, and you are sure to revel in the food, music, dance and entertainment that make Statia unique.

Reliving History

Statia has some of the best re-created historical sites in the Caribbean, thanks to the efforts of the Sint Eustatius Historical Foundation, the Center for Archeological Research (SECAR) and the local government. Realizing that their island was rich in historical artifacts and structures, these organizations have preserved and still maintain historic homes, churches and forts open to the public.

Among the highlights are the 18th-century Simon Doncker House, now the site of the **St. Eustatius Museum**; the **Honem Dalim**, the second-oldest Jewish synagogue in the Western Hemisphere; and the many homes and buildings included in the **Historic Core Renovation Program** in Oranjestad. For more information, see the Historical Foundation's website at www.steustatiushistory.org.

Another historic site available for tour is the **Lynch Plantation Museum** at Lynch Bay. Also called the **Berkel Family Plantation**, this residence and museum illustrates 19th-century life through antiques, photographs and equipment. One of the family members is available for guided tours if you phone ahead. ☎ 599-318-2338.

St. Eustatius Museum

TAKE PART IN A REAL DIG

Statia is regarded as one of the richest sites of historical artifacts and structures in the Caribbean. During the colonial period, it was also one of the richest trade centers in the region, so prosperous that it became known as "the Golden Rock." During its heyday, trading ships arrived daily to fill the more than 600 warehouses along Statia's coastline with goods from all over the world. At the same time, wealthy traders and merchants built elaborately furnished and decorated homes. When the revenue from trading dried up, the warehouses, and sometimes the goods stored in them, were abandoned, and many of the formerly wealthy families left the island. The result is a historical record as important to today's archaeologists as sugar and rum were to colonists. To preserve this record, the always-forward looking island established **St. Eustatius Center for Archeological Research** as a permanent archeological resource on the island.

Visitors who have a yen to dig can volunteer with the Center's **Excavation Experiences** program and participate in excavations underway at Fort Amsterdam and the Pleasures Estate plantation, among others. The volunteers pay for tuition, food and accommodations in exchange for valuable instruction and experience in archeology. The program is offered from mid-January to the end of August. Volunteers excavate in the morning and process artifacts in the afternoon. It's a one-of-a-kind experience for those who love history.

To find out more, contact SECAR, ☎ 599-524-6770, fax 599-318-3631, www.secar.org.

Statia

Where to Stay

Hotels & Small Inns

Statia – small island, small hotels. If you're looking to get lost in the anonymity of a mega-resort, Statia is not for you. Statia is about close, personal encounters with the innkeepers, who send you home with warm impressions of the Statians' hospitality and simplicity. Here are the four hotels, in alpha order, that offer comfortable lodgings to visitors.

Here are the four hotels that offer comfortable lodging. Unlike the other islands, hotels here don't charge different rates for high and low season. The Country Inn is a real bargain at $60 a night, and the other three range from $110 to $190 a night for a double, proving that Statia really is paradise for those on limited budgets.

Country Inn

This is the low-budget housing alternative, with room rates like the US used to have in the '60s and '70s. The six rooms are nestled into a tropical garden with a view over Zeelandia Bay. Owner Iris Pompier makes sure her guests are content and enjoy the best Statia has to offer.

Location: Concordia, center of the island.

Rooms: Six, all with cable TV, AC and alarm clocks.

Rates: EP, with breakfast, lunch and dinner available upon request.

Features: Single or double rooms, no credit cards accepted.

☎ 599-318-2484, www. statiatourism.com/ countryinn.

Golden Era Hotel

Nestled at the edge of the sea in an 18h-century warehouse, this charming, small hotel offers comfortable rooms and a good restaurant. The beach is about a half-mile away,

Golden Era Hotel

and when you are in the restaurant or by the pool the waves are just a short walk away.

Location: Oranjestad.

Rooms: 20 in all, including singles, doubles, suites and efficiency suites. All have refrigerators and cable TV.

Rates: EP.

Features: Restaurant, pool, pool bar, dive shop next door.

☎ 599-318-2455, fax 599-318-2445, www.statiatourism.com/goldenera.

Kings Well Resort

This small resort overlooks Oranje Bay and distinguishes itself as an animal-lovers paradise. Owners Win and Laura keep five macaws and a variety of cats, dogs and iguanas on-site for everyone to enjoy; they're even present at meals. The resort has the ambiance of a private villa. Win and Laura are on hand to cater to individual needs; they also operate a restaurant open to the public for lunch and dinner.

Oranje Bay, seen from Kings Well Resort

Kings Well Resort

www.kingswellstatia.com.

Location: Oranje Bay.

Rooms: 12 in all, including seaview, seafront and garden-view rooms. All have private balconies, refrigerators, ceiling fans and cable TV; some have AC.

Rates: BP.

Features: Restaurant, pool, hot tub.

☎ 599-318-2538,

The Old Gin House

The Old Gin House

Housed in a refurbished 18th-century gin factory, the hotel is an historic landmark, often referred to as the "luxury" inn and the best place to stay on the island. Rooms are furnished with colonial reproductions for a charming tropical atmosphere. Closed in September.

Location: Oranjestad.

Rooms: 14 garden-view, two ocean-view and two one-bedroom suites, all with balconies, ceiling fans, AC and cable TV. Suites have a separate study and living room, refrigerator and DVD players.

Rates: EP.

Features: Restaurant, pool.

☎ 599-318-2319, US 800-634-4907, fax 599-318-2135, www.oldginhouse. com.

Cottages

If you are looking for simplicity and a back-to-nature feel, you should check out the cottages. Expect to pay $110 per night for a double in all seasons.

Statia Lodge

This collection of 10 bungalows near Oranjestad offers great family-friendly accommodations. The one- and two-bedroom cottages made of exotic woods have a restful and yet elegant atmosphere. On the grounds are a pool and pool house, and the views overlook the sea. ☎ 599-318-1900, fax 599-318-2873, www.statialodge.com.

Statia Lodge

Where to Eat

RESTAURANT PRICE CHART	
$	Cheap eats, normally quick meals or take-out foods; US$8 or less per entrée.
$$	Good value, lots of West Indian cuisine; US$9-$14 for a plate of food.
$$$	A nice place with gourmet aspirations; US$15-$24 for a satisfying entrée.
$$$$	Positively elegant, usually requiring some dressing up; entrées range from US$25 to $50, depending on the island.

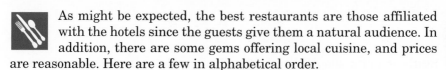

As might be expected, the best restaurants are those affiliated with the hotels since the guests give them a natural audience. In addition, there are some gems offering local cuisine, and prices are reasonable. Here are a few in alphabetical order.

Blue Bead Restaurant and Bar

A delightful, small restaurant, the Blue Bead offers French Creole and Italian favorites in a pleasant setting near the dive shops. Lower Town, Gallows Bay. ☎ 599-318-2873.

Chinese Bar and Restaurant

There are a number of Chinese restaurants on the island, and this is one of the best of them. It offers typical favorites in a nice downtown setting. Oranjestad on H.M. Queen Beatrixstraat. Open for dinner.

Statia

Kings Well Restaurant

At this restaurant, which is part of the Kings Well Resort, owners Win and Laura serve German cuisine alongside their wry and candid observations on the state of the world. If you don't like eating in a dining room that accepts dogs and cats roaming around, you should look elsewhere. Lower Town. Open to patrons for breakfast, lunch and dinner; open to the public for lunch and dinner only. ☎ 599-318-2538.

Old Gin House Restaurant

This is considered one of the island's top restaurants. The historic setting is romantic, the Belgian chef is Michelin-trained, and the wine list is good. A prix fixe three-course dinner is offered nightly; you can also order à la carte. Lower Town, Oranjestad. Open for dinner only. A snack bar serves breakfast and lunch across the street. ☎ 599-318-2319.

Ocean View Terrace

On a terrace overlooking Fort Oranje, this warm and inviting restaurant serves a selection of local dishes with a beautiful sunset view. Government's Guest House, Ft. Oranje. Open for (**more info). ☎ 599-318-2934.

Smoke Alley Bar and Grill

A favorite for those who like to hang out in a relaxed atmosphere, Smoke Alley serves Tex Mex favorites as well as grilled hamburgers, ribs, fish and steaks. It's located on the water and hosts live music on Friday nights. Lower Town, Gallows Bay. Open for lunch and dinner, closed Sundays. ☎ 599-318-2002.

Superburger

Statia's version of fast food offers a menu of hamburgers, shakes, sandwiches and ice cream. They also have breakfast and hot local dishes during lunch. Oranjestad. Open for breakfast and lunch. ☎ 599-318-2412.

Shopping

Statia is not a shopper's paradise. In fact, there is only one gift store, **Mazinga Gift Shop** on Fort Oranje Straat, where you can buy souvenirs, books and sundries.

Nighlife

Again, Statia is not the place to go if you love an active nightlife. **Smoke Alley** and some hotel restaurants have live music on the weekends, and the **Old Gin House** hosts barbecues on Wednesday evenings. Also, **Cool Corner**, a local bar in the center of Oranjestad across from the museum, is a fun place to hang out and share stories with the locals and your fellow travelers.

The Beaches of Statia

The beaches in Statia are not the typical Caribbean long, wide strands with offshore reefs coaxing a gentle surf to shore. Most beaches are just small strips of sand, and strong undertows make some unsuitable for swimming.

Oranje Bay

This is considered the best beach on the island. It has no strong current or undertow to fear, and you'll be safe from stinging or biting creatures. Lots of rocks line the beach, and at times the sand is sparse due to currents and tides. There are grassy areas for blankets and chairs.

Zeelandia Beach

This beach on the eastern or Atlantic side features black and tan sands good for sunbathing. However, there often is a danger-ous undertow and swimming is not recommended

Lynch Beach

This small beach on the Atlantic side with shallow waters suit-able for wading is ideal for chil-dren. However, there is some undertow in the deeper areas, so stay near shore and swim with caution.

Zeelandia Beach

Crooks Castle Beach

Snorkelers like this golden sand beach where you can see sea fans and various corals plus some interesting fish. It's on the Caribbean side just south of Oranjestad.

Corre Corre Bay

Getting to this beach involves a half-hour hike down Mountain Road on the southeastern side of the island. It's good for sunbathing, but the surf is often too rough for swimming.

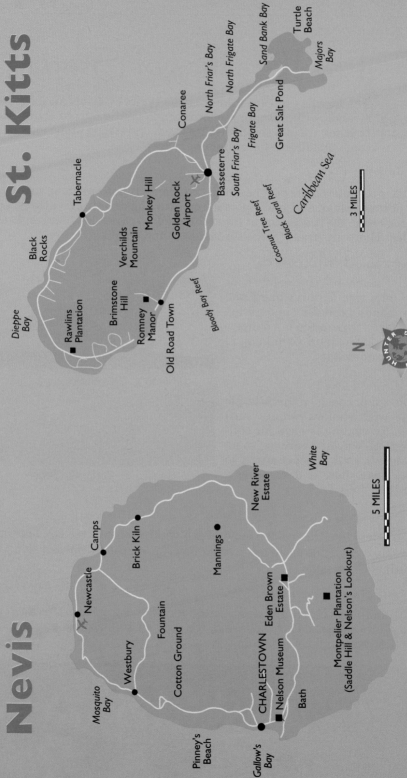

Nevis

Mosquito Bay

Newcastle

Camps

Brick Kiln

Westbury

Fountain

Cotton Ground

Mannings

New River Estate

CHARLESTOWN

Eden Brown Estate

Nelson Museum

Bath

Montpelier Plantation
(Saddle Hill & Nelson's Lookout)

White Bay

Pinney's Beach

Gallow's Bay

5 MILES

N

St. Kitts

Black Rocks

Tabernacle

Dieppe Bay

Rawlins Plantation

Brimstone Hill

Romney Manor

Old Road Town

Bloody Bay Reef

Verchilds Mountain

Monkey Hill

Golden Rock Airport

Conaree

Basseterre

South Friar's Bay

Frigate Bay

North Friar's Bay

North Frigate Bay

Sand Bank Bay

Great Salt Pond

Turtle Beach

Majors Bay

Coconut Tree Reef

Black Coral Reef

Caribbean Sea

3 MILES

St. Kitts & Nevis
The Allure of the Islands

Up until a few years ago, St. Kitts and Nevis were the type of islands that tourists delighted in "discovering." Seemingly untouched by modern times, they seemed like the "old" Caribbean – small, intimate hotels, pristine beaches, uncluttered roads, with acres of cane fields and rainforests dominating the landscape. But with the coming of two large chain hotels – the Marriott in St. Kitts and the Four Seasons in Nevis – the landscape, the ambience and the pace have changed rapidly and irrevocably.

Now everywhere you look on these two islands there are new developments going up. The emphasis is on five-star resorts, many of which start with sales of private villas to help finance building of the amenities and resort as a whole. Along with the resorts have come three golf courses, a new cruise ship port area with duty-free shops and a marine park.

But you still find hints of the old laid-back islands here, especially in the delightful plantation inns on

St. Kitts from space

St. Kitts, South Range and Basseterre

both islands. These small hotels, built around historical buildings and sugar mills, still have a colonial charm. They are furnished with Caribbean antiques and emphasize the old-fashioned standards of warm, personalized service. So it is possible to sample both the charm of the old world and the activities of the new.

If you stay on St. Kitts, be sure to allow at least one day to visit Nevis, which is just a short ferry ride or a 10-minute flight away. The main port city there, **Charlestown**, is a study in historic preservation. Many of the 'skirt-and-blouse' structures – where the first level is stone and the second is wood siding – are still standing and are now being used for offices and stores. The stately old churches such as **St. John's Anglican** and the historic **Cottle Church** reinforce the sense of history. In addition, the **Nevis Botanical Gardens** offer a beautiful respite from the world, where you can learn about the unique plants of the Caribbean and enjoy the beauty of carefully designed displays of orchids, roses, bromeliads and fruit trees. While the wild vervet monkeys are endemic to both islands,

Nevis

they are more frequently sighted in Nevis, running across roads (and the golf course at the Four Seasons) or sitting in trees.

Here's what to look for according to the type of traveler you are

The Perfect Cruise Passenger will of course head to either the St. Kitts Marriott Resort or the Four Seasons in Nevis, where everything you want is right at your fingertips. Although they aren't all-inclusives, they have a number of restaurants, beautiful beaches, boutiques, a spa, a golf course, and everything else that matters. For day-trips, take a ferry to Nevis, or join one of the many water or land tours offered by local operators.

The Boots-On Adventurer will want to head uphill for hiking tours into the rainforests of Mt. Liamuiga in St. Kitts and Mount Nevis in Nevis. In St. Kitts, the Bird Rock Hotel or the Timothy Beach Club offer comfortable accommodations at great prices. In Nevis, the Oualie Beach Hotel is definitely your spot, since it's adjacent to Mountain Bike Rentals and Windsurfing Nevis, official headquarters for the many triathlons and bike races on the island throughout the year. Also, don't miss the scuba diving and deep sea fishing around both islands.

The Cultural Explorer will find many historic places on both islands, as well as craft centers and museums. The St. Kitts Carnival and Music Festival are two great events not to miss, and Culturama and the NICHE events on Nevis always draw

St. Kitts & Nevis

crowds. You'll especially love Nevis, where you can tour Heritage Village and the beautiful Botanical Gardens.

The "I Like What I Like" Traveler will find bliss at any of the multitude of comfortable and spacious villas on either island, or the villa resorts, which have good lodgings plus some important amenities. No reason to give up your golf, because St. Kitts has two great courses, and Nevis has a Robert Trent Jones-designed course. If strange cuisines don't appeal to your palate, stick with the familiar at the St. Kitts Marriott Royal Grille Steakhouse.

The Incurable Romantic should check out the gracious plantation inns on both islands. The Sugar Mill honeymoon suite at the Rawlings Plantation Inn and just about any suite at the Golden Lemon will really get you in the mood. As far as restaurants go, you can't miss with the Royal Palm at Ottley's, Diana's Restaurant or Waterfalls in St. Kitts, and Coconut Grove or the Montpelier Terrace Restaurant in Nevis. Don't miss a visit to the Mango Orchard Spa at Ottley's Plantation for a couples' massage in the gazebo.

The Family Social Director will welcome the availability of villas and villa resorts in St. Kitts, and the Oualie Beach Hotel in Nevis. Children are welcomed at most of the resorts, with the exception of the Golden Lemon Inn in St. Kitts. Among the activities kids will love are the new Marine Park at South Frigate Bay Beach in St. Kitts and the Under the Sea Sealife Education Centre in Nevis. Along the way, the ferry ride from St. Kitts to Nevis is fun, as is looking for the elusive green vervet monkeys almost everywhere on both islands.

The Ultimate Shopper will revel in the delights of the new Port Zante duty-free center and the downtown area of Basseterre in St. Kitts. Also, be sure to plan a trip to Romney Manor in St. Kitts, where Caribelle Batik has a demonstration shop and boutique. In Nevis, check out the Cotton Ginnery Complex for a number of shops offering local goods, as well as the shops and galleries throughout Charlestown. There are also some great boutiques at the St. Kitts Marriott and the Nevis Four Seasons hotels.

A Brief History

The history of St. Kitts and Nevis is largely the same as their Leeward Island neighbors. They too were initially occupied by the Carib and Arawak Indians. The Indian name for St. Kitts was "Liamuiga" or "fertile land," in recognition of the rich soil that remained from ancient times when the central 3,792-ft peak was an active volcano.

The modern name of the two islands is said to have originated with Christopher Columbus (who else?), who bestowed the name St. Christopher on the larger island in honor of the patron saint of travelers. This seemed especially appropriate later, since the island's visibility and position made it a major stopping point in the early days of heavy transatlantic migration. British soldiers later shortened the name to St. Kitts.

Nevis was named for its appearance. Because the continuous cloud cover that shrouded its 3,232-ft peak suggested a snow cap, it was given the Spanish name *Nuestro Senor del las Nieves* or Our Lady of the Snows. That was later shortened to Nevis (pronounced Nee-vis).

From 1493 until the early 17th century, the original inhabitants gradually disappeared as they fell victim to European diseases, repeated Spanish, French and British attacks, and forced labor. Official colonization began in 1623 when Sir Thomas Warner and his family occupied the island for Great Britain. French settlers arrived in 1625, and in 1626 a combined militia of the two groups wiped out the remnants of the Caribs in a massacre at Bloody Point. From this island, the British fanned out to settle on Nevis, Antigua, Barbuda, Tortuga and Montserrat, and the French occupied Martinique and Guadeloupe.

The islands prospered as centers for tobacco and sugar production, while ownership seesawed back and forth between the British and the French.

ATTAQUE DE BRIMSTOMHILL.

Battle of Brimstone Hill (1782 engraving)

Horatio, Lord Nelson

The struggle culminated in a battle, won by the French, at the massive British fortifications of Brimstone Hill in 1782. A year later, the islands were returned to the British under the terms of the Treaty of Versailles.

With its natural conditions conducive to the growth of sugar cane, and the knowledge of sugar crystallization brought to the island by the Sephardic Jews, the sugar industry made Nevis fantastically wealthy, earning it the title "Queen of the Caribees." Production in St. Kitts was equally profitable, and St. Kitts became known as "Sugar City." However, sugar was a labor-intensive industry that required far more workers than the colonists could provide, so the slave trade became essential to the islands. By 1700, about three-fourths of the residents were slaves.

Nevis' sugar production declined in the mid-1700s, as frequent battles between the colonizing powers led to emigration of available workers, and depletion of the soil lowered production. But the island's beauty and great climate attracted rich Europeans who built grand estate houses – many of which survive today as the plantation inns. Some of the notable inhabitants of Nevis during that period were Alexander Hamilton, who was born here in 1757, and Horatio, Lord Nelson, who distinguished himself in naval battles and married a local beauty named Fanny Nisbet.

Fanny Nisbet

St. Kitts' experience with sugar production lasted much longer. It survived the economic crisis that other islands went through when slavery was abolished in 1834, although soil depletion and the high costs of labor reduced production somewhat. Still the island managed to keep sugar as the primary income-producing export into the 20th century. The government got into the business, creating the St. Kitts Sugar Manufacturing Corporation in 1911 to modernize the industry. The estate owners built a narrow-gauge railroad to bring the cane harvest from the outlying areas to the processing plants. In the 1970s, the individual owners ran into severe hardships and government nationalized all the cane fields. By then St. Kitts faced a world economy where other nations were growing and processing the crop in less expensive ways and Great Britain still insisted on preferred prices that didn't allow for much profit.

The industry hobbled along, trying to provide a livelihood for the 1,500 citizens. By the year 2000, the government realized this industry was no longer tenable, and in 2005 St. Kitts ended all sugar production, the last holdout in the Caribbean.

In the meantime, the two islands were seeking their independence from British rule. In 1967, together with Anguilla (which later that year seceded), they were awarded the status of Associated Statehood in the United Kingdom, paving the way for their ultimate independence as a sovereign state in 1983. Unhappy with being overshadowed by its larger sister island, Nevis has attempted to separate from St. Kitts, most recently in 1998. But the secessionist forces have never marshaled the majority vote needed for independence.

As with other Leeward Islands, St. Kitts and Nevis looked to tourism to replace the revenues lost when sugar production declined. The islands' beauty, ideal climate and hospitality began to attract visitors from the US, Canada and Europe and by the mid-20th century the islands had developed into a prime Caribbean destination. Tourism is the dominant industry today.

The Facts

Population: 39,129, with African being the predominant race; there are also British, Portuguese and Lebanese inhabitants, along with many US and Canadian ex-pats or part-time residents.

Language: The official language is English, spoken with the West Indies lilt that is so appealing.

Main City: The primary city in St. Kitts is Basseterre (pronounced boss-tear), and the main port in Nevis is Charlestown.

Government & Economy: The unified federation is an independent Commonwealth Realm member, with Queen Elizabeth II as the titular head of state. She is represented in the country by a Governor-General who acts on the advice of the Prime Minister and cabinet. The PM is the leader of the majority party of the unicameral National Assembly. This body has 14 members, 11 popularly elected representatives (three from Nevis), and three appointed senators.

St. Kitts & Nevis

Tourism and related services comprise 71% of the economy, with the rest coming from export-related manufacturing and offshore banking. Right now, St. Kitts is experiencing significant real estate development and construction activity related to tourism.

People & Culture: The Kittians and Nevisians are gracious, welcoming people who take significant pride in their island. Native artisans produce art glass, glass jewelry and batik fabrics. A group of local fashion designers are building a reputation throughout the Caribbean and beyond.

One particular and unique point of pride in St. Kitts' is boat building. Since 1968, Phillip Walwyn has been building classic wooden multi-hull boats with his company Pleasant Boat Company. In addition, Indigo Yachts Ltd. produces large catamarans. Their combined activity makes St. Kitts the second-largest boat building island in the Eastern Caribbean (outranked only by Trinidad).

St. Kitts is a nation of rabid cricket fans. The Warner Park cricket stadium underwent a large-scale renovation in 2006 in anticipation of the crowds of Australians, South Africans, Dutch and Scottish fans that arrived for the 2007 ICC Cricket World Cup.

Another event that brings international attention to these small islands is the annual St. Kitts Music Festival, which attracts major stars to the

Southern tip of St. kitts, with Nevis in the distance (Kakokayo)

island from a range of genres for several days of musical revels. Among past participants have been South African flugelhorn player Hugh Masekela, the Sun Win-Ching Chinese Ensemble, American R&B stars Kool and the Gang, big band leader Bobby Caldwell, country singer Kenny Rogers, and Reggae standouts Dennis Brown and local legend Crucial Bankie.

Geography: The federation includes 69-square-mile St. Kitts and 36-square-mile Nevis. Both are volcanic in origin, with single large peaks, Mt. Liamuiga in St. Kitts and Mount Nevis in Nevis, forming the center of the islands and creating rainforest areas. St. Kitts' shape resembles a baseball bat and Nevis is round like a ball. The larger island's Southeast Peninsula ends at The Narrows, a two-mile-wide channel that separates it from Nevis' northernmost point.

Climate: The tropical climate keeps the islands at 75-88°F year-round, with the rainy season occurring during the summer months. The trade winds guarantee constant breezes so many of the hotels, particularly the plantation inns in the foothills of Mount Nevis, need no air conditioning.

Flora & Fauna: One of the most distinguishing denizens of the islands is the green vervet monkey. It is said that the monkey population outnumbers humans two to one. You occasionally catch sight of them scampering across roads or running up tree trunks. But the creature you see scurrying across the road is more likely to be a mongoose, which has virtually eradicated snakes on the island.

Green vervet monkey

The rainforest areas draping the central peaks include an abundance of tropical plants and trees, including the coconut palm, flamboyant, white cedar, breadfruit, mango, sour sop and silk cotton trees, with bushes of sea grapes and wild cherries. The showiest of these is the beautiful flamboyant, which bursts into bright red flowers during the summer months and is the national flower of St. Kitts and Nevis. You can see a good sampling of flora, including orchids, bromeliads and exotic tropical flowers, at the Nevis Botanical Gardens.

The southeast peninsula of St. Kitts is a dry area with an abundance of cactus and century plants. The shoreline is dotted with mangroves, whose valuable eco-system sustains young fish, crustaceans, and sea birds. Birds that can be seen in that area include ospreys, chicken hawks, stilts, herons and ducks. You may also see the national bird, the brown pelican, as it performs some amazing aerial high-dives in search of food.

Nevis is also justifiably proud of the more than 60 types of butterflies and over 300 types of moths found on the island. The bird population is equally abundant. If you're counting, there are about 149 species on the island.

In a limited number of weeks in the fall and spring, more than 30 species of whales and dolphins can be seen off the coast of the islands. Sea turtles are also constantly appearing in the waters, delighting snorkelers and divers.

St. Kitts

Travel Information

When to Go

 Like Antigua, St. Kitts and Nevis' modern history is relatively hurricane free. So travel to the islands is good year-round. The summer months are hotter and sticky with high humidity, and the traditional high season runs from December through April.

Getting There

St. Kitts receives tourists by air and by sea, having both an international airport and a major new cruise ship dock. All incoming travelers must show a valid passport and onward or return ticket. The departure fee collected at the airport is US$22 or EC$60, payable in cash or by credit card at the airport.

By Air

St. Kitts' modern **Robert Llewellyn Bradshaw International Airport** (airport code SKB) receives major carriers' flights from Europe, the US and Canada, as well as regional carriers such as LIAT, Caribbean Star, Caribbean Sun and Caribbean Airlines. It is recognized as the best mid-sized airport in the Caribbean, and has the latest technology for flight information and baggage handling.

The major North American operators, who can also book connecting flights with the regional carriers, are:

Air Canada, with direct and non-stop service to St. Kitts from Toronto. ☎ 800-744-2472 or www.aircanada.com.

American Airlines, flying non-stop from Miami to St. Kitts three days a week, and with connecting service from San Juan every day. ☎ 800-433-7300, www.aa.com.

Continental, offering non-stop flights from Newark and Houston to San Juan, and from Newark to Antigua. ☎ 800-231-0856, www.continental.com.

Delta, with non-stop flights from Atlanta to St. Maarten, Antigua and San Juan. ☎ 800-241-4141, www.delta.com.

United, flying daily non-stop from Chicago to San Juan, and non-stop several days a week from Orlando, Miami, Tampa and Baltimore to San Juan. ☎ 800-864-8331, www.united.com.

US Airways, with non-stop flights from Charlotte to St. Kitts three days a week, a non-stop from Charlotte into Antigua, and non-stops from Chicago and Philadelphia into San Juan. ☎ 800-622-1015, www.usairways.com.

If you are looking for a connecting flight or want to do some island-hopping, these inter-island carriers operate into St. Kitts:

Air Jamaica, with flights from Jamaica to St. Kitts. ☎ 800-523-5585, www.airjamaica.com.

Caribbean Airlines (formerly known as BWIA), with flights from Trinidad and Tobago to St. Kitts. ☎ 800-538-2942, www.bwee.com.

Caribbean Star offering twice-daily flights from Antigua to St. Kitts. ☎ 866-864-6272 in the US, 800-744-STAR in the Caribbean, www.flycaribbeanstar.com.

Caribbean Sun, flying once a week to St. Kitts. ☎ 866-864-6272 or www.flycsa.com.

LIAT, offering twice-daily non-stop flights from Antigua to St. Kitts. ☎ 268-480-5610 or www.fly-liat.com. (At press time, LIAT was in merger talks with Caribbean Star, and a new airline is likely to have been created by the time this book appears.)

Customs

 Personal belongings are exempt from duty when visitors enter the island, but they place restrictions on certain items. Visitors are permitted to bring up to 200 cigarettes and 100 cigars, or 250 grams of tobacco; 1.136 liters of wine and spirits, and 170 ml. of perfume. If you pass through customs either in St. Kitts or Nevis, you won't have to repeat the process when you visit the other island.

St. Kitts & Nevis

Special Events & Holidays

 Kittians start their year off with a bang. The **National Carnival** starts in mid-December and ends with the festive Grand Parade on January 2 and Las Lap on January 3. Other major events during the year include the internationally renowned **Music Festival** in late June, **Independence Day** in September, and the **St. Kitts Tourism Week** in October. Communities host their own festivals throughout the year with parades, street dances and entertainment from jazz and soca to calypso and steel pan music.

Calendar of Events (to see specific dates for particular years, see the Calendar in the official tourism site, www.stkitts-tourism.com):

January
New Year's Day – Public holiday.
Carnival Grand Parade and Las Lap.

February
Inner City Festival – Community festival.

March
ICC Cricket World Cup (2007 only) – See www.cricketworldcup.com for schedule. (**need to update this)

April
Sandy Point Easter-Rama – Community festival.
Good Friday – Public holiday.
Easter Monday – Public holiday.

May
Labor Day, May 1 – Public holiday.
Cricket Test Matches begin – See www.icc-cricket.com for detailed schedule.
Cayon-Green Valley Festival – Community festival.

June
Whit Monday, June 5 – Public holiday.
St. Kitts Musical Festival, late June – See www.stkittsmusicfestival.net for entertainment lineup and schedule.

August

Festab – Community festival.

Emancipation Day, August 7 – Public holiday.

Saddle Fest – Community festival.

September

Festival de Capisterre – Community festival.

National Heroes Day, September 16 – Public holiday.

Newtown Fest – Community festival.

Independence Day, September 19 – Public holiday.

October

Fiesta de St. Peters – Community festival.

St. Kitts Tourism Week.

November

Guy Fest – Community festival.

Village O'Rama – Community festival.

St. Kitts Masquerades, Christmas

December

National Carnival – Begins mid-December. See www.stkittscarnival.com for details.

Health

 The primary hospital, **Joseph N. France General Hospital** in Basseterre (☎ 869-465-2551), was completed in 2003. Many hotels also have a physician on call for their guests' emergencies. If you need to get to the US or elsewhere for health care in a hurry, an **Air Ambulance** service is available (☎ 869-465-2801). There are several pharmacies on the island to serve your medication and cosmetic needs.

Pets

 To bring a pet into St. Kitts or Nevis, you must apply in writing to the Chief Veterinary Officer (CVO) for an import permit. Your application must include the species, name, age, sex, breed, color and microchip number (which is a requirement for all pets). In addition, you must provide lab reports plus a health certificate from the exporting country that details the animal's rabies vaccinations and general health. The animal must also be treated for parasites within 48 hours of travel.

St. Kitts & Nevis

For more information, contact the CVO at PO Box 39, Veterinary Services, Department of Agriculture, Basseterre, St. Kitts, West Indies, ☎ 869-465-2110, fax 869-465-2928.

Crime

 The incidence of crime on the island is relatively low. However, as in most of the Caribbean islands, minor crimes like theft and breaking-and-entering are on the rise, so proper precautions should be taken at all times.

Electricity

 Most of the residences are on a 220-volt current, but many of the hotels have a 110-volt current available. If you are staying in a villa, bring along a converter just in case.

Tipping

 Hotels normally include a 10% service charge in their bills. In restaurants, it's customary to leave a 10-15% gratuity. Tipping taxi drivers is not customary.

Money Matters

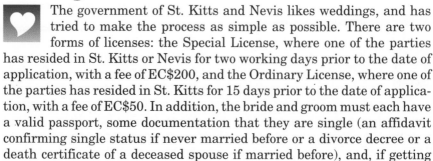 The economy of St. Kitts is based on the Eastern Caribbean dollar, or EC. In addition, the US dollar (but not US coins) is widely accepted at the resorts, restaurants and shops, as are major credit cards. The current rate of exchange is approximately EC$2.70 to US$1. ATMs dispensing US dollars are available at the **Royal Bank of St. Kitts** in Basseterre and at the Marriott hotel. VISA and MasterCard holders can obtain EC at several locations, including 24-hour ATMs at the **Bank of Nova Scotia**, **First Caribbean International**, **Royal Bank of Canada**, **St. Kitts Nevis-Anguilla National Bank**, **Development Bank of St. Kitts**, **RBTT**, **Royal Bank of St. Kitts**, and **Barclays Bank**.

Weddings

The government of St. Kitts and Nevis likes weddings, and has tried to make the process as simple as possible. There are two forms of licenses: the Special License, where one of the parties has resided in St. Kitts or Nevis for two working days prior to the date of application, with a fee of EC$200, and the Ordinary License, where one of the parties has resided in St. Kitts for 15 days prior to the date of application, with a fee of EC$50. In addition, the bride and groom must each have a valid passport, some documentation that they are single (an affidavit confirming single status if never married before or a divorce decree or a death certificate of a deceased spouse if married before), and, if getting married by a priest or minister, a letter from your minister in your home country attesting that you are single and have received religious counseling.

For more information as well as a list of wedding coordinators, see the St. Kitts Tourism Authority website at www.stkitts-tourism.com.

Internet Access

St. Kitts has entered the digital age, and many of the hotels now offer WiFi service for those who can't leave their computers at home. Some, like the Marriott, have an Internet hookup in each room and charge a fee for daily access. Check with your hotel for technology updates.

Communications

Cellular service to the island is provided by Cable & Wireless and Digicel. Since C&W has a reciprocal agreement with some US carriers, you can use your Cingular cell phone in St. Kitts. For others, you may need to get an additional SIM card.

Media

St. Kitts and Nevis has a daily newspaper, the *St. Kitts Sun* (www.sunstkitts.com), and three primary weekly newspapers, *The Democrat* (www.pamdemocrat.org), *The St. Kitts and Nevis Observer* (www.stkittsnevisobserver.com), and *The Labour Spokesman* (www.labourspokesman.com); all are available in print and online. In addition, the prime minister's office publishes the latest information on government initiatives and changes at www.cuopm.org.

Sources of Information

For more information, refer to www.stkitts-tourism.com, the official site of the Tourism Authority. For materials, contact the offices below.

In the US

St. Kitts Tourism Authority, 414 East 75th St, Suite #5, New York, NY 10021, ☎ 212-535-1234, fax 212-734-6511, toll free 800-582-6208; **St. Kitts Embassy**, 3216 New Mexico Ave. NW, Washington, DC 20016-2745, ☎ 202-364-8123, fax 202-364-8126.

In Canada

St. Kitts Tourism Authority, 133 Richmond St W, Suite 311, Toronto, ON M5H 2L3, ☎ 416-368-6707, fax 416-368-3934, toll free 888-395-4887.

St. Kitts & Nevis

In St. Kitts

St. Kitts Tourism Authority, PO Box 132, Pelican Mall, Bay Road, Basseterre, St. Kitts-West Indies, ☎ 869-465-4040, fax 869-465-8794.

Getting Around

As with most of the former British colonies, St. Kitts and Nevis follow the British model of driving on the left. Since both are relatively small islands and it's easy to figure out where everything is, you may want to try the brave new world of "if you're left, you're right" and get a rental car. With the island in the shape of a baseball bat with a high mountain in the middle, you can picture the road. It's one big loop with an extension going down the handle (known as the Southeast Peninsula). There aren't a lot of street signs, but there are some fairly good maps that show all historical points, beaches, and hotels.

Taxis are plentiful, and the drivers are the unofficial guides to the islands, full of interesting facts and figures. They also can tell you a lot about how the islands used to be when sugar was still a mainstay of the economy.

Airport

The **Robert L. Bradshaw International Airport** just underwent significant renovation as part of Kittian initiatives to enhance tourism. You can easily pick up a taxi here, and if you choose you can arrange to pick up your rental car here, although reports are that's not always a reliable choice. It's easier to take a taxi and have the rental agency deliver the car to your hotel or villa. Your taxi driver will know the quickest way to get to your destination, and you won't have to figure out how to get around until after you have rested from the trip.

Taxi Service

Taxis – mostly vans or mini-buses – are everywhere and offer reliable transportation with the added convenience of a knowledgeable guide to the historical and cultural sights.

SAMPLE FARES FOR 1-4 PEOPLE
Airport to Basseterre .... US$12, EC$32
Airport to Frigate Bay hotels .... US$12, EC$32
Airport to Half Moon Bay (Marriott) .... US$10, EC$27
Airport to Dieppe Bay (Rawlins) .... US$22, EC$58
Half-Island Tour......................... US$60, EC$159
Full-Island Tour .... US$80, EC$212 (excluding SE Peninsula)
Basseterre to Turtle Beach.................. US$26, EC$69
Frigate Bay to Ottleys .... $22 US, EC$58
Frigate Bay to Brimstone Hill.............. US$50, EC$133

Car Rentals

Available vehicles range from luxury cars and vans to "jeeps" or mid-sized SUVs. You must obtain a drivers' permit from the Traffic Department for EC$64.80 (about US$24). The car rental agencies can assist with this transaction. You will need a valid license from your home area to obtain a license in St. Kitts. There are eight gas stations scattered about on the island, so you don't need to worry about finding fuel. Gas prices as of late 2006 were about EC$10.50 a gallon, or roughly US$3.90.

MAJOR CAR RENTAL COMPANIES	
Avis Rent-A-Car	☎ 869-465-6507
Courtesy Car Rentals	☎ 869-465-7804
Delisle Walwyn Auto Rentals	☎ 869-465-8449
Sunshine Car Rental	☎ 869-465-2193
Thrifty/TDC Car Rentals	☎ 869-465-2991
G & L Car Rentals	☎ 869-466-8040
Caines Rent-A-Car	☎ 869-465-2366
Hanley's Car Rental	☎ 869-465-0545
Cool Profile	☎ 869-465-4448

Scooter Rentals

If you want to add a little zip to your travels, consider renting a motor scooter. The roads aren't steep here, so this is an easy and fun way to get around. You must obtain a drivers' license just as you would for a car rental. A lot of drivers don't give scooters much respect so you need to exercise caution.

SCOOTER RENTAL AGENCIES	
Fullview Scooter Rentals	☎ 869-465-5123
Island Scooter Rentals	☎ 869-465-8545
Islandwide Scooter Rentals	☎ 869-466-7841
St. Kitts Motorcycle Rental Ltd.	☎ 869-465-5533
Sunny Blue Scooter Rentals	☎ 869-466-3772, smackysmacks@yahoo.com

St. Kitts & Nevis

Exploring

On Foot

Mt. Liamuiga, the 3,792-ft peak at the center of the island, dominates St. Kitts. The peak serves as a huge natural playground where you can follow rainforest paths up to the volcano crater to view its large lake and sulphur vents. The panoramic views of neighboring islands and St. Kitts' coastline from the crater rim are in themselves worth the trip. Tour operators offer a number of trips of varying duration and difficulty.

Mt. Liamuiga

Hiking Tour Operators

Duke of Earl's Adventures has two tours, one for experienced hikers that lasts six hours and goes up to the crater, and a second that spends more time in the rainforest areas and lasts 2½ hours. ☎ 869-465-1899 or 869-663-0994.

Greg's Safaris offers a five-hour Mountain Rainforest Safari trek through a hidden canyon with Indian petroglyphs and a 10-hour rigorous Volcano Safari up to the Mt. Liamuiga crater. ☎ 869-465-4121 or 869-465-5209.

Off the Beaten Path's owner Oliver Spencer leads tours to the ruins of an abandoned coffee plantation. He'll fill you in on the folklore and flora, including traditional herbal remedies, along the way. ☎ 869-465-6314.

On Wheels

Overland Tours

Going overland in St. Kitts primarily involves the rainforest and historic plantation areas; the route is just hilly enough to be fun.

Fun Bikes has guided tours using their all-terrain quad bikes which they promote as being perfect for those who "are adventurous and outgoing." The trips go through rainforests, local villages and rarely-seen plantations. They stop at Lodge Great House, a recently renovated historic plantation now open to the public. Fun Bikes provides all equipment and safety gear, and you get a brief training session on the bikes before you set out. ☎ 869-662-2088, www.stkittsactivities.com.

Greg's Safaris offers a tour that takes you off the beaten path in modified Land Rovers, where you explore the coastal areas of St. Kitts. This tour includes lunch at the Lodge Great House, and takes a total of seven hours (see contact information above).

Jungle Byke Tours has tours through cane fields and up into the rainforest using all-terrain quad bikes. ☎ 869-664-2204.

Scenic or Historic Tours

Between the plantations, the battlements and the modern day sights, there's a great deal to see in St. Kitts. See *Seeing the Sights* later in this chapter for more details. Many taxis drivers are certified as guides by the St. Kitts Tourism Authority (☎ 869-465-4040, www.stkitts-tourism.com), or you can contact the following private tour operators.

Big Banana Tours uses open-sided trucks that can carry up to 20 people on island and rainforest tours. ☎ 869-466-7930, cell 869-663-5115.

Caribbean Journey Masters offers a ton of different tours, including island and plantation tours, hikes up the volcano, and some offbeat tours like Bob & Elvis' Bar Crawl with Dinner tour or a Beer Tasting Tour. ☎ 869-466-8110, cell 869-662-7848, www.caribbeanjourneymasters.com.

Chariot Tours & Taxi Services, owned by Christian Rameshar, does island tours from a long-time resident's point of view. ☎ 869-466-9310, rummustdrink@yahoo.com.

Flamboyant Tours offers full-island and half-island historic and adventure tours, as well as a unique Sugar City Style cultural evening tour and a City and Beach Tour where you shop and tan all in one trip. ☎ 869-466-3910, www.tdclimited.com/tours.

Grey's Island Excursions, run by Thenford Grey, uses high-roof, 16-seat air-conditioned vans for knowledgeable tours around the island. It's the complete circuit, and he can tailor the stops and narration to your particular group. ☎ 869-465-2152, cell 869-664-7972, thenang06@yahoo.com.

Kantours operates a fleet of taxis that take visitors on historic tours of Basseterre, Brimstone Hill, Romney Manor and other sites. They also guide hikes up Mt. Liamuiga and offer snorkeling and dive tours. ☎ 869-465-2098, 869-465-3054, www.kantours.com.

Royston Tours is run by Royston Stevens, a highly recommended tour guide who really knows the island. He will customize tours to your particular interests. ☎ 869-663-4529, www3.sympatico.ca/dougjp/royston.html.

Tropical Tours has a full range of tours on land and sea, including a 3½-hour island tour that hits all the highlights. ☎ 869-465-4039, www.tropicalstkitts-nevis.com.

By Train

One of the most unusual and interesting ways to see St. Kitts, especially with reference to its sugar plantation past, is to take the **St. Kitts Scenic Railway**. This narrow-gauge railway was built from 1912-1926 to transport cane from the fields to the mill in Basseterre. The tracks have been refurbished and luxurious railcars brought in to make this a major attraction. The 30-mile trip winds through villages, abandoned sugar estates and farms, and skirts the base of Mt. Liamuiga, so you get a complete view of the interior of the island. The rail cars are double-decked, with an open-air observation deck up top, and an air-conditioned lower lounge with a service bar and restroom. Entertainment and a colorful narrative history of the island are presented during the 3½-hour trip. ☎ 869-465-7263, www.stkittsscenicrailway.com.

By Bicycle

Mountain bikes or all-terrain quad bikes are a great way to explore the trails up into the rainforests or through the cane fields. There are two companies in St. Kitts that rent this type of transportation: **Fun Bikes** (ATVs), ☎ 869-466-3202, or **Meadville Bike Rental**, ☎ 869-469-5235.

On Water

Scuba Diving

St. Kitts' incredible array of undersea sites are mostly off the leeward western and southwestern shores of the island. **Paradise Reef**, which lies off the coast adjacent to Brimstone Hill, is the island's only marine reserve, and is very popular with divers. Rays, turtles, sharks, barracudas, lobsters, eels and a wide vari-

Royal gramma (Clark Anderson/Aquaimages)

ety of fish are seen in sites ranging from 30 to 120 feet. There are about 400 wrecks ringing the island, and lots of striking coral, vents and other structures to make dives interesting. St. Kitts' law forbids unsupervised divers, so you must be accompanied by one of the dive instructors on the island.

Dive St. Kitts has teamed up with Bird Rock Beach Hotel to offer special stay-and-dive packages. As with all the operators, they have their own special, little-used sites they take clients to explore, and have a full range of PADI classes and equipment. ☎ 869-465-1189, www.divestkitts.com.

Kenneth's Dive Center has 40-ft and 50-ft custom dive cats and a 32-ft speedboat to use for tours to sites off St. Kitts and Nevis. Owner Kenneth Samuel has been diving in St. Kitts for over 35 years and has full PADI instructor certification. He can provide instructions, equipment and gear as well as tours. ☎ 869-465-2670 or 869-465-7043, www.kenneth-divecenter.com.

Pro Divers has a 38-ft dive catamaran and a 34-ft V-hull powerboat for tours. They also offer a full range of PADI courses. The dive shop at the Ocean Terrace Inn in Basseterre has all the equipment and gear you need. If you're not sure you want to dive, Pro Divers'

Wreck of the MV River Taw
(Clark Anderson / Aquaimages)

free introductory class, offered two days a week, may help you decide. ☎ 869-466-DIVE (3483), www.prodiversstkitts.com (see this site for details on the 19 major dive sites around the islands).

St. Kitts Scuba and dive master Barry Svendsen offer all types of courses and dives and will pick up customers from the major resorts. ☎ 869-466-8744, www.sttkittsscuba.com.

Snorkeling

Many of the dive sites include shallow areas where snorkelers can see an abundance of life, including turtles, rays and the usual shallow reef denizens. The dive operators mentioned above offer snorkeling tours and provide equipment. Also, most water tour companies include snorkeling in their daily activities, and provide equipment on board. In addition, the major tour operators like **Caribbean Journey Masters** and **Tropical Tours** have kayak and snorkeling trips and provide all equipment.

If you have your own gear and want to go it alone, there are interesting reefs off the shores of Belle Tete, Dieppe Bay and White House Bay beaches.

Flamingo tongue skeet on a sea fan
(Clark Anderson/Aquaimages)

Marine Park: The newly constructed **Marine World** at South Friar's Bay is a four-acre park with a stingray lagoon, dolphin encounters, watersports center, aviary, and restaurant. A break wall enclosure was built out into the bay to limit impacts on the shoreline and surrounding ecosystem, while still providing a natural setting for the dolphins and rays.

Watersports

 Taking a sail around the island may be okay for one day, but you really want to get *in* the water. All of the resorts provide non-motorized equipment like kayaks, Hobie Cats and sunfish; for a faster pace, you can rent jet skis from **Mister X Watersports**, next to the Timothy Beach Resort. ☎ 869-762-3983, www.mrxshiggidyshack.com. You can also rent kayaks and snorkeling equipment at **Turtle Beach Bar & Restaurant**. ☎ 869-469-7611, www.turtlebeach1.com.

Water Tours

The waters off the southwestern peninsula see a lot of action from boat tours, since the water is clear, reefs for snorkeling are plentiful, and the vistas to St. Kitts and Nevis are beautiful.

Banana Boat Tours offers sunset cruises and snorkeling trips on a 34-ft inflatable Scarib boat. They also are available for private charters and St. Kitts-to-Nevis transfers. ☎ 869-465-0645, www.bananaboattours.com.

Blue Water Safaris' fleet of custom catamarans are used for sunset, moonlight, party and other fun tours as well as private charters. They usually include a stop at one of the reefs for snorkeling, and have all equipment on board. ☎ 869-466-4933, www.bluewatersafaris.com.

CatFanTaSea is the catamaran trip offered by Caribbean Journey Masters on their own boat, with a stop for lunch at Pinney's Beach in Nevis. ☎ 869-466-8110, www.caribbeanjourneymasters.com.

Turtle Tours specializes in eco-tours in kayaks along the southeastern peninsula starting at Turtle Beach. Tour guides point out the sights, such as turtles, pelicans, cormorants, frigate birds, wild mountain goats and monkeys. They also provide stops for snorkeling. For the uninitiated, they can give introductory snorkeling lessons. ☎ 869-469-9094.

Wahoo Water Tours does the complete tour, with sailing, snorkeling and a barbecue. ☎ 869-465-7474.

Deep-Sea Fishing

 Off the shores of St. Kitts and Nevis are reefs and canyons where large fish thrive, making this a prime destination for deep-sea fishing. Among the fish you'll snare are wahoo, marlin, yellow fin and black fin tuna, mahi-mahi and kingfish.

No Problem Boat Charter offers the expertise of captains Larry Betance and Jonathan Winterburn aboard the 35-ft *Miss Ashley* sport fisher, with all the latest gadgets such as GPS. They take you out to depths between 300 and 3,000 feet. Full- and half-day charters are for two to six people, and they'll even fillet some of your catch for dinner. ☎ 869-466-4933 or 869-466-7515, www.fishstkittsandnevis.com.

Caribbean Journey Masters offers four- and eight-hour fishing trips where you can haul in the big ones. ☎ 869-466-8110, www.caribbean-journeymasters.com.

Kantours has a small open fisherman's boat with canopy or a larger Cabin Cruiser dedicated to fishing trips. ☎ 869-465-2098, 869-465-3054, www.kantours.com.

Tropical Tours offers a 4½-hour morning or a three-hour afternoon trip out to the deep waters for mackerel, snapper, king-fish, dolphin, wahoo or barracuda. ☎ 869-465-4039, www.tropicalstkitts-nevis.com.

Boat Charters

The major tour operators mentioned previously have connections to many of the boat charter operators and can set up what you need. In addition, **Leeward Island Charters** has two 70-ft catamarans perfect for day cruises. They come with refreshments, music and great hospitality. ☎ 869-465 7474, www.leewardislandcharters.com.

Tropical Dreamer, a glass-bottom sailing catamaran, is also available for charters. ☎ 869-465-8224.

VIP Charters offers day charters as well as circumnavigation tours, snorkeling trips, and, of course, fishing trips, aboard a 48-ft luxury sport fishing yacht called *Reel Thing*. ☎ 869-762-5410, www.vipcharters.net.

If you want quick passage to Nevis (it's only two miles away) or a day of fishing in an informal setting, a few boats are available for charter at the dock in front of **Turtle Beach Bar & Grill** (☎ 869-469-7611, www.turtlebeach1.com) at the southernmost end of the island.

St. Kitts & Nevis

On Horseback

Tropical Tours and **Caribbean Journey Masters** (see details above) offer horseback rides through rainforest and cane fields. In addition, **Trinity Stables** (☎ 869-465-3226) provides guides for horseback beach rides and trips into the rainforest.

Playing & Watching Sports

Golf

The major course on St. Kitts is the **Royal St. Kitts Golf Course**, situated between Frigate Bay and the Marriott hotel. The course is host to the St. Kitts Open in early June, and in 2005 started a Pro-Am tournament. They also offer the Royal Golf Academy, with instruction for all levels of skill by PGA certified instructors. The course plays as an 18-hole, par 71 course at 6,900 yards from the back tees. It's a beautifully landscaped and scenic course, with water hazards, lots of palm trees, and holes on both the windward and leeward sides of the island. You can play nine or 18 holes, with rates varying in low and high season. Guests at the Marriott next door get a reduced rate. They have a three- and five-day pass, a seven-day weekly pass, and lower fees for twilight play (after 2 pm). ☎ 869-466-2700 or toll-free in the US 866-STK-GOLF, www.royalstkittsgolfclub.com.

Royal St. Kitts Golf Course

The newest 18-hole course on the island is **La Vallee**. The plans are to develop an entire community around the course, including villas and a hotel.

Golfers also visit Nevis, to play on the **Four Seasons**' legendary Robert Trent Jones 18-hole course. The views to the Caribbean Sea are beautiful, and the course is quite challenging. ☎ 869-469-1111.

Tennis

 There are courts at **Ottley's Plantation**, **the Sugar Bay Club**, **Rawlins Plantation** (grass), and the **St. Kitts Marriott**. Check with the hotels to see what their non-guest fees are to play a set or two.

Horseracing

 Horseracing has always been big in the Caribbean, and the new **Beaumont Park Racetrack**, located in Dieppe Bay, is generating new excitement for the sport on St. Kitts and throughout the region. In addition to a six-furlong thoroughbred racing track, they also have a greyhound racing park. Other amenities include a private Jockey Club, restaurant, bar, day room for children, as well as TV broadcasts of major sports events and simulcast racing from around the world. ☎ 869-465-1627, www.beaumontpark.kn.

Race fans also visit Nevis on holidays when races are held at the **Indian Castle Racetrack**. Check the Nevis information on page 352 for more details.

Cricket

As in all the Caribbean islands, watching cricket – and cheering on or bemoaning the state of the West Indies team – is a national pastime. The main cricket grounds at the **Warner Park stadium** were recently renovated in anticipation of the ICC Cricket World Cup matches played there in March 2007. The stadium seats 8,000 spectators and has new facilities for the media and players. It will be the scene for international test matches as well as regional play. Check local papers for the schedule of matches.

Seeing the Sights

Sampling the Culture

As with most of the Leewards, St. Kitts' heritage and culture derives from the history of sugar plantations, slavery and European colonialism. What survives is a colorful, multifaceted celebration of music, dance, costume and food displayed most effectively at **Carnival** time. This annual celebration during the Christmas season features clowns, stilted figures called "Moko Jumbies," Big Drum Bands, dramatic presentations, Masquerade, calypso bands, pageants, an early morning celebration called "Jump Up" or "J'Ouevert" (pronounced Juvee), and West Indian food and lots of it (for a more detailed explanation of the various components, see www.stkittsculture.org). The festivities begin mid-December and last

Downtown Basseterre
(Clark Anderson / Aquaimages)

through New Year's Day, so if you are planning to be on the island during this time, take full advantage of this amazing cultural exposure. See www.stkittscarnival.com for a complete schedule of events.

The love of costuming and color carries through in one of St. Kitts' developing industries, **fashion design**. In recent years, St. Kitts-based designers have distinguished themselves throughout the world of fashion. Look for designs by **Caribelle Batik**, John Warden's **Island to Island** fashions, Judith Rawlins and her **Brown Sugar** line, Patrice Bartlette with **Raymonde Signature Designs**, and Sandra Bowry and her **Fashion Caribe** line. For an up-close look at the art of batik, stop by **Romney Manor**, where Caribelle artisans demonstrate how these colorful graphic fabrics are created with the clever use of dyes and beeswax.

The **St. Christopher Heritage Society** is tasked with keeping the artifacts of culture and history alive, and is working to create the **National Museum** at the Old Treasury Building.

The Crafthouse provides a workshop and resource center for the nation's cottage industry of local craft production. You can see some of the products at this facility in the **CAP Southwell Industrial Park**, as well as at vendors' booths throughout the island.

St. Kitts Music Festival

What started out in 1996 as a celebration of local music has turned into a major international music event that attracts artists and audiences from around the globe. This four-day event held in late June features a mix of music, from Caribbean soca and American R&B to African rhythms and gospel music. Past headliners have included Shaggy, Air Supply, Dionne Warwick, and Yolanda Adams, as well as Caribbean reggae and soca stars. For information on coming festivals and the talent line-ups, see www.stkittsmusicfestival.net.

Reliving History

There is no escaping history on this island, as witnessed by the 200 historical sites here. Among the most popular are:

Brimstone Hill. The British built this fortress to repel the French from the island. It stands high above Basseterre, surprisingly well preserved and worth the hike up the steps to the top. There the panorama makes it all worthwhile.

Bastion at Brimstone Hill
(discover-st-kitts-nevis-beaches.com / Amicia Mussenden)

Basseterre. Many of the buildings surrounding Independence Square are original 17th-century structures, and all have colorful tales to tell. The square itself was the center for slave trading, and surrounding buildings such as the Georgian House warehoused slaves and were integral to the commerce of the city.

Basseterre (J. Stephen Conn)

Plantations. There are still plantations to be seen around the island in addition to those converted to hotels. The most notable structures still existing are the **Lodge** and **Shadwell Great Houses** and the **Belmont Estate Yard**.

Churches. Religious structures are key to any history, and on St. Kitts they reflect the battles between the English, French and Spanish forces. The Roman Catholic **Church of the Immaculate Conception**, built in

St. Kitts & Nevis

1927, replaced an earlier church built around 1856. The **St. George's Anglican Church** dates back to 1848.

Bloody Point. In 1626, the British and French colonies on the island had reached a size that was intolerable to the native Caribs, who liked raiding and pillaging. In a final resolution at Bloody Point, the colonists massacred the Indians, ending the cycle of raids and paving the way for truly settled communities.

Half Way Tree Village. When the established British colony allowed a French ship to stop and make repairs after a battle with a Spanish warship, they opened the door for the French to settle on the island. By the mid-1600s, amity turned into suspicion and the island was divided, using a large tamarind tree in Half Way Tree Village as the marker. It remained a point of contention until the whole ownership business was settled in the 19th century.

Where to Stay

Luxury With Limits

$$$$ – These resorts range from a massive American-chain resort to charming plantation inns. They are self-contained and offer rates ranging from US$420-$525 in high season, and US$350-400 in low season, European Plan.

St. Kitts Marriott Resort & Royal Beach Casino

The construction of this large Marriott changed the ambiance and image of St. Kitts forever. It consists of a five-story hotel above a sprawling collection of villas that extend to the Atlantic at North Frigate Bay. There is a wide selection of room sizes and styles, eight restaurants, and a choice of activities, including a Vegas-style casino, a 15,000-sq-ft spa and fitness center, three pools, and an adjacent golf course. It's all marble and glass, with luxury baths and bed linens, but it's still a Marriott and not really an authentic local experience; it would be a mistake to just stay on the property and not venture out to see the real St. Kitts.

Basseterre (J. Stephen Conn)

Location: North Frigate Bay, Atlantic side.

Rooms: 523 rooms and 113 suites, with luxury marble baths, refrigerators, private balconies, AC, TV, and Internet access (fee).

Rates: EP only.

Features: Eight restaurants, three lounges including dance club and cigar and rum bar, 35,000-sq-ft Royal Beach Casino, three pools, Jacuzzi, Kids' Club, Teens Game Room, beach, Emerald Mist Spa, two tennis courts.

☎ 869 466 1200, 800-228-9290 US and Canada, fax 869 466 1201, www.stkittsmarriott.com.

Ottley's Plantation Inn

This beautiful gem of a small hotel is family-run and exemplifies the best of St. Kitts. Originally a 17th-century sugar plantation, the estate has been converted into a restful retreat where you are pampered at every turn. From the breakfast where each plate is a visual delight, to the rooms furnished in English colonial style, you are surrounded by

Ottley's Plantation Inn

beauty. While not directly on a beach, they have a free shuttle that takes you to Hermitage Bay nearby.

Location: Mid-island, just outside Lodge village.

Rooms: 24 standard, super-deluxe and supreme rooms, two-room Royal Suite cottages (some with private plunge pools), three-bedroom Grand Villa, all with AC in bedrooms. TVs available upon request for some rooms.

Rates: AI, MAP or EP.

Features: Royal Palm Restaurant, spring-fed pool, shuttle to beach and Basseterre, hard-surface tennis court, croquet lawn, Mango Orchard Spa.

☎ 869-465-7234, 800-772-3039 US, fax 869-465-4760, www.ottleys.com.

Rawlins Plantation Inn

As you pass miles of cane fields, you wonder if you'll ever reach this sedate inn on the northern end of the island. But the trip is well worth it. The cottages have views to the sea and Nevis, and are furnished in mahogany antiques and enclosed by wood shutters. You may have to walk through a

Rawlins Plantation Inn

visiting herd of cows, and you are warned to close and secure the shutters at night lest the monkeys make a raid, so you know you are really "out there." The overall ambiance is serene and relaxed, the food in the restaurant is excellent, and service is first-rate. The owners are adding on to the resort with new villas, but they are being built in England and assembled on-site to minimize the impact to visitors. They have also purchased the land between the existing resort and the sea, so look for beach facilities and further favorable developments.

Location: Northern coast, just past Dieppe Bay Towne.

Rooms: 10 in all, with deluxe cottage rooms, deluxe garden cottage, honeymoon suite in old sugar mill, two-bedroom garden suite cottage, and two-bedroom deluxe garden cottage, individually decorated with mahogany reproductions and antiques, private bath, ceiling fans and verandahs.

Rates: EP or MAP.

Features: Restaurant, spring-fed pool, grass tennis court, croquet court.

☎ 869-465-6221, fax 869-465-4954, www.rawlinsplantation.com.

Reasonable & Comfortable Hotels

$$$ – Accommodations in this range include a small inn and a full-service resort, ranging from US$300-$450 in high season, and US$150-$300 in low season.

Golden Lemon Inn

This romantic inn sits on a beautiful windward-side, reef-protected beach and features the design excellence of Arthur Leaman, former decorating editor for *House and Garden* magazine. He built the main house on the stone foundation of the original 17th-century house, and then added one- and two-bedroom villas with plunge pools. Just recently, he redecorated, keeping the period furniture and adding to the charm with bright colors in contemporary patterns. The inn has been recognized by major travel magazines as one of the most romantic in the Caribbean. No children under 18 years of age permitted.

Location: Dieppe Bay, northeast end of the island.

Rooms: 26 in all, in single or double rooms in the Great House and one- and two-bedroom villas; some air-conditioned bedrooms are available.

Rates: AI or EP.

Features: Restaurant, pool, beach.

☎ 869-465-7260, fax 869-465-4019, www.goldenlemon.com.

Golden Lemon Inn (Cynthia Blair)

Sugar Bay Club

Located in the busy Frigate Bay area, this family-friendly low-rise resort offers comfortable lodgings in a centralized location. It's a self-contained resort with windward-side beach and a landscaped pool with waterfall forming the center of the property. The pool-view cottage suites have a separate living room and a small porch, and the oceanfront rooms open right on the beach.

Location: North Frigate Bay.

Rooms: 20 garden, 40 poolside, 18 oceanfront rooms and 22 poolside cottage suites, all with refrigerators, private terraces or balconies, AC, TVs.

Rates: AI or EP.

Features: Two restaurants, two bars, two pools, Children's Club, beach, tennis court and fitness center.

☎ 869-465-8037, 800-858-4618 US, fax 869-465-6745, www.sugarbayclub.com.

Sugar Bay Club

Good Value Hotels

$$ – Accommodations in this range are room-only and offer good value as well as some nice sea views. Rates range from US$200-$280 in high season, and US$150-$200 in low.

Frigate Bay Resort

Frigate Bay Resort

This 64-room resort sits on a hillside overlooking the Caribbean. It's done in the plantation style, although not with the charm of the original plantation inns. Families will be comfortable in a two-bedroom condominium suite with a full kitchen, living and dining areas, two full baths, and two balconies. It's a three-minute walk to Frigate Bay beach on the Caribbean.

Location: Southern Frigate Bay area.

Rooms: 64 total, in hillside and poolside rooms, poolside studios, one- and two-bedroom condominium suites, all with ceiling fans, AC and TV. The studios and suites have full kitchens plus living and dining areas. Internet access can be added to the room for a fee.

Rates: EP with BP and MAP packages available.

Features: Pool, adjacent to golf course.

☎ 869-465-8935, 800-266-2185 US, fax 869-465-7050, www.frigatebay. com.

Ocean Terrace Inn

This hotel has the advantage of sitting right on the edge of Basseterre overlooking the harbor and the disadvantage of being in an area where there is no beach. Places to shop and dine in the

Ocean Terrace Inn

city are an easy stroll away, and there are beautiful views of Nevis and the downtown area from the room balconies. The 71-room hotel has three restaurants, a fantasy pool with a waterfall and Jacuzzi, and other nice touches.

Location: Basseterre.

Rooms: 71 rooms, including standard, superior, superior one-bedroom suites and deluxe rooms based on view and size; all are equipped with coffee/tea service, refrigerators and dataports, AC, TV.

Rates: EP.

Features: Three restaurants, three bars, three pools, fitness and health club, car rental and dive shop on-site.

☎ 869-465-2754, 800-524-0512 US, fax 869-465-1057, www. oceanterraceinn.com.

Timothy Beach Resort

Timothy Beach Resort is identified by the distinctive blue buildings nestled into the side of a hill on Frigate Bay Beach, with a beautiful view of the sunsets. Built as a condominium resort, the units are now available for vacation rentals so there are some very comfortable accommodations for families or those requiring a full kitchen and home-like atmosphere.

Timothy Beach Resort

Location: Frigate Bay Beach.

Rooms: Mountain-view and ocean-view rooms; studio, large studio, one- and two-bedroom suites, and two-bedroom townhouse apartment are available. All have balconies, AC and TV; studios and suites have full kitchens and living and dining areas.

Rates: EP.

Features: Restaurant, ocean-side pool, watersports, adjacent to golf course.

☎ 869-465-8597, 877-94-BEACH (US), 800-288-7991 Canada, fax 869-466-7085, timothybeach.com.

No-Frills Hotels

$ – These are low-cost accommodations in the range of US$100-$125 in high season, US$80-$100 in low season.

St. Kitts & Nevis

Bird Rock Beach

Bird Rock Beach

This small hotel is on a secluded beach at the edge of Frigate Bay. All rooms look out over the Caribbean, either toward Basseterre or toward Nevis. The rates are reasonable and the two- and three-bedroom suites make it ideal for a large family.

Location: Frigate Bay, near Basseterre.

Rooms: Superior rooms with king beds, and studio, one- , two- and three-bedroom suites. All have balconies, AC and TV; suites have kitchens and sitting areas.

Rates: EP.

Features: Two restaurants, pool, watersports, Dive St. Kitts on-site.

☎ 869-465-8914, 888-358-6870 US & Canada, fax 869-465-1675, www.birdrockbeach.com.

Palms Hotel

This neat, nicely decorated hotel in Basseterre can serve as a base for all sorts of activities, from shopping to historic tours and beach days. Its 12 suites have all the basic requirements, including television, air conditioning and Internet access.

Location: Downtown Basseterre.

Rooms: 12 in all, including junior, one- and two-bedroom suites with coffeemaker, minibar, AC, TV and Internet access.

Rates: EP.

Features: Bar, walking distance to restaurants and shopping.

☎ 869-465-0800, fax 869-465-5889, www.palmshotel.com.

Villa Resorts

Villa resorts, or villatels, as they are called, are the coming thing in St. Kitts. There are many projects underway, with villas for sale now and the promise of extensive amenities added when the villas are mostly sold and the hotel on the property is built. Most are in the Frigate Bay area near the Marriott, but the large and relatively undeveloped Southeastern Peninsula will be the site of many more of these in the future.

Island Paradise Village is a sedate condominium development on the North Frigate Bay beach next to Sugar Bay Club. The units are available with one, two or three bedrooms, and amenities include a pool. ☎ 869-465-8035, fax 869-465-8236, www.islandparadisevillage.com.

Sealofts is adjacent to the Royal St. Kitts Golf Club. The property is on the beach and offers unusual tri-level villas where the bottom level is a pedestal containing a shower and laundry, and the bedrooms are on the top two floors. The complex has two tennis courts and a pool. ☎ 869-465-2075, fax 869-466-5034, www.sealofts.com.

St. Christopher's Club is an ambitious multi-use project under development with privately owned condominium units available for vacation rentals. On the North Frigate Bay beach, it has a pool and is immediately adjacent to the Royal St. Kitts Golf Club. Plans are to add a hotel, restaurant, casino, tennis courts and shopping arcade, so check the extent of development at the time you are planning to go.
☎ 869-465-4854, fax 869-465-6466, www.stchristopherclub.com.

Individual Villas & Condo Rentals

There are many private villas on the island, and more are being added every day. Check the **St. Kitts Tourism Authority** website for a few of these (www.stkitts-tourism.com), **St. Kitts Realty** (www.stkittsrealty.com), or **B. Kassab & Associates Realtors** (www.bkassab.com) for availabilities.

Buying in Paradise

If your dream is to own a piece of paradise, now is the time to act. Four Seasons, Newfound Property International, Auberge and other big names in resort real estate are building new luxury developments that start with villa sales and then progress into full resorts with a hotel and all its amenities. St. Kitts is an international banking center, and has come up with a way for land purchasers to have Kittian passports and rights as full citizens (see www.skbfinancialservices.com for a full explanation of this). Developments open for tours and sales include Kittian Heights and La Vallee developments on the north coast, Calypso Bay Resort, Ocean's Edge and Half Moon Heights in the center of the island, Sundance Ridge and the 1,700-acre Auberge development on the Southeast Peninsula, Turtle Beach Estates on the southernmost end of the island, and on Nevis, the Four Seasons Resort Estates. The really good news is after all this construction is done, St. Kitts and Nevis will have significantly more hotel and villa accommodations available for the vacation traveler.

St. Kitts & Nevis

Guest Houses

These accommodations include breakfast and offer extremely low-cost daily rates – from $40 to $60 for a one-bedroom unit.

Culture House is a three-story building on Conaree Bay that offers en-suite rooms (private bathroom included), a restaurant, bar, and meeting facilities. The rooms are simply furnished. ☎ 869-466-1940, www.stkittsculturehouse.com.

Inner Circle Guest House is the creation of event promoter DJ Morrishaw, and features simple one or two bedrooms in a complex that is used for various entertainment events. ☎ 869-466-5857, www.djmorrishaw.com.

Day Spas

The Body Haven Spa & Beauty Store emphasizes well-being and rejuvenation. It offers massages, hand and foot reflexology, hand collagen treatments, pedicures, paraffin treatments for hands and feet and beauty services. The spa is in The Sands complex on Newtown Bay Road. ☎ 869-465-4418, www.sknvibes.com/bodyhaven.

Emerald Mist Spa is a sleek full-service spa and fitness center occupying 15,000 square feet at the Marriott. The spa offers a range of health and beauty treatments, including massage, body scrubs, body wraps, therapy baths, facials, manicures/pedicures, paraffin hand treatments and waxing. Other facilities in the spa include a sauna, hot and cold tubs, steam room and hair salon. The fitness center provides counseling as well as fitness and yoga classes. ☎ 869-466-1200, ext 7630.

The **Mango Orchard Spa** is a new addition to the Ottley's Plantation Inn. The first-class spa is housed in a small and brightly painted chattel house surrounded by fantastic tropical greenery. You can opt to have a massage in the gazebo where you'll feel as if you're right in the rainforest, looking out for monkeys. Among the services are massage, body wraps, manicures, pedicures and facials. ☎ 869-465-7234, www.ottleys.com.

Dining Around St. Kitts

While you won't find any super-premium, high-style restaurants (yet), St. Kitts offers a great selection of dining choices. Dressing up means "casual elegance." The fancy restaurants are still relaxed and, in many cases, very romantic, with views and gorgeous settings. Many of them are in hotels, and the ones at the plantation inns are especially good. There are also a lot of good lunch spots in downtown Basseterre.

RESTAURANT PRICE CHART	
$	Cheap eats, normally quick meals or take-out foods; US$8 or less per entrée.
$$	Good value, lots of West Indian cuisine; US$9-$14 for a plate of food.
$$$	A nice place with gourmet aspirations; US$15-$24 for a satisfying entrée.
$$$$	Positively elegant, usually requiring some dressing up; entrées range from US$25 to $50, depending on the island.

Dressing Up to Eat Out

Diana's Restaurant

The atmosphere is romantic and the food has a distinct French influence, following the resort owners' guiding philosophy of "love, life and happiness." $$. Bird Rock Beach Resort. Open for breakfast, lunch and dinner. ☎ 869-465-8914, www.birdrockbeach.com.

The Golden Lemon Inn

Arthur Leaman brings the same elegant good taste that distinguishes his inn to this restaurant. Many of the recipes have been featured in *Bon Appetit*, and the settings on the front terrace or inside in the dining room hark back to more elegant times. $$$. Dieppe Bay. Open for breakfast, lunch, dinner and Sunday brunch. ☎ 869-465-7260, www.goldenlemon. com.

Marshalls

This elegant restaurant poolside at the Horizons Villa Resort offers classic seafood such as pan roasted Chilean sea bass and grilled lobster or shrimp plus steak, rack of lamb and duck breast. The desserts are worth the extra calories. $$$. Horizons Villas, Southeast Peninsula. Open for dinner. ☎ 869-466-8245, www.marshalls-stkitts.com.

Rawlins Plantation Inn

Sitting on the patio overlooking the lawn and cane fields that lead to the sea, you get an overwhelming sense of what life used to be like in St. Kitts. The restaurant is outstanding, with one seating for four courses at dinner, and a very popular West Indian buffet for lunch. It's one of those "don't miss it" experiences. $$$. Northern end of the island. Open for lunch and dinner. ☎ 869-465-6221, www.rawlinsplantation.com.

Royal Grille Steakhouse

If you're not staying at the Marriott, plan an evening here at this elegant steakhouse, and then move into the casino for some fun before going back to your hotel or villa. The menu includes prime beef and seafood, classically prepared. $$$. Frigate Bay. Open for dinner only. ☎ 869-466-1200.

St. Kitts & Nevis

The Royal Palm at Ottley's

This upscale restaurant is set within the stone walls of an old sugar factory. Bouquets brighten each table, and the cuisine features tastes from around the world. The Sunday Champagne Brunch is a stand-out. $$$. Near Lodge, on the eastern coast. Open for breakfast, lunch, dinner and Sunday brunch. ☎ 869-465-7234, www.ottleys.com.

Waterfalls

Taking advantage of a beautiful setting overlooking Basseterre, this patio restaurant is highlighted by waterfalls, of course. The cuisine is described as a modern interpretation of classic Continental and West Indian tastes. They offer a West Indian buffet on Friday evenings and Sunday afternoons. $$$. Basseterre. ☎ 869-465-2754, www.oceanterraceinn.com.

Relaxing on the Water

Blu Seafood

Blu Seafood

This newly-renovated terraced restaurant on the beach at the Marriott offers a stellar selection of seafood. Dinner starts with a complimentary signature "Blu Wave" aperitif. $$$. Marriott, Frigate Bay. Open for breakfast and lunch seasonally and dinner daily. ☎ 869-466-1200

Fisherman's Wharf

Overlooking the lights of Basseterre, this restaurant lets you sample the best of the local seafood in a relaxed setting (the picnic tables are a clue to the dress code). The conch chowder is a specialty. In addition to grilled fish, they serve steak and chicken. $$. Ocean Terrace Inn, Basseterre. ☎ 869-465-2754, www.oceanterraceinn. com.

Sunset Café

Sunset-watching is a major activity at this pleasant café tucked into the Timothy Beach Resort. Frigate Bay. ☎ 869-465-8597.

Turtle Beach Bar & Grill

You know you are in a really special place when you see the giant (and alive) pig standing by the walkway into the restaurant. You may question just how special when a curious monkey glides through the rafters of the dining room perusing your dinner. But it's all in good fun at this popular beach bar that offers grilled fish and lobster, ribs and burgers. $$. Far end of the Southeast Peninsula, near Nevis. Open for lunch and dinner. ☎ 869-469-7611, www.turtlebeach1.com.

Turtle Beach Bar & Grill

Ethnic Foods & Favorites

The Ballahoo Restaurant

This long-standing downtown restaurant is a favorite meeting place. It's breezy and bright, and it overlooks the Circus at the center of Basseterre. The food is a mix of burgers, salads, pastas, seafood and vegetarian dishes. $$. Downtown Basseterre. Open for breakfast, lunch and dinner. ☎ 869-465-4197, www.ballahoo.com.

King's Palace

This favorite Chinese restaurant is elegant and enjoyable. The menu is extensive and there is usually a long list of specials to choose from as well. $$. Porte Zante complex, Basseterre. Open for lunch and dinner. ☎ 869-466-3685.

PJ's Restaurant

PJ's is all about Italian, so you'll find pasta and pizza on the menu. There is a loyal clientele who come here for the hand-rolled pasta and freshly made bread. Takeout is available. $$. Frigate Bay. Open for dinner, Tuesday through Sunday. ☎ 869-465-8373.

Star of India

This is the only Indian restaurant on the island, and it offers the usual fare of curries and tandoori selections. They put out a popular Friday buffet and are open on Sundays and holidays. $. Victoria Road, Basseterre. Open for lunch and dinner. ☎ 869-466-1537.

Stonewalls Tropical Bar & Eating Place

The name is a nod to the thick walls that encircle the dining area, and the food is basic Caribbean pub – ribs, grilled fish and steak. It's a relaxed atmosphere in a garden setting, near the historic district of Basseterre. $$. Princess Street, Basseterre. Open for dinner only. ☎ 869-465-5248.

West Indian Cooking

Manhattan Gardens

This bright gingerbread cottage is hard to miss, and the food from owner-chef Rosalind Walters is pure Caribbean, including grilled lobster. She offers a Saturday night Caribbean Food Fest and a Sunday barbecue. Be sure to make reservations, because she doesn't open on the days when she has no reservations. $$. Old Road Town. Open for lunch and dinner. ☎ 869-465-9121.

Oasis Café

In a garden setting that includes a tiki bar, you'll find this small but interesting café good for a filling breakfast or lunch. $$. TDC Mall on Fort Street, Basseterre. Open for breakfast and lunch. ☎ 869-465-7065.

Spratnet

Ask a Kittian what is his or her favorite restaurant, and they will direct you here. It's an unassuming little place by the side of the road (watch so you don't miss it), and you are guaranteed to get authentic West Indian cooking. $. Old Road, in Basseterre. Open for dinner. ☎ 869-466-7535.

Serendipity Restaurant & Lounge Bar

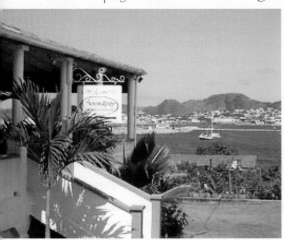

Serendipity Restaurant

Situated on the Fortlands highlands overlooking Basseterre Bay, this relaxed restaurant offers memorable meals featuring dishes with Caribbean flavorings. Among the lunch entrées are Caribbean bouillabaisse and coconut coated tiger shrimp along with burgers, pastas and salads; dinner entrées are equally eclectic. $$. Fortlands, above Basseterre. Open for lunch and dinner. ☎ 869-465-9999, www. serendipitystkitts.com.

Quick Bites

Bambu's Café

For a quick lunch while shopping in Basseterre this is a good bet. In addition to burgers, they offer conch fritters and other West Indian staples. $$.

Bank Street, near the Circus in Basseterre. Open for lunch and dinner. ☎ 869-466-5280.

Gourmet Galley Deli

This full-service deli/restaurant/pizzeria is a first for the island. Among the selections are calzones, fresh bread and pastries, deli meats, cheeses and various coffees and teas. They also do condo provisioning, and will fill your kitchen with a customized list of goodies. $$. Frigate Bay, Sugar's complex. Open for breakfast, lunch and dinner. ☎ 869-465-4049.

Shopping

Between the Circus area of downtown Basseterre and the new duty-free shops of Port Zante, shoppers have a wealth of selections. Within a three-block area in Basseterre alone you can cruise through **Island Hopper** for gorgeous silks and batiks, **Glass Island** for locally made glass jewelry and art pieces, **Island Fever** for resort wear, and **Ashburry's Duty Free** for watches, jewelry, fine china and leather goods.

Port Zante Complex

Shops at Port Zante include **Diamonds International, Dupont Jewelry, Kay's Fine Jewelry, Linen & Gold, St. Kitts Rum Shop, Amina Crafts Market**, and **Island Treasures**.

Other shopping centers include the enclosed **Pelican Mall** at the edge of Port Zante, the **TDC Mall** on Fort Street near the Circus, and the boutiques at the **Marriott Hotel**. A little farther out, you can purchase lovely, locally made clothing, accessories and home decorations from **Carabelle Batik** at Romney Manor. And be sure to visit the gift shop at **Stonewalls** for the latest designs from Island-to-Island.

If collecting local art is your hobby, there are several galleries in Basseterre, including **Spencer Cameron Gallery**, the **Sugar Mill Gallery**, and **Kate Design**.

Nighlife

Even though it has a reputation as a quiet island, the nightlife in St. Kitts rocks. From the beach rum shacks to the high-style disco at the Marriott, there are a lot of options for a great time at night.

Royal Beach Casino

Royal Beach Casino

The main attraction at the Marriott is the 35,000-square-foot casino. It's the largest Vegas-style casino in the Caribbean, with 400 slots and 34 gaming tables, plus a lounge area with 10 large-screen televisions for viewing sports events. ☎ 869-466-1200, www.stkittsmarriott.com.

Mr. X's Shiggidy Shack

For a good lime (relaxing evening with friends), head for this granddaddy of all the beach bars on Frigate Beach. While it's a restaurant with great grilled lobster, it's also a major party place. On Thursdays they do a beach bonfire and have live music, on Saturdays they let people make fools of themselves with Karaoke, on Sundays they host a live band, and if you're lucky enough to be there during a full moon, you can take part in their special celebration and bonfire. ☎ 869-762-3983, www.mrxshiggidyshack.com.

BET Soundstage

This nightclub opened in 2005 and has become a favored night spot for Kittians and visitors. The three-story building in Basseterre offers karaoke, dancing, video games and music ranging from jazz to hip-hop. ☎ 869-465-6802.

BET Soundstage

Bobbsy's

Dancing is big here, and they encourage people to have fun, with nights dedicated to Latin music and karaoke. The club occupies the second floor of a building on Frigate Bay Road and from the patio you can see the Caribbean. Call to see what's on tap for the week you are there. ☎ 869-466-6133.

Turtle Beach Bar

With the slogan "Live de Life," this is an all-day and all-night gathering place, with beach volleyball, boats to take out for fishing, kayaks and snorkeling equipment for rent, and a great atmosphere for just limin' and having fun. It's at the southernmost tip of the island. ☎ 869-469-7611, www.turtlebeach1.com.

Bob & Elvis Party Bus

Take a bunch of friends and hop on the bus that promises "what happens on de bus, stays on de bus." The renovated school bus with a dynamic sound system and bar takes you first to the Southeast Peninsula for a sunset champagne moment, and then tours around to favorite bars, stopping for dinner at one of the best restaurants. One

drink at each stop is complimentary, and on the bus they provide unlimited "Purple Mu Foo" cocktails (their own secret blend). ☎ 869-466-8110, www.caribbeanjourneymasters.com.

Pirates of the Caribbean Theme Night

For a lively evening of food, entertainment and games, make a reservation for Pirates Night at the Lodge Great House. It's a cabaret-style format, with a West Indian buffet, live music, fire-eaters, and all the drinks you can handle, for one price. ☎ 869-465-6548, www.stkittsactivities.com.

The Beaches of St. Kitts

At last estimate, there are 19 beaches to enjoy in St. Kitts, with the majority on the Southeast Peninsula. While not as plentiful as those in Antigua, the beaches are beautiful by any standard – soft sand, relatively calm waters, offshore reefs, and the occasional beach bar. All beaches are public, even though many developers try to partition sections for the exclusive use of their guests.

Banana Bay

Banana Bay

This beautiful beach at the southernmost tip of the island has not yet been discovered by the hordes. Fringed by palm trees, the beach is inviting, with soft sand and pretty much everything you would want except the crowds – and no beach bars.

Belle Tete

Belle Tete

The black sand beach at Belle Tete is at the far northern part of the island. It is made up of two spits of land – the leeward side is relatively calm (although there are some strong undercurrents), and the windward side has some rough surf and high waves good for surfing.

Cockleshell Bay

Right on the Narrows between St. Kitts and Nevis, this two-mile strand gives you great views of Nevis. If you get thirsty, the Lion Rock Beach Bar is right there. It has become a favorite spot for beach picnics on public holidays.

Conaree Beach

On the windward side of the island, this is a favorite beach for those who love body-surfing and snorkeling. The sand is black/grey, reflecting its volcanic origins.

Dieppe Bay

This picturesque black sand beach in front of the Golden Lemon Inn is protected by a reef, so the swimming is good and the snorkeling is great. Since it's on the northern coast, you can see both the Atlantic and Caribbean.

Cockleshell Bay

North Frigate Bay

If you are staying at the Marriott or any resort nearby, you are on North Frigate Bay beach. It used to be a lovely dune-protected beach edged with sea grapes, but the developers decided this was a very picturesque area, so you know how that goes. The services are great and the sand is soft, but you deal with a lot more crowds.

Majors Bay

This relatively unknown beach at the far end of the Southeast Peninsula now has a beach bar, so what was a secluded stretch of sand may be a bit more crowded these days. The bay is also popular as an anchorage for yachts, and as a place where you can fish from the shore.

Sandy Bank Bay

This windward-side beach is surprisingly calm and relatively uninhabited. If you like being left to your own resources, with no beach bars or watersports suppliers, you'll like this beach.

Majors Bay

South Friar's Bay

This beach on the edge of the Southeast Peninsula facing the beautiful Caribbean is said to be the best on the island. The swimming and snorkeling is good, and the beach is home to a number of beach bars, including the Shipwreck Bar & Grill, Sunset Beach Bar, Bikini Beach Bar & Grill and others. The ambiance here is likely to change, however, when the planned Dolphin Marine Park, which requires construction of a new sea wall, opens.

South Frigate Bay

When you first arrive in St. Kitts, this is probably the first beach you will encounter. It sits on the edge of the St. Kitts Royal Golf Course on the leeward side, and is popular with sunset-watchers and swimmers. The Monkey Bar, Mr. X's Shiggidy Shack and the Sunset Café are among the popular beach bars located here.

South Friar's Bay

Turtle Beach

The Turtle Beach Bar, the docks lined with boats for charter and the plenitude of watersports and beach activities here add up to a popular beach that's a lot of fun. It's at the end of the Southeast Peninsula, and you can easily see Nevis across the two-mile-wide Narrows.

White House Bay

While this beach has a rocky shoreline, it's still popular as a prime snor-

South Frigate Bay

keling spot since there are a number of reefs and wrecks just offshore. Boat captains of small boats favor it as a sheltered anchorage.

Nevis
Travel Information

Only information that is different from St. Kitts is included here.

Getting There

Nevis has its own airport, as well as a ferry dock in Charlestown that welcomes daily voyages from St. Kitts.

By Air

The airport is near the town of Newcastle, so it is called the **Newcastle Airport**. It has a short landing strip and can accommodate only small planes. Among the carriers that fly in and out are **WinAir** (daily flights from St. Maarten and St. Kitts), **American Eagle** (daily flights from San Juan), and **LIAT Airlines** (daily flights from Antigua). See the St. Kitts listing above and the St. Maarten and Antigua chapters for airlines that regularly fly to these destinations so you can plan your trip accordingly.

By Water

The most common (and some would say most enjoyable) way to get to Nevis from St. Kitts is by ferry, a 45-minute crossing from Basseterre to Charlestown with beautiful views of both islands. There are four companies operating the ferries, including **M&M Transportation** aboard the *Carib Surf* and *Carib Breeze*, **Wesk Agency Ltd**. on *Sea Hustler* and *Mark Twain*, **St. Kitts and Nevis Fast Ferries** with the *Geronimo Express*, and **F&F Transportation** with the *MV Carib Queen*. Since the ferries depart St. Kitts every half-hour from 6:30 am to 5 pm, and Nevis every half-hour from 7 am to 5:30 pm, the easiest option is to report to the Ferry Terminal at the dock when you are ready to go. They will sell you a ticket for the next departing boat, and you simply get on board.

Special Events & Holidays

Nevis stands on its own in many respects, and one of the cultural differences is that the island celebrates its own form of Carnival, called **Culturama**. In addition, whenever there is a holiday, you can count on horseracing events at the Indian Castle Race Track. There are also a lot of activities related to history and culture sponsored by the Nevis Historical and Conservation Society.

January

New Year's Day – Horseracing at Indian Castle Race Track. Nevis Turf and Jockey Club, ☎ 869-469-3477.

Carnival Day and Last Lap in St. Kitts – Public holiday.

Alexander Hamilton Birthday, January 11 – Celebrations hosted by the Nevis Historical and Conservation Society, ☎ 869-469-5786.

February

Tourism Week – Events include competitions, public discussions, and cultural presentations. Ministry of Tourism, ☎ 869-469-0109.

Nevis Olympic/Sprint Triathlon. Nevis Cycle & Triathlon Club, ☎ 869-469-9682, www.neviscycleclub.com.

March

B. Weber Memorial Cross Channel Swim – Nevis Cycle & Triathlon Club, ☎ 869-469-9682, www.neviscycleclub.com.

Agricultural Open Day and Exhibition – Showcases Nevis' best quality crop and animal produce, locally made processed items and a rich blend of local foods and cultural displays. Nevis Ministry of Agriculture, ☎ 869-469-5603/7302.

April

Good Friday – Public holiday. Kite flying contest.

Easter Sunday – Horseracing at Indian Castle Race Track. Nevis Turf and Jockey Club, ☎ 869-469-3477.

Easter Monday – Public holiday.

Nevis 'King of The Road' bike race – Nevis Cycle & Triathlon Club, ☎ 869-469-9682, www.neviscycleclub.com.

Earth Day – Activities organized by the Nevis Historical and Conservation Society, ☎ 869-469-5786, www.nevis-nhcs.org.

Labor Day Racing at Indian Castle Race Track – Nevis Turf and Jockey Club, ☎ 869-469-3477.

May

Labor Day, May 1 – Public holiday.

4th Annual Church Ground Community Club 10km Road Run. ☎ 869-469-3398.

Round the Island Team Relay Race – Nevis Cycle & Triathlon Club, ☎ 869-469-9682, www.neviscycleclub.com.

June

Tourism Awards Presentation & Banquet – Nevis Tourism Authority, ☎ 869-469-7550, info@nevisisland.com.

Whit Sunday Horseracing at Indian Castle Race Track – Nevis Turf and Jockey Club, ☎ 869-469-3477.

Whit Monday – Public holiday.

World Environment Day, June 4 – Activities organized by Nevis Historical and Conservation Society, ☎ 869-469-5786, www.nevis-nhcs.org.

July

Fruit Festival – Exposition of food and drinks made from locally grown tropical fruits. Nevis Department of Agriculture, ☎ 869-469-5603/7302.

Emancipation Day, July 31 – Beginning of Culturama Activities. ☎ 869-469-1992, www.nevisculturama.net.

August

Culturama Horseracing at the Indian Castle Race Track – Nevis Turf and Jockey Club, ☎ 869-469-3477.

Culturama Activities, Parade and Last Lap – Two-day public holiday. ☎ 869-469-1992, www.nevisculturama.net.

Caribbean International Food Fair – St. George's Rectory, ☎ 869-469-3441.

September

14th Annual Coastal Cleanup – Nevis Historical and Conservation Society, ☎ 869-469-5786, www.nevis-nhcs.org.

National Hero's Day, September 16 – Public holiday.

Independence Day Anniversary, September 19 – Public holiday. Military parade, horse race, and other activities.

October

Annual Sports Fishing Tournament at Oualie Beach Hotel – Nevis Yacht Club, ☎ 869-469-9690.

World Food Day Activities – Nevis Department of Agriculture, ☎ 869-469-5603/7302.

NICHE Nevis International Culinary Heritage Exposition.

November

2nd Nevis Half-Marathon – Nevis Cycle & Triathlon Club, ☎ 869-469-9682, www.neviscycleclub.com.

December

Christmas Day, December 25 – Public holiday.

Boxing Day, December 26 – Public holiday. Horseracing at Indian Castle Race Track. Nevis Turf and Jockey Club, ☎ 869-469-3477.

Health

The 54-bed **Alexandra Hospital** in Charlestown (☎ 869-469-5473) is the main healthcare facility for the island. Ten doctors are currently practicing on the island and there are two dental clinics. The three pharmacies on the island serve visitors' needs for medicines and cosmetics.

Money Matters

As outlined above, St. Kitts and Nevis use the Eastern Caribbean Dollar, with an exchange rate of EC$2.71 to the US dollar. Twenty-four-hour ATMs using the Cirrus and Plus networks are available at the **Bank of Nevis, Ltd.**, **Bank of Nova Scotia**, **First**

Caribbean International Bank, **National Bank**, **RBTT** and **Newcastle Airport** (open when airport is open).

Internet Access

Caribsurf is the main provider of Internet access on the island. There are terminals available for use at **Cable & Wireless** (☎ 869-469-5000), the **Nevis Public Library** (☎ 869-469-5521), and **Downtown Cybercafé** (☎ 869-469-1999). WiFi networks are currently being established and many of the hotels offer connections in their lobby areas, if not in the rooms.

Sources of Information

For more information on Nevis refer to www.nevisisland.com, the official site of the Nevis Tourism Authority. For materials, contact the offices below.

In the US & Canada

Nevis Tourism Authority, toll free 866-55-NEVIS (63847).

In Nevis

Nevis Tourism Authority, Main Street, Charlestown, Nevis, ☎ 869-469-7550 or 866-55-NEVIS, fax 869-469-7551.

In the UK

Glynis Watts, ***Nevis Island Estates***, Elm House, Park Lane, Lower Froyle, Alton, Hamphire GU34 4LT, ☎ 01420 520810, fax 01420 22071, Glynis.watts@virgin.net or office@nevisislandestates.com.

In Italy

Ian Rooks, Via Sant Alessandro, 688, Caronno Pertusella, 21042 Varese Italy, ☎ (+39) 0296451070, irooks@nevisisland.com.

Getting Around

Airport

The small Newcastle Airport is modern and bright. You can easily pick up a taxi outside the main doors. Two of the rental agencies have offices in Newcastle, and the other ones are happy to meet you at the airport with your rental.

Taxi Service

Taxis are plentiful and the congenial drivers are knowledgeable about the island. You can easily locate a driver either at the airport or at your hotel, and often they will give you their card so that you can call them whenever you need a pick-up to go out to dinner or sightseeing. You can also contact the taxi stands in Newcastle (☎ 869-469-9790) or Charlestown (☎ 869-469-1483/5631) for assistance.

SAMPLE TAXI FARES	
Airport to Charlestown	$15 US/$40 EC
Airport to Pinney's Beach area	$15 US/$40 EC
Airport to Montpelier Plantation Inn	$25 US/$68 EC
Pinney's Beach to Racetrack	$18 US/$49 EC
Nisbet Plantation to Botanical Gardens	$18 US/$49 EC

Car Rentals

You can rent "jeeps" (small SUVs like the Suzuki Grand Vitara or the Toyota RAV4), sedans and minivans from several agencies on the island. They will assist you in getting a driver's permit from one of the island's police departments, for a cost of US$24. Please note you need a valid driver's license from your home area to get a Nevisian license.

MAJOR CAR RENTAL COMPANIES	
Hertz	☎ 869-469-7467
Gajor's	☎ 869-469-5367/1439
M&M Rental	☎ 869-663-2013/469-9798
Nevis Car Rental	☎ 869-469-9837
Noel's	☎ 869-469-5199
Parry's	☎ 869-469-5917
Stanley's	☎ 869-469-2597
Strikers	☎ 869-469-2654
TDC	☎ 869-469-5430
Teach	☎ 869-469-1140

Exploring

On Foot

The island's eco-system is dominated by Nevis Peak, the 3,232-ft mountain at its center. Many describe the island as a "sombrero" because of the way the land circles the peak in the middle. While trails up the peak are accessible to all, island officials advise it's safer (as well as more meaningful) to go with a tour guide.

One hike that is easy to do on your own is the **Golden Rock Nature Trail**, at the Golden Rock Plantation Inn (☎ 869-469-3346). The trail is

Nevis Peak

not difficult; it starts in an area thick with monkeys and then winds up through the rainforest. The inn has a handout that identifies sights along the way, including all the fruit trees, medicinal plants, bushes, and even a termite's nest.

Another developing hiking trail that when completed will be truly impressive is the **Upper Round Road** project. The Nevis Historical and Conservation Society received grants from RARE, Center for Tropical Conservation, to renovate a nine-mile road through the center of the island as a hiking, riding and mountain biking trail. It stretches from the Golden Rock Plantation Inn on the windward side of the island to the Nisbet Plantation Beach Club on the northern tip. Along the way, visitors pass through local villages, West Indian houses, the rainforest and orchards.

Hiking Tour Operators

Eco-Rambles are the specialty of historian David Rollinson, who offers walking excursions to explore the landscape and history of the island. Tours include rainforest and ruins as well as an historical view of downtown Charlestown. ☎ 869-469-2091, droll@caribsurf.com.

Michael Herbert, a local "bush doctor" with a remarkable knowledge of natural remedies, shares his insights during **Herb's Nature Tours'** treks up the mountain. ☎ 869-469-3512.

Biologists Jim and Nikki Johnson of the **Top to Bottom** tour company host educational hikes all over the island, taking visitors on walks along a ghaut (a creek bringing water down from the mountains), climbs on Mt. Nevis, and trips to the beach for stargazing. They are especially attuned to children, and their trips are as entertaining as they are educational. ☎ 869-469-9080, www.walknevis.com.

Sunrise Tours, owned by local resident and eco-lover Lynnell Liburd and his wife Earla, take groups into the little-known areas, including Devil's Copper, a volcanic vent that leads into an area with dramatic waterfalls. Earla, a teacher, leads a tour through the village of Rawlins, known as "the breadbasket of Nevis." She shows how life was earlier in the 20th century and how the Nevisians grow and process their food. ☎ 869-469-2758, www.nevisnaturetours.com.

On Wheels

Car or Jeep

While there are not many tour operators that specifically offer land tours on this 36-square-mile island, it is small enough that most of the taxi drivers have a working knowledge of the sights. In fact, many are very knowledgeable about the island's history and culture and make excellent guides. In addition to the historical sights mentioned below, they can get you to the beautiful Botanical Gardens, Newcastle Pottery and the beaches.

Teach Tours offers customized tours in minibuses (☎ 869-469-1140). If you want to go a little more upscale, **Islander 1** has Lincolns to chauffeur you around the sights (☎ 869-469-5203).

Bicycle Rentals

With one main road that circles the island, and lots of trails going off of it up Nevis Peak, the island is ideal for mountain biking. Two shops in Nevis offer rentals: **Mountain Bike Rentals** at Oualie Beach (☎ 869-469-9682, www.mountainbikenevis.com), the headquarters for the Nevis Triathlon activities, and **Meadville Bike Rental** on Craddock Road (☎ 869-469-5235).

On Water

Scuba Diving

There are good dive sites off the shores of Nevis all around the island, but some of the best are on the eastern side, off Pinney's Beach and then north toward St. Kitts. Although Nevis is not generally recognized as a great dive destination, many feel that's due to lack of publicity more than anything else. Among the favorite sites are the wreck of the *River Taw*, Monkey Shoal, Booby High Shoals, and the Fish Bowl. Divers report seeing lobsters, turtles, nurse sharks, sea plumes and colorful sponges as well as wrecks, anchors and cannons sunk during sea battles.

Scuba Safaris is a PADI- and NAUI-certified dive shop and school, located on Oualie Beach. With three dive boats, they offer daily dives to the outer reefs and best dive sites around the island as well as specialty dives such as deep, night, wreck and advanced diving. ☎ 869-469-9518, scubanev@caribsurf.com.

Southeast coast of Nevis, protected by coral reefs (Aaron Vos)

Snorkeling

To get the most out of snorkeling on Nevis, visit Barbara Whitman's **Under the Sea Sealife Education Centre** on Oualie Beach. An animal behaviorist and marine biologist, Whitman emphasizes education. Before she takes you out on a snorkeling tour, she invites you into her sea lab to see how various creatures interact in their natural setting. That way, you'll not just drift around looking at the beautiful animals, but you'll be watching for interactions and enjoying the tour a lot more. Whitman is pioneering a method of introducing rescued turtles back into their natural habitat and happily shares stories about the project. She'll also invite you to "walk a turtle," which is an incredible experience. She conducts a Sea Camp for ages six-12, and a Marine Biology Course for ages 15-18. ☎ 869-469-1291, cell 869-662-9291, www.undertheseanevis.com.

Another snorkeling highlight, if you are on the island between January and April, is the Whale and Dolphin Snorkel Safari offered by **Scuba Safaris**. This 3½-hour educational tour uses hydrophones so you can listen for the clicks and whistles that indicate the presence of whales.

Among the best beaches on the island for snorkeling are Oualie Bay, Gallows Bay, Herbert's Beach and Nisbet Beach.

Windsurfing

The strong breezes that blow almost continuously off Nevis make it a great place for windsurfing. **Windsurfing Nevis** is the headquarters for the sport and owner Winston Crooke actively promotes the destination as a testing ground for new equipment and as a site for regattas and competitions. Windsurfers primarily use Oualie Bay, which benefits from consistent trade winds that create the ideal "bump & jump" conditions windsurfers enjoy. ☎ 869-469-9682, www.windsurfingnevis.com.

Watersports

If you just love being in the water, if you want to water-ski or if you want to just play around, there are a few ways for you to do this in Nevis. Most of the hotels have the usual range of Hobie Cats, Sunfish, kayaks and snorkeling gear available as part of their normal watersports.

If you want a little more action, **Jamestown Watersports** can take you skiing; they also have water toys such as tubes and banana boats for rent. ☎ 869-469-5977. The hotels have connections to other suppliers.

Deep-Sea Fishing

The waters off Nevis have some of the best fishing in the Caribbean, and each year the Nevis Yacht Club hosts an annual fishing tournament in late October. There is an assortment of both reef fish and game fish, including wahoo, tuna, king fish, marlin, and sailfish.

Jumby, a fishing boat operated by **Nevis Charters**, offers trips that include deep-sea and bottom fishing as well as snorkeling. The charter company also runs a casino run, taking passengers to the St. Kitts Marriott, waiting while they gamble, then returning them to Nevis. ☎ 869-662-9499, mattlloyd@sisterisles.kn.

Nevis Watersports, with Captain Julian Rigby at the helm, will take you out for a full or half-day of fishing on the *Sea Brat*, a 31-ft Bertram. They also offer hourly power boat charters, snorkeling trips, and water taxis to Turtle Beach and Basseterre. ☎ 869-469-9690, www.fishnevis.com.

Venture II is captained by experienced fisherman Claude Nisbett on his 28-ft Sea Sport. You can choose to fish the windward or leeward side, and Nisbett will guide you to the best spots. ☎ 869-469-9837.

Water Tours

There are no formal sea tour operators in Nevis, although you can check at Oualie Beach to see if Captain Lennox Wallace is sailing his catamaran *Caona* out to St. Kitts for the day with a group wanting to swim and snorkel. Also, **Turtle Tours** (☎ 869-469-8503) offers kayak tours of Nevis' coastline as well as snorkeling tours.

Boat Charters

There are a few boats available for charter, but many are on an informal basis. You can check to see if your hotel has an arrangement with boats for charter, or go down to Oualie Beach or Newcastle Bay Marine to see who is available on any given day.

Captain Matt Lloyd, a professional fisherman, offers to take people out on the 50-foot *Deep Venture* for an authentic fishing adventure. The catch is his to use in Le Bistro Restaurant in Charlestown, but he is generous in sharing. ☎ 869-469-5110, mattlloyd@caribsurf.com.

Sea Nevis Charter Boat Ltd. and captain Les Windley offer a sailboat for day-sails with snorkeling and refreshments. ☎ 869-469-9239.

Star Charters' owners Steve and Irene Macek take you on a day-sail aboard the schooner *Star*, complete with gourmet brunch. ☎ 869-469-2716.

Tucket Mist is a 46-ft Morgan sloop available for charters for up to eight people. ☎ 869-469-0200.

On Horseback

The **Hermitage Stables** adjacent to the Hermitage Inn takes you on rides up Saddle Hill. For a real treat, ask about their tour of Gingerland in hand-carved mahogany carriages. ☎ 869-469-3477, nevherm@caribsurf.com.

The **Nevis Equestrian Centre** near Pinney's Beach offers 10 different types of rides, from leisurely beach rides to trail rides up the hills. ☎ 869-469-9118, alitalk@caribcable.com.

Playing & Watching Sports

Horseracing

At the far southeastern end of the island is the **Indian Castle Racetrack**, a major gathering point for Nevisians and visitors during holidays. The Nevis Turf & Jockey Club sponsors races 10 to 12 times a year on the wild and windswept course, and each race is an event in itself with local food vendors, lots of limin' in the stands, music, and a general good time. Check the local newspapers for times and dates.

Golf

CondéNast Traveler magazine has dubbed the 18-hole Robert Trent Jones course at the **Four Seasons Resort** as the seventh-best course in the world. The course is open to the public for play, except during the peak seasons of December and January, when only hotel guests can use it. ☎ 869-469-1111, www.fourseasons.com/nevis.

A smaller 12-hole, par-3 executive course is available at **Cat Ghaut Chip'n Putt** in Newcastle. The 15-acre property includes a nature trail. ☎ 869-469-9826.

Triathlons & Mountain Biking

Nevis is becoming a center for mountain biking and triathlons. The Nevis Cycle and Triathlon Club hosts numerous events throughout the year (☎ 869-469-9682, www.neviscycleclub.com). The interest in these sports has largely been attributed to Winston Crooke, owner of Wheel World Cycle Shop at Oualie Beach, who has built the racing teams and conducts ongoing training programs that anyone can join.

Seeing the Sights

Sampling the Culture

Culturama

Emancipation of the slaves whose labor drove the sugar economy was, as you can imagine, a big event in the history of the Leeward Islands. The commemorations are cultural events of sizeable proportion, and give visitors the opportunity to see, smell, taste and enjoy what it is to be a native.

In Nevis, the celebration is called **Culturama**, and it takes place over a seven-day period beginning in late July. Among the events are drama presentations, pageants, street fairs with food and music, and a grand parade. The heart of the festival is the cultural village. To see the full schedule, go to www.nevisculturama.net or call ☎ 869-469-1992.

Culturama

Out of these celebrations has come a musical heritage that visitors can experience at any time. **String bands** or "scratch bands" are small groups of musicians with guitars, mandolins, a baho or bass pipe made from bamboo or PVC, a fife, and percussion instruments such as a triangle and a guiro gourd with ridges that are scratched (hence the name). There are currently three scratch bands on the island, and they perform at the hotels and restaurants on a regular basis. Other musical traditions include **calypso** (or Kaiso as it is known in Nevis) and **steel pan** bands, which also provide entertainment at hotels and restaurants.

Among the local crafts are **pottery**, **wood carving** and **textiles**. Visitors can purchase locally made souvenirs at the **Nevis Craft House** in Pinneys and at **Newcastle Pottery** in Newcastle. Also, don't miss a visit to **Café des Arts** in Charlestown (☎ 869-469-7098), a delightful restaurant and gallery that features locally created artwork.

The Nevis Botanical Gardens

As a delightful respite from the real world, the Nevis Botanical Gardens rate among the top attractions in the Leewards. The gardens have thousands of tropical and subtropical species displayed on seven acres of land. The species are clustered into separate display areas, such as the Orchid Terraces, the Cacti Garden, the Tropical Vine Garden, the Fruit Orchard and the Rainforest Conservatory. Interspersed among the blooms are ponds with fountains, shaded walkways and benches. If you have any curiosity about identifying various tropical flowers, trees and fruits, this is the place to answer your questions. The on-site restaurant, Martha's-in-the-Garden, overlooks the gardens and is a great place for lunch. Call ahead to see when the Gardens and the restaurant are open, as the schedules change from season to season. ☎ 869-469-3509, www.botanicalgardennevis.com.

Reliving History

Everywhere you turn on Nevis, you see history – from the wonderfully preserved buildings throughout Charlestown to the plantation inns and historical sites around the island. Among the highlights are:

Downtown Charlestown

Considered by many historians to be the best remaining example of the colonial era in the Caribbean, downtown Charlestown retains many wonderful original structures, preserved today as offices and retail outlets. The old stone **Cotton Ginnery** near the ferry boat pier has seen new life as a shopping mall and place for the

Main Street, Charleston (Aaron Vos)

Museum of Nevis History, Charleston (Aaron Vos)

exhibit of local crafts. At the edge of town the **Museum of Nevis History** occupies a portion of the Hamilton House, the birthplace of Alexander Hamilton. The second floor of the Hamilton House serves as the meeting room for the Nevis House of Assembly.

Another interesting historical site at the edge of Charlestown is the **Bath Hotel and Spring House**. Built in 1778, the hotel was a major tourist attraction for those who came to enjoy the hot spring baths on the property. After the decline of the sugar plantations, it was used as a hotel from 1912 to 1940, and then as a training center for the West Indian regiment. Today it is the temporary headquarters for the Nevis police. The Spring House bath structure still stands, but was badly damaged in recent hurricanes. A restoration group has constructed an open outdoor pool near the building so people can still enjoy the reputed healing powers of the water there.

Plantation Ruins

Cottage at the entrance to the Montravers Estate (Aaron Vos)

The **Hamilton** family was prominent in Nevis, and you can visit the ruins of the family's sugar plantation just outside Charlestown. What remains are foundations of the Great House, the windmill, the cistern, the boiling house and steam engine. The **Eden Brown Estate**, about 30 minutes from Charlestown, has a checkered past and is rumored to be haunted, attracting many visitors. At **Montravers Estate** archeologists have uncovered the ruins of a layered house; the original construction is from the 17th century, a middle layer was added in the 18th century, and the building was finally completed in the 19th century. Other plantation ruins include the **New River** and **Coconut Walk** estates on the road past Golden Rock Plantation Inn. In addition, the plantation inns such as Golden Rock, Montpelier, Old Manor, Hermitage and Nisbet all have proud histories they are delighted to share with visitors. Montpelier is especially interesting because Lord Horatio Nelson wed Nevisian widow Frances Nisbet on that site in 1787.

Nevis

Nevisian Heritage Village

Intent on showing both visitors and locals how life was like in past eras, the Nevisian government has reconstructed a village on the grounds of a former sugar plantation near Gingerland. Among the points of interest are a Carib chief's thatched hut with actual relics of tools and food implements; wattle-and-daub structures showing how the slaves lived; and a post-emancipation chattel house displaying artifacts from that era. There are also backyard gardens, a blacksmithy, a shoemaker's shop and a rum shop. A guide is usually on hand to walk you through the village and give you an oral history. Future plans for development include a small restaurant and a still to illustrate how rum is made.

Historic Churches

Nevis has many outstanding examples of colonial-era churches, some of which are still being used by congregations. One of the most interesting is the ruins of **Cottle Church**, near the Mt. Nevis Hotel. John Cottle built the church in 1824 so that his family and his slaves could worship together at a time when it was illegal for slaves to go to church. Other churches of note are **St. John's Fig Tree Church**, **St. James Windward Church**, **St. Thomas' Lowland Church** and **St. Paul's Anglican Church**.

Where to Stay

Luxe Hotels

$$$$$ – For a beachfront double, expect to pay a nightly rate of about US$650-$1,150 in high season, and US$450-$750 in low.

Four Seasons Resort

 The Four Seasons is the first true-five-star resort on Nevis and it's been a big boost in attracting high-end tourists. It aims to be a world unto its own and would appear to have succeeded in many ways – only about 13% of guests leave the resort to dine elsewhere on the island. The property sits on the leeward Pinney's Beach, one of the best on Nevis, and also boasts its own Robert Trent Jones golf course, which

Four Seasons Resort

attracts many from St. Kitts who come to play for the day. Rooms and public facilities are done in typical British colonial style, with lots of mahogany furniture, bright colors and quality appointments.

Location: Pinney's Beach, western coast.

Rooms: 196, including mountain-side, mountain-view, ocean-side and ocean-front rooms, and executive, luxury and ocean suites, as well as three villas. All have refrigerated private bars, luxury bedding, AC, TV, DVD player and high-speed Internet.

Rates: EP, with several packages available.

Features: Four restaurants, one lounge, 24-hour room service and concierge, spa, sports pavilion with weight training and studio classes, 10 tennis courts (four clay, six hard surface), Robert Trent Jones golf course, watersports, volleyball and basketball.

☎ 869-469-1111, 800-332-3442 US, 800-268-6282 Canada, fax 869-469-1112, www.fourseasons.com/nevis.

Nisbet Plantation Beach Club

Once the home of Fanny Nisbet, the wife of Admiral Horatio Nelson, this reclaimed plantation is one of the few plantation inns on Nevis that is actually on the beach. The view from the Great House down the Avenue of the Palms to the beach is memorable, as are the beautifully appointed rooms. In 2006, the interior of the Great House was renovated, air conditioning was installed, a hot tub that seats 10 was added near the pool, a fitness center was built, all rooms were updated with new furniture and baths, and

Nisbet Plantation Beach Club

The Palms Spa was opened. The resort is a regular on *CondéNast Traveler*'s Gold List.

Location: Near Newcastle on the northeast coast.

Rooms: 34 total, including 14 superior rooms, 10 deluxe suites, and 12 premier junior suites. All have minibars, tea/coffee service, AC.

Rates: BP, automatic complimentary MAP upgrade on stays of three nights or more.

Features: Two restaurants, beach bar, pool, hot tub, tennis court, lawn croquet, fitness center, spa, and non-motorized watersports.

☎ 869-469-9325, 800-742-6008 US and Canada, fax 869-469-9864, www. NisbetPlantation.com.

Luxury With Limits

$$$$ – *These comfortable and unique properties offer deluxe rooms from US$400-$550 in high season, and US$250-$450 in low.*

Hermitage Plantation Inn

The Hermitage is an intimate inn offering relaxed and secluded accommodations in one of the oldest preserved wooden houses in the Caribbean. The Lupinacci family provides excellent management, and the cottages and rooms are comfortable and perfectly suited to the tropical setting. Goosepen Cottage has a patio that faces the rainforest where you can lie in a hammock and wait to catch a glimpse of a passing

Cottage at Hermitage Plantation Inn

monkey. Furnishings include a lovely mahogany four-poster bed wrapped in mosquito netting, a separate living room surrounded by wooden shutters, and a small bar/kitchenette area. All around the property are fruit trees and gardens. A bell is rung to summon guests to the dining verandah for dinner. Blink, and you'll think you're back in the 17th century.

Location: Inland near Gingerland, at the southern end of the island.

Rooms: 12 cottages, two hillside rooms, and the three-bedroom Manor House, all with ceiling fans, refrigerators, tea/coffee service, and antique and heirloom furniture. Luxury cottages have TV/VCR, CD players and kitchenettes.

Rates: BP.

Features: Restaurant, lounge, library, pool, room service for dinner, tennis court and stables.

☎ 869-469-3477, 800-682-4025 US, fax 869-46-2481, www. hermitagenevis.com.

Montpelier Plantation Inn

Montpelier Plantation Inn

This lovely inn sits up in the hills on a historic 60-acre estate at a 750-foot elevation, with views from some of the cottages out to the sea. The Montpelier has a lot to recommend it: A very high level of service, 17 unique rooms, and a restaurant (The Terrace) considered one of the best on the island. For something special, ask for a reservation in The Mill dining room, which seats only 12 people. There is one seating a night. The Inn will shuttle guests to its own beach facility, bar and restaurant. Only children over the age of eight are welcomed.

Location: Inland near Saddle Hill, on the southern end of the island.

Rooms: 17, including premier rooms, suites and two-bedroom suites. All have bright, colorful furnishings, private balconies, small refrigerators and AC.

Rates: BP plus afternoon tea; many packages available, including a "Babymoon" Package for expectant parents.

Features: Restaurant, beach bar, tiled pool, private beach with shuttle, massage services.

☎ 869-469-3462, fax 869-469-2932, www.montpeliernevis.com.

Mt. Nevis Hotel & Beach Club

Built in 1989 on the Round Hill Estate, this informal hotel features suites and adjoining rooms in four two-story, white stucco pavilions, with future plans for four more buildings. They have a shuttle to their own beach and restaurant on Newcastle Bay (they provide cell phones so you can call when you're read to go back to the Inn). The grassy areas surrounding the hotel lack trees for shade or a sense of the tropics, but provide a nice view to the ocean.

Location: Inland near Round Hill, in the northern area.

Rooms: 28 rooms, including deluxe rooms and junior, superior and two-bedroom suites. All have TVs, VCR, AC and balconies. Suites have full kitchens.

Mt. Nevis Hotel & Beach Club

Rates: BP, with packages available.

Features: Two restaurants, pool, private beach with watersports.

☎ 869-469-9373/4, 800-75-NEVIS (US and Canada), fax 869-469-9375, www.mountnevishotel.com.

Reasonable & Comfortable Hotels

$$$ – These relaxed and casual accommodations start at US$380 in high season, US$280 in low.

Oualie Beach Hotel

Oualie Beach Hotel

If you want to be right on a terrific sheltered, soft-sand beach with access to all kinds of water and land-based sports, in a relaxed setting where everyone from the youngest to the oldest will have a good time, you need to look at this hotel. The rooms are clean and well-furnished with mahogany four-poster beds. All rooms face the sea and are housed in charming gingerbread cottages with screened verandahs. The service is warm and welcoming, the restaurant has a great reputation, and they bring in local bands to entertain a few evenings a week. Barbara Whitman, the noted marine biologist, has her teaching aquarium adjacent to the property, and the bay is heavily used by snorkelers, windsurfers and watersports lovers. Almost everyone who visits Nevis ends up here at some time during their stay.

Location: Northeast coast.

Rooms: 32 in all, with deluxe, studio and premier levels. All have four-poster beds, small refrigerators, tea/coffee service, TV, AC, Internet (free WiFi). Studios have full kitchens, and are adjacent to deluxe rooms with a common door so they can be booked together as a family suite. Premier rooms have larger baths with double vanities.

Rates: EP, BP, MAP and AI available.

Features: Restaurant, spa, watersports, live entertainment two nights a week, adjacent activities center with windsurfing instruction and equipment, mountain bike rentals, scuba instruction and dive and snorkeling tours.

☎ 869-469-9735, fax 869-469-9176, www.oualiebeach.com.

Old Manor Plantation Inn

Creative restoration has built the charm back into this inn nestled into the foothills of Mt. Nevis at an elevation of 700 feet. The cut-stone buildings built towards the end of the 17th century have been transformed into rooms with stone walls, high ceilings and hardwood floors. The Plantation Suites are large and open with comfortable furnishings, although some rooms need a little refurbishing. Among the more charming aspects are the round pool that was once a cistern and the antique tools of the sugar factory lying about like sculpture.

Old Manor Plantation Inn (Kent E. St. John)

Location: Inland at the southern end of the island.

Rooms: 13 total, including Plantation Suites and deluxe rooms. All have ceiling fans, mini-refrigerators and tea/coffee service.

Rates: BP, with packages available.

Features: Restaurant, pool, trails to the rainforest, complimentary shuttle to Pinney's Beach, spa treatments can be arranged.

☎ 869-469-3445, fax 869-469-3388, www.oldmanornevis.com.

Good Value Hotels

$$ – These value-priced hotels offer accommodations at about US$215-$250 in high season, US$150-$175 in low.

Golden Rock Plantation Inn

A sense of history pervades this plantation inn, where many of the original buildings have been kept intact and put to good use. The remarkable bar is set inside what used to be the hearth of the Great House kitchen and the sugar mill has been converted into a suite with single beds and chairs downstairs, and a native-made

Golden Rock Plantation Inn (Kent E. St. John)

'more-than-king-sized' bed on the second floor. Most of the beds and some of the other mahogany and bamboo furniture were made on the island.

Location: Nevis Peak foothills on the eastern side.

Rooms: 14 rooms, including doubles in cottages with views to the sea and the Sugar Mill Suite. All have four-poster beds, verandahs and en-suite bathrooms.

Rates: EP and MAP.

Features: Restaurant, bar, pool, separate restaurant at Pinney's Beach with shuttle from hotel.

☎ 869-469-3346, fax 869-469-2113, www.golden-rock.com.

Villas & Condos

Cliffdwellers is a collection of individually owned villas overlooking Tamarind Bay available for vacation rentals. The complex has its own 100-ft pool and Bananas Restaurant, one of the best eateries on the island. ☎ 869-469-8262, fax 869-469-8195, www.cliffdwellers.org.

Four Seasons Resort Estates further expands the luxury offerings of the Four Seasons in two- to five-bedroom privately owned villas that can be rented according to the owners' schedules. These are dramatic luxury homes on the hills above the golf course and overlooking the resort, where all activities and amenities are available to villa guests. ☎ 869-469-1111, www.fsestatesnevis.com.

Howells Realty has a wide selection of large villas for rent, and also brokers sales of homes on Nevis. ☎ 869) 469-5648.

Oualie Realty represents a number of villas for vacation rentals, including Dolphin House, Tamarind Tor, Stone House and Coral Gate. ☎ 869-469-9403, fax 869-469-9817, www.oualierealty.com.

Seashell Properties is the agent for 16 colorful and interesting villas throughout the island. ☎ 869-469-1675, fax 869-469-1288, www.nevisvillas.com.

Villa Paradiso is a collection of three four-bedroom luxury villas, with dramatic thatched roofs and private pools near Pinney's Beach. ☎ 888-710-2528, www.villaparadisonevis.com.

Wimco, the international villa company, has several large luxury villas available on Nevis. ☎ 800-449-1553, www.wimco.com.

Guest Houses

These small properties offer a more intimate encounter with the Nevisians as well as a relaxed lifestyle where you are pretty much on your own. Expect to pay $120-$200 a night for a room, depending on size and location.

Banyan Tree Bed & Breakfast is a small inn with three bedrooms available in two structures on a hill overlooking the sea. ☎ 869-469-3449 or 603-448-5467, www.banyantreebandb.com.

Pinney's Cottages are three two-bedroom cottages with kitchenettes and living/dining rooms close to Pinney's Beach. ☎ 869-469-1811, www.pinneyscomplex.com.

Tranquility Annexe, on the slopes of Mount Nevis near Zetlands, is a new apartment complex offering nine short-term units. Each has a full kitchen and balcony with views to the mountains. ☎ 869-469-2304, tranquility2@caribsurf.com.

Yamseed Inn, near the airport in Newcastle, is a beachfront bed-and-breakfast with two rooms in the main house and two small cottages on the grounds. ☎ 869-469-9361.

Day Spas

In addition to the serene and gorgeous spas that are available to guests and non-guests alike at the Four Seasons Hotel, Nisbet Plantation and Hermitage Plantation, there are two independent spas on Nevis.

F.I.T. Fitness Center Ltd. is a complete fitness complex in Charlestown, offering workout equipment, classes, physical therapy and full spa services. The massages and manicure/pedicures can be done in your room or villa, a convenience that sets this service apart from others. ☎ 869-469-3481, www.fitwellnesscenter.com.

Jade Spa combines a wellness center with Tui Na facials and Shaitsu and other types of massages. The garden restaurant serves salads, sandwiches and local dishes. It's located in Newcastle, near the airport. ☎ 869-469-9564.

The brand new **Spa Nevis** is located in The Condo at Nelson Springs development. It offers massages, facials, body and foot treatments and nail services in a tranquil setting. ☎ 869-469-1127, www.spanevis.com.

RESTAURANT PRICE CHART	
$	Cheap eats, normally quick meals or take-out foods; US$8 or less per entrée.
$$	Good value, lots of West Indian cuisine; US$9-$14 for a plate of food.
$$$	A nice place with gourmet aspirations; US$15-$24 for a satisfying entrée.
$$$$	Positively elegant, usually requiring some dressing up; entrées range from US$25 to $50, depending on the island.

Eating Out

Dressing Up to Eat Out

The Four Seasons Dining Room

The Dining Room has the distinction of being the most expensive, and arguably the best, restaurant on the island. The cuisine is best described as "fusion," with French and Asian influences. The room is beautifully done with mahogany furniture and dark wood walls. Bright bouquets of flowers add color. It's definitely the place to show off your best "island couture." $$$$. Pinney's Beach. Open for dinner only, reservations required. ☎ 869-469-1111, www.fourseasons.com/nevis.

Hermitage Plantation Inn

The latticed porch of the Great House is the scene of this lovely open-air dining room. The cuisine – conch cakes with lobster sauce and marinated shrimp on black bean cakes – is classic with local accents. The kitchen produces outstanding baked goods, so don't miss the dessert menu. $$$$. Southern area of the island, near Gingerland. Open for breakfast, lunch, afternoon tea and dinner, with dinner reservations required. ☎ 869-469-3477, www.hermitagenevis.com.

Miss June's Cuisine

Oprah Winfrey is said to have talked Miss June into opening this restaurant. It is located in Miss June Mestier's home on the road between the airport and the Four Seasons. Dining here is more like going to an intimate dinner party than a restaurant, and the grand lady's hospitality makes everyone feel relaxed and welcomed. Miss June lays out a fantastic West Indian buffet and treats everyone to a running commentary on the food and her life. This is a place not to be missed – but you must make reservations since room is limited and the place doesn't open if there aren't reservations on the books. Jones Bay. Open for dinner only, a few days a week. $$$$, www.nevis1.com/miss-junes-restaurant.html, ☎ 869-469-5330.

Montpelier Plantation Inn

Montpelier Plantation Inn

Even if the food didn't have the outstanding reputation it does, the location of this dining room would attract a big following. The inn sits at the top of a hill, and the open-air terrace off the main room of the historic Great House looks out over the island. Those in the know try to arrange for seating in the Sugar Mill, where only 12 fortunate guests get to dine each night. The cuisine includes local seafood and produce, featuring a lot of island fruits such as mango, pineapple and coconut. $$$$. Southern end of the island. Open for breakfast, lunch and dinner, with reservations recommended for lunch and dinner. ☎ 869-469-3462, www.montpeliernevis.com.

The Great House at Nisbet Plantation Inn

If you are seeking elegant dining in air-conditioned comfort in a beautiful historic setting, this should be your first choice. Stone walls, art and antiques provide the ambiance while you enjoy a stellar five-course meal. $$$$. Nisbet Beach, northeastern corner of the island. Open for dinner only, reservations required. ☎ 869-469-9325, www.nisbetplantation.com.

Relaxing on the Water

Chevy's Calypso Bar

This has become the new "in" spot on Pinney's Beach, a lively place with good food in big portions at reasonable prices. The cuisine is a mix of seafood, West Indian favorites, and burgers. They've created a signature drink, the Pantie Dropper, meant to compete with Sunshine's (see below) Killer Bee for the title of best rum drink on the island. Wednesday night is karaoke night, and on Sunday afternoons the beach party starts at 4. $. Pinney's Beach. ☎ 869-665-2533/664-9474, chevvi@yahoo.com.

Coconut Grove Restaurant & Wine Lounge

As you settle in at your table under the thatched roof of this Balinese structure steps away from Nelson's Spring beach, you are presented with intriguing choices, including Passionate Scallops, Seafood Napoleon, and Wahoo "Meli Melo." The choices aren't easy, but the setting is beautiful and the service is good. It is said to have the only wine cellar on the island outside of the Four Seasons. $$$. Pinney's Beach. ☎ 869-469-1020, www.coconutgrovenevis.com.

Gallipot Restaurant

This fairly recent addition to the Nevis dining scene has been well received by visitors and locals. The seafood is guaranteed fresh, since owner Julian Rigby also owns the deep sea fishing charter boat operating from Oualie Beach. The daily catch is really the daily catch. The menu also includes burgers, salads, steaks and chicken curry. Sunday lunch is a treat for Brits, with roast beef and Yorkshire pudding. $$. Tamarind Bay. Open for lunch seven days a week, dinner Mondays through Saturdays. ☎ 869-469-8230.

Oualie Beach Hotel

This relaxed dining room is just steps from Oualie Beach, the most active beach on the island. Lobster is always done well here, the conch chowder is regarded as the best on the island, and the West Indian Buffet is popular, making this place a favorite for locals as well as visitors. They have live entertainment three nights a week, when local string bands and steel pan bands strut their stuff. Breakfast is also very good, and includes the lightest banana pancakes you'll ever eat. $$. Northwestern coast. Open for breakfast, lunch and dinner. ☎ 869-469-9735, www.oualiebeach.com.

Pizza Beach

This outpost of the Mt. Nevis Hotel offers one of the few places to get pizzas on the island. It has a great beachside setting, but they haven't sorted out whether they are actually an Italian or Mexican restaurant, so in addition to pizza and pasta, you can order quesadillas, tacos and flautas. $$$. Newcastle Marina. Open for dinner only. ☎ 869/469-9395, www.mountnevishotel.com.

Sunshine's Beach Bar & Grill

Everybody knows Sunshine and his famous Killer Bee drink. This beachside bar at Pinney's Beach is a local hangout, the place you go for a good lunch of barbecued chicken or lobster while you relax and gaze out at the water. Bonfires are lit most nights, and the full moon gives rise to a Full Moon Bash. $$. Pinney's Beach. Open for lunch and dinner in high season; no lunch; dinner by reservation only in low season. ☎ 869-469-5817, www.sunshinenevis.com.

Ethnic Foods & Favorites

Neve

Neve

For Italian dining at its best, this Four Seasons restaurant is a good choice. Glass spheres filled with candles are the focal point of the open-air room. The dining is casual, and they also feature a good breakfast buffet. $$$. Pinney's Beach. Open for breakfast every day, and dinner Sunday through Tuesday. ☎ 869-469-1020, www.fourseasons.com/nevis.

Seafood Madness

Of course, it's all about seafood here, with Creole spices working their magic. Other specialties include chicken, steak and ribs. Ask about their exotic drinks like the "Booming Madness" or "Tropical Illusion." $$. Pinney's Road near Charlestown. Open for breakfast, lunch and dinner. ☎ 869-469-0558.

West Indian Cooking

Bananas Restaurant

Owner Gillian Smith describes the cuisine here as "West Indian with a twist." Look for the familiar fish cakes, jerk pork and lamb shanks, along with some surprises like Molten Chocolate Cake for dessert. The beautiful setting is high on a hill and overlooks the water. $$$. Hamilton Estate, central part of the island. Open for dinner only. ☎ 869-469-1891.

Mango

West Indian food at the Four Seasons? This breezy restaurant right on the beach features Creole and other flavors in a menu that delights both guests and island residents. It's also a great place to watch sunsets. $$$. Pinney's Beach. Open for lunch, dinner and Sunday brunch. ☎ 869-469-1020, www.fourseasons.com/nevis.

Rumours Bar and Grill

This restaurant on the main road near the airport is "rumoured" to have the best conch chowder on the island. The fare is primarily West Indian, and the atmosphere is relaxed

Mango

and casual. On Friday nights they have a West Indian buffet with stewed mutton, curried chicken, goat water, black pudding, macaroni pie and all those other goodies the islands are famous for. $. Main road, near Newcastle. ☎ 869-469-9436.

Unella's by the Sea

When you are in Charlestown, this is an ideal spot for lunch or dinner on the waterfront. The specialties are West Indian, but there are a lot of other choices as well. $$. On the Charlestown Waterfront. Open for breakfast, lunch and dinner. ☎ 869-469-5574.

Café des Arts

Delight in Doing Lunch

Café des Arts

This small café on the edge of Charlestown is adjacent to Hamilton House and displays the works of local artists in its gallery. The salads and sandwiches are beautifully presented, and the setting outside under shade trees is very pleasant, causing you to linger. $$. Open for breakfast and lunch. ☎ 869-469-7098.

Martha's in the Garden

Talk about a gorgeous garden setting! Here you are completely surrounded by fantastic gardens of orchids, roses, cacti, palms and tropical flowers in the main house of the Botanical Gardens. After a stroll through the displays, you can stop here for a light lunch in the best Caribbean style. The offerings include a Ploughman's Lunch, Tapas Plate, and even an English Tea with Scones. Nevis Botanical Gardens, southern end of the island. Open for breakfast and lunch, seasonally. ☎ 869-469-3399.

A WEEK OF CARIBBEAN WINE, FOOD & CULTURE

If you love learning about new wines and cooking techniques native to a region, you'll want to plan your visit to Nevis for late October when the annual **Nevis International Culinary Heritage Exposition** is held on the island. Activities include daily cooking demonstrations, gourmet lunches and dinners prepared by leading Caribbean and international chefs, along with informative sessions on cheeses, wines and Caribbean foods. Tickets can be purchased to attend all events for the week, three days of events, or single days. ☎ 869-469-7550 or toll-free 866-55-NEVIS, www.nevis-niche.com.

Shopping

While not a major duty-free port, Charlestown offers some interesting shopping for those in search of special keepsakes and island wear.

The **Cotton Ginnery Complex** is one of the first stops for shoppers. The old buildings have been converted into a retail center with a few stores of interest, such as **The Blue Magic Photo Studio and Gift Shop**, **Caribbean Styles and Tings** for clothing, **Chapter One** for books, and **Jeveren's Fashions**.

Elsewhere along Main Street are the **African Arts Shop**, **Bocane Ceramics**, **Caribco Gifts**, the **Gallery of Nevis Art**, **Island Hopper**, **Pemberton's** and **Kids N Things**.

If you love gathering local crafts, the **Nevis Craft Cooperative** on Main Street just outside Charlestown provides a workshop and store for local artisans working in wood, ceramics and rug weaving. They also have a small store in the Cotton Ginnery.

Those staying in villas or rooms with kitchens who are ambitious enough to try cooking West Indian style like to visit the **Public Market** and **Fisherman's Wharf** at the waterfront. This colorful marketplace offers gems you won't see in your local markets, like huge avocados (called pears), fresh coconuts, plantain, christophene, tannia, papaya and mango. The market is open every day except Sunday; Friday and Saturday are the days to go if you really want to feel immersed in the culture.

Nighlife

On Nevis, there is something going on every night of the week. It may be a live band and beach barbecue at Oualie Beach on Tuesday nights, a string band and roast pig barbecue on Wednesdays at the Hermitage Plantation, a bonfire and beach party at Sunshine's on Sunday evenings, or an evening out at one of the following:

Double Deuce is a gathering place for locals and visitors on Pinney's Beach. The main attractions of this rum shack are good, simple food, fancy cocktails, and a somewhat Hemingwayesque feeling. Thursday night is karaoke night. ☎ 869-469-2222, www.doubledeucebar.com.

Eddy's Bar & Restaurant in downtown Charlestown bar is a Wednesday night favorite, starting with a lively happy hour, dinner, and then the main attraction: karaoke and dancing. ☎ 869-469-5958.

Mango is a good choice is you're looking for a more sedate night on the town. The outdoor lounge in the Four Seasons has a piano bar, reasonable menu and exotic drinks, all of which keeps this place busy. ☎ 869-469-1111.

Water Department Barbecue jumps on Friday nights when everyone is out in the streets enjoying ribs and chicken hot off the grills. One of the biggest draws is the barbecue put on by the local water department on Pump Road at the Gathering Place to raise funds for trips. It's lots of limin' and greeting old friends, as well as playing dominos and enjoying the moment. There is no contact phone so just follow the crowds.

The Beaches of Nevis

Although Nevis is a tiny island, it boasts a number of beautiful beaches that offer great snorkeling, swimming and leisure activities as well as services such as rum shacks and restaurants. The sand is either a golden brown or white, owing to the island's volcanic origins combined with coral growth in the surrounding reefs. Most beaches are lined with palms, giving a very tropical feel to the scenery (as well as some shade).

Cades Bay Beach

Beach at Cades Bay

This beach is fronted by the Inn at Cades Bay and the popular Tequila Sheila's bar and restaurant, which has live entertainment during Sunday brunch. The swimming on this long stretch of sand is very good, and the beach is perfect for walking.

Indian Castle Beach

Near the racetrack at the southern end of the island is this windward beach. Some windsurfing is done here when the waves are good and the wind is high.

Lovers Beach

This northern-end beach can only be reached by a short trail, keeping it secluded. Bring a picnic lunch, since there are no bars or restaurants.

Newcastle Beach

This more lively neighbor to Lovers Beach is the site of a marina and bar. Some like to come and watch the infrequent takeoffs and landings at the airport just south of the beach.

Nisbet Beach

The Nisbet Plantation Beach Club maintains this beautiful beach in peak condition and there's a beach bar right off the sand. The snorkeling offshore is good, and the calm Caribbean waters are perfect for swimming.

Oualie Beach

With a very good sandy beach, calm waters, offshore reefs for snorkeling, and a pier for

Oualie Beach

boats to moor, this is the watersports headquarters for the island. Suppliers of windsurfing and watersports equipment are just off the beach, and Barbara Whitman's snorkeling tours begin here. The Oualie Beach Resort's restaurant and bar provides sustenance. It's a great place for families to spend the day.

Pinney's Beach

Many frequent visitors feel this is one of the best beaches in the entire Caribbean, with four miles of soft golden sand, calm and clear water, fringes of coconut palms for shade, and, of course, Sunshine's Beach Bar. Four Seasons thought so highly of it that they put their resort here. It's definitely a beach to visit, if only for an afternoon.

Windward Beach

As the name implies, this is an eastern coast beach popular with windsurfers and surfers. It's not recommended for those who like to lounge around and take a leisurely swim.

Oualie Beach

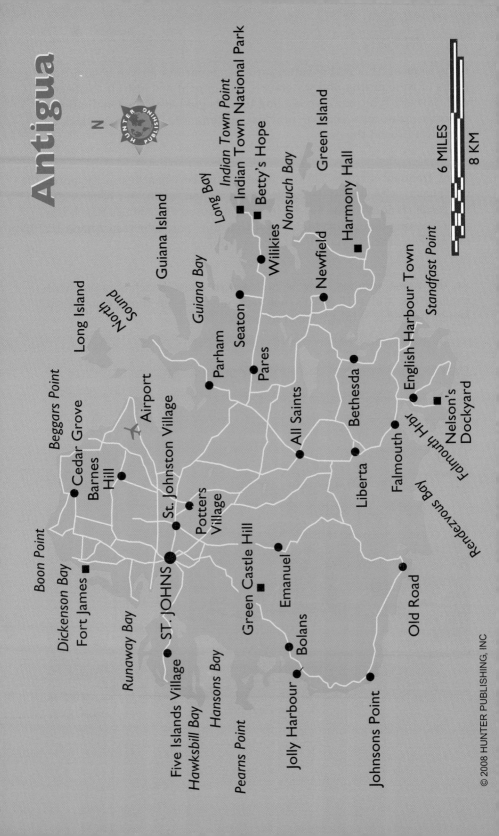

Antigua

N

North Sound

Boon Point

Dickenson Bay

Fort James

Runaway Bay

Five Islands Village

Hawksbill Bay

Hansons Bay

Pearns Point

Jolly Harbour

Johnsons Point

Old Road

Rendezvous Bay

Falmouth Hrbr.

Nelson's Dockyard

Standfast Point

English Harbour Town

Falmouth

Liberta

Bethesda

Harmony Hall

Green Island

Nonsuch Bay

Newfield

Willikies

Betty's Hope

Indian Town National Park

Indian Town Point

Long Bay

Guiana Bay

Guiana Island

Long Island

Beggars Point

Cedar Grove

Barnes Hill

Airport

St. Johnston Village

Potters Village

ST. JOHNS

Green Castle Hill

Emanuel

Bolans

All Saints

Pares

Seaton

Parham

6 MILES

8 KM

© 2008 HUNTER PUBLISHING, INC

Antigua & Barbuda
The Allure of the Islands

The country of Antigua (pronounced an-TEE-ga) and Barbuda (pronounced bar-BYU-da) is the kind of place you discover almost by accident and then come back to year-after-year because it seems like home. In fact, many of the hoteliers will tell you they have patrons who have been coming here the same week of each year for 15, 20 or 25 years.

What makes it such a desirable destination? Well, for starters, the main island of Antigua has a jagged coastline

marked with numerous bays and inlets, and most of these have their own beautiful white sand beaches. In fact, the Antiguans boast of having 365 beaches, one for every day of the year. Although you'd be hard pressed to count them all, each has its own combination of soft white sand, crystal clear warm water and other attractions that draw people to idle away the hours. Many bays only have one resort on them, and all beaches are public, so you can explore at will.

Accommodations for the most part are in small boutique hotels aimed at travelers who want to be pampered. Sandals is the only international hotel chain with a presence on the island (although that may have changed by the time this book goes to press), and the largest hotel, the Royal Antiguan, was constructed by the government. For the most part, you find intimate, comfortable lodgings where you get to know the owners, managers and staff, as well as other patrons. If you stay at a certain hotel more than once, you'll find that the staff remembers you from one time to the next – that's a unique part of the Antiguans' charm.

Internationally, Antigua is known for its annual **Sailing Week** in late April, when large yachts and sailing vessels from around the world gather

Antigua from space

to enjoy races and camaraderie that envelopes the entire island. For the yachting community, it's one of the major parties of the year.

As the operating base for regional airlines such as LIAT, the country has become a major hub for travel to the surrounding Caribbean islands. You can easily come into Antigua on major carriers, stay a while, and then visit other islands without a lot of preplanning or hassle.

Here's What to Look For According to the Type of Traveler You Are

The Perfect Cruise Passenger will love the all-inclusive resorts like Curtain Bluff, Blue Waters, St. James Club, Galley Bay, Occidental Pineapple Beach, and Sandals, where you never have to leave to get all that you want. St. John's is a perfect shopping port of call, and the glittering casinos provide cruise-type entertainment.

The Boots-On Adventurer should head to the hills for a climb up Boggy Peak into the rainforest or to the sea where wrecks turn a dive into a real exploration. For a soft adventure, check out the Antigua Rainforest Canopy Tour, where you coast along zip lines through the trees. If you're looking for basic accommodations, try South Coast Horizon, Antigua Yacht Club, the Catamaran Hotel or Coco's, where the living is easy but not glamorous or super-pricey. A side-trip to Barbuda is recommended to see the amazing frigate bird colony and do some diving among the numerous wrecks that circle the island. If you want day-long adventures, inquire about 4x4 overland tours or the circumnavigations on catamarans.

The Cultural Explorer will love downtown St. John's, where the Vendor's Mall and Farmer's Market let you meet the Antiguans. Start your historical explorations at the Museum of Antigua and Barbuda, then visit St. John's Cathedral. Further immerse yourself in history by staying at the Copper and Lumber Hotel or Admiral's Inn in Nelson's Dockyard, from where you can explore all the preserved naval fortifications of English Harbour.

The "I Like What I Like" traveler would do well to choose either an all-inclusive hotel or one of the private villas where you can set yourself up with all the comforts of home. For the ultimate in luxury, Jumby Bay or Carlisle Bay will satisfy all your needs. The array of restaurants includes steak houses, seafood restaurants and all sorts of ethnic cuisines. The casinos, while small, do their best to resemble Las Vegas. Golfing is great at either Cedar Valley or Jolly Harbour.

The Incurable Romantic has a wealth of accommodations to choose from, since Antigua is considered one of the most romantic islands in the Leewards. Choose Sandals for a honeymoon-type atmosphere (and gorgeous sunsets), Blue Waters for solicitous service, The Beach Club on Barbuda for an "out at the end of the world" experience, or sedate Cocobay or Coconut Beach Club if you want to be left utterly alone on a beautiful beach. You cannot get more romantic than dining on the beach at Coconut Grove, or in high style at The Pavilion. For an evening or two of sheer privacy, charter a yacht for your own custom cruise around the islands, stopping wherever your bliss takes you.

The Family Social Director will find kid-friendly resorts like The Verandah, Sunsail Club Colonna, South Coast Horizons, Hawksbill or Jolly Beach to everyone's liking. Or if you know you need a kitchen and a home-like setting, look at the villas or cottages at Jolly Harbour, Galleon Beach, South Coast Horizon or Antigua Village, where many activities are offered within the properties. Everyone should enjoy a day in the rainforest riding zip lines along the tree canopies or acting out on the Pirates of Antigua's *Black Swan*. There are fast-food restaurants such as Subway and KFC, and Big Banana or Mauro's will satisfy any and all pizza lovers. Don't forget to take the little ones to Stingray City and Nelson's Dockyard.

The Ultimate Shopper will revel in the boutiques lining the streets of downtown St. John's, especially at Heritage and Redcliffe Quays. If you don't need a beach, stay at Heritage Hotel right downtown. If you require a little sun and sand, stay in the Dickenson Bay area, just a short ride from St. John's. Plan a lunch at Harmony Hall where, in addition to a delightful al fresco Italian/Caribbean meal, you'll find an art gallery filled with paintings, prints, sculptures, jewelry, hand-made clothing and crafts by artists from Antigua and other Caribbean islands.

A Brief History

The history of Antigua and Barbuda began long before Columbus sighted the previously uncharted island in 1493 and named it after Santa Maria de la Antigua. In fact, he "discovered" a place with a history thousands of years old. According to artifacts found in the Jolly Beach area, the first Amerindian tribes landed here from South America around 1775 BC. Then the island again went through an uninhabited era until the Arawak Indians began migrating from South America. These rural, peaceful people organized an advanced agrarian society until fresh water became scarce, and they began to come under attack from the marauding and warlike Carib Indians. The Caribs did not settle here, but used the island as a base for collecting food and causing trouble.

When the major colonial powers in the region turned their attention to Antigua in the 16th century, they found little in the way of valuable resources or fresh water. They had to weather attacks by the Caribs as well. Finally, in 1625, Antigua, St. Kitts, Nevis and Barbuda were taken under the protection of England. However, the island wasn't colonized until 1632, when the English sent over an exploration party from St. Kitts and Captain Edward Warner established a settlement at Falmouth, claiming the island for the British Crown.

The Caribs continued their harassment, and the colonists lived much as the Arawak Indians had, cultivating cassava, sweet potatoes, ginger and maize and taking food from the sea. Finally, the Caribs disappeared, paving the way for a quiet period when planters began growing tobacco as a major cash crop for export. When the prospects for that tobacco declined due to overproduction, the farmers turned to a crop imported from Brazil – sugar cane. Thus began the plantation system and importation of slave labor from Africa, setting the course of history in the island and throughout the Leewards.

As sugar became increasingly important to Europe, other countries became interested in Antigua. In 1665 the Dutch attacked, and then the following year the French laid siege, destroying sugar plantations, taking slaves and devastating the island. Finally, in 1666, the Treaty of Breda ended the war and the island was given to Britain once again. This began an era of prosperity where large sugar plantations were the focal point of the economy, and the British fortified their holding in a key strategic area of the Caribbean. Over 40 military installations were created along the rugged and frequently indented coastline – and a few of the defensive structures such as Nelson's Dockyard and Shirley Heights survive to this day.

One of the largest landholders was Sir Christopher Codrington, who in 1665 also leased land on Barbuda from the English crown. This established the link that eventually led to the crown annexing Barbuda to Antigua in 1860.

During the time when sugar was in its prime, the slave labor system flourished and the slaves were subjected to brutal conditions. When slavery was abolished by the British Parliament in 1807, there were over 23,000 slaves, 2,000 whites and 4,000 free colored on the island. Since the land was still in the hands of plantation owners, the freed slaves gathered in the villages and shanty towns around St. John's.

Reliving History

Mills at Betty's Hope

To get a glimpse of what life was like during the time when sugar reigned, be sure to visit **Betty's Hope**, a recreated plantation with demonstrations of colonial life and the Caribbean's only authentic and functional windmill. Factory Road just south of Pares village. ☎ 268-462-1469.

During WWII, the Americans established a military base that brought construction jobs, and Antigua began a new phase of prosperity, fueled by growth and tourism. The island also saw a rise in labor unions that sought improvement in working conditions and wages. In 1956, a ministerial system of government was introduced, which led to the appointment of a chief minister in 1961.

In 1966, Vere Bird represented Antigua as the chief minister in a constitution conference held in London, which resulted in Antigua and Barbuda becoming the first associated British state in the Caribbean. That in turn led to the islands achieving full sovereign independence in 1981. Antiguans now had total control of their external and internal affairs, with Vere Bird as their prime minister. He held office until 1994, when he stepped aside and his son Lester Bird and the Antiguan Labour Party took over the reins. In the face of widespread rumors of corruption and graft as well as severe problems with the country's infrastructure, the ALP lost their majority to the United Progressive Party in 2004, and Baldwin Spencer assumed the office of prime minister. The next elections will be held in 2010.

The Facts

Population: 68,722, primarily descendants of African slaves and indigenous Indians, with a growing number of residents from other Caribbean islands such as Guyana, Montserrat, Jamaica, Barbados and Trinidad. There is also a flourishing community of retirees from Canada, the US and Europe, giving the island a truly international flavor.

Language: English, with a West Indies lilt.

Main City: St. John's.

Government & Economy: The country gained its independence from Britain on November 1, 1981. It now follows the British parliamentary system, with a prime minister over a bicameral legislature comprised of 17 elected members in the House of Representatives and 17 appointed members in the upper Senate. Elections are held at intervals of no more than five years. The British monarchy is represented by a governor-general, who advises the government, appoints the members of the Senate and plays a largely ceremonial role.

The economy of the islands is changing. In recent history, 70% of the economy was based on tourism and about 10% came from fishing and agriculture. But with the growth of Antigua's online gaming industry and large-scale construction, other sectors are experiencing significant growth.

People & Culture: Antiguans and Barbudans are proud people who care greatly about their appearance, their families and their country. The population is the size of a large town and yet the country is independent and has a seat in the UN. Citizens participate in the everyday dealings of the government, and you only have to listen to one of the local radio talk shows to hear how passionately those citizens take their politics.

The villages of Antigua were formed around churches, many of which stand to this day as graceful reminders of the past and interesting focal points for local culture. Whenever you are around and about, you will see village entrepreneurs at roadside stands offering food and drinks, local produce and crafts. Be cautious about patronizing the local food stands; they are unregulated and sanitary conditions may not be optimal.

One of the highlights of the year for native Antiguans is Carnival, a wild and colorful celebration of music, dance and costumes held at the end of July and beginning of August. For Barbudans, the annual festival is Caribana, held in late May and early June. Also highly important to the islanders is the national sport of cricket. The country hosts test matches on the International Cricket Conference circuit. In 2007 it was one of nine Caribbean venues for the ICC World Cup; the new stadium is said to be one of the top five in the world.

Carnival

Geography: This island nation is composed of three islands – Antigua, Barbuda and Redonda. Antigua is the largest at 108 square miles, and is comprised of natural harbors, flat lands, rolling hills and Boggy Peak (1,319 ft altitude), with surrounding rainforest at the southwestern end. The island is fringed with smaller islands and coral reefs that make navigation tricky at times.

Barbuda, at 66 square miles, is a low-lying coral island 26 miles north of Antigua, geographically distinguished by pink sand beaches and Codrington Lagoon. It is home to 1,500 residents and the largest population of frigate birds in the Lesser Antilles, along with 400 other bird species.

Redonda, only a mile long and a third of a mile wide, is a volcanic cone with steep cliffs. While active as a phosphate mining center in the past, the island is now uninhabited.

The center of commerce is the capital city of St. John's, which welcomes large numbers of cruise ships in its deep harbor. At the southern end of the island, English Harbour is visited by yachtsmen from all over the world, as well as tourists visiting the historical sites at Nelson's Dockyard and Shirley Heights.

Climate: The weather is delightfully tropical, with highs averaging from 81°F in the coldest months of January and February to 87°F in the hottest months of July and August. Evening temperatures rarely fall below 72°F. The rainfall is heaviest in the summer months.

Flora & Fauna: The islands go through periods of sufficient rainfall that turn everything green, and then periods of drought when vegetation dries up quickly. However, nature here has adapted to the cycles. Among the most noted plants is the large **agave**, known as the "dagger log" because its leaves are shaped like daggers. Once in its lifetime the plant sprouts a spike, often reaching 20 feet high and topped with yellow florets. The Antiguans have named it their national flower.

The **Antiguan black pineapple**, the national fruit, is cultivated in the rainforest area along with bananas. There is also some production of sugar cane, squash, yams, cucumbers, mangoes, coconut, papaya, citrus and other food crops for local consumption.

Guiana Island, just off the northeast coast of Antigua, is still heavily forested (although the island is being considered for development) and supports a large colony of nesting seabirds. The marshes and salt ponds around the island are home to stilts, egrets, pelicans and other water birds, while the many lush gardens attract several species of hummingbirds. Unfortunately, development may have begun by the time this book is published.

Agaves in bloom

A major attraction for bird watchers is **Codrington Lagoon** on Barbuda, where the dramatic frigate birds have one of the largest colonies in the world. Boat tours will

Goat Point

Barbuda

Goat Island

Kid Island

Hog Point

Two Foot Bay

Goat Island Flush

Dark Cave

Frigate Bird Sanctuary

Pigeon Cliff

Codrington Lagoon

Low Bay

Airport

CODRINGTON

Darby Cave Sinkhole

THE HIGHLANDS

Martello Tower

Dulcina

N

The River Landing

Palmetto Point

Salt Pond

The Castle

Coco Point

Gravenor Bay

Spanish Point

6 MILES

8 KM

© 2008 HUNTER PUBLISHING, INC

take you close to the nesting areas so that you can see the snowy white chicks and their ebony parents, socializing and feeding the young ones.

Sea turtles, including the green, loggerhead, hawksbill and leatherback species, are native to Antigua and Barbuda. The loggerhead is considered a vulnerable species, and the other three are

Great Bird Island

endangered, so there are protections in place to prevent people from disturbing them. Various ecological groups study them and conduct nighttime watches to track nesting patterns.

Antiguan racer

The Antiguan racer, one of the rarest snakes on earth, is found on **Great Bird Island**. This area also has one of the largest mangrove systems in the Lesser Antilles. Elsewhere on the island you can find mongoose and several species of lizards as well as roaming herds of goats and cows and an occasional horse or donkey. To the chagrin of many visitors who like quiet at night, the tree frogs, with their nocturnal loud chirping habits, are everywhere.

On Barbuda, after Hurricane Luis in 1995, iguanas began showing up in wooded areas. Residents reported seeing some with lengths of up to six feet. Fallow deer, wild boar, wild donkeys, red-footed tortoises, turtles, and guinea fowl are also seen wandering on the island.

The islands are fringed with coral reefs, home to a wide variety of fish, coral and other sea life. Snorkeling and scuba diving are popular pursuits for those wishing to see the colorful array firsthand. In addition, some 27 species of whales and dolphins have been observed in the warm waters of Antigua and Barbuda.

Travel Information

When to Go

The climate, and its history of being relatively free of hurricane damage, makes the island hospitable year-round. The warmest months are the summer, when the trade winds die down and the humid air results in sticky conditions. Traditional high season begins in mid-December and runs through the end of April, to include the world-renowned Sailing Week.

Getting There

There are two ways to enter Antigua, by air or by sea. All incoming travelers via air must show a valid passport and an onward or return ticket. Departure tax collected at the airport is US$20 or EC$50, and exact change is required.

Barbuda can only be entered by air or ferry boat from Antigua, or by first going through customs at one of the harbors mentioned below for private boats.

By Air

All travelers land at **VC Bird International Airport**, in the island's northeast corner, about 20 minutes by vehicle from St. John's. The airport is large enough to receive 747s and wide bodies from Europe, Canada and the US, as well as smaller inter-island jets from various US and Caribbean operators.

Among the major North American operators, which can also book connecting flights with the regional carriers, are:

Air Canada, with direct service from Toronto to Antigua. ☎ 800-744-2472, www.aircanada.com.

American Airlines, with daily connecting service on American Eagle from San Juan, Puerto Rico and a daily direct flight from Baltimore. ☎ 800-433-7300, www.aa.com.

Continental Airlines, flying non-stop from Newark to Antigua one day a week, and with several non-stop flights from Newark and Houston into San Juan each week. ☎ 800-231-0856, www.continental.com.

Delta Airlines, with non-stop service from Atlanta two to three days a week (depending on season) as well as non-stop flights from Atlanta into St. Maarten and San Juan several days a week. ☎ 800-241-4141, www.delta.com.

United, offering daily non-stop service from Chicago to San Juan, and non-stop flights several days a week from Orlando, Miami, Tampa and Baltimore to San Juan. ☎ 800-864-8331, www.united.com.

US Air, flying non-stop from Charlotte and Philadelphia into Antigua, plus non-stop from Charlotte into St. Kitts and St. Maarten, and from Charlotte, Chicago, Tampa and Philadelphia into San Juan. ☎ 800-622-1015, www.usair.com.

If you are traveling to islands beyond Antigua, or are looking for a connecting flight when carriers don't offer direct flights, these inter-island carriers operate to and from Antigua:

Air Jamaica, ☎ 800-523-5585, www.airjamaica.com.

Caribbean Airlines, ☎ 800-538-2942, www.bwee.com.

LIAT, ☎ 268-480-5610, www.fly-liat.com.

By Sea

Antigua enjoys an international reputation as a port not only for cruise ships, but also for international yachts and mega-yachts. The cruise ships dock either at Heritage Quay in the center of St. John's, or at the cruise terminal at Deep Water, two miles away.

Private boats enter the country at either English Harbour, Jolly Harbour or St. John's, all of which have customs stations where you can obtain cruising permits to go anywhere in Antiguan waters, including Barbuda. Captains of the boats must present their papers plus passports for each passenger and crew member before they can leave the craft. Full-service marinas are located at English Harbour, Nelson's Dockyard, Falmouth Harbour, and Jolly Harbour.

Customs

Visitors to the island are allowed 200 cigarettes, two 26-oz bottles of wine or spirits, and five ounces of perfume duty-free. Your bags may be inspected upon arrival, and if any goods are identified as meant for sale on the island, you may be charged duty. Plants, flowers, fruit, guns and illicit drugs are forbidden and will be confiscated.

Special Events & Holidays

The first major event of the year in Antigua is Sailing Week, held annually in late April. Expect rooms and reservations to be hard to find during this time, as the yachting set from around the world descends upon English Harbour for the largest regatta in the Caribbean.

Sailing Week

In late July and early August, the entire island focuses on Carnival. This bacchanalia includes beauty pageants, parades through St. John's, and tons of food and liquor and limin' (West Indian for celebrating and socializing with friends), akin to Mardi Gras in the US.

The island nation celebrates its Independence Day on November 1 with parades, speeches, concerts and a day of celebration.

To see specific dates for particular years, see the Calendar at the official tourism site, www.antigua-barbuda.org.

January

New Year's Day – Public holiday.

Official start of cricket season. ☎ 268-462-9090.

February

Valentine's Day Regatta – Jolly Harbour Yacht Club. ☎ 268-461-6324, www.jollyharbouryachtclub.com.

Power Boat Rally – Antigua Yacht Club. ☎ 268-460-1799, www.antiguayachtclub.com.

March

Antigua International Laser Open – Antigua Yacht Club, English Harbor. ☎ 268-460-1799, www.antiguayachtclub.com.

Antigua Open Golf Tournament – Cedar Valley Golf Course. ☎ 268-462-0161.

Antigua and Barbuda National Dressage Challenge – Spring Hill Riding Club. ☎ 268-773-3139.

April

Annual Model Boat Race Competition – Sponsored by the Ministry of Tourism. ☎ 268-462-0480.

Walk for Nature, Earth Day commemoration – Sponsored by the Environmental Awareness Group. ☎ 268-462-6236.

Good Friday – Public holiday.

Easter Monday – Public holiday.

Antigua Classic Yacht Regatta – English Harbour. One of the foremost classic yacht regattas of the world. ☎ 268-460-1799, www.antiguaclassics. com.

FEI World Dressage Challenge – Spring Hill Riding School. ☎ 268-773-3139.

Mega Yacht Regatta – Sponsored by Antigua Yacht Club. Yachts must be more than 100 ft. in length to compete. ☎ 268-460-1799, www. antiguayachtclub.com.

Guadeloupe to Antigua Race – Sponsored by Antigua Yacht Club as start of Sailing Week activities. ☎ 268-460-1799, www.antiguayachtclub.com.

Antigua Sailing Week – English Harbour. Parties, barbecues, races, Lord Nelson's Ball and more. ☎ 268-562-3276, www.sailingweek.com.

May

Labor Day – Public holiday.

International Cricket One-Day Internationals – Antigua Recreation Grounds. ☎ 268-481-2450/51/52, www.windiescricket.com.

Antigua Tennis Week – Curtain Bluff Hotel. Includes professional players from around the world. ☎ 268-462-8400.

Antigua & Barbuda Sports Fishing Tournament – Falmouth Harbour. ☎ 268-460-7400 or 268-762-4400.

Barbuda Caribana – Codrington. ☎ 268-460-0077, www.barbudaful.net.

June

International Cricket Test Match – Antigua Recreation Grounds. ☎ 268-481-2450/51/52, www.windiescricket.com.

Whit Monday – Public holiday.

International Amateur Badminton Tournament – Perry Bay Multicultural Center. ☎ 268-560-9981/773-2649, 44-208-808-7679 UK.

July

Caricom Day – Public holiday.

Caribbean Sailing Association Dinghy Championship – Antigua Yacht Club, English Harbour. ☎ 268-460-1799, www.antiguayachtclub.com.

Antigua Carnival – Activities begin in late July. ☎ 1 268-462-4707, www. antiguacarnival.com.

August

Antigua Carnival – Includes public holidays in early August. ☎ 268-462-4707, www.antiguacarnival.com.

Antigua Carnival

September

Jolly Harbour Annual Regatta – Jolly Harbour. Held on last weekend of the month. ☎ 268-461-6300, www.jollyharbouryachtclub.com.

October

De Jam Festival, various venues. DJs from around the world play the best of urban music. www.dejamfestival.com.

National Warri Festival – ☎ 268-461-6400 or 268-461-1615.

Heritage Day (National Dress Day), October 31 – Parades of residents in local costume. Sponsored by the Ministry of Culture. ☎ 268-562-5303.

November

Independence Day, November 1 – Public holiday. Special events throughout the day, including a parade, church service and speeches.

December

Antigua Charter Yacht Show – ☎ 268-460-1530, www.antigua-charter-yacht-meeting.com.

VC Bird Day – Public holiday commemorating the life of the late V.C. Bird, first prime minister of Antigua.

Christmas Champagne Party, December 25 – Nelson's Dockyard. ☎ 268-462-4601.

Christmas Day, December 25 – Public holiday.

Boxing Day, December 26 – Public holiday.

Health

Most hotels have doctors on call for guest emergencies, and there are top-notch physicians, dentists and eye specialists available on the island. **Holburton Hospital** near St. John's is the main health facility, and there is a private hospital, **Adelin Clinic**, on Ft. Road near St. John's. **Mount St. John's Medical Center**, the imposing new hospital high above St. John's, is scheduled to open in 2008. The **Spring**

readily available for your transfer to a hotel or resort. The trip can take 10-20 minutes if you are headed to Dickenson, Runaway Bay or Deep Bay resorts and up to 30-40 minutes if you are going to the southern part of the island.

Taxi Service

Taxis are the most common means of transportation for visitors, especially since driving is done on the left side of the road. Most of the drivers are well versed in locations and sights to be pointed out, and are very accommodating in making whatever arrangements you need. If you are going out to dinner, for example, they will arrange to meet you at a set time to take you back to your accommodations.

Sample fares, one-way:

- Airport to Jolly Harbour area, US$24, EC$64
- Airport to Dickenson Bay, US$16, EC$42
- Airport to Nelson's Dockyard, US$31, EC$82
- Jolly Harbour area to St. John's, US$18, EC$48
- Dickenson Bay resorts to St. John's, US$12, EC$32
- Nelson's Dockyard area to St. John's, US$24, EC$64

Car Rentals

A car rental is ideal for traveling around the island on your own schedule. To drive, you will need to have a valid license and major credit card, and you will be required to pay US$20 for a temporary Antiguan driver's license. These are available through the rental company or at any Antiguan Police Station.

There are many gas stations in the St. John's area, but once you travel out into the countryside they become scarce, so be sure to fuel up before you set out. Expect to pay about US$5 for a gallon of gasoline. However, since the island is only about 12 miles at the widest point, and you can't go more than 40 mph on the rough roads, you won't be using fuel in the same way you do at home.

Although the available maps are clear and informative, there are few street signs; keep an eye out for landmarks in order to find your way. If you get lost, the Antiguans are very accommodating about directions.

Car Rental Companies

ATS Car Rental & Limousine, ☎ 268-562-1709

Avis Rent-a-Car, ☎ 268-462-2840

Budget Rent-A-Car, ☎ 268-462-3009

Dion's Rent-A-Car & Taxi, ☎ 268-462-3466

Dollar Rent-A-Car, ☎ 268-462-0362

Hertz Rent-A-Car, ☎ 268-481-4440

Lion's Car Rental, ☎ 268-562-2708
Oakland Rent-A-Car, ☎ 268-462-3021
St. John's Car Rental, ☎ 268-462-0594
Thrifty Car Rental, ☎ 268-462-9532

Exploring
On Foot

The geography and history of the island have produced many interesting hiking trails. Walkers can spend a day strolling through St. John's and visiting the many historical sights there, or go out into the largely undeveloped countryside. Trails in the National Park at English Harbour take you around the battlements at Nelson's Dockyard and Falmouth Harbor. In the National Park at Half Moon Bay, you can start from one of the most beautiful beaches on the island and then climb into the hills for vistas to Guadeloupe (look for the stone arch rising 150 feet from the ocean). Another popular trail takes you through the rainforest on the southwestern end of the island, from Wallings Dam to Rendezvous Bay.

Two organizations hosting hikes on a periodic basis are the **Historical & Archaeological Society** (☎ 268-462-4930/1469), and the **Environmental Awareness Group** (☎ 268-462-6236). Antigua is also fortunate to have a chapter of the **Hash House Harriers** (☎ 268-461-0686), an international group that offers hikers a fun trek of five-seven miles, ending with suitable libations.

Zip-Lining

Many of the prime rainforest areas in the Caribbean have found that people love soaring through the canopies on zip lines, and Antigua is following the trend with a new **Rainforest Canopy Tour**. You simply hook on the harness, put on a helmet, and then zoom along lines, some more than 300 feet long and 200 to 300 feet high, as you cross

Rainforest canopy zip-lining

gorges and view the tree tops of the canopy. If you don't savor the idea of flying through the air with little protection, the tour also includes short trails, rope elements, suspension bridges and the "Leap of Faith," a 36-ft controlled vertical descent. Tours run from 45 to 150 minutes, and are offered seven days a week. ☎ 268-562-6363, www.antiguarainforest.com.

On Wheels

Outside St. John's and the villages, the terrain can get hilly and rough, but back-road trails often lead to some of the best attractions such as secluded beaches, archeological sites and historical ruins.

Car or Jeep

Off-road sightseeing can be very rewarding. Most car rental companies offer 4WD vehicles if you want to go it on your own.

Overland Tour Operators

Adventure Off-Road Tours uses All Terrain Vehicles (ATVs) to take visitors through old sugar estates and into the center of the island. ☎ 268-464-9253.

Estate Safari Tours has 4X4 Nissan Patrol vehicles driven by knowledgeable guides. They'll take you on routes showing the hidden highlights and great views, then end with a meal at the Safari Bar and Grill, their own restaurant in Parham. ☎ 268-462-4713, 268-727-8815.

Happy Trails Tours specializes in off-road and historical tours using air-conditioned 4x4 vehicles. In addition to visiting the rainforest areas, you can combine a land tour with Paddles Eco-Tours for a complete day. ☎ 268-726-4273/ 464-2089, www.happytrailsantigua.com.

Island Safari stands out because of their custom-built safari-rigged 4x4 Land Rovers, complete with roll bars and Bobcat seats and belts. Their rides take you into rugged territory for a view of the southern and western sides of the island. ☎ 268-480-1225, www.tropicalad.com.

Scenic & Historic Tours

Among the highlights of ground tours are Devil's Bridge, Betty's Hope plantation, the rainforest area and the English Harbour/Nelson's Dockyard area. For more details, see *Seeing the Sights* on page 404.

Carib-World Travel acts as an Antiguan tour operator, offering a number of day tours, including one to Cades Pineapple Plantation and day-trips to Montserrat complete with air travel. ☎ 268-480-2999, fax 268-480-2995, www.carib-world.com.

Elvis George & Sons Tours has been offering tour services for 17 years. They offer taxi tours around the island as well as serve as agents for water-based or special tours. ☎ 268-461-5660

Jackson Taxi & Tours is another long-standing tour operator, having been in the business for 40 years. They offer 47- and 24-seat buses as well as smaller vans, for beach and scenic tours. ☎ 268-728-3953, www.jackstaxi.com.

Lawrence of Antigua has both vans and buses, all air conditioned, for individual, family or group tours. They can also provide custom tours to your specifications. ☎ 268-463-3238, www.lawrenceofantigua.com.

Scenic Tours Antigua offers a number of land-based tours using a large and comfortable air conditioned bus. Groups of 8-10 are ideal, but if you have less, give them a call and they can customize something or fit you into an ongoing tour. ☎ 268-764-3060 or US 888-380-1234, www.scenictoursantigua.com.

HISTORY AWAITS

Nelson's Dockyard Museum

The Antigua & Barbuda National Parks oversees the collection of historic sites in the southern part of the island around English Harbour. Your first stop in exploring this area should be **Nelson's Dockyard**, where there are many original buildings on display. Your admission ticket will also admit you to the **Dow's Hill Historical Center**, high on the hill above the Dockyard, which offers a multi-media presentation about Antigua's history. The Parks Service also offers four guided tours, including a walk through Nelson's Dockyard and a hike to explore the fortifications at **Fort Berkeley**, a water tour to see the **Pillars of Hercules** rock formation and the **Dockyard** as sailors see it, an archeology trek in 4WD drive vehicles, and an eco-historical tour.

All must be arranged in advance, and there are fees involved based on the size of your group and extent of the tour. Call ☎ 268-481-5021 to discuss your preferences, and they will create a personalized tour for you. To preview the tours, see www.nationalparksantigua.com/new.

Bicycle Rentals

The rolling hills and scenery may inspire you to pick up some mountain bikes and find your own trails. Bike rentals are available at **Bike Plus** in St. John's (☎ 268-462-2453/6050), or at **Paradise Boat Sales Rentals & Charters** in Jolly Harbour (☎ 268-460-7125).

On Water

The clear, bright turquoise waters, the colorful and expansive reefs with their teeming tropical life, the brilliant white sand beaches accessible only from the water – these are the things most visitors come for. And on Antigua, there are a multitude of ways to explore the depths and the beaches.

Snorkeling

Antigua has great beaches and all of them are open to the public. But the real attraction for snorkelers is the reefs sitting just off many of these beaches, providing underwater sightseeing that doesn't involve a boat. The best beaches for this are **Half Moon Bay**, **Cades Bay**, **Hawksbill**, **Freeman's Bay**, **Long Bay** and **Turner's Beach**. **Cades Reef** and **Bird** and **Green Islands** are prime destinations for most of the boat tours that offer snorkeling, so check to see which you will be visiting.

If you don't bring your own equipment, most of the tour boats and hotels offer it free. If you are going on your own, you can rent equipment from **Sea Sports WatersPorts** at Dickenson Bay (☎ 268-462-3355, www.seasportsantigua.com), or purchase it from **Aqua Sports**, a retail store in Heritage Quay (☎ 268-480-3090, www.aquasportsantigua.com).

Scuba Diving

Antigua's dive offerings are excellent, with coral canyons, sea caves and teeming ocean life as well as numerous boat wrecks. Depths vary from the wreck of the *Jettias* at 25 feet, to Sunken Rock at 120 feet or more. Prime sites also include **Cades Reef**, **Ariadne Shoal**, and **Sandy Island**, as well as **Bird Channel** and the **Pillars**

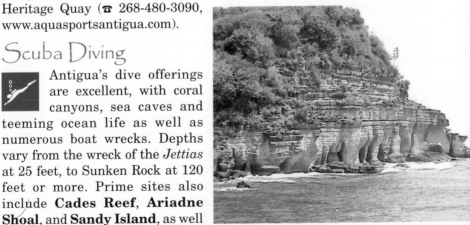

Pillars of Hercules

of Hercules. Go to www.123dive.com/Antigua to read a discussion of the various sites.

In addition to the dive operators listed below, many hotels such as the St. James Club, Curtain Bluff, and Sandals have their own PADI instructors and dive tours.

Dive Operators

Antigua Scuba Center has two locations – English Harbour and Long Bay. ☎ 212-380-1502 or 268-729-4698, www.antiguascuba.com.

Deep Bay Divers is in St. Johns, so it's convenient for cruise ship passengers. ☎ 268-463-8000, www.deepbaydivers.com.

Dive Antigua offers instruction, equipment and dives at Dickenson Bay. ☎ 268-462-3483, www.diveantigua.com.

Dockyard Divers specializes in dives off the south coast, along with instruction and equipment. Nelson's Dockyard. ☎ 268-460-1178/729-3040.

Indigo Divers offers dives on Cades Reef, as well as instruction in English and German. Jolly Harbour. ☎ 268-729-3483, www.indigo-divers.com.

Jolly Dive operates out of Jolly Beach Hotel, but anyone can use the equipment and go on the dives. ☎ 268-462-8305, www.jollydive.com.

Long Bay Dive Shop is at Long Bay Hotel and operates dives not only on the eastern side but throughout the island's perimeter. Closed in September. ☎ 268-463-2005.

Water Tours

Whether you want to circumnavigate the island or just take a sunset cruise, water tours are the best way to get acclimated to the island and all it has to offer. Genial and knowledgeable crews love to get a good party going and many provide lunch as well as all the rum punch you can drink. Most offer snorkeling equipment at no extra charge, but if you have your own, feel free to bring it along.

Water Tour Operators

Adventure Antigua specializes in eco-tours to the northern outer islands using a 50-ft power catamaran. The company also offers Xtreme Navigation circumnavigation tours in a high-speed 40-ft boat that stops at Sting Ray City, Green Island, Nelson's Dockyard, and Rendezvous Bay. ☎ 268-726-6355, www.adventureantigua.com.

Antigua Seafaris does exhilarating four-hour circumnavigations in 40-ft high-speed boats as well as individual snorkeling tours using personal water scooters (for ages 12 and up). ☎ 268-726-4435, www.antiguaseafaris.com.

Antigua Paddles Eco Kayak Tour explores the northern islands' ecosystems using kayaks. ☎ 268-463-1944, www.antiguapaddles.com.

Creole Cruises has lobster lunches on a deserted island or snorkeling cruises in 30-ft Pirogues with bimini tops for shade. ☎ 268-460-5130, www.creolecruisesantigua.com.

Excellence and **Tiami Cruises** sail to Barbuda, run tours to Cades Reef or circumnavigate using high-speed catamarans. ☎ 268-460-1225, www. tropicalad.com.

Miguel's Holiday Adventure has day tours with lunch on Prickly Pear Island. ☎ 268-460-9978/ 772-3213, www.pricklypearisland.com.

Pirates of Antigua delights families with tours on the *Black Swan*, a refurbished 89-ft sailing schooner. Kids can hoist the mainsail, learn pirate-speak and even choose to make a sibling or friend walk the plank. Tours include lunch, refreshments and a stop for snorkeling. ☎ 268-562-7946, www.piratesofantigua.com.

SeaSports Tours also uses high-speed 40-ft boats for customized tours or visits to Barbuda, Redonda and the outer reefs. ☎ 268-462-3355, www. seasportsantigua.com.

Wadadli Cats has the largest and newest fleet of catamarans, offering circumnavigation, triple-destination, Bird Island or Cades Reef tours plus alfresco lunches and entertainment. The staff is entertaining, the boats give a smooth ride, and the tours are great. ☎ 268-462-4792, www. wadadlicats.com.

FOR THE KIDS - SWIM WITH GLIDING MONSTERS

An unusual adventure that opens up the underwater world to children is Stingray City. The owners have built an offshore natural habitat for these gliding monsters of the deep, and offer guided snorkeling tours that are safe and perfect for the smaller set. Boats depart from a dock at Seatons four times a day, and snorkeling equipment is included. ☎ 268-562-7297, www.stingraycityantigua.com.

Watersports

The choice on most of the Leeward Islands is whether to spend time under the water on or top of it. Here are some ways to do the latter in sailboats or on windsurfers, kite boards or other joyous means of transportation.

Kite Antigua, the only dedicated kite boarding operation in Antigua, offers lessons and rental equipment. Jabberwock Beach. ☎ 268-727-3983.

Jolly Harbour Watersports has equipment for windsurfing, water cycling, skiing, kayaking or sailing as well as jet skis and wave runners. Near Castaways Beach Bar. ☎ 268-764-6501.

Sea Sports Watersports, next to Sandals, has equipment for waterskiing, parasailing, windsurfing and Sunfish sailing, as well as jet skis, jet bikes and kayaks. Dickensor Bay. ☎ 268-462-3355, www. seasportsantigua.com.

Sunsail Club Colonna offers a wide array of watersports to guests and non-guests for a fee. Activities include windsurfing, catamaran or dinghy sailing (with lessons), yachting, snorkeling and canoeing. Hodges Bay. ☎ 268-462-6263, www.sunsail.com.

Windsurfing Antigua, based at the Lord Nelson Hotel on the north coast, offers lessons and rent gear. ☎ 268-462-9463.

Hotel Guest for a Day

Just because you are staying in a villa or private home doesn't mean you can't enjoy the beaches and watersports at major resorts. Many hotels, including Sandals, Hawksbill and Grand Pineapple Beach, offer a day-use package that often includes all non-motorized watersports, use of beach lounges, and dining privileges.

Deep-Sea Fishing

There is some serious fishing to be done off the coast of Antigua. Boats available for charter include the following:

Missa Ferdie is a 38-ft Phoenix Sports Fisherman with a wide range of gear. Available for full- and half-day charters for up to six people. ☎ 268-462-1440/460-1503.

Nightwing is a 35-ft Bertram with a spacious cabin. Available for half-day, three-quarter-day and full-day charters, as well as billfish charters. ☎ 268-464-4665.

Obsession is a 45-ft Hatteras that has the distinction of being the first and only boat in Antigua to catch all five billfish species. ☎ 268-462-3174/464-3174, www.charternet.com/charters/obsession.

Overdraft, a fully equipped 40-ft fishing boat with capacity for six people, is available for deep-sea fishing. ☎ 268-462-1961/464-4954, www.antiguafishing.com.

Boat Charters

This home to the international yachting set has an impressive number of large and small boats moored in Jolly Harbour, Falmouth Harbour and English Harbour. Many are available for charters.

Antigua Yacht Charters Ltd. offers motor and sailing yachts of all sizes. ☎ 268-463-7101, www.antiguayachtcharters.com.

Exotic Destination Day Charters uses mini-boats with outboard motors that you captain yourself. ☎ 268-562-4905, exoticdestination@candw.ag.

Horizon Yacht Charters has yachts for charter, either crewed or bareboat, for vacations throughout the Leeward Islands. ☎ 866-439-1089 (toll free US), 268-562-4725, www.antiguahorizon.com.

Jabberwocky Yacht Charters offers day or overnight charters on a 50-ft Beneteau cruising yacht with comfortable accommodations. ☎ 268-764-0595, www.adventurecaribbean.com.

Miramar Sailing has day and term charters aboard a 40-ft Beneteau Oceanis 400, for sunset cruises or inter-island jaunts. ☎ 268-770-6172, www.miramarsailing.com.

Nauti Yachts offers a number of yachts for charter, including 40- to 100-ft motor yachts and catamarans. They make all arrangements, from pickup at the airport through provisioning and crew. ☎ 941-400-5679 (FL), 480-277-3435 (AZ) or 805-748-4440 (CA), www.nautiyachts.com.

Nicholson Yacht Charters, the Caribbean office of the Nicholson Yacht Charter Management Company based in Newport, RI, manages charters of yachts from 45- to 200-feet throughout the Caribbean. ☎ 268-460-1530, www.nicholson-charters.com.

Sea Spa Charters, using a 40-ft Sea Ray Sundancer, will fit the trip to your specifications. ☎ 268-562-5340.

See by Sea has day charters and sunset cruises. ☎ 268-462-1474, seebysea@hotmail.com.

Sentio is a 50-ft sailing yacht available for charter for up to 18 people. www.sail-antigua.com.

Yachting Party of the Year – Antigua Sailing Week

While Antigua may not be a household word to most travelers, yachtsmen know it as the site of one of the best regattas and parties held throughout the world. Each year, Antigua Sailing Week draws large sailing yachts for a week of competition, revelry and rowdiness that everyone on the island enjoys. In a typical year, more than 180 boats representing 27 countries compete for prizes in 19 classes according to size.

The week starts on the last Thursday in April with the Guadeloupe-to-Antigua Race. Then on Sunday, the races around

the island begin, with Division A yachts setting off from English Harbour. In the following five days, the boats follow various courses, including a circumnavigation for the larger boats, and shorter courses along the southern and western coasts for smaller boats.

After Day Three, everyone takes a rest during Lay Day, and Pigeon Point Beach becomes a playground with music, food, drinks (lots of drinks), and games. Then it's back to work until Saturday, when the grand Lord Nelson's Ball is held to award the trophies.

The entire island gets involved in this event, and food vendors vie for spots at Dickenson Beach and Jolly Harbour for the festivities at the end of certain days' races. School children take part in a design competition to come up with the best posters for the race. Other vendors supply clothing, hats and memorabilia for the racing crews to collect.

While you can't see the yachts as they are racing, since island-ringing reefs prevent them from coming close to shore, you can catch sight of them in various venues. Early Sunday morning you can view the promenade of Class A yachts out of English Harbour from the vantage point of Shirley Heights. You may get fortunate and have someone invite you onto one of the party boats that run out beyond the reefs just to get a view of the colorful spinnaker sails as the racers pass by. Or you can join the end-of-race-day parties held at Dickenson Bay beach on Sunday and at Jolly Harbour Marina on Thursday.

It's a great time to be in Antigua, especially if you love sailing. For more information and this year's schedule of events, see www.sailingweek.com.

On Horseback

 If your idea of heaven is seeing beautiful countryside and beaches atop a noble steed, the **Spring Hill Riding Club** in Falmouth could become your favorite spot on the island. This home of the Antigua Barbuda Horse Society and part of the Fédération Equestre Internationale offers trail rides with professionally trained instructors and quality horses. ☎ 268-460-7787.

By Air

One of the best ways to see the topography and layout of Antigua is by hovering above it. **Caribbean Helicopters** in Jolly Harbour offers tours for all needs and budgets, including a 15-minute half-island tour, a 30-minute full-island tour, and an overhead view of the active Montserrat volcano. The Bell 206 copter can seat four-six people and cruises at 130 mph, giving you a ride – and a view – unlike any other on the island. ☎ 268-460-5900, fax 268-460-5901, www.caribbeanhelicopters.net.

Playing & Watching Sports

Cricket

Antiguans are incredibly enthusiastic about their national sport, with good reason. Cricket in the Caribbean is unlike the sport in any other area of the world – the day-long matches are one big party, with everyone limin', jammin' and having a great time.

The country has become a noted international venue due to the construction of the Vivian Richards Cricket Stadium for the ICC Cricket World Cup Super 8 matches held in April 2007. Another venue is the Antigua Recreation Grounds, now used for inter-island competitions and concerts.

Many around the world believe the inauguration of the Stanford 20-20 matches here in summer 2006 breathed new life into the sport. These matches pit the various Caribbean island teams against each other and are held at the Stanford Cricket Grounds adjacent to the Sticky Wicket restaurant at the airport.

Prime cricket season is January through August, so check daily newspapers for specific matches taking place while you are there.

Golf

Cedar Valley Golf Course

With its sunny days and tropical fauna, Antigua is ideal for golf. There are two 18-hole courses on the island, both open to the public. Concierges at most of the hotels can arrange for your day of play. **Cedar Valley Golf Course**, an 18-hole par-70 course located on the northern end of the island, has beautiful rolling greens and plenty of hills for a real challenge. A fully stocked pro shop has rental clubs and carts, and the clubhouse includes a bar and grill. ☎ 268-462-0161. **Jolly Harbour Golf Course**, an 18-hole par-71 course located within the Jolly Harbour residential complex, is beautifully landscaped and includes seven lakes. The club includes a driving range and a clubhouse with pro shop, restaurant, bar and locker rooms. ☎ 268-462-7771.

Tennis

 While most hotels have at least one court, some are equipped for tournament play and offer lessons. These include **St. James Club**, **Carlisle Bay**, **Jolly Beach** and the **Royal Antiguan**. **Curtain Bluff** hosts an annual Pro-Am tournament in May and also sponsors many young players headed to camps and competitions in the US. In addition, at Jolly Harbour, the **BBR Sports Center** offers play on two clay and two AstroTurf courts, as well as a squash court, and all are open to the public. ☎ 268-462-6260. In English Harbour, **Temo Sports** has synthetic grass tennis courts and two glass-backed squash courts. ☎ 268-463-6376.

Seeing the Sights

Sampling the Culture

Antigua is home to a thriving colony of artists, including world-renowned painters, potters and sculptors. Their crafts are presented at many places on the island, including the gallery at Harmony Hall and shops in English Harbour, Redcliffe Quay, Heritage Quay and Woods Centre. In addition, tourists can find typical Caribbean island goods such as colorful wraps, hand-made steel pans, carved wood figures and bead jewelry at the Vendors Mall in St. John's and in the displays presented by enterprising vendors on almost every beach on the island.

One of the most noted craft production centers is Sea View Farm Village, where potters create native pottery. Their pots, protected with green grass, are fired in open fires in the yard. The results are sold there in the village as well as in galleries and gift stores throughout the island.

Other important displays of Antiguan culture are presented in the streets during Carnival (early August) and the Inde-

Antigua Carnival

St. John's

pendence Celebration (around November 1). Antiguans use these events as times to remember their roots and celebrate the food, clothing, and music that make the island unique.

Reliving History

The island teems with historical sites from the British colonial period. These are centered primarily around St. John's and English Harbour. In addition, there are some interesting 17th- and 18th-century churches that form the center of villages throughout the island – most notably **St. Peter's Anglican Church in Parham, Our Lady of Perpetual Help Church** in Tyrells, **Olivet**

Pentacostal Church in Liberta, **and St. George's Anglican Church** in Fitches Creek. Maps of Antigua that you receive from car rental companies and hotels display all these sites, and taxi drivers are familiar with them.

St. John's

Your first stop in the city should be the **Museum of Antigua & Barbuda**, on lower Long Street. The museum is housed in the Court House Building, which was constructed in 1747 and renovated after earthquake damage in 1974. Here you will find exhibits about the sister islands' history from geological birth through the 20th century. Next, walk up Long Street,

St. John's Cathedral

looking to your left for the tall twin spires of **St. John's Cathedral**. This magnificent structure started as a wood building in 1720 and was rebuilt in stone in 1848. You can walk around the grounds and see the unique interior encased in pitch pine to protect against further earthquake and hurricane damage.

English Harbour

Looking down on English Harbour

This center of naval fortifications at the southern end of the island now serves as the main historical center while still vitally active as an international yachting base. The highlight is **Nelson's Dockyard**, the only working Georgian naval dockyard in the world, where many of the original buildings remain. Other sites include the **Dow's Hill Interpretation Centre** where a multimedia presentation takes you through Antigua's history; **Fort Berkeley** at the western entrance to English Harbour; and the ruins of fortifications around **Shirley Heights**.

Where to Stay

Luxe Hotels

As with most of the Caribbean, Antigua resorts price their accommodations according to high season, which runs from early January to mid-April, and low season, from mid-April to mid-December. Most now offer another tier of highest rates during the Christmas holiday period, from mid-December to early January, taking advantage of cold-climate snowbirds who dream of a green Christmas. Please note that all hotels add tax and service charges of 18½% to all bills.

Here are the major beach resorts; they are grouped according to relative costs, which usually indicate the quality of the accommodations and service.

$$$$$. – All of these except Carlisle Bay are on an all-inclusive (AI) or Full American (FAP) plan, where all meals, bar drinks and watersports are included in the rates. High-season rates run from US$850-$1,200 per night, and low season rates from US$520-$850.

Blue Waters

This elegant self-contained resort, one of the longest established on the island, will have you convinced you don't need to wander anywhere else. Renovated in 1998, the rooms, public areas and restaurants are true to traditional West Indian design – lots of wicker, bright fabrics, and warm wood accents. The grounds are a study in what a tropical garden should look like, and the pools and beach areas are spread out enough so you

Beach at Blue Waters

never feel you're part of a crowd. For those who like accolades, Blue Waters was voted "Best Hotel in Antigua" in the 2003 and 2005 World Travel Awards.

Location: Northwestern coast.

Rooms: 77, including hillside superior and junior suites, beachfront deluxe junior and luxury suites, and one-, two- and three-bedroom beachfront villas. Also noted for the Rock Cottage, a four/five-bedroom villa perched on a rocky outcrop with gorgeous ocean views. TV, ceiling fans, patio or balcony and AC in all rooms.

Rates: Breakfast Plan, MAP or All-Inclusive rates.

Features: Two restaurants, two bars, beach, three pools, spa, tennis, gym, watersports, golf (nearby), Internet access, gift shop, game room.

☎ 800-557-6536 US, 44 (0) 870 360 1245 UK, fax 44 (0) 870 360 1246, www.bluewaters.net.

Carlisle Bay Club

Carlisle Bay Club

Eschewing the British colonial school of interior design so popular in the West Indies, the owners of Carlisle Bay aimed for serenity and freshness with Indonesian design. White is the predominant color, accented by dark Balinese furniture and unexpected splashes of color. Once you walk across the bridge between koi ponds and into the reception hall, an amazing sense of calm settles on you. The Blue Spa is one of the best on the island for helping you attain the serenity you seek. The East restaurant features dark grey walls and coral pink chair covers for a bi-chromatic theme intended to keep your focus on the outstanding food rather than your surroundings. They recently added a Cool Kids program and built a clubhouse just for the junior set complete with paddling pool, swing set, and mini-tennis courts.

Location: Southwest corner of the island in St. Mary parish, near the rainforest.

Rooms: 80, including beach suites, ocean suites and three-bedroom Carlisle suites. AC, TV, Internet in all rooms.

Rates: EP (includes only the room). Note that this is one of the few hotels in this rate category that is not all-inclusive.

Features: Two restaurants, three bars, beach, pool, spa, tennis courts with pro shop, gym, watersports library, screening room, gift store.

☎ 800-628-8929 US, fax 201-712-1279, ☎ 268-484-0002 Antigua, fax 268-484-0003, www.carlisle-bay.com.

Curtain Bluff

Taking its name from the way the surf makes a pattern on the shoreline, this venerable hotel has been setting the standards for customer service and appreciation on the island for many years. In 2002, *CondéNast Traveler* named it one of the top 10 resorts in the Caribbean, and the hotel is regularly listed in *Travel & Leisure*'s top five Caribbean resorts. The rooms are done in light wickers and bright colors, and a sense of relaxation and energy pervails. It has been owned for 47 years by the dynamic duo of Howard and Chelle Hulford. The Hulfords are very much present during all hours of the day to make sure guests feel at home. Major renovations in 2006 included the addition of air conditioning to all bedrooms and a new on-site 5,000-sq-ft spa on the beach.

Terrace at Curtain Bluff

Location: Old Road, southwest area of the island near the rainforest.

Rooms: 72, including deluxe rooms, terrace suites, beachside junior suites and 3-level executive suites. Ceiling fans, patios or balconies, AC and Internet in all rooms.

Rates: AI, all meals, drinks and non-motorized watersports, plus the use of a boat to take guests out to Cades Reef for snorkeling, are included.

Features: Two restaurants, two bars, two beaches, pool, spa, four tennis courts, squash court, putting green, croquet lawn, gym, watersports, television in an activity room above the tennis shop.

☎ 888-289-9898 US; ☎ 268-462-8400 Antigua, fax 268-462-8409, www.curtainbluff.com.

Galley Bay

Galley Bay

As you walk across the long bridge that leads through the lagoon and bird sanctuary into the reception area, you know you have come to a special place. The lush tropical grounds are beautifully manicured, the rooms are impeccably furnished in wicker and bright colors, and the beach is all that you've dreamed of. Three-quarters of the rooms are directly on the beach. Take a look at the unusual Gauguin cottages that line the lagoon and feature dual thatched-roof rondavels housing a bedroom in one and bathroom in the other. This resort is designed for couples only, but children are allowed to stay at Christmas and New Year's.

Location: Five Islands, just outside St. John's.

Rooms: 70, including Gauguin cottages with private splash pools, and superior, deluxe and premium suite beachfront rooms. Ceiling fans, balconies and AC in rooms.

Rates: AI.

Features: Two restaurants, two bars, beach, pool, spa, tennis, game room, air-conditioned fitness center, watersports, library with Internet access, beauty salon, gift boutique.

☎ 800-858-4618 US, 0870 160 9645 UK, fax 954-481-1661, ☎ 268-463-0302 Antigua, fax 268-462-4551, www.eliteislandresorts.com.

Hermitage Bay

This is the newest addition to the island's luxury all-inclusive resorts. Hermitage Bay offers luxurious individual cottages with expansive verandahs facing the sea either right at the water's edge or up on the hill. The style recaptures the Antigua of old, with shingled roofs, dark wood floors and trim and lots of colonial touches – but it also includes high-tech amenities like LCD televisions, iPod docks, DVD players and in-room high-speed Internet access.

Location: On the Caribbean coast, just south of St. John's Harbour.

Rooms: 25 cottage suites, with eight on the beach and the rest hillside. All have separate living and sleeping areas, large verandahs, AC, TV, iPod docks, DVD players and Internet access.

Rates: AI.

Features: Restaurant, bar, beach, pool, non-motorized watersports and spa.

☎ 268-562-5500, fax 268-562-5505, www. hermitagebay.com.

Hermitage Bay

Jumby Bay

Jumby Bay

At this resort, you have your own 300-acre private island to explore. Long known as a playground for the rich and famous, Jumby Bay offers luxurious, relaxing accommodations and a staff attentive to your every need. The resort was purchased by the Rosewood Hotel chain in 2002 and underwent a significant renovation, making it one of the most beautiful places to stay in Antigua. The rooms are done in the British colonial style, with dark mahogany four-poster beds and replica furniture. It's easy to see why the resort has garnered an incredible array of awards, including *CondéNast Traveler* Gold List; a Harper's Hideaway Report listing as one of the top 20 international resort hideaways in the world; *Travel + Leisure's* World's Best Award and World's Best Service Award; and a World Travel Awards listing as Antigua and Barbuda's Leading Hotel for 2005. They recently introduced two family-friendly services, The Pampered Parent program for children aged two-nine, and a Nanny program providing care for infants and children.

Location: Jumby Bay island.

Rooms: 40 suites and 11 villas with private plunge pools. Some of the private villas on the island are also available for rent. 24-hr room service, ceiling fans, mini-bar, coffee maker, luxury baths, stereo radio with CD player, dial-up Internet and AC in all rooms. TVs and DVD players available.

Rates: AI.

Features: Two restaurants, two bars, three beaches, pool with individual cabanas, tennis, fitness center, watersports, bicycles for getting around the island, daily *NY Times*, evening movies, business center with high-speed Internet access.

☎ 888-767-3966 US, ☎ 268-462-6000 Antigua, fax 268-462-6020, www. jumbybayresort.com.

Sandals Antigua Caribbean Village & Spa

Sandals

This is the most extensive resort on the island, and is situated on what many believe to be the best beach on the island. As with all Sandals establishments, it is a couples-only, all-inclusive resort as well as a self-contained village. Amenities include the luxurious Red Lane Spa, five pools, five whirlpools, a fitness center, five restaurants and five bars. The rooms recently underwent renovation, and the rondavals**(explain)(a favorite with honeymooners) were upgraded with private plunge pools. If you are looking for a resort where your every need is anticipated and you don't need to go anywhere else, this is the place for you.

Location: Dickenson Bay, northwest area of the island.

Rooms: 193, including beach and garden rondovals, ocean-view suites, verandah suites and beachfront concierge rooms. All rooms have clock radios, AC, TV. Some have CD players and other upgraded amenities.

Rates: AI.

Features: As mentioned above, plus non-motorized watersports and tennis court.

☎ 888-SANDALS, ☎ 268-462-0267 Antigua, fax 268-462-4135, www.sandals.com/main/antigua.

Sandals Mediterranean Village

In a complete departure from the regional norm of West Indian style, Sandals has created this new, elaborate high-rise resort adjacent to Sandals Caribbean Village. While it shares some of the amenities like restaurants, beach and spa, it also has its own pool and whirlpool (said to be the largest in the Eastern Caribbean), three restaurants, a pizzeria, and retail space. The 180 luxury suites include one-bedroom villas with private plunge pools and waterfall walls, as well as penthouse suites with great views over Dickenson Bay and the sunsets to the west. All suites feature Mediterranean-style accents, Jacuzzi tubs for two, four-poster mahogany beds and flat screen TVs.

Location: Dickenson Bay, northwest area of the island.

Rooms: 11 one-bedroom villa suites with private pools, 21 one-bedroom penthouse suites, 14 executive suites and 134 junior suites, AC, TV.

Rates: AI.

Features: As listed above, plus non-motorized watersports.

☎ 888-SANDALS, 268-462-0267 Antigua, fax 268-462-4135, www.sandals.com/main/antigua.

Luxe With Limits

$$$$ – These are a mixture of all-inclusives and other meal plans. High-season rates run from US$450-$675 per night, and low season rates from US$320-$575.

Dian Bay Resort & Spa

One of the newest hotels in Antigua, this northeast coast hotel offers a small-hotel feel with some big-hotel features. Rooms have views of Dian Bay, the Atlantic and Lovers' Beach, which they will gladly take you to by boat. The pool is three-tiered, with a waterfall, making for pleasant afternoon sunning activities. The spa is a definite highlight, with a full array of massage, body treatments, body scrubs, facials and salon services, as well as Ayurvedic treatments. This is an adults-only resort, so no children are allowed.

Dian Bay

Location: Dian Bay, northeast coast.

Rooms: 50, of which 16 are pool-view/garden-view, and 34 ocean-view, all with private terraces, coffee makers, ceiling fans, clock radios, AC and TV.

Rates: EP or AI.

Features: Restaurant, bar, pool, small beach with transport to larger beach across the bay, nonmotorized watersports, spa.

☎ 268-460-6646, fax 268-460-8400, www.dianbay-antigua.com.

Halcyon Cove by Rex Resorts

One of the major draws of this classic resort is its location on Dickenson Bay, one of the best beaches in Antigua. The water is calm, warm and crystal clear, the sand is soft, and there are plenty of watersports to keep everyone busy. This is a non-smoking, family-friendly resort with a Children's Club to keep the little ones occupied during the day. The all-inclusive plan is a good bet since it covers not only meals at the newly reno-

Halcyon Cove

vated Warri Pier and the Arawak Terrace, but also the restaurants at the other two Rex Resort properties on the island, Blue Heron and Hawksbill. The property underwent redecoration of the rooms and renovation of the swimming pool in 2006.

Location: Dickenson Bay, east side of the island.

Rooms: 210, including standard, superior, poolside, beachfront rooms and beachfront suites. These latter two room categories are not available for families with children. Mini-fridge, AC and TVs in all rooms.

Rates: EP or AI.

Features: Two restaurants, three bars, tennis, non-motorized watersports, golf (nearby), Internet in lobby.

☎ 800-255-5859 US, 44 (0) 20 8741-5333 UK; 268-462-0256 Antigua, fax 268-462-0271, www.rexresorts.com.

Hawksbill by Rex Resorts

This long-time favorite all-inclusive has an interesting feature: One of its four beaches is a clothing-optional beach. The beaches face to the west, ideal for sunset-watching. There is a look-out over a large rock in the shape of – what else – a giant hawksbill turtle's head. Room choices include cottage club rooms set among the palms and near the beach, which are the only air-conditioned rooms and, for many loyal guests, the best in the

Hawksbill

house. The hotel recently converted to a smoke-free environment in all rooms and is family-friendly.

Location: Five Islands, just outside St. John's on the western coast.

Rooms: 111, including standard with garden-view, superior sea-view rooms and beach club rooms. The hotel also has a Great House, a three-bedroom villa, ideal for a large family or group. All rooms have mini-fridges and ceiling fans, AC only in beach club rooms.

Rates: AI.

Features: Three restaurants, two bars, four powdery sand beaches, tennis court and Wellness Center, golf nearby, Internet access in lobby.

☎ 800-255-5859 US, 268-462-0301 Antigua, fax 268-462-1515, www.rexresorts.com.

Occidental Grand Pineapple Beach Resort

This all-inclusive is on Long Bay on the eastern/Atlantic side of the island and away from the bustle of St. John's and the airport. The 1,600-foot white sand beach is outstanding. As a self-contained resort, it offers two oceanside pools (the "tranquility pool" is adults-only), four tennis courts, an air-conditioned gym and a spa, plus several restaurants and bars.

Occidental Grand Pineapple

Don't miss The Outhouse, a snack bar high up on the hill above the resort, overlooking the ocean. The rooms are basic – neat, clean and well appointed; about 75% have ocean views. In 2007 it was announced that the hotel was sold to the Beaches chain, so you may see some changes in the future.

Location: Long Bay, eastern coast.

Rooms: 180, including standard, garden-view, ocean-view, waterfront and beachfront. AC, TV.

Rates: AI.

Features: Three restaurants, three bars, two snack bars, two pools, four tennis courts, air-conditioned fitness center, spa, non-motorized watersports, game room, daily activities program, nightly entertainment, gift shop.

☎ 800-858-4618 US, 0870 160 9645 UK, 268-462-2006 Antigua, fax 268-462-2452, www.eliteislandresorts.com.

St. James Club

This is another of Antigua's venerable all-inclusive hotels with clientele that returns year-after-year because of the high standards of service and beautiful setting. Occupying 100 acres on the southern coast, this resort is like a small city divided into two main areas: the

St. James Club

Club, with rooms, restaurants and recreation, and the Village, with residential-type villas. The resort is on the Atlantic side, so one beach is rough surf and the other is calmer, although the water is murky at times. A family-friendly resort, it offers a Kids' Club and accommodations that are very comfortable for children.

Location: Mamora Bay on the southern coast.

Rooms: 250 in all, including club, premium and beachfront rooms, new Bay suites, and two-bedroom villas. All rooms have alarm clocks, ceiling fans, private balcony or patio, AC and cable TV.

Rates: AI or EP

Features: five restaurants, five bars, four pools, two beaches, six tennis courts, small casino, beauty salon and spa, gym, volleyball and croquet, Internet café and WiFi hot spots.

☎ 800-858-4618 US, 0870 160 9645 UK, 268-460-5000 Antigua, fax 268-460-3015, www.eliteislandresorts.com.

Sunsail Club Colonna

This hotel is part of the Sunsail chain. It specializes in sailing instruction that takes advantage of the windswept northern coast, as well as yacht charters. A village done in Mediterranean style, it recently underwent substantial refurbishment and added a Kids' Club facility, a Caribbean Pirates Galleon play area, fully equipped fitness room, and the Serenity Spa with sauna, steam room and Jacuzzi. It's also said to have one of the largest pools on the island.

Cabana at Sunsail Club

Location: Hodges Bay on the north coast.

Rooms: 74 double rooms plus 27 one-bedroom apartments and 16 two- and three-bedroom villas. All have mini-fridges, coffee/tea service, AC, TV.

Rates: AI.

Features: Two small beaches, game room, open-air restaurant and bar, pool, fitness room, watersports, tennis court, spa.

☎ 888-359-3568 US, 44 (0) 870 428 4196 UK, 268-462-6263 Antigua, www.sunsail.com.

The Verandah

The Verandah restaurant

This eco-friendly resort is one of the newest hotels on the island. It is beautifully situated on 30 waterfront acres along the northeast coast adjacent to a national park and within walking distance of Devil's Bridge. True to its name, the hotel features rooms with large verandahs, decorated in Caribbean style. It's also a family-friendly resort, with a Kids' Club and one restaurant dedicated to the little ones.

Location: Dian Bay, on the northeast coast.

Rooms: 200 bay-view and ocean-view suites with kitchenettes, dual vanities, satellite TV, AC, Internet in rooms.

Rates: AI and EP (not available December 31-January 3).

Features: Four restaurants (including a coffee shop and the children's restaurant), five bars, two freshwater pools, children's pool, two tennis courts, fitness center, spa, children's activities, watersports, mini-cinema, game rooms, Internet café.

☎ 800-858-4618 US, 44 (0) 870 160 9645 UK, www.eliteislandsresorts.com.

Reasonable & Comfortable Hotels

$$$ – These are a primarily room-only resorts and hotels, although there are a few all-inclusives. High season rates run from $250-$415 per night, and low season from $150-$380.

Antigua Village

This property, on Dickenson Bay, began as a residential village where all the units were sold to individual owners. Today about half the units are rented out as hotel rooms. There are few amenities on-site, so the owners have created an "Owners Club" where owners and visiting guests can take advantage of special meal plans and discounted rates on activities like golf, tennis, watersports, tours and boat charters.

Location: Dickenson Bay, northwestern coast.

Rooms: One-bedroom studios, suites and villas; all with kitchens, TV, AC. Villas and studios can be combined for larger families or groups.

Rates: EP only.

Features: Pool, special 'dine-around' arrangements with Hemingway's

Antigua Village

and Le Bistro restaurants; other restaurants and bars within walking distance, watersports and tennis at adjacent facility.

☎ 877-877-1317 US, 268-462-2930 Antigua, fax 268-462-0375, www. antiguavillage.net.

Antigua Yacht Club

Antigua Yacht Club

Another recent addition to the Antigua hospitality scene is Antigua Yacht Club, located on a hill overlooking Falmouth Harbour. The club is unique in that the rooms in the six buildings on the hill have been designed to easily accommodate yachting crews or wedding groups, with one central two-story executive suite adjoining four individual studios. There is also one building housing 19 traditional hotel rooms. The décor is cool Indonesian, with lots of dark wood and white Italian luxury fabrics, as well as the latest accessories, such as flat-panel TVs and luxurious baths. The restaurants and activities of English Harbour are just a short taxi ride away.

Location: Falmouth Harbour.

Rooms: 19 hotel rooms, 24 studio apartments and six one-bedroom executive suites with balconies, kitchenettes, DVD/CD players, satellite TV, AC, Internet in rooms.

Rates: EP only.

Features: Health spa, Turkish steam bath and fitness center; restaurants, bars, grocery/liquor store and boutiques are immediately adjacent.

☎ 268-562-3030, fax 268-562-3031, www.aycmarina.com.

Cocobay Resort

Cocobay Resort

This resort, designed to resemble a Caribbean village but with a distinctly laid-back "Big Sur" sensibility, offers comfortable accommodations at a very reasonable rate. A favorite with honeymooners because of the relaxed and romantic atmosphere, highlights include outdoor showers and hammocks on the verandah in each room. There are two restaurants, one for the All-Inclusive meals, and the high-style, high-priced Sheer, which is open to the public. The infinity pool has a beautiful view over the water, and a cute little Wellness Cottage sits perched on a bluff over the bay.

Location: Valley Church area, west coast.

Rooms: 41 one-bedroom cottages plus four hilltop two-bedroom plantation houses, all with mini-fridges, ceiling fans, coffee/tea service, no TV.

Rates: AI.

Features: Pool, two beaches, two restaurants, bar, watersports, Wellness Cottage for massages and treatments.

☎ 800-816-7587 US, 268-562-2400 Antigua, fax 268-562-2424, www.cocobayresort.com.

Coconut Beach Club

This resort, completely renovated in 2004 by the owners of the Cocobay Resort, emphasizes low-key relaxation in a beautiful setting. All rooms are considered beachfront and have rustic balconies with hammocks. The resort is all-inclusive, and children are not permitted except during the Christmas holiday.

Coconut Beach Club

Location: Yepton Beach, west coast.

Rooms: 44, including deluxe rooms, junior suites with separate living areas, and deluxe suites with kitchenettes. All have coffee/tea service, mini-fridge, and AC.

Rates: AI.

Features: Restaurant, pool, poolside bar, tennis court, entertainment three nights a week, watersports, hiking trail, Wellness Cottage, lounge with cable TV, Internet desk in lobby, sundries shop.

☎ 800-361-4621 US, 268-462-3239 Antigua, fax 268-462-3240, www. coconutbeachclub.com.

Coco's Hotel

View from Coco's

This low-key small hotel is best known for the friendly staff and good food and is highly rated as a romantic getaway. The 19 gingerbread cottages are on a steep hill, with the highest priced ones also the highest on the hill. Those who can't walk up a steep incline for any length of time should request the lower rooms. The décor is rustic and the rooms are homey, with one king bed and an open-air shower. The mini-fridge is stocked at all times with drinks.

Location: Lignum Vitae Bay, next to the Jolly Beach Resort.

Rooms: 19 one-bedroom cottages, with choice of standard, superior or premium, based on the view.

Rates: AI only.

Features: Restaurant, pool, two beaches, restaurant, beach bar service, library, Internet available in guest service room.

☎ 268-462-9700, fax 268-462-9423, www.coconutbeachclub.com.

Inn at English Harbour

This distinguished resort is nestled into the hillside above Freeman's Bay within Dockyard National Park. Done in the British colonial style with lots of stone work, rattan and mahogany furniture, it's a welcome respite from the world. You have the option of a room up on the hill or beachfront, depending on how close you want to be

Inn at English Harbour

to the water. A spa and gift shop were added in 2006.

Location: Freeman's Bay at the entrance to English Harbour, southern coast.

Rooms: 10 hillside ocean-view and beachfront rooms, 24 beachfront junior, superior and deluxe suites. All with ceiling fans, minifridges and coffee/tea service, TV.

Rates: EP, BP, MAP or AI.

Features: Two restaurants, one bar, free-form infinity pool, two tennis courts, watersports, fitness center and spa, Internet access in lobby.

☎ 800-970-2123 US, 44 (0) 1935 873344 UK, 268-460-1014 Antigua, www.theinn.ag.

Jolly Beach Resort

This large resort on the western coast is very popular with Europeans and is geared toward those looking for a lot of activity. It has a great beach and an activities staff to get people going with volleyball, cricket, beach soccer, Caribbean dance lessons and mixology classes. The pool is one of those large freeform things with a big waterfall in the middle, billed as a "fantasy" pool.

Jolly Beach Resort

Location: Lignum Vitae Bay, west coast.

Rooms: 462 in all, including supersaver, standard, superior, king superior and junior suites. All rooms have AC, satellite TV; some rooms have small refrigerators and coffee/tea service.

Rates: AI.

Features: Five restaurants, seven bars, 8,000-sq-ft pool, four tennis courts, gym, watersports, Kidz Club, activities and entertainment, WiFi access for fee.

☎ 954-919-0191 US, 44 (0) 1372 469878 UK, 268-462-0061 Antigua, www.jollybeachresort.com.

Pool at Siboney Beach Club

Siboney Beach Club

This small locally owned all-suite hotel is on the island's best beach. Extensive and lush landscaping surrounds the buildings and pool and creates the feeling of an oasis. The club's on-property restaurant, the award-winning Coconut Grove, is a perfect place for watching sunsets and enjoying a romantic dinner right on the beach.

Location: Dickenson Bay, west coast.

kitchenette and air-conditioned bedroom; choice of superior, deluxe and deluxe ocean-view.

Rates: EP.

Features: Pool, beach, restaurant with bar, beach lounges and snorkeling gear, free WiFi access.

☎ 268-462-0806, fax 268-462-3356, www.siboneybeachclub.com.

Good Value Hotels

$$ – These are primarily room-only or self-catering units. High-season rates run around $250 per night, and low-season from $125-$200.

Galleon Beach

Galleon Beach

This is one of the island's best kept secrets, probably because it is an older hotel and somewhat in need of refurbishing. But the cottages with kitchens and separate living rooms are comfortable and roomy, the on-site Calabash Restaurant is very good, and the snorkeling right off the beach is great. There is some development of villas going on at the far end of the property, but it doesn't seem to intrude on the serenity of the place.

Location: Freeman's Bay, adjacent to English Harbour.

Rooms: 28 in all, including beachside one- and two-bedroom cottages, garden one- and two-bedroom cottages and rondavels; three-bedroom private villas on hill. All have patios, kitchens and ceiling fans.

Rates: EP.

Features: Restaurant with bar, two tennis courts, beach, watersports, small commissary, Internet access and WiFi available at Reception.

☎ 268-460-1024, fax 268-460-1450, www.galleonbeach.com.

South Coast Horizon

This is billed as an "eco-friendly resort" because it actively maintains a large palm garden and lagoon with mangroves. The resort offers, for varying fees, educational tours of Fantasy Pyramid Park and the Boardwalk and Lagoon. Also on-site are Cades Reef Kayaking and Cades Reef Snorkeling. The resort, the closest to Cades Reef, offers its guests daily boat rides to the reef.

Location: Cades Bay, southern coast.

Rooms: One-bedroom suites with private patios, fully equipped kitchens, Jacuzzi/shower.

Rates: EP or AI.

Features: Restaurant, secluded beach, lagoon and garden with educational tours, access to Cades Reef for snorkeling or kayaking, peddle boats.

☎ 268-562-4074, fax 268-562-4075, www.southcoasthorizons.com.

No-Frills Hotels

$ – These are basic hotels with room-only rates. High-season rates run from $125-$180 per night, and low season from $125-$140.

Anchorage Inn

While naming itself an inn, this property has recently expanded to 40 rooms, making it more of a hotel, and a very comfortable one at that. It is not a beachfront property but rather is across the road from Dickenson Bay. It's still a good location since the many restaurants and activities of the northwest coast are only a walk away, and St. John's is a 10-minute drive.

Location: Dickenson Bay Road, northwest coast.

Rooms: 40, including seven self-contained units with kitchens; superior and standard rooms, some with ocean views. All rooms have ceiling fans, coffee/tea service, mini-fridges, microwave ovens, TV, AC, Internet access.

Rates: EP.

Features: Restaurant (breakfast only), two bars, pool.

☎ 268-462-4065, fax 268-462-4066, www.antiguaanchorageinn.com.

Catamaran Hotel

This Falmouth Harbour hotel is another good value – especially for families. Two of its rooms, the Captain's Cabin and Bruno's Cabin, have a queen four-poster bed plus a queen sofa bed, both with kitchens. The view out to the yachts in the marina is great, and Rickert's Club restaurant is near by. English Harbour is just a short drive away.

Location: Falmouth Harbour, southern coast.

Rooms: Two cabins, eight ocean-view and six beachfront rooms, all with kitchenettes, ceiling fans, AC, TV.

Catamaran Hotel

building offering a choice of lagoon-view, mountain-view or ocean-view (upper floors), plus 12 one-bedroom cottages. All rooms have clock radios, AC and TV.

Rates: EP or AI.

Features: Three restaurants, six bars, large pool, beach, Internet

Rates: EP.

Features: Beach, pool, Internet café on-site; restaurant adjacent to the property, plus grocery store and ice cream parlor within walking distance.

☎ 268-460-1036, fax 268-460-1339, www.catamarain-antigua.com.

Grand Royal Antiguan

The largest hotel on the island, the Royal Antiguan was originally built by the government and is now in the capable hands of the Grand Royal hoteliers. The rooms are bright and airy, and the one-bedroom cottages are among the best accommodations in the hotel. It overlooks a lagoon, but the southwestern side has a very good beach where you'll find the Andes restaurant and access to all watersports.

Location: Five Islands, just south of St. John's.

Rooms: 265 in an eight-story

Beach at Grand Royal Antiguan

café, spa, fitness room, boutique, eight tennis courts, children's activities, watersports, nightly entertainment, small electronic casino.

☎ 268-462-3733, fax 268-462-3728, www.grandroyalantiguan.com

Heritage Hotel

If you love being in the center of activity around a major tourism hub, you'll like Heritage Hotel. It is in Heritage Quay, the welcoming point for all cruise ship passengers and a major shopping area in downtown St. John's. The rooms have nice views of the harbor and the

Heritage Hotel

massive cruise ships that dock nearby, but there is no beach readily available so you'll have to take a taxi or drive to the sand.

Location: Heritage Quay, St. John's.

Rooms: A range of options including executive king or queen, standard, deluxe one-bedroom suite with kitchen and living area, and studio suite with kitchenette; AC, TV, Internet access.

Rates: BP.

Features: Duty-free shops, vendors' mall, restaurants, King's Casino, ferry to Barbuda and other activities literally right outside your door.

☎ 268-462-1247, fax 268-462-1179, www.heritagedowntown.com.

Small Inns

These represent real value accommodations for the budget-minded. For double accommodations, usually with either a queen or king-sized bed, you can expect to pay $100-$130 per night in low season, and $145-$200 in high season. Some include breakfast in the rate, sweetening the deal.

Admiral's Inn

The Admiral's Inn in historic Nelson's Dockyard is a step back in time. The weathered brick walls and nautical décor of a building originally constructed in 1788 constantly remind you of the past, while at the same time providing luxurious comfort. As an added attraction, you are right in the

Rooms: 13 rooms plus "Joiner's Loft" two-bedroom apartment; choice of minimum, moderate or superior rooms, with AC in moderate and superior rooms.

Rates: EP.

Features: Restaurant and bar, free transfers to Freeman's Bay and Pigeon Point beaches (plus towels and chairs); use of small sailboats within English Harbour.

☎ 268-460-1153, fax 268-460-1534, www.admiralsantigua.com.

Admiral's Inn

Copper & Lumber Store Hotel

Again, Nelson's Dockyard is the site of an intimate inn wrapped in history and charm. This building, originally done in 1783, has been recognized as one of the finest examples of Georgian architecture in the Caribbean. Each room is furnished in antiques and cleverly named after one of Lord Nelson's ships. The breeze – and the views – from the Harbour are delightful.

Copper & Lumber Store Hotel

Location: Nelson's Dockyard, southern coast.

Rooms: 14 suites or studios, choice of Georgian suite or studio or contemporary suite or studio. All have kitchenettes and living areas, AC and TV.

Rates: EP.

Courtyard at Copper & Lumber Store Hotel

Features: Restaurant and bar; use of beach and watersports equipment at Galleon Beach Hotel across the bay; access to shops, restaurants and watersports offered at Nelson's Dockyard.

☎ 268-460-1058, fax 268-460-1529, www.copperandlumberhotel.com.

Harmony Hall

More noted for its restaurant, Harmony Hall also offers six inn rooms for those wanting to stay on the Atlantic side of the island. The hospitality is warm, and the property offers a beach and a pool as well as a boat that takes people out to Green Island for snorkeling.

Location: Just past Freeman's Village on Brown's Bay, eastern coast.

Rooms: Six, in two villas, with high ceilings, king beds, private patio, minibar, coffee/tea service.

Rates: BP.

Features: Restaurant and bar, beach, pool, massage hut, kayaks, boat to Green Island.

☎ 268-460-4120, fax 268-460-4406, www.harmonyhall.com.

Inn La Galleria

This small inn sits high on a hill above the Royal Antiguan. The views from the restaurant and ocean-view rooms look out at Deep Bay and a large salt pond. The accommodations are simply furnished, and the deluxe and ocean-view rooms are available with or without a kitchenette.

Location: Just outside Five Islands, western coast.

Rooms: 12 rooms, choice of standard, deluxe and ocean-view. All have mini-fridge, AC and TV.

View from Inn La Galleria

Rates: BP.

Features: Restaurant, bar and Internet access on-site; beach, watersports, tennis and horseback riding nearby.

☎ 268-460-6060, fax 268-461-6317, www.innlagalleria.com.

Villas, Condos & Apartments

For those who want a more home-like atmosphere, as well as access to full kitchens, booking a villa or apartment may be the best bet. The prices are often better than hotels but, unless you choose a villa resort, you'll likely sacrifice amenities such as beaches, pools and on-site restaurants. For individual private villas, check out these websites: www.antiguanice.com; www.rentors.com, www.cyberrentals.com; or www.ownersdirect.co.uk. Here are some agencies and villa resorts that offer a range of accommodations.

Antigua Villa Rentals/Tradewinds Realty represents a number of private villas, including Treetops Cottage, Jasmine Hill, Carib House and Villa Mamora. ☎ 268-460-1082, fax 268-460-1081, www.antigua-villa-rentals.com.

Antigua Villas represents two- and three-bedroom villas in Paradise View, overlooking Dickenson Bay. ☎ 604-224-9144, fax 604-224-9117, www.antiguavilla.com.

Caribrep Villas has a collection of cottages and one- , two- and three-bedroom villas all over the island. ☎ 268-463-2070, fax 268-560-1824, www.caribrepvillas.com.

Terrace at Emerald Springs Villas

Emerald Springs Villas has two villas, a three-bedroom home overlooking Nonsuch Bay on the eastern side of the island, and a three-bedroom home in Cedar Valley, adjacent to a golf course and near St. John's. ☎ 268-461-6323, fax 905-884-1465, www.emeraldspringsvillas.com.

Jolly Harbour is the largest all-villa resort on the island, with luxury two-bedroom townhouses sitting on the water, some with their own docks, and all with patios that end at the water's edge. The complex has a beach, tennis court, swimming pool, shops, grocery store, golf course and several restaurants, including the Castaways Beach Bar and Grill. ☎ 268-462-7771/3, fax 268-462-7772, www.jollyharbourantigua.com.

Marina Bay Beach Resort is on Dickenson Bay and has a good beach. There are 27 studio, one- and two-bedroom units with views to the ocean.

Units have full kitchens and air conditioning. ☎ 268-462-1309, fax 268-462-2151.

Palm Bay Beach Club, on Nonsuch Bay on the eastern coast, is a laid-back collection of seven two-bedroom villas with large porches. The resort has a small beach, a pool and a tennis court. ☎ 268-460-4173, fax 268-562-3804, www.palmbayantigua.com.

Pelican Isle Villas, on the southern end of the island, offers seven furnished one- and two-bedroom villas overlooking a white sand beach on one side and a tropical reef on the other. ☎ 268-462-8385, 800-965-2440 US, fax 268-462-4361, pelican@candw.ag.

Serendipity Cottages has 10 beautifully colored gingerbread cottages set in a secluded garden in the central area of the island with a view to the sea. The units have kitchenettes and modern conveniences such as Internet access and air conditioning. ☎ 268-562-6500, fax 268-562-6502, www.serendipityantigua.com.

Sun Villas Antigua is an agent representing many villas in English Harbour, St. James Club, Falmouth and Jolly Harbour. ☎ 268-561-1075, 44 (0) 01342 776102 UK, www.sunvillasantigua.com.

Sunset Cove is a condominium development that makes its 33 units available for vacationers. All units have kitchens, air conditioning and cable TV, and some units can be combined to accommodate families or small groups. The property has a nice beach and pool, but it's located next to a lively night club so those who value quiet evenings may have a problem with that. ☎ 268-462-3762 fax 268-462-2684.

Sunset Cove Villa

Day Spas

If you just cannot imagine sunbathing and working out without having a spa to repair sun damage or make you gorgeous again, but you aren't staying at a resort with an on-site spa, Antigua has many solutions for you.

Akparo is open during high season and has some on-call services in low season. Services include massages, facials, manicures/pedicures, waxing, hair services and chiropractic visits. Nelson's Dockyard, ☎ 268-460-5705.

Alternative Body Care is open year-round, and offers aromatherapy and therapeutic massage as well as hot stone and pregnancy massages.

They also provide reflexology, body polishes, essential oil wraps, facials, body waxing and other beauty treatments. Redcliffe Quay, ☎ 268-460-8748.

Blue Spa at the Carlisle Bay Hotel is the most luxurious spa on the island and is often featured in spa magazines throughout the world. With 17,000 square feet of space, it offers six treatment rooms and a wide range of massage and holistic therapies, facials, body and beauty treatments. Carlisle Bay, ☎ 268-484-0025.

Equilibrium Health Spa gives massages, facials, waxing and body wraps on a year-round basis. They also can book appointments with a physiotherapist for those needing treatment for sports or other injuries, as well as 'body slim' treatments using electrotherapy. St. John's, ☎ 268-462-7919.

Red Lane Spa at Sandals uses renowned Pevonia botanical products in its massage and beauty services. It offers a long list of massages, body wraps and beauty treatments as well as a tropical nail bar with Pedi Coladas and Margarita Manicures. Dickenson Bay, ☎ 268-462-0267.

Touch Therapies has an airport location for massages as well as two other places that provide facials, manicures, pedicures, waxing, body wraps and scrubs, laser treatments and eye treatments. Owner Karen Grannum makes sure her clients are accommodated and even offers some Sunday hours. Fort Road, ☎ 268-562-1286; Hawksbill Resort, ☎ 268-562-5144.

Tree House Body Shop looks after the whole body with massages, osteopathic services, hair services for Caucasians (no braids or twists), waxing, manicures and pedicures. The only MD in the English Harbour area also sees patients in the shop here three days a week. English Harbour, ☎ 268-460-3434.

Eating Out

Antigua attracts well-heeled visitors from Europe, North America, the Middle East and Asia and has developed many outstanding restaurants to cater to their cosmopolitan tastes. The restaurants are competitive with the finest five-star restaurants in the US, England and France, so expect the prices to be equivalent. There are also some great beach-side restaurants, ethnic eateries and something for just about every hungry visitor to enjoy. Unless noted, most restaurants are open on Sundays, although this may vary in high and low season.

RESTAURANT PRICE CHART	
$	Cheap eats, normally quick meals or take-out foods; US$8 or less per entrée.
$$	Good value, lots of West Indian cuisine; US$9-$14 for a plate of food.
$$$	A nice place with gourmet aspirations; US$15-$24 for a satisfying entrée.
$$$$	Positively elegant, usually requiring some dressing up; entrées range from US$25 to $50, depending on the island.

Dressing Up to Dine Out

Admiral's Inn

This special-occasion restaurant is in one of the historic buildings at Nelson's Dockyard and provides an intimate dining experience. Diners sit and overlook the beautiful yachts in the harbor, soaking up the special atmosphere. The menu features traditional dishes such as pumpkin soup, red snapper and lobster thermidor, all with Caribbean influences for a unique taste. $$$. Open for breakfast, lunch and dinner. ☎ 268-460-1027.

Antigua Yacht Club

Overlooking Falmouth Harbor and the beautiful mega-yachts moored there, this restaurant offers a relaxing lunch or dinner experience. The room is furnished in warm mahogany, the views are stunning, and the Italian/Caribbean cuisine emphasizes fresh seafood. You may even be fortunate enough to have piano music playing in the background, creating the perfect ambience. $$$. Open for lunch and dinner. ☎ 268-460-1797, www.aycmarina.com.

Bellagio

Looking for a special evening out, where you can really dress up and have fun? Head to the Grand Princess Casino, a one-of-a-kind building on the island with Corinthian columns, crystal chandeliers, marble floors and the works. First have dinner in the five-star Bellagio restaurant, noted for its Italian cuisine and luxe air-conditioned setting. Then head downstairs to the casino, which has been described as the most opulent casino floor in the Caribbean. $$$$. Jolly Harbour. Open for lunch and dinner. ☎ 268-562-9900.

Grand Princess Casino

Hideout.

At the crossroads leading to Mamora Bay, this subtle little restaurant is building a nice reputation as a "must-do" in Antigua. Max Freling, a talented chef in the French style, and his effervescent wife Nicola, welcome you to a setting that you would swear is their home, except for the art gallery gracing one corner of the room. Rack of lamb is done with panache, and fresh fish is always cooked to perfection. Since there are only about 12 tables, be sure to make reservations. $$$. Located on the road leading from Willoughby Bay to Mamora Bay. Open for dinner only, closed on Sundays. Closed May through September. ☎ 268-460-3666.

Le Bistro

Le Bistro

This establishment has long been touted as one of the best dining experiences in Antigua, as evidenced by its place on numerous recommended listings from *Gourmet Magazine* and other gastronomic guides. Award-winning head chef and owner Patrick Gauducheau incorporates the best of Caribbean and haute French cuisine with wonderful results. If you want to sample the local lobster, Le Bistro grills it to perfection. The crispy Long Island duckling flamed with Grand Marnier is another memorable dish. Reservations are a must, especially in high season. $$$$. Hodges Bay, on the north side of the island. Open for dinner only, closed on Mondays. ☎ 268-462-3881.

The Pavilion Antigua

This elegant restaurant, sitting on the hill overlooking the airport, sets a new standard for dining in Antigua. Executive chef Andrew Knoll honed his craft to perfection working alongside Emeril for many years. Knoll produces an imaginative and intriguing menu described as southern

The Pavilion Antigua

cuisine with a French flair, which translates into combinations that cele-brate local produce and startle you with the unexpected. The beautiful setting is equal to the superb food. The restaurant is in a new building that resembles a fine classic plantation house. The intimate dining room seats only 24 at a time. Jackets and ties for men are required, as are reser-vations. $$$$. At the Airport in Coolidge. Open for dinner only, Tuesday through Saturday. ☎ 268-480-6800, www.thepavilionantigua.com.

Sheer

Perched on a cliff adjoining Cocobay Resort, this is one of the islands best-kept dining secrets. It's an intimate restaurant where 24 tables are set in six private pavilions overlooking the ocean. They only do one seating a night. Chef Nigel Martin comes up with some amazing combinations in a cuisine heavily influenced with Pan Asian and South American flavors, using many local ingredients such as dasheen, okra, plantains and pine-apple. Of course, reservations are required. $$$$. Cocobay Resort, on the West coast south of Jolly Harbour. Serves dinner only, Tuesday through Saturday. ☎ 268-562-2400.

The Cove Restaurant

One of the newest additions to the Antigua restaurant scene, this elegant oceanfront restaurant has carved out its niche in the fine dining category. Chef Pascal Bionaz delights with entrées such as rack of lamb, beef ten-derloin and duck breast done in classical European style. They also offer a unique Sunday afternoon dinner from 1 to 4 pm. Reservations are highly recommended. $$$$. Boon's Point on northwest coast, near Blue Waters. Open for dinner Monday through Saturday, and Sunday afternoon dinner. ☎ 268-562-2683, www.thecove-antigua.com.

Relaxing on the Water

Calabash

The outdoor dining deck near the beach makes this a good choice for a delightful luncheon setting. Dinner is served there or in the large dining room across the road. The food is a mixture of Creole and high-style, and comes highly recommended by those who frequent Galleon Beach Hotel. $$. Adjacent to Galleon Beach Hotel, near English Harbour. Open for lunch and dinner. ☎ 268-562-4906.

Coconut Grove

For a romantic and exotic setting, this is your place. The calm waters of Dickenson Bay swirl just a few yards away, and the menu of fresh seafood – especially the coconut shrimp – leaves you satisfied and serene. $$$. At

Siboney Beach Club. Open for breakfast, lunch and dinner. ☎ 268-462-1538, www.coconutgroveantigua.com.

Coco's

This hillside restaurant overlooking Valley Church Bay has a very romantic feel, and chef Tyrone Astaphan's creations add to the atmosphere. The ever-changing menu includes Caribbean flavors and ingredients. $$. On Valley Road just outside St. Mary's next to Coco's Hotel. Open for breakfast, lunch and dinner. ☎ 268-462-9700.

Harmony Hall

Sitting on the terrace in the shade of an old sugar mill, gazing out over the azure expanse of Nonsuch Bay, you'll feel you have truly found paradise. Then a delectable plate of homemade mozzarella, ripe tomatoes and fresh basil is placed in front of you, and you are convinced this is heaven on earth. The Italian cuisine with West Indies accents served here is definitely one of the best on the island. Before lunch, hop on their boat for a snorkeling expedition to Green Island, or visit their pool or beach for a quick dip. After lunch, enjoy a stroll through the art gallery and gift shop, where local artists display their latest creations. It's a delightful way to spend an afternoon. $$$$. East side of the island near the village of Freetown. Open for lunch every day, and dinner on Fridays and Saturdays only. Closed from May through September. ☎ 268-460-4120, www.harmonyhall.com.

The Last Lemming

The Last Lemming

This restaurant is tucked under the new Antigua Yacht Club hotel, on the waterfront of Falmouth Harbour. Gaze over an incredible array of yachts while you choose from a menu featuring seafood; lunch offers light entrées, sushi and salads. They offer live music on Tuesday and Friday evenings, as well as a martini and wine bar every night. $$$. Falmouth Harbour, open for lunch and dinner, closed Sundays. ☎ 268-460-6910.

Miller's by the Sea

It's a restaurant, it's a major entertainment venue, it's a beach bar all rolled into one. Located on a powdery white sand beach near Fort James, the place is popular with locals and often hosts special musical events.

Cuisine includes island favorites like conch chowder, plus a wide selection of seafood and meat entrées. $$. Near Fort James, just outside St. John's off the Dickenson Bay Road. Open for lunch and dinner. ☎ 268-462-9414.

The Beach

This large restaurant is one of a local chain owned by the Big Banana Holding Company. It is very relaxed and hospitable for parties, business meetings or gatherings after work. The food is a notch above a typical beach bar, and the setting is outstanding. Cuisine includes tastes from the Mediterranean, America and Pacific Rim countries. There's live music on Friday nights. $$$. On Dickenson Bay, next to Antigua Village. Open for breakfast, lunch and dinner. ☎ 268-480-6940.

Turner's Beach Bar & Grill

A favorite for cruise ship tours, Turner's offers a great beach and open-air atmosphere. The curried conch and lobster salad are not to be missed; there is a covered area for indoor evening dining. Turner's rents beach lounges and has shade huts, so you can make a day of it on one of the best west coast beaches. $$. At Johnson's Point, just past the Blue Heron hotel. Open for lunch and dinner. ☎ 268-462-9133.

Turner's Beach Bar & Grill

Antigua & Barbuda

Culinary Alert! Spiny Lobster

Your visit to Antigua or Barbuda will not be complete without tasting the spiny lobster, THE local delicacy. Unlike the northern lobsters, this crustacean has no large front claws, but rather two long spikes that serve as a major defense mechanism. This sweet-fleshed creature of the sea is one of the major export products of Barbuda, and Antigua to a lesser extent. You'll find it featured on the menu of most upper-end restaurants; it is also a staple at food stands that are ever-present along roadsides and in villages. The spiny lobster is best when halved, brushed with butter, and grilled, but you'll also find it in salads, mixed into pasta dishes, and offered as medallions with a lush cream sauce.

Ethnic Foods & Favorites

Alberto's

This Willoughby Bay favorite is like an old hideaway, hard to see from the road but delightful once you get inside. The Ravenello family offers a varied cuisine using fresh local seafood and vegetables, with a lovely open-air setting and an extensive wine cellar. $$$. Red Hill, Willoughby Bay. Open for dinner only. ☎ 268-460-3007.

Café Napoleon

While you're in St. John's for shopping, plan to do lunch at this French spot. You'll find the usual favorites like salad Niçoise and baguette sandwiches as well as daily specials. $$. In Redcliffe Quay, downtown St. John's. Open for lunch and dinner. ☎ 268-562-1820.

George

This downtown restaurant offers an eclectic menu of salads, burgers, snacks, pastas and full entrées in a contemporary open-air setting. The Caribbean Seafood Salad is intriguing and the burger selection is good. On Saturdays they feature a true West Indian menu with fungi, salt fish and all the rest. $$. Corner of Market and Redcliffe streets. Open for breakfast, lunch and dinner. ☎ 268-562-4866.

HQ2 Piano Bar & Restaurant

HQ2 Piano Bar & Restaurant

Located in the old Officers' Quarters at Nelson's Dockyard in English Harbour, HQ2 reeks of history and atmosphere. The jazz band at the bar and dinner seating on the verandah overlooking the marina combine for a very pleasant evening, as does the French and Asian fusion menu. $$$. Open for lunch and dinner, closed on Mondays.
☎ 268-562-2563.

Le Cap Horn

Owners Gustav and Helene describe their cuisine as Modern French, but you'll also find dishes reminiscent of the best in classic French cooking.

Make sure to leave room for dessert because Helene, daughter of a baker, produces some wonderful pastries. $$$. Dockyard Drive in English Harbour. Open for dinner, closed on Thursdays. ☎ 268-460-1194.

New Thriving Restaurant

You'll see many branches of this authentic Chinese restaurant throughout Antigua, but the ones downtown in St. John's and on Airport Road seem to do the best business. The dining rooms are spacious and pleasant, and the menu items range from the expected to the sublime. Look for several dishes using conch, as well as the standards. $$. Open for lunch, dinner and carryout, closed Sundays. ☎ 268-562-0046 (Airport Road), 268-462-4611 (Long Street).

Peter's BBQ Restaurant

This long-time favorite of the Jolly Harbour crowd offers steakhouse fare, including seven varieties of steak, with some German and Swiss influences. Situated on the marina, the restaurant offers patio seating so you can gaze at all the yachts while enjoying your meal. $$. At the Jolly Harbour commercial complex. Open for breakfast, lunch and dinner. ☎ 268-464-6026.

West Indian Cooking

Commissioner's Grill

During lunch here you may unknowingly be sitting next to a minister of the government, a senator or an ambassador. It's the gathering place for those who want authentic Antiguan food in a breezy, pleasant atmosphere. $$$. On Lower Redcliffe Street, across from Redcliffe Quay. Open for lunch and dinner. ☎ 268-462-1883.

Home

Chef Carl Thomas creates dishes strongly influenced by his Antiguan roots, but also with touches of foreign cuisines. Don't be surprised if Chef Thomas stops by your table to chat. Home was named "Best Restaurant in Antigua" by the BBC. $$$. In Gambles Terrace, near St. John. Open for dinner, closed Sundays; closed for one month in summer. ☎ 268-461-7651, www.thehomerestaurant.com.

Hemingway's

High above St. Mary's Street on a verandah where you can watch cruise ship passengers descend upon the town, this restaurant offers local specials along with great salads, sandwiches and seafood entrées. Lowell and

Ann's hospitality is unsurpassed, and the coconut crushes are wonderful. $$$. Lower St. Mary's Street. Open for lunch and dinner, closed Sundays. ☎ 268-462-2763.

Russell's

Not only is the West Indian food great here, but you also have a magnificent view out to St. John's Harbour and sunsets over Runaway Bay. To spice up the joint, Russell has added Sunday afternoon live jazz. $$$. On the grounds of Ft. James, at the southern end of Runaway Bay. Open for lunch and dinner. ☎ 268-728-1998.

STOP FOR A TASTE OF BLACK PINEAPPLE

If you're looking to immerse yourself in real local tastes, make **The Culture Shop** on Fig Tree Drive a must-do stop while you are out and about on the island. Here you can find super sweet Antiguan black pineapples just harvested from the Cades pineapple plantation, as well as guavas, mangoes, bananas, huge local avocados, and a selection of seasonal fresh juices. Owner Elaine started this local fruit stand with a small harvest. It has now grown into a shop offering local jams and hot pepper sauces for sale. At the entrance to Wallings Dam, on Fig Tree Drive. ☎ 268-460-3949.

Sports Bars

Gladiator Sports Bar

As part of the impressive Grand Princess entertainment complex at Jolly Harbour, this relaxed bar also has organized activities such as bingo and karaoke. The menu is what you'd expect, with lots of sandwiches, salads and light bites. Huge plasma screens allow you to watch your favorite teams in comfort. On Saturdays they feature an 'all you can eat' buffet for EC$50, a great value since that's about US$19. $$. In the Grand Princess building, Jolly Harbour. Open for lunch and dinner. ☎ 268-562-9900.

Sticky Wicket

You can't miss The Wicket as you drive out of the airport. It's part restaurant, part West Indies Cricket Hall of Fame, and part cricket stadium that in 2006 saw the inauguration of the Stanford 20/20 Tournament. The food is high-quality, with emphasis on smoked meats, prepared on the premises, as well as the best burgers on the island. There are five TV screens in the main dining room, so you can keep tabs on the latest matches while eating. $$. At the airport. Open for lunch and dinner. ☎ 268-481-7000, www.stickywicket.com.

Sticky Wicket

Steely Bar & Restaurant

Situated next to the pool in the Jolly Harbour BBR Sportive complex, this relaxed bar offers a mix of local and international cuisine. Plan to be there on Tuesday evenings for entertainment by the Halcyon Steel Orchestra, or Saturday for karaoke. $$. ☎ 268-462-6260. In the BBR Sportive recreation complex at Jolly Harbour. Open from 8 am until late.

Quick Bites

Bellyful's

It may not look like much of a restaurant when you walk in, but once you discover that they do one thing only and do it better than anyone on the island, you forget the sparse decor. Here you'll find crisp, flaky Jamaican patties, just pulled from the oven, filled with beef or chicken. The price is very low and the flavor is impressive. One or two make a complete meal. $. Open for lunch and dinner. ☎ 268-562-4098 (Market Street across from Court's); ☎ 268-562-6921 (High Street in St. John's); ☎ 268-562-5433 (English Harbour).

Big Banana Pizzas in Paradise

This old favorite recently moved from its cramped location at Redcliff Quay to a sleek new two-story building further up Redcliffe Street. But the pizza is of the same high quality and the service is great. $$. On Lower Redcliffe Street, next to the British American Mall. Open for lunch and dinner, closed Sundays. ☎ 268-480-6985, www.bigbanana-antigua.com.

Franciane's French Bakery

With four locations scattered throughout St. John's and environs, this is a local favorite for fresh-baked baguette sandwiches and other baked goods.

Antigua & Barbuda

$. Old Parham Road; Jasmine Court; Long Street and Cross Street; Heritage Quay. Open for lunch, closed Sundays. ☎ 268-462-2253.

Famous Mauro's Pizza

With more than 30 different pizzas, produced from a wood-burning brick oven – Mauro's is paradise for pizza aficionados. Authentic Italian and freshly grown local ingredients make for the best pizza on the island. $$. Cobbs Cross. Open for lunch and dinner, closed Wednesdays. ☎ 268-460-1318.

Papi's

If you love chicken but don't want it Kentucky Fried, go across the street from the KFC on Fort Road to Papi's for flame-grilled chicken or pan-fried fish with delectable sides. The prices are reasonable, the food is healthy, and the atmosphere is very pleasant for families and groups. $$. Fort Road just outside St. John's. Open for lunch and dinner. ☎ 268-562-7274.

The island, demonstrating its affinity with the US, also has a **Subway** in downtown St. John's (one of the few eateries there open on Sundays) and three **KFC**s, on Fort Road, downtown near the Deluxe Cinemas, and on Old Parham Road.

Vegetarian

Mama Lolly's Vegetarian Café

This small café in Redcliffe Quay is a local favorite for lunch and dinner. The vegetable lasagna is the best, and they offer an assortment of hot and cold dishes you can mix and match for a complete meal. Right outside their door is a separate juice bar where freshly made carrot and fruit juices as well as smoothies are offered. $. In Redcliffe Key, behind the Pottery Shop. Open for lunch only, closed Sundays. ☎ 268-562-1552.

Kalabashe

Just across the street from Redcliffe Quay in the Vendors' Mall building is this small storefront café, offering an assortment of entrées and salads as well as juices and smoothies. The emphasis is on "island spice," so expect some hot Jamaican influences. $. #10 Vendors Mall, Lower Redcliffe Street. ☎ 268-562-6070.

Shopping

There's a reason St. John's is one of the premiere cruise ship stops on the Eastern Caribbean tour. The duty-free delights, including perfumes, liquor, jewelry and clothing, are centered around the colorful open-air malls of Heritage Quay and Redcliffe Quay. Boutiques line the streets beginning at the entrance to Heritage Quay, east on St. Mary's Street, and then both north and south on Market Street.

Heritage Quay

This two-story mall features stores you see in many other duty-free ports – **Lipstick, Columbian Emeralds, The Body Shop, Benetton, Longchamp, Abbott's Jewelry** and **Diamonds International**. In addition, you can supplement your beachwear/tropical evening wear at **Gingerlily** or **Sunseakers**, and find all you need for playing on the beach at **The Beach Store**. For gifts to take back home, try **Shipwreck, the Linen Shop** or, for something completely unusual, **Island Arts**, which features prints of works by Star Wars animator Nick Maley.

Shops on Heritage Quay

Redcliffe Quay

Redcliffe Quay shops

Among the most interesting stores here is **Exotic Antigua**, where you'll find great bargains on Tommy Bahama shirts, linen ensembles, stylish handbags and hats. If you have a special evening event coming up, be sure to stop in at **Noreen Phillips Couturière**, where the venerable Noreen offers incredibly bejeweled and sparkly original evening gowns and cocktail dresses. **Deshaun**, a talented young designer, also displays her latest creations in a storefront here. For elegant casual clothes, especially linens and cotton, **A Thousand Flowers** is a favorite of locals as well as visitors. For souvenirs, try **Jacaranda**, which offers prints and mats designed by Caribbean artists, along with gift packages of coffee, tea, and Tortuga Rum Cake, a real delicacy.

St. Mary's/Market Streets

Street vendor in St. John's

The first exciting women's clothing boutique you'll encounter is **Rain**, which offers a range from daily business clothing to dressy evening wear. The selection of jewelry, sandals and shoes is also very good. Another boutique with great style is **It**, at the corner of High and Thames Streets, just down from Heritage Quay. Numerous other clothing and shoe stores line Market Street, extending all the way down to the Farmer's Market.

Vendor's Mall

This open-air mall is the government's solution to crowded downtown streets, that is, take all the street vendors off the sidewalks and put them in one place. As you leave Heritage Quay going toward Redcliffe Quay, you are assaulted by a cacophony of ladies vying to get your attention to look at their booths. There you'll find an array of beach wraps, t-shirts, hats, jewelry, craft items, and inexpensive treasures you can take home to those who weren't lucky enough to come on your vacation.

Other interesting shopping can be found at the **British-American Mall** on lower Redcliffe Street, a two-story structure that houses a pharmacy, a Chinese herbalist's shop, the Best of Books bookstore, and Made in Antigua, a gift store with authentic island crafts. If you're looking for more practical stores, **Woods Centre** on Friar's Hill Road houses the **Epicurean Grocery**, one of the largest on the island, along with a pharmacy, **Radio Shack**, **Harper's Office Supply**, a toy store, children's and adults' shoe stores, a gallery of local artists' works, an optician, and a branch of the **Antigua Post Office**.

For local produce, as well as some local crafts, don't miss the **Farmer's Market** and **Public Market**, on Market Street going out of St. John's. This busy commercial hub features individual tables and booths where local farmers and craftsmen bring the fruits of their labors for sale. Also nearby are the **Meat Market** and **Fish Market**, where you can purchase everything you need to create superb meals while capitalizing on the local marketplace (and its cheaper prices).

English Harbour, since it is a distance from St. John's, also has some local shopping choices, such as the boutique, food and liquor store, and nautical gear shops at Falmouth Harbour. On your way off the island, you'll be able to do some last-minute shopping in the Departures Lounge at **V.C. Bird International Airport**, where **King Progress Music Shop** offers a good selection of Caribbean music, **Abbott's Perfumery** gives you a last chance at duty-free perfumes, **Coco Shop** sells clothing and dolls, and **Columbian Emeralds** saves you from forgetting an important souvenir for someone you love.

Nighlife

Casinos

 One of the major draws of Caribbean islands like Antigua and St. Maarten are the casinos, where you can legally fritter away your money in a tropical atmosphere. There are no lavish shows, but the odds are good and the action is lively at the following:

Grand Princess Casino

This glittery casino is the major draw of the Jolly Harbour entertainment complex, which resembles a marble palace. With 250 slot machines and 24 live tables, it's the largest gaming enterprise in Antigua, and the most convenient, since the building also houses two restaurants and a nightclub. Plan to spend an entire evening. In Jolly Harbour. Open seven days a week. ☎ 268-562-9900, www.grandprincessentertainment.com.

King's Casino

Located in Heritage Quay, this large casino has long been an attraction for visitors. You can play craps, roulette, blackjack, baccarat and Caribbean stud poker, or feed a range of 'state of the art' slots, including the largest slot machine in the world. They offer live entertainment, and major sporting events are broadcast all day from satellite feeds. On the waterfront in Heritage Quay. Open seven days a week. ☎ 268-462-1727, www.kingscasino.com.

St. James Casino

Offered as a convenience for guests, this small casino is also open to visitors from other hotels. It bills itself as a "Monte Carlo style" entertainment center and is frequented by a low-key but elegant crowd. In the St. James Club, southern end of the island. ☎ 268-460-5000.

Nightclubs

 The scene is ever-changing, but the clubs are a major draw for young and old. Be sure to dress up so you'll fit in with the local crowd.

Abracadabra Disco Bar

This is the social center of English Harbour, with themed parties, live bands and DJs, in an outdoor patio setting. It closes down for the summer, but during Sailing Week it sees as much action as during all the other weeks combined. Just outside Nelson's Dockyard. ☎ 268-460-1732.

Liquid Nightclub

Capping a night of dining and gambling, your final stop at the Grand Princess complex should be Liquid. Here the stylish and hip go to dance, lime, and generally have a good time – but be forewarned, the action starts well after 11 pm. Second Floor of the Grand Princess Casino, Jolly Harbour. ☎ 268-562-9900.

Rush Nightclub

This unassuming building has a striking décor, and the music bellows out across Runaway Bay. Open Thursdays through Sundays, starting at 10:30 pm. On Runaway Bay, next to Sunset Cove. ☎ 268-562-7874.

The Coast

This nightclub opened in 2006, adjacent to the King's Casino in Heritage Quay. It's a combination restaurant and venue for live entertainment, and is popular with locals as well as visitors. In Heritage Quay, next to the casino on the waterfront

The Place to Be on Sunday Nights

Many visitors and locals feel the best party open on to allon Antigua is Sunday night at **Shirley Heights**. It starts at around 6 pm with a steel band performance, usually by Halcyon Steel Orchestra. As darkness falls, the stage lights up and the place starts jumping with the music of one of the islands' talented soca bands. Then it's dancing out under the stars for a colorful crowd that includes Europeans, Canadians and Americans as well as Antiguans. Also available is a barbecue dinner, with choices ranging from hamburgers to chicken to ribs and fish. Admission/cover charge is EC$20 per person.

Barbuda

Antigua's flat limestone and sand sister island, 27 miles to the north, is a place where time seemingly stands still. It is not highly developed, and has just three hotels (only one of which is open to the general public) and a few restaurants in the main village of Codrington. But the pink sand beaches are spectacular, and the ring of coral reef around the island makes snorkeling and diving exceptional. If you plan a day-trip to the beach, take your time and travel by ferry from St. John's (about a 90-minute ride). Be sure to bring your drinks, food and shelter, since there are none of these on the beaches.

History

Even though Barbuda is a small, flat island, it has a colorful and interesting history. As with many of the Leeward Islands, Barbuda's first settlers were Amerindians, including the warlike Caribs. There are 19 known archeological sites and ancient petroglyphs or rock drawings are still found in some of the highland caves.

The first European settlers came in 1625, when Britain claimed Barbuda, along with Antigua, Nevis and St. Kitts. Both the British, and later the French, found habitation difficult because of the lack of arable land and the continuous attacks by Caribs. Finally, by 1666, some settlers (although no one is sure of what nationality) built a strong enough settlement, at what is now Codrington, to defend against the attacks.

In 1680, King Charles II of England granted a 50-year lease to Christopher and John Codrington. Their first settlement was again attacked by Caribs, and it wasn't until four years later that they could lay claim to another 50-year lease on the land, with a payment to the Governor of

Barbuda seascape

Antigua at a rate of "one horse annually." They were also given the rights to all wreckage on the island, a considerable gift since at the time there were over 150 known shipwrecks on the reefs surrounding the island. Plundering these wrecks became the settlers' main source of income.

When John Codrington died in 1688, Christopher became the sole lease-holder. He also had large sugar plantations in Antigua, and decided to use Barbuda as a stock farm for the provisioning of Antigua. The island was rich in game, including fallow deer, wild boar and guinea fowl, all of which still roam the island today. According to local legends, the island was also used as Codrington's breeding farm for slaves, producing tall, strong men. The Codrington family managed to hold on to the lease despite a devastating attack by French privateers in 1710, family squabbles over owner-ship, a downturn in the sugar market, and the abolition of slavery.

However, by 1860, with the freed slaves living in poverty because the Codringtons could not pay them, Britain began looking for a way to get rid of the island because of the lack of products and the welfare demands of the residents. They turned ownership over to Antigua, and in 1870 the Codrington family relinquished all claims on the lease.

Antigua merged Barbuda's activities with its own, building up the tourism and agriculture infrastructure. The island was declared a crown estate in 1903, and a warden was put in place to oversee it. Then in 1976 the warden was replaced with the Barbuda Council, a governing body that exists to this day to take care of day-to-day concerns of the 1,500 residents. The island also sends representatives to the Antiguan Parliament and is active in the dual-island's politics and governance.

One of the main economic mainstays of the island is sand mining, where for years tons of sand have been strip-mined from Palmetto Point for export to the construction trades in Antigua and around the Caribbean. In 2006, after much complaint from environmentalists about the damage the sand mining was doing to the island's ecosystem, a temporary end to the practice threw the island's economic picture again into doubt. Sand mining has since restarted. Who knows when it will finally stop.

Travel Information

Getting Around

There are only three ways to get to Barbuda. You can take the **Barbuda Express** ferry that leaves several times a day from St. John's (☎ 268-764-2291, www.antiguaferries.com). **Carib Aviation** offers 15-minute flights twice daily from **V.C. Bird Airport** (☎ 268-481-2400, caribav@candw.ag). Or you can **charter a boat** for a cruise to the island (see the boat charter listings earlier in this chapter).

Once you are on the 62-square-mile island, it's not far to any point. The best way to get around is to hire one of the taxi drivers, who will pick you up from the airport, ferry dock, or anywhere along the shoreline they can reach by road. They are well informed and can direct you to the caves and historical sights. They are particularly skilled in traversing the rough roads of the island. They also can arrange for your tour of the Codrington Lagoon, if you want to see the frigate birds (see below).

If you want to go it alone, you can hire a bicycle from **Griff Walker** (☎ 268-460-0539), who has adult mountain bikes available.

TAXI SERVICES ON BARBUDA
■ Byron Askie, ☎ 268-460-0164, or cell 268-773-6082.
■ Crystal Bay Tours, ☎ 268-460-0059, or cell 268-724-7490.
■ Eric Burton, ☎ 268-460-0465.
■ eXtra Taxi Service, ☎ 268-460-0408, or cell 268-772-0917.
■ George Burton, ☎ 268 460 0103, or cell 268-772-1209.
■ Paradise Tours, ☎ 268-773-9957.

Exploring

On Foot

From the airport or ferry dock, it's a short walk into **Codrington village**, where you'll find restaurants, bars and stores. From there, it's a three-mile walk to **Martello Tower** and **River Fort**, one of the major historical sites on the island. One of Barbuda's most spectacular beaches, about 11 miles long, can be reached by walking west of the Tower out to Palmetto Point, near The Beach House resort.

Another great hike (not a sedate walk) starts at the **Highland House** ruins on the Atlantic (eastern) side of the island, which is also the highest point on the island. A rocky trail to the north leads to **Dark Cave**, a deep, rock-lined sinkhole ending in a freshwater pool. It's a treacherous climb down, so hiring a guide is advisable. To the south, you can walk through the Highlands to **Darby Cave**, another deep sinkhole surrounded by the luxuriant growth of palmetto palms.

On Water

Most activity on this island centers around the water and the beautiful turquoise reefs that teem with sea life.

Wreck Diving & Snorkeling

Since fishing is prohibited from any boat other than a Barbuda vessel and no spearfishing is allowed, there are tons of fish to see, along with eagle rays, sting rays and turtles. It is said that wherever you anchor off the coast, you are within short swimming distance of a great reef, although most reefs cannot be reached from the beach. Among the most popular reefs are Spanish Point and White Bay. Equipment and tours are available from **George Burton's Scuba**, ☎ 268-460-0103, cell 268-772-1209. Snorkels can also be rented from **Byron Askie**, ☎ 268-460-0164 or at the **Green Door Tavern** in Codrington.

Fishing

Kingfish, dolphin, mahi mahi, tuna and barracuda are commonly found in the waters off Barbuda, making for great sport. On the outskirts of Codrington Lagoon, you'll find bonefish, tarpon and 10-pounders. However, in order to fish you must be aboard a locally owned vessel. Contact **Mcarthur Nedd**, who has a boat for rod and reel fishing (☎ 268-460-0059, cell 268-724-7490).

Watersports

Kayaks, lasers and Hobie Cats are available for fun right off the beaches. The only supplier is **Byron Askie**, ☎ 268-460-0164. Jet skis are not permitted because of their potential to damage some of the shallower reefs.

Eco-Travel

Barbuda attracts those who are looking for unique eco-experiences, and rewards them well with two primary activities.

Bird Watching

The Codrington Lagoon is home to one of the largest colonies of **frigate birds** in the world. The birds, with an adult wingspan of over six feet, are totally creatures of the sea. Their small feet don't allow them to walk or swim, so they spend their time perched in trees or reconnoitering the seas for flying fish or for opportunities to steal fish from passing pelicans and gulls. During mat-

Frigate birds on Barbuda

ing season, the eligible males blow up their bright red neck pouches like balloons. Knowledgeable guides such as **George "Prophet" Burton** (☎ 268-460-0103) are the only ones authorized to take you into the lagoon for observation of these amazing creatures.

The lagoon is also the home of about 170 other species of birds, including the Barbuda warbler, found only on this island, the whistling duck, an endangered species, and the tropic bird, found in large numbers in the cliffs and caves of Two Foot Bay.

Cave Exploration

The island boasts some fascinating underground structures that can be toured with a guide. These include **Dark Cave**, a massive sinkhole 180 feet deep that leads to a 440 foot by 60 foot cavern. The cavern continues through a passageway that ends in five freshwater pools – habitats for a species of crustaceans found nowhere else in the world. **Darby's Cave**, in the northern highlands, is another sinkhole, about 350 feet wide and 70 feet deep. At Two Foot Bay, easily reached by taxi, are a series of caverns including **Indian Cave**, **Drop Cavern** and **Bat Chambers**. Here you can see the vestiges of Amerindian rock carvings, the only ones on Antigua and Barbuda.

Where to Stay

Given its size and small population, Barbuda is not known for a great number of places to stay and eat. There are three main hotels, all five-star, luxurious, all-inclusive and expensive; a two-villa enclave; and a number of small guesthouses and cottages for rent by the locals at very reasonable rates. Three more hotels are expected to be available by 2008. Both of the hotels available to the general public now have daily rates from $900-$1,000 and more. And if you expect TVs in the rooms, forget it. This is a place for quiet reflection, beach walking, reading and sea excursions, the assumption being that you'll be so blissed out, you won't miss your favorite shows.

The Beach House

Club house at The Beach House

This elegant resort captivates with contemporary architecture, stark white walls, and dark wood accents. The service is impeccable, with Service Ambassadors assigned to each guest to take care of any needs. The resort is situated on Palmetto Point, where long lengths of pink sand beach stretch in two directions away from the Point, giving guests many miles of walkable, deserted shore. But, with the excellent restaurant, beautiful reflecting pool and lovely rooms, you may not want to stray at all. This is an adults-only resort, but children may be allowed to stay when the new two-bedroom villas with plunge pools are completed.

Location: Palmetto Point, southwestern coast.

Rooms: 20 ocean-view junior suites and one one-bedroom suite, with private terraces, air conditioning and coffee/tea service; guests provided with cell phones while there; airport transfer included in rate; resort closes from early September to mid-November every year.

Rates: MAP.

Features: Restaurant and bar, saltwater pool, two beaches, boat available for going to reefs, fishing right off shore, massage services, horseback riding.

☎ 631-537-1352, 888-776-0333 US, fax 631-537-1352, www. thebeachhousebarbuda.com.

Coco Point

Unless you have stayed here before, or been initiated into the lore of Coco Point by parents or friends, you may have a hard time learning much about this place. The management is well known for discouraging any media coverage about the hotel, preferring rather to attract full occupancy just by word of mouth and faithful returnees. It's a beautiful place, with all the activities you could imagine, so you should definitely consider contacting them about rates.

Coco Point

Location: Southernmost tip at Cocoa Bay.

Rooms: 34, in beachside cottages.

Rates: AI.

Features: Two all-weather tennis courts; deep-sea and reef-fishing (tackle and guide provided); Sunfish sailing; windsurfing; waterskiing; sea-kayaking; snorkeling (equipment provided); and informal trap-shooting; air transfers from Antigua airport to private landing strip at hotel.

☎ 212-986-1416, fax 212-986-0901, www.cocopoint.com.

North Beach

This private enclave of two West Indian-style villas on the beach plus a dining pavilion is set on a peninsula at the northern tip of the island; it is only accessible by boat. The beach is spectacular, and you get a pronounced feel of "getting away from it all."

Location: On the northern coast.

☎ 212-689-9688, www.northbeachbarbuda.com.

Guest Houses

You can obtain an up-to-date listing of guest houses from the Antigua-Barbuda Tourism Office or www.barbudaful.net, but here are some highlights:

Cerene Deazle's Guesthouse. Single & double rooms. ☎ 268-775-1349.

John Hartford's Guesthouse. Single & double rooms, one with kitchenette. ☎ 268-460-0498.

Lynton Thomas' Guesthouse. Five single rooms with private baths. ☎ 268-773-9957.

Nedd's Guesthouse. Four double rooms with shared sitting room and kitchen. ☎ 268-460 0059.

Francis Guesthouse. Single & double rooms plus triple with kitchenette. ☎ 268-460-0346.

The Island Chalet. ☎ 268-460-0065.

Ilene Nedd. One-bedroom house and three-bedroom house. ☎ 268-460-0419.

Del's Place. Small two-bedroom cottage outside the village. ☎ 268-460-0042.

Dining Out

Palm Tree Restaurant

 This small but very pleasant restaurant run by Cereme Deazle offers a great lobster lunch as well as terrific breakfasts and dinners. Codrington. Open for breakfast, lunch and dinner. ☎ 268-775-1349.

Wa O'Moni

This restaurant is one of the newer ones on Barbuda and is a friendly place for lunch or dinner. Again, the specialty is Barbudan lobster, but they also serve other seafood, plus salads, sandwiches, burgers and desserts. Codrington. Open for lunch and dinner seven days a week, and breakfast on Sundays. ☎ 268-562-1933.

RESTAURANT PRICE CHART	
$$	Good value, lots of West Indian cuisine; US$9-$14 for a plate of food.

The Beaches of Antigua & Barbuda

 Antigua' shape would be roughly a circle, except the island's shoreline is crimped by inlets, bays and creeks. These indentations, combined with offshore reefs that virtually ring the island, set up the perfect geographic model for idyllic white sand beaches. Long ago, some marketer who noticed this decided to create the image of "365 beaches, one for every day of the year." While in fact there may not be quite that many, the beaches of Antigua are a concentration of some of the best in the Caribbean, with powdery white sand, clear aqua-hued water, and fringes of palms or other trees to provide shade.

All beaches in Antigua are public, and recently the government mounted an effort to provide more facilities at the ones recognized as national parks such as Fryes Beach and Half Moon Bay. Most maps available on the island show all the beaches, but the specific road to some may not be clear. Locals are used to people asking about them, so don't be afraid to stop in a village or at a roadside stand to get clear directions.

Here's a quick rundown of some of the best on the islands.

On Antigua

Cades Beach

On the Caribbean side, southwest corner. Because the beach and sand base eventually leads out to Cades Reef, this is a popular beach for snorkelers. It is accessible only by boat, as it is surrounded by mangroves.

Darkwood Beach

On the Caribbean side, southwest corner. This beach sits just off the road leading to Fig Tree Drive, making it very popular for Sunday afternoon picnics. Facilities include a beach bar and toilets, plus a few shade huts.

Deep Bay

On the Caribbean side, mid-island. This beach, adjacent to

Darkwood Beach

the Grand Royal Antiguan hotel, is lined with palm trees and has great snorkeling.

Dickenson Bay

On the Caribbean side, northwest coast. Said to be the most popular, it is lined with resorts such as Sandals and Halcyon Cove. The shallow, sand-lined area goes far out, the water is warm and clear, and the surf is pretty tame.

Fryes Bay

On the Caribbean side, southwest corner. As one of the truly public beaches, with open access for Antiguans, this is very popular. It can be windy at times, and right now has no beach bar or restaurant. The government is working to improve the area.

Galley Bay

On the Caribbean side, mid-island. This is a beautiful but small strand, not easily accessible unless you are staying at the Galley Bay resort. Ask the locals about the side-road that gives you access.

Half Moon Bay

On the Atlantic side, southeast corner. You have to spend some time getting to this beach, which was recently designated a national park. The crescent-shaped strand has something for everyone – rough surf for boogie boards and surfboards on the southern end, and calm, clear and warm waters with little surf on the protected northern end. Until the government resolves the disposition of the hurricane-wrecked Half Moon Bay Resort, there will be little in the way of facilities so plan to bring a cooler and picnic basket.

Hawksbill Bay

On the Caribbean side, mid-island. The Hawksbill resort sits on a collection of four beaches facing this bay, each with great sand and warm waters. The beach farthest south is the only clothing-optional beach on the island. The distinguishing hawksbill-shaped rock sits just offshore.

Jolly Beach/Lignumvitae Bay

On the Caribbean side, southwest corner. This popular, wide beach serves the Jolly Beach Resort and the townhouse complex of Jolly Harbour. There is a separate road in the middle of the two developments for beach access. The water can be cloudy here, a condition due to, some say, filling in a natural salt pond to create more land.

Long Bay

On the Atlantic side, northeast corner. Another popular spot for snorkeling, this long strip of beach is used by guests of both the Long Bay Hotel and the Occidental Grand Pineapple Beach Resort. There are amenities such as a public restaurant, beach vendors, and toilet facilities.

Pigeon Beach

In English Harbour, southern side. Most people know about this beach because it's closest to the hotels and inns of Nelson's Dockyard and English Harbour, and because it's the site of great parties for Sailing Week. Expect a multitude of sailing yachts anchored just offshore.

Rendezvous Bay

Rendezvous Bay

On the southern end, where the Caribbean and Atlantic meet. This secluded, charming beach is actually four beaches separated by rocky outcroppings and is accessible only by an arduous hike or a four-wheel drive down a less-than-ideal trail. But, because there are no resorts or hotels on the bay, it's surrounded by green hills and gives you an "out of this world" feeling.

Runaway Bay

Runaway Bay

On the Caribbean side, northwest coast. Just south of Dickenson Bay is this less-populated and beautiful beach. There are numerous access points, and a few restaurants on the beach, such as the Lobster Shack.

Turner's Beach

On the Caribbean side, southwest corner. Farther

Turner's Beach

down from Darkwood is this wide stretch of soft sand, popular with cruise ship passengers as well as locals, especially on Sunday afternoons. Avoid it when the cruise ships are in, because the restaurant is inundated. You can rent beach lounges and use the shade huts.

On Barbuda

Palmetto Point

Palmetto Point Beach

The beaches of Barbuda are even more spectacular than those of Antigua, with soft pink sand, wide shallow areas for wading, and little surf because of the off-shore reefs. The longest strip of beach starts at Palmetto Point and extends northward up Low Bay to Luis Beach near the Codrington Lagoon. Bring all your drinks and food, because there are no facilities on this or any other strip of beach on Barbuda.

Jumby Bay

On Long Island, off the northeast coast of Antigua. While all beaches are public, access to this beautiful beach is problematic unless you have a boat. The ferry to the exclusive Jumby Bay resort is limited to guests, so there is no easy way to get there unless you intend to have lunch at the one restaurant open to the public. If you're on a boat, Pasture Bay on the opposite side of the island is less social and more sedate.

Jumby Bay

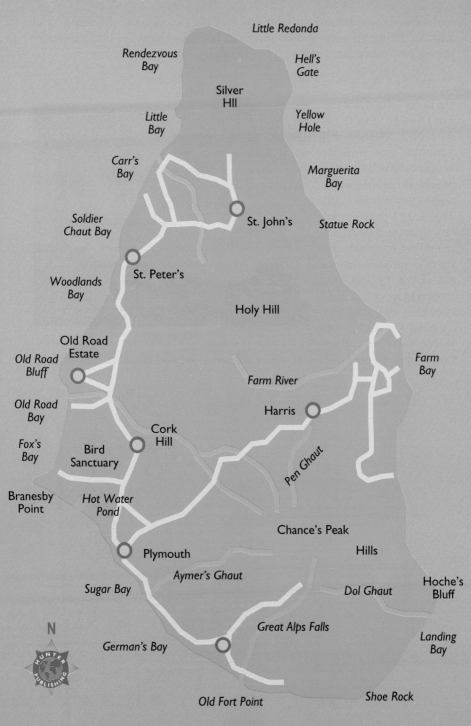

Montserrat
The Allure of the Island

Montserrat is a study in human courage in the face of Mother Nature's fury. Since 1995, the Soufrière Hills volcano has been wreaking havoc on this small island, driving away the many who have lost homes, businesses and relatives. Today, it is a country divided between the lush area north of the Exclusion Zone where determined citizens have stayed on to build new homes and villages, and the barren area south of the Zone, where gray ash covers the main town of Plymouth.

But the pyroclastic flows that buried the island's airport, golf course, schools, and port have spawned a new tourist attraction – visitors to Montserrat today almost always want to get as close to the volcano as allowed – and there is a new concentration on diving, mountain hiking and eco-discovery, all enhanced by Soufrière Hills' eruption. But the fragile optimism is underscored by the knowledge that Lady Soufrière and her rapidly growing lava dome can decide to pitch another fit at any time and rain acidic, metal-scorching ash down onto forests, crops and roofs, sowing devastation, fear and doubt.

Montserrat's volcanic landscape

The best way to approach Montserrat is to base yourself in Antigua, and fly to Montserrat for two to five days. There are some delightful hotels and restaurants, and the island remains reminiscent of the "old Caribbean," where hospitality ruled and visitors weren't in pursuit of the next great fad. The northern area is lush, green and beautiful. People stop to talk to you on the street and display great pride in their island; crime is almost nonexistent. However, unless you are a hiking or diving enthusiast, there is little to do after you tour the Exclusion Zone, visit the Montserrat Volcano Observatory, and go to Jack Boy Hill to watch the growing dome.

What to Look For According to the Type of Traveler You Are

The Perfect Cruise Passenger won't really find a lot here. There are no all-inclusive hotels. The Vue Pointe Hotel and Tropical Mansions Hotel both have restaurants and pools, but no beach to speak of.

The Boots-On Adventurer will love this island, because so much of it is devoted to eco-tourism and exploring the natural wonder of an active volcano. You can hike a multitude of trails up Centre Hills, go bird or turtle watching, take part in some incredible dives, and get a great view of a glowing volcano at night. The guesthouses are a great value and perfect for those who don't need a high level of comfort.

The Cultural Explorer should look at the events calendar and plan to be on the island during St. Patrick's Day, the Calabash Festival or the Queen's Birthday. Many of the restaurants serve traditional goat water (stew) and other West Indian delights. And shopping at the Montserrat National Trust Gift Store and the arts and crafts store will net you some treasured mementos.

The "I Like What I Like" Traveler could rent one of the elegant villas scattered around the north end of the island, where you can while away the days in your own little slice of heaven.

The Incurable Romantic should enjoy some of the small guesthouses, particularly the Sugar Mill Suite at the Montserrat Moments Inn. Dinner by candlelight at the Vue Pointe Hotel is also on the romantic radar.

The Family Social Director can choose brood-suitable accommodations from numerous three- and four-bedroom villas, many with pools and views to the ocean. You can organize a trip to the Montserrat Volcano Observatory, along with hikes that will allow the kids to view tropical flora and fauna up-close.

The Ultimate Shopper won't find a lot of duty-free shopping, but will enjoy some of the small boutiques such as Luv's Sea Island Cotton shop where handmade accessories celebrate a time when cotton was a vital part of the local economy.

A Brief History

The current difficulties brought on by the volcanic activity are just the latest in a long history of natural and man-made disasters visited upon this small island over the years. As with most of the Leewards, Montserrat was originally inhabited by the Arawak and Carib Indians, and it was given its current name by Christopher Columbus, who had a grand time naming islands after places he had been – in this case a Spanish monastery – or people he wanted to honor.

The first European settlers who found their way to Montserrat's shores were English and Irish Catholics, carried there from St. Kitts in 1632 by Englishman Thomas Warner. This was one of the few Caribbean islands that tolerated Roman Catholics at that time, so it became a haven of sorts for the Irish – hence the name "Emerald Isle of the Caribbean." This influx was assisted by Oliver Cromwell, who sent Irish political prisoners to the island after his victory at Drogheda in 1649.

From then on, Montserrat history is a seesaw of good times and disasters, much of it stemming from the competition between England, the Netherlands and France for control of the Leewards, with an occasional raid from the fierce Caribs. In 1662 the French, aided by the Caribs and the Irish, attacked the British-held island. The captured English were sent to Jamaica and most never returned. The English eventually retook the island, and then a severe hurricane destroyed what was left after the battles.

Interspersed among the manmade carnage were the natural disasters – hurricanes, earthquakes and floods. The detailed and concise history compiled by William G. Innanen (see innanen.com/montserrat/history) outlines the pattern of strife and natural disasters that caused the population to shrink and swell at various times.

By the 1700s, small farms gave way to large plantations as sugar became the dominant crop. King Sugar brought African slaves to the island as workers; it also marginalized the Irish, who did not have the financial backing to create large farms and were in fact prohibited from owning land unless they swore allegiance to the British Crown. The Irish, who tended to side with anyone who was not British, allied themselves with the French, Spanish, and slave populations. Later, the island embraced its Irish heritage and today it is the only country outside of Ireland that recognizes St. Patrick's Day as a public holiday (and they spend a week celebrating it).

By 1729, slavery had tipped the racial demographic toward blacks, with 1,100 whites and 5,800 blacks on the island. Principal exports were sugar, molasses, rum, cotton, indigo and lime juice, although Montserrat did not

Montserrat

produce sugar in the volume the other Leewards did during this time. When England and Spain went to war again in the 1740s, the island received minimal support from England and became a base for privateers.

In the late 1700s the Leewards were parceled out among various European owners. The 1783 Peace at Versailles permanently and finally gave Montserrat to Britain, and the island government abolished civil restrictions against the Irish and Roman Catholics and began working at building civil order and the economy. (The British suggested making Montserrat part of Antigua, but Antigua wasn't having it.) The emancipation of slaves in 1834 drove the plantation owners, and hence the government, to bankruptcy. Post-emancipation, an "apprenticeship" system required slaves to remain at the plantation as apprentices for four years. After serving their time, a large number of freed slaves fled Montserrat for other Caribbean islands, most notably Trinidad.

The island hit rock bottom in the 1840s, a decline hastened by natural disasters, including a devastating earthquake in 1843 and a severe drought and smallpox epidemic in 1849. Partial salvation arrived in the 1850s when Joseph Sturge visited the island and hit upon the idea of exporting lime juice as a cash crop. Sturge began buying up the sugar plantations and planting lime trees, and the lime industry lifted Montserrat out of its doldrums. In 1866, the island was established as the first British Crown Colony of the Leeward Islands.

The struggle to develop a successful economy and government, however, continued to be an up-and-down affair, with hurricanes, earthquakes, droughts and scale infestations of the lime trees constituting a good portion of the "down." In 1899, an extremely destructive hurricane in the Leewards destroyed the lime industry, and 2,000 unemployed workers migrated to Panama to work on the canal. Again, the innovative Sturges family scratched their heads and came up with the idea of growing and exporting Sea Island cotton. Some lime and sugar industry remained, but by the 1930s, cotton was the primary cash crop for the island. Also during 1930s, frequent earthquakes reshaped the mountains in the southern part of the island and eventually resulted in the present day Soufrière Hills volcanic activity.

By this time, slavery was illegal, but the wages paid to cotton plantation workers were so low that workers began to unionize to improve pay and working conditions. Montserrat's population peaked at 14,000 in 1946, but thereafter declined as thousands migrated due to economic, social, and, ultimately, natural forces. By the late 1950s, labor strife and worker migration, primarily to England, combined with crop-eating pests, had decimated the cotton industry. In time, wages sent home by émigrés became the major source of income for the island.

In the 1960s, the traveling world discovered this lush, quiet little island, and visitors from England, the US and Canada begin arriving. Real estate development and construction became the major industries, scheduled air service opened the island to tourism, and regular inter-island freight and passenger shipping began. In the 1970s, Beatles producer George Martin opened AIR Studios Montserrat, a recording studio that drew international rock stars like Eric Clapton, Elton John, Mick Jagger and Sting to the island.

View of the volcano

Then Hurricane Hugo hit in 1989, damaging over 90% of the structures on the island. A mere six years later, in 1995, the previously dormant Soufrière Hills volcano erupted and buried the capital of Plymouth in 40 feet of mud, wiping out the airport and dock, and covering the southern part of the island in ash. The subsequent and continuing ash venting and pyroclastic flows forced the government to designate a no-travel zone, known as the Exclusion Zone.

The Facts

Population

It is estimated that more than 8,000 residents left Montserrat in the late 1990s. The current population stands at 9,400, compared to the 12,000 who lived here in 1995 before the Soufrière Hills activity. About 90% of the population is black or mulatto; the remaining 10% is white, many of Irish descent. There is also a large expatriate population of US, UK and Canadian origin.

Montserrat

Language

As a British territory, the language is English, with a distinct West Indian lilt.

Main City

The official capital, **Plymouth**, now sits under a solid layer of ash, like a modern-day Pompeii. The governmental offices have been moved to **Brades**, and most restaurants and shops are centered around Brades and **Little Bay**.

Government & Economy

The island is now a United Kingdom overseas territory, with Queen Elizabeth II as the head of state. A resident governor represents the British Crown in a largely ceremonial post. All residents are considered to be citizens of the UK. The day-to-day business of the country is run by the popularly elected legislature, with a chief minister at the helm, advised by an appointed cabinet of ministers. The election of 2006 put Dr. Lowell Lewis in as chief minister.

The primary sectors of the economy are tourism, real estate development, some agriculture, and light industry.

People & Culture

The best word to describe the Montserratians is "plucky." In spite of the volcano that looms over their daily lives, they are upbeat and optimistic about the future and very proud of what they offer to the world. As you tour the island, you will constantly be greeted by locals who seem genuinely happy to share their island with you. In fact, the population is so small, you will notice that your taxi driver or guide knows almost everyone he or she passes; there are constant quick beeps of the horn to say hello (and to warn drivers about oncoming traffic on the numerous hairpin turns in the roads).

The main preoccupation on the island since 1995 has been rebuilding the infrastructure and convincing native islanders and tourists to return. Montserratian builders are well-qualified and proud of the work they are doing to rebuild their island. At the slightest encouragement they will point out examples of the tacky, inadequately built structures the British built in the late 1990s, as opposed to the sturdy and more appropriate buildings the islanders have built since.

Soufrière Hills volcano (Patrick Smith)

The island also promotes its Irish heritage in a big way. Your passport is stamped with a shamrock as you enter the "Emerald Isle of the Caribbean" and St. Patrick's Day is an official holiday, with a week of celebrations to enjoy. The history of good relations between the Irish and the slaves and the modern-day influx of Brits, Yanks and Canadians, have resulted in a harmonious, multiracial society.

Geography

This mountainous island is 39 square miles, and sits 27 miles southwest of Antigua. Its pear shape – 12 miles long and seven miles wide at the southern end – is still being altered by the pyroclastic flows of ash as they extend out into the sea and reshape the coastline. Montserrat's highest point is the 3,000-ft Soufrière Hills, the site of major volcanic activity.

The northern area is rain forest-like, lush and green, with hills, winding roads and a number of crystal-clear creeks (called ghauts) that bring water down from the mountains. The forests teem with fruit trees, birds, lizards and other life you associate with a tropical island. The northernmost extinct volcano, Silver Hill, is the site of a vibrant new housing community built to encourage natives to return home. Montserrat has fewer beaches than the other Leewards, and what beaches they have are of black volcanic sand, with the notable exception of white-sand Rendezvous Bay, the best beach on the island.

DRINK FROM THE FOUNTAIN OF RUNAWAY GHAUT

The water that flows from the mountain streams of Montserrat is some of the best in the Caribbean. For a taste, ask your guide to stop at the tap along the roadside at Runaway Ghaut. This unassuming little piece of plumbing is an important landmark to Montserratians. It provides not only a refreshing drink, but legend says that if you drink from this fountain, you will be drawn back to Montserrat again and again.

The Montserrat coastline (T. Gilligan)

The southern half of the island is defined by the Exclusion Zone boundary that cuts through the Centre Hills and runs north of St. George and Garabaldi Hills. In contrast to its lush northern neighbor, the southern terrain is as barren as the surface of the moon. The buildings and homes of the capital city of Plymouth are still buried in ash, with just an occasional spire or tall roof peeking through the rubble. Flora and fauna start to recover only to be wiped out again by volcanic venting that blankets the area in more caustic ash.

Climate

In the island's delightful tropical climate, temperatures never go lower than the 70s. Ocean breezes keep the summer heat at a reasonable level.

Flora & Fauna

The northern area is filled with wildlife, including 34 species of resident land birds, an array of lizards including the rare galliwasp, and a species of large bullfrogs known as "mountain chickens." Among the trees you'll see are various species of palms as well as tropical fruit trees, including mango, papaya, cashew, golden apple and banana.

The rich volcanic ash that shot out into the bays and sea during the eruption has actually enhanced underwater life. A recent article in one of the dive magazines declared that the diving here is as good or better than Saba. You'll see large formations of barrel sponges, lots of turtles, and rare fish such as the flying gournod.

The flying gournod

Travel Information

When to Go

Montserrat is hospitable year-round, and follows the same weather patterns as the other Leewards. The summer months are warmer and have more rain, the winter months are ideal, and the hurricane risks are greatest from June to the end of October. Before leaving home, consult the Montserrat Volcano Observatory website at www.mvo.org to see what the current alert level is and how active the volcano has been recently.

Getting There

The ferry between Antigua and Montserrat no longer runs, so the only way to get to the island currently is by air. A new airport opened in 2005 at Gerald's. Two airlines operate charter flights and one offers daily service from Antigua and St. Maarten, along with a helicopter service. There is also some discussion about renewal of the ferry on a smaller scale. Check the tourism website at www.visitmontserrat.com for the latest information. The airlines flying in are:

WinAir, with four flights per day from Antigua, and two from St. Maarten. This airline is a code share partner with most of the major airlines flying into Antigua and St. Maarten, so you can set up the entire trip at one time if you are traveling on **USAir**, **Air Canada**, **Air France**, **Continental**, **KLM**, **LIAT**, **Lufthansa** or **Caribbean Star/Caribbean**

The airport, at left

Sun. Side-trips can be arranged in Antigua by contacting Port Services Ltd., VC Bird International Airport, ☎ 268-462-2522/2523, fax 664-462-5185, www.fly-winair.com. In St. Maarten, contact WinAir, Princess Juliana International Airport, ☎ 599-545-4273/4230/4210, reservations@fly-winair.com.

Air Montserrat started operating private charter flights and selling "consolidator" tickets for passenger service on charter flights in 2006. To book a flight, check their website at www.airmontserrat.com. Air Montserrat has reps in Antigua at Carib-World Travel, Woods Centre, ☎ 268-480-2999, info@carib-world.com and in Montserrat at Travel World International, Davy Hill, ☎ 664-491-2713, travelmni@candw.ms.

Carib Aviation has charter flights between Antigua and Montserrat. Contact in Antigua is ☎ 268-481-2401/2404, fax 268-481-2405, caribav@candw.ag; www.candoo.com/carib.

Caribbean Helicopters offers charter flights, medivac services, and volcano-viewing trips from Antigua. ☎ 268-460-5900, fax 268-460-5901, helicopters@candw.ag, www.caribbeanhelicopters.net.

 Note that there is a departure and airport security tax of US$21 (EC$55) for all except Caricom nationals, who pay a lower rate of US$13 (EC$35).

Customs

 Visitors to the island are allowed 200 cigarettes, 50 cigars, half a pound of tobacco, 40 ounces of alcoholic beverages and six ounces of perfume duty-free. Gift articles up to a value of US$185, including these allowances, are duty-free, and personal items are exempt from duty.

Special Events & Holidays

Montserratians celebrate two big events each year with week-long celebrations: St. Patrick's Day and Christmas. In 2006, they began a Calabash Festival to honor their native culture, food and crafts. The Calabash promises to be a yearly event and is held in July to compete with other islands' Carnivals. To see specific dates for particular years, see the Calendar at the official tourism site, www.visitmontserrat.com.

January
New Year's Day Parade – Public holiday.
On Shore Fishing Competition.

March
St. Patrick's Day Week of Celebration, including Freedom Run, concerts, masquerades.

April
Good Friday – Public holiday.
Easter Monday – Public holiday.
Montserrat Open Fishing Tournament, end of April and first of May.

May
Labor Day, May 1.
Whit Monday, last Monday in May.

June
Queen's Birthday Celebration, second Saturday in June.

July
Look Out Day.
Calabash Festival, late July.
Cudjoe Head Day, July 28-30.

August
August Monday – Public holiday.
St. Peter's Parish Bazaar, early July.

October
Tourism Week.
Credit Union Week.
Museum Week.
Police, Fire, Search & Rescue Community Week.

December
Christmas Festival.
Christmas Day, December 25 – Public holiday.
Boxing Day, December 26 – Public holiday.
St. John's Day, December 27.
Festival Day, December 31.

Montserrat

Health

Glendon Hospital can handle most medical emergencies. It is in the village of St. John's (☎ 664-491-2552/7404). There are private physicians on the island specializing in dermatology, general medicine, general surgery and gynecology. A dentist operates a dental clinic. For more serious problems, arrangements can be made to quickly transfer patients to Antigua or Guadeloupe. **Lee's Pharmacy** in Brades can fill any medication needs.

Pets

To bring a dog or cat to the island, you must obtain a Veterinary Health Certificate issued within 72 hours prior to travel from a competent veterinary authority in the country where the animal resided for a period of at least three months prior to travel. The certificate must certify that the animal is free from contagious diseases. In addition, you must get approval of the importation by notifying the Veterinary Officer of Montserrat and providing time of arrival and port of entry at least 48 hours prior to arrival time. Animals may be subject to house quarantine. For further details, contact the Department of Agriculture, P.O. Box 272, Brades. ☎ 664-491-2546/2075, malhe@candw.ms.

Crime

With such a small population, the incidence of crime is very low. However, you should take the normal precautions of locking doors and securing valuables wherever you are staying.

Electricity

Since the island is a British territory, the primary voltage is 220. Some hotels have a 110-volt plug available for computers, and private villas vary according to the nationality of the owners. If you are from the US or Canada, bringing a converter will make life easier.

Tipping

Most restaurants add a 10% service fee to the bill. Higher amounts and all other tipping is at your discretion, but it's always good to tip taxi drivers, tour guides and housekeepers, who work hard to make your trip more enjoyable.

Money Matters

 The Eastern Caribbean Dollar is the predominant currency for Montserrat. The exchange rate is fixed at EC$2.70 to US$1. Most stores and restaurants will take either currency. Go to the banks for the best exchange rate.

 Convert EC to US in a Flash: To figure out the US$ equivalent of a price given in EC, just divide the EC cost in half, then deduct 25% or one-fourth of that figure. Example: EC$68 would be US$34 minus US$8, for a rough estimate of US$26.

There are two banks on the island, the **Bank of Montserrat** in St. Peters and **Royal Bank of Canada** on the Brades Main Road. They offer currency exchange and follow traditional banking hours, which means they close by 2 pm, except on Wednesdays, when they are open until 1 pm, and Fridays, when they are open until 3 pm. Neither is open on Saturdays.

The only ATM on the island is at the Royal Bank of Canada. Federal Express, UPS and DHL offer services on the island for quick transfer of documents.

Weddings

Montserrat has some beautiful settings for weddings. For non-nationals visiting the island, the government requires a minimum stay of three working days in Montserrat before application can be made to obtain a Special or Governor's marriage license. Application for the license is made through the Department of Administration. Documents required include the Marriage Application Form (issued by the Department of Administration), passports of both parties, original absolute divorce decree (if divorced), original death certificate of deceased spouse (if widowed), and a non-marriage certificate (if applicable). For more information, contact the Department of Administration, PO Box 292, Government Headquarters, Brades, Montserrat, B.W.I. ☎ 664-491-2365. The office is open Monday through Friday from 8 am to 4 pm.

Internet Access

WWW The two hotels on the island offer in-room Internet access if you bring your own laptop. More and more of the guest houses and villas are adding this feature. There are also two Internet cafés on the island: **Andy's Internet Café and Repairs** on the Brades Main

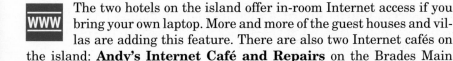

Road (www.andysinternetcafe.com), and **Grant Enterprises and Trading** in Brades.

Communications

Cellular service is available through two platforms: TDMA (D amPS on 800 Mhz) and GSM 850. Purchase of a local SIM card is US$6 and a temporary phone rental is US$20 monthly through Cable and Wireless. ☎ 664-491-2112 (ext 250), mnisupport@cwmni.cwplc.com.

Media

The island has one newspaper, *The Montserrat Reporter* (published weekly, www.themontserratreporter.com), and a monthly *Montserrat Newsletter* with information on special programs and activities (www.montserrat-newsletter.com).

Sources of Information

For more information, see www.visitmontserrat.com, the official website of the Montserrat Tourist Board. For additional materials, contact the offices below.

In the US

Caribbean Tourism Organization, 80 Broad St., 32nd Floor, New York, NY 10024, ☎ 212-635-9530, fax 212-635-9511, get2cto@dorsai.org.

In the UK

Montserrat Government (UK) Office, 7 Portland Place, London WIB 1PP, ☎ (44) 020-7031-0317, fax (44) 020-7031-0318, j.panton@montserratgov.co.uk.

In Germany

Montserrat Tourist Board, Basic Services Group, Bahnhofplatz 4, D-55116 Mainz, Germany, ☎ +49-6131-99332, fax +49-6131-99331, www.visitmontserrat.de.

In Montserrat

Montserrat Tourist Board, # 7 Farara Plaza, Buildings B&C , PO Box 7, Brades, Montserrat, WI, ☎ 664-491-2230/8730, fax 664-491-7430, info@montserrattourism.ms.

Getting Around

Airport

The small new airport at Gerald's is still developing services, but you'll be able to catch a taxi or rent a car there. The trip to a destination anywhere in the north takes 10-20 minutes at the most; be prepared for hairpin turns and beautiful scenery.

> **For Safety's Sake:** When you arrive at the airport, you should receive a brochure titled "Guide to Volcanic Hazards," issued by the government. It explains the science and outlines the hazards associated with the Soufrière Hills Volcano. It identifies the Exclusion Zone and the Safe Zone, and explains how you will be alerted of developing danger from the volcano. The brochure also provides a list of emergency contact numbers. Read it, and keep it handy.

Taxi Service

Taxis are the most common means of transportation on Montserrat, especially since driving is done on the left side of the road and the roads are a jumble of sharp curves and narrow passages. Most of the drivers are well versed in locations and sights to be pointed out and are very accommodating in making whatever arrangements you need.

Sample fares:

- Airport to Vue Pointe Hotel, US$25, EC$68.
- Airport to Tropical Mansion Suites, US$8, EC$22.
- Vue Pointe Hotel to Montserrat Volcano Observatory, US$10, EC$27.
- Tropical Mansions to MVO, US$24, EC$65.
- Vue Pointe Hotel to Jack Boy Hill, US$27, EC$72.
- Tropical Mansions to Jack Boy Hill, US$10, EC$27.

Car Rentals

Driving in Montserrat is an interesting experience – you drive on the left and there are no stop lights, but there are plenty of hairpin turns and switchbacks. Basically, the roads run in a horseshoe shape from Jack Boy Hill on the eastern side to Old Towne on the western side, all dead ending at the Exclusion Zone.

In deference to the quality of the roads, a number of agencies (all are locally owned) offer 'jeeps' or small 4WD SUVs. You can obtain a temporary Montserrat driver's license from the police department in Brades or

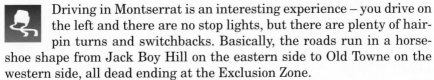

Salem for US$20; you'll need to show your current license from your country of origin.

There are only two gas stations on all of Montserrat, and the second one was built in 2005. Expect to pay about US$5 for a gallon of gasoline. However, since the part of the island you can drive on is only about six miles long and you can't go more than 25 mph on the winding roads, your fuel is likely to last a lot longer than it does at home.

Maps of the current roads haven't been redone in a while, but there are road signs to direct you to certain landmarks, and the Montserratians are extremely gracious about giving directions. Just remember, you cannot go into the Daytime Entry Zone without a qualified guide, you can't enter the Exclusion Zone at all, and you need to be aware of the alert level to know where it is currently safe to go.

Car rental companies:

- Be-Beep's Car Rentals, ☎ 664-491-3787, cell 664-492-1083.
- Danny Lyons Rentals (jeeps), ☎ 664-491-6216 or 664-492-1455.
- Equipment & Supplies Ltd. (cars/vans), ☎ 664-491-2402, farara@hotmail.com.
- Ethelyne's Car Rental (cars/jeeps), ☎ 664-491-2855.
- Grant Enterprises & Trading (cars/jeeps), ☎ 664-491-9654, granten@candw.ms.
- Jefferson Car Rental (cars jeeps), ☎ 664-491-2126, jeffersonrental@candw.ms.
- Joel Osborne & Associates Ltd. (jeeps), ☎ 664-491-6300 or 664-492-1555, joelo@hotmail.com.
- KC's Car Rentals (cars), %%664-491-5756, kccarrental@hotmail.com.
- Lea Car Rentals (cars), ☎ 664-491-8533 or 664-493-5640.
- Montserrat Enterprises Ltd. (cars/jeeps), ☎ 664-491-2431/2, melenter@candw.ms.
- Neville Bradshaw Agencies (cars), ☎ 664-491-5270/2070, nbvillas@candw.ms.
- M.S. Osborne Ltd. (jeeps), ☎ 664-491-2494/5/3288, msosborne@candw.ms.
- Pickett Van Rentals (vans), ☎ 664-491-5513, johnsonwp@candw.ms.
- Zeekies Rentals (cars), ☎ 664-491-4515, cell 664-493-5281.

Exploring
On Foot

Hiking

With so many trails that lead into the lush hills of the northern part of the island, Montserrat is a hiker's paradise. Two major government initiatives insure that the natural beauty of the island is preserved and enhanced – The Darwin Centre Hills Project and the Montserrat National Trust. Trails in the Centre Hills area include:

Oriole Walkway. This sometimes steep, sometimes wide-open trail, goes through a habitat rich in wildlife and lush with vegetation. You may see the Montserrat oriole, along with other avian species such as the forest thrush, the mangrove cuckoo, the trembler and the purple throated carib. Watch underfoot for unusual amphibians such as the galliwasp lizard.

Trail to "The Cot". This heritage trail goes through an old banana plantation and along the ruins of a Sturge family cottage

Along the Oriole Walkway

called "The Cot." Continue up into the hills for a scenic view that includes some villages in the Exclusion Zone.

Blackwood Allen Trail. This trail is ideal for the experienced hiker. It runs from the Grand View Bed and Breakfast to Mongo Hill and meanders alongside a stream and through dense vegetation that includes the heliconia, Montserrat's national flower. A viewing platform allows panoramic views of the coastline and some northern villages.

Runaway Ghaut. A ghaut (pronounced "gut") is a deep ravine carrying rainwater down from the hills to the sea. This is an easy trail that is good for strolling or picnics.

Trails on other parts of the island include:

Volcanic fissure

Silver Hills Trail. At the northern tip of the island is the long-dormant Silver Hills volcano, the oldest on the island. From here, it's possible to envision what the southern part of the island may look like in the next million years. You hike from Drummond through forests, across fields and up hills, passing many beautiful vistas of land and sea. One highlight is the breeding colony of frigate birds at Pelican Point.

Trail to Rendezvous Bay. Rendezvous Bay has the distinction of being the only white sand – and the most beautiful – beach on Montserrat. The beach is not accessible by road, so you have to hike in along a steep trail over a bluff (it's not an easy walk). Before starting out, check with a Forest Ranger to see if it's passable. If you anticipate being too tired to hike out after a day on the beach, you can arrange to have a boat come and return you to land.

 Pick Your Trail Carefully: The level of endurance and skill required for each trail varies. Part of the Oriole Walkway is little more than a trampled path and climbs steeply, so it is not ideal for the inexperienced hiker or someone with limited stamina. Be sure to check with a guide from the MNT as to the level of difficulty. Wear comfortable hiking shoes and take a supply of water with you.

Eco-Adventures

Bird Watching

Many people come to Montserrat to observe the 34 species of resident land birds and migrant songbirds that inhabit the island. The most elusive of these is the Montserrat oriole, the country's national bird, which is seen only rarely. Knowledgeable guides such as James "Scriber" Daley can "call" the birds to you. The MNT or the Centre Hills Project office can get you in touch with these guides, as well as provide you with a colorful plastic guide to help identify each species.

Turtle Watching

The island's black sand beaches serve as nesting sites for the green turtle, loggerhead, and hawksbill sea turtles. From August to September, you may be fortu-

Montserrat oriole (female)

nate enough to spy a female turtle coming in on the surf under the protection of darkness to lay her eggs. The MNT offers some treks to the beaches for this activity, so contact them to learn dates and times.

The Darwin Centre Hills Project

The need for protection of the ecosystem in Montserrat extends beyond just preservation from volcanic activity. The Centre Hills are the last viable habitat for many species of globally threatened and endemic wildlife. The Hills are also the source for the local water supply. The protected species found there include the oriole, mountain chicken (a frog), the rare galliwasp lizard, and several species of plants. In addition, resident species include tree frogs, anoles, ground lizards, dwarf geckos and iguanas.

Funded by the UK Darwin Initiative for the Survival of the Species and led by the Royal Society for the Protection of Birds, the Centre Hills Project staff conducts socioeconomic assessments, provides outreach and education, and carries out ecological research. The Project is also assisting in building a strong local organization to manage the protected areas and maintain the beauty of the Centre Hills.

The Project's work is also supported by the Montserrat Tourist Board, the Ministry of Agriculture, the Montserrat National Trust (MNT), the Durrell Wildlife Conservation Trust and the Royal Botanic Gardens at Kew. To find out more, contact the MNT (☎ 664-491-3088, www.montserratnationaltrust.com) or visit their museum and botanical gardens on the Salem Main Road.

Montserrat

On Wheels

Car or Jeep

Right now, there is not much in the way of overland trails for motorized vehicles. At times it will seem like just driving around the island is enough of an adventure, with plenty of sharp turns and no idea of what is coming at you.

Scenic Tours

Of course, the main land-based tours take you to see the volcano in action and to visit the villages. Most taxi drivers are knowledgeable about all the attractions of the island. However, if you want to go into the Daytime Entry Zone to see the devastation of Plymouth, be sure to ask if the driver is approved to go into the zone. These drivers must carry drinking water and other supplies, and must check in with the police to find out the latest conditions in the Belham River Valley area. For more discussion of interesting sights and historical areas you can visit, see the discussion under *Seeing the Sights* later in this chapter.

Tour Operators

Avalon's Taxi-Tours, ☎ 664-491-3432, cell 664-492-1565, citrusseeker@gmail.com; **Clifford "Shaw-Duck" Ryan**, ☎ 664-492-1849; **Eustace A. Dyer**, ☎ 664-491-2721; **Grant Tours**, ☎ 664-491-9654, granten@candw.ms or casselj@candw.ms; **'JIG' Tours/Jadine Glitzenhirn**, ☎ 664-491-2752, cell 664-496-2752, jigproms@hotmail.com; **Rose Willock**, ☎ 664-491-6652, willockr@candw.ms; **Slym Tours & Taxi Service**, ☎ 664-491-4479, cell 664-492-2878.

Bicycle Rentals

Montserrart's hills and winding roads are like catnip to mountain bikers. You don't have to leave the main road to find your way to the many interesting villages and beautiful scenery. For bike rentals, there are two sources: **Gingerbread Hill guest house** in St. Peter's, ☎ 664-491-5812, www.volcano-island.com and **Imagine Peace Bicycle Shop** in Brades, ☎ 664-491-8809, ghbikes@hotmail.com.

On Water

Swimming & Beach-Going

The island has several beautiful beaches; all but one has volcanic pearl-gray sand.

Little Bay is a popular swimming beach. There are several bars and restaurants adjacent to the beach, including the Green Monkey and the Good Life Restaurant.

Bunkum Bay is a large shallow bay popular with snorkelers; it has a beach bar.

Woodlands Beach is on the Caribbean Sea side, but can have some waves.

Lime Kiln Beach is a secluded beach that also draws snorkelers.

Old Road Bay, in front of the Vue Point, has changed because of the ash flows coming down the Belham River Valley.

Rendezvous Bay is a white sand beach; it is accessible only by hiking a rugged trail or by boat.

Scuba Diving

The volcanic ash and boulders spewed into the sea by the volcano built new natural reefs and enhanced Montserrat's already beautiful dive sites. In addition, maritime exclusion zones have been defined to protect marine species. The dive areas reach from Old Road Bluff in the west to North West Bluff, around the northern shoreline towards Hell's Gate, and then along the eastern shore to the border of the Exclusion area. Bryan Cunningham is the owner of Seawolf Diving School and a certified instructor with years of experience in South Africa, the Red Sea, the Virgin Islands and the Bahamas. Cunningham says that the island is a natural teaching area because there are such varied sites, from shallow and level areas to deep reefs with caves and huge barrel sponges. Among the highlights are:

- A shallow coastal reef reached from the shore of Woodland Bay, with a small cave.
- A reef with a depth of 90 to 140 feet off Bunkum Bay.
- Carr's Bay, with a reef that be accessed from shore.
- Potato Hill reef, with a shallower dive area but lots of color.
- Rendezvous Bay – very popular because of the bat cave dive and the reef system that extends from here to the Northwest Bluff.

The best way to see these spots and others is through a dive trip with one of the two dive shops on the island. **Seawolf Diving School** operates out of the Vue Pointe Hotel and also offers a villa called Diver's Haven with six en-suite bedrooms for diving groups. Equipment is provided (☎ 664-491-7807, www.seawolfdivingschool.com). The **Green Monkey Inn and Dive Shop**, on the beach at Little Bay, has equipment and dive packages, along with rental dive kayaks, sea scooters and snorkeling rafts. Owner Troy Deppermann is a Master Scuba Diver Trainer and can certify divers as well as guide them to the best spots around the island (☎ 664-496-2960, www.divemontserrat.com).

Snorkeling

Among the favorite snorkeling areas on the island are **Bunkum Bay**, **Rendezvous Bay** and **Lime Kiln Bay**. All three have shallow reefs and ledges leading out to deeper waters where the divers head. Snorkeling equipment is available from the two dive shops, and the Green Monkey can also provide sea scooters and snorkeling rafts.

Deep-Sea Fishing

There are many spots for shore fishing along the coasts, including Old Road Bay, Little Bay and Rendezvous Bay. But if you dream of landing a marlin, wahoo or tuna, you must head out to the deep sea. In fact, each year in September the Montserrat Fisherman's Cooperative hosts an International Fishing Tournament that attracts anglers from all over the world. There are several fishing boat operators for hire, including: **Danny Sweeney**, aka Jumpin' Jack, ☎ 664-491-5645, mwilson@candw.ms; **Carlton O'Garro**, ☎ 664-491-8902 and **Bruce Farara**, ☎ 664-491-8802, farara@hotmail.com.

Seeing the Sights

Volcano Viewing

The largest attraction (literally) on the island is the Soufrière Hills Volcano, which rumbled to life in July 1995. The blast began with earthquake swarms followed by pyroclastic flows. Hot ash and gases flowed down at a rapid pace, igniting and burying structures in its path. The magma dome at the top of the mountain began a cycle, continuing today, of growing, occasionally venting, and sometimes exploding and raining ash and danger down. The area of Plymouth has been evacuated three times, most recently in April of 1996. Then, as people continued their lives in the eastern and central areas around the W.H. Bramble Airport, pyroclastic flows began moving into the northern ghauts. Although the residents were warned to stay out of the area, many returned during the day to take care of their homes and gardens, unknown to the government officials. Nineteen people were killed when a series of flows moved quickly down the mountain, burying the villages and the airport.

Since then, no one has been allowed in the southern Exclusion Zone. You may enter the Day Time Entry Zone in the suburbs north of Plymouth below Old Town to view Plymouth at a distance and see some homes that were buried in ash. Entry to this zone is across the Belham River Valley, for-merly the site of the island's only golf course, now covered in layers of ash and mud. When conditions

The remains of Plymouth, buried in ash

are too wet, the road is not passable, so you need a knowledgeable guide. Also, having a guide is useful when you start smelling sulphur and need guidance as to whether to get out of the area quickly.

The prime viewing spot to see the growing magma dome is on the eastern side at Jack Boy Hill, which overlooks the buried Bramble Airport and the destroyed villages on the eastern side. The government has built a view-ing area with a small snack bar, toilet facilities, picnic tables and a high-powered telescope. Many like to visit this area at night, when you can see the volcano glowing red in the darkness.

To really immerse yourself in volcanology, visit the **Montserrat Volcano Observatory** in Flemmings, where scientists observe, report and fore-cast the activities of the volcano on a daily basis. A new Visitor Interpreta-tion Center shows video footage of actual events and traces the history of the eruptions and ventings through interactive kiosks. The windows of the center also give a good view of the growing dome. For more informa-tion, go to the MVO's website at www.mvo.ms (the site has some dramatic photos and the latest information on alert levels and activity).

Sampling the Culture

Montserratians celebrate their culture in many special events throughout the year. **Festival Village**, the Carnival grounds, also sees a lot of activ-ity during the St. Patrick's Day week of events, Christmas events and the Queen's Birthday celebration.

If you're in town for the St. Patrick's Day festivities, you'll want to take a **Freedom Hike**. The hike into the hills, led by guides, is as cultural as it is physical. At the end of the hike you'll be treated to a traditional Creole breakfast that includes salt fish, Johnny cakes, bush tea and other West Indian delights. In addition, many of the local rum shops and roadside cafés serve traditional West Indian goat water, coconut tarts and salt fish.

For local crafts and handiwork, visit the **Montserrat Arts and Crafts Association store** in Brades, where you'll find handmade textiles, wood carvings and pottery, as well as local honey and jams. **Luv's Cotton Store** in Salem is the last holdover from the time when sea island cotton ruled the Montserratian economy.

For performing arts, check the schedule (www.visitmontserrat.com) of the newly completed 700-seat **Cultural Centre** in Little Bay.

Reliving History

The Montserratians are working hard to uncover and recreate the artifacts of their heritage lost to mud and ash. Central to the recovery is the Montserrat National Trust (MNT), which operates out of the **Oriole Complex** headquarters in Olveston.

In the Complex is a **Botanical Garden** with a recreated ghaut, orchid conservatory and plantings of historic and medicinal plants. The **Natural History Centre** on-site shows historical photographs and items to help preserve memories of the island as it was before 1995, along with special revolving exhibits. A small reference library and videos on the history of the island are available for use by visitors and students. A gift shop gives you the chance to pick up helpful guides and videos about the island.

The Trust oversees the Darwin Centre Hills Project and is working on developing trails and other ways for tourists to enjoy the many diverse and interesting areas of the now-thriving northern Safe Zone. To learn about opening hours and exhibits at the Complex, contact the MNT, Salem Main Road, ☎ 664-491-3086, mnatrust@candw.ms, www.montserratnationaltrust.com.

Where to Stay

Hotels

There are only two hotels on the island, one a longstanding favorite, the other built in 1999. Both are in the $150 price range for a double room.

Tropical Mansion Suites

This modern hotel sits on a bluff overlooking the sea and offers pleasant rooms in a breezy location. There is a restaurant on-site and the grounds include an old sugar mill and gardens planted with herbs and fruit trees. In the center of the complex is a pool and fountain named "The Little Alps" in memory of the waterfalls at the southern end of Montserrat that were destroyed by the volcano. All rooms are now air-conditioned and a recent upgrade spruced up the furnishings and amenities.

Tropical Mansion

Location: In Sweeney's, close to Little Bay and the airport.

Rooms: 18, including honeymoon suite with four-poster bed, deluxe with kitchenettes, and standard rooms. All have balconies (some have two), AC, TV, and Internet access.

Rates: EP.

Features: Restaurant and bar, pool, small conference room.

☎ 664-491-8767, fax 664-491-8275, www.tropicalmansion.com.

Vue Pointe Hotel

Cedric and Carol Osborne have worked hard at keeping this hotel going in spite of its location near the Daytime Entry Zone and the occasional blankets of ash that fall in the zone. The hospitality is warm and welcoming. You'll feel like an old friend even if it's your first visit. The site overlooks the volcano and the Belham River Valley (where the golf course used to be). The individual guest cottages are staggered up the hillside to take advantage of the view of Old Road Bay; most were renovated by 2007.

 A note of caution: The hotel closes when the threat level from the volcano is at 4 or 5, so call ahead.

Location: In Old Towne, on Old Road Bay.

Rooms: 18 cottages and rooms, 12 with kitchenettes; all have cable TVs and WiFi.

Rates: EP.

Features: Restaurant and bar, Jumpin' Jacks beach restaurant adjacent to property, pool, two tennis courts, library, conference center, Sea Wolf Diving School. Internet access is available in the lobby.

☎ 664-491-5210, fax 664-491-4813, www.vuepointe.com.

Guest Houses

While you won't find any mega-chain hotels, you will find some delightful guest houses brimming over with typical Montserrat hospitality. Rates in these intimate inns are very reasonable, running from $65 to $125 per night for double occupancy. Some of the best are:

Erindell Villa Guesthouse

Erindell

Owners Lou and Shirley Spycalla turned their home into a guesthouse after their jobs disappeared under the volcano flow. As it turns out, the Spycalla's are natural hosts and their good humor and hospitality keep things lively and interesting. They regard all visitors as family, and will entertain you as well as feed you (Lou is the cook). *Location:* On Gros Michel Drive in Woodlands.

Rooms: Two, each with private entrances, twin beds, en-suite bathrooms, hair driers, cable TV, phone, radio, ceiling fans, small fridge, coffee & tea-making facilities, and microwave/toaster oven.

Rates: EP.

Features: Small café, pool, laundry, a variety of table games, karaoke fun, beach & pool towels, beach mats & chairs, snorkeling equipment, use of a cell phone when hiking or going to the beach, Internet access on-site.

☎ 664-491-3655, www.erindellvilla.com.

Gingerbread Hill

The Lea family has created a comfortable and memorable home where you can relax and truly enjoy yourself. The Heavenly Suite comes with a 360-degree view of the rainforests, mountains and sea. The Villa has two bedrooms and two baths. The Tree House Room is surrounded by banana and papaya trees, and the Backpacker's Special offers bunk beds. The Leas are well connected on the island and can help arrange tours and activities to suit your interests. Be sure to ask David about the series of videos he shot documenting the volcano eruptions and history of the island.

Location: In St. Peters.

Rooms: Described above, suite and villa include full kitchens, others have small fridges and coffee/tea service, cable TV, complimentary WiFi Internet access.

Rates: EP.

Features: Complimentary airport transfers, rental cars and bicycles available on-site, volcano tours with David Lea.

☎ 664-491-5812, fax 305-422-0222, www.volcano-island.com.

Grand View Bed & Breakfast

The views from the upper stories of this inn are indeed grand. The tropical gardens, a pet project of owner Theresa Silcott, are filled with fruit trees and exotic plants. The rooms are simply and uniquely furnished. Ham radio operators love to stay here because of the excellent reception (the family operates its own radio station here). Also, you can walk to the Montserrat Volcano Observatory.

Location: on Baker Hill.

Rooms: Two suites and three bedrooms, all with private baths, cable TV, ceiling fans.

Rates: CP.

Features: Restaurant and bar, Certified Tour Guide on-site.

☎ 664-491-2284, fax 664-491-6876, www.grandviewmni.com.

Montserrat Moments Inn & the Old Sugar Mill

This small inn is built around a 17th-century sugar mill. One of the rooms is actually in the mill, other rooms are scattered across the property. The views from the pool and terrace are spectacular. The main house can be rented as

Montserrat Moments

a three-bedroom villa (including the mill suite). When it's not rented, the main house is used to serve breakfast for the other residents.

Location: In Manjack Heights, overlooking the Caribbean and the Centre Hills.

Rooms: 12 rooms, some suites with kitchenettes, some have air conditioning; Internet access available.

Rates: CP.

Features: Large pool, gardens, laundry facilities.

☎ 664-491-7707/492-1743, flogriff@candw.ms.

Travellers Palm Guest House

Terrace at Travellers Palm

Another gem in the crown of Montserrat hospitality, Travellers Palm offers bright accommodations and a great view to the sea. It is centrally located, so you can get to Old Road Bay, Bunkum Bay, Woodlands Bay and the Daytime Entry Zone quickly and easily.

Location: In Olveston.

Rooms: Three, two with fridges, coffee/tea service and cable TV, one without TV.

Rates: CP.

Features: Pool with terrace, gardens with fruit trees, laundry facilities, complimentary airport shuttle.

☎ 664-491-4816, www.travellerspalmmontserrat.com.

Villas

In the 1960s, the island economy turned on the sudden interest of US, UK and Canadian residents in buying property on Montserrat for vacation homes. Often these large and graceful homes are for rent when the owners aren't in residence. Many are situated on bluffs overlooking the sea or have nice sea views, and most have their own private pools and some yard or garden areas.

For a listing of individual villas, see the Tourism Board website at www.visitmontserrat.com. Agencies that handle villa rentals include the following:

Montserrat Enterprises, Ltd. has a number of two- to four-bedroom villas, most with pools. ☎ 664-491-2431/2, www.montserratenterprises.com.

Montserrat Villas manages four villas, including the Waterworks Estate. ☎ 664-491-7060, fax 664-491-8553, www.montserratvillas.com.

Tradewinds Real Estate has some elegant villas scattered across the bluffs on the Caribbean side of the island. ☎ 664-491-2004, fax 664-491-6229, www.tradewindsmontserrat.com.

Tropical Island Real Estate, Ltd. is a development company that manages many of the villas it built. ☎ 664-491-2819; US & Canada 786-319-9672, fax 664-491-7821, www.sunislandrealestate.com.

Where to Eat

 Since the list of restaurants is relatively short, I'll just put them in alpha order. For such a small population, the range of choices is pretty good.

RESTAURANT PRICE CHART	
$	Cheap eats, normally quick meals or take-out foods; US$8 or less per entrée.
$$	Good value, lots of West Indian cuisine; US$9-$14 for a plate of food.
$$$	A nice place with gourmet aspirations; US$15-$24 for a satisfying entrée.

Jumping Jack's Beach Bar & Restaurant

While the beach is not really there any more, the ambience and hospitality are still great at this place because of the efforts of owners Danny and Margaret Sweeney. Danny catches the fish and Margaret cooks them (the fresh tuna sandwich comes highly recommended). Don't miss Friday night dinner; it's the only night the restaurant is open for dinner and it can turn into quite a party. $$. Old Road Beach, just past the Vue Pointe Hotel. Open for breakfast and lunch every day and dinner on Friday. ☎ 664-491-5645.

Tina's Restaurant

This local favorite on the Brades main road is a good choice for simple food in a relaxed and very pleasant setting. You can sit indoors to enjoy the air conditioning or outdoors to enjoy the breezes. Choose from a menu of local dishes and seafood specialties, including lobster burgers. Desserts are excellent. $$. Open for lunch and dinner. ☎ 664-491-3538.

The Attic

In a small white wooden building in a neighborhood setting sits the Attic, an outstanding place for lunch. The rotis are quite good and quite large. Be sure to ask what local juices are on the day's menu. The gooseberry juice is outstanding – my husband drank the entire supply the day we visited. $. Olveston Estate Drive, off the Salem main road. ☎ 664-491-2008.

Vue Pointe Hotel & Restaurant

This hotel restaurant sits on an open-air patio overlooking the pool with views out to Old Road Bay. It's a very romantic setting, especially by moonlight, and the food is well prepared. Wednesday night barbecues always draw a crowd, so you'll need reservations. Friday night's menu emphasizes Chinese choices, and Monday night is game night. $$$. Old Towne, on Old Road Bay. Open for breakfast, lunch and dinner every day. ☎ 664-491-5210, vuepointe@candw.ms.

Windsor Restaurant

Windsor offers a mix of Caribbean and Italian cuisines from its perch on a hillside overlooking the lush forests of the Centre Hills. A buffet lunch is served Tuesdays and Thursdays. $$$. Cudjoe Head, on the main road. Open for breakfast, lunch, dinner and afternoon tea. ☎ 664-491-2900, lena@candw.ms.

Ziggy's Restaurant

Many residents consider Ziggy's to be the best restaurant on the island. It offers a menu of international cuisine served in high style. It also has an outstanding wine list. The restaurant is not always open regular hours, so be sure to call for reservations. $$$. Woodlands. Open for dinner only, by reservation. ☎ 664-491-8282, ziggs@candw.ms.

Shopping

Shopping opportunities occur primarily around the villages of Brades and Salem, where there are some small boutiques and retail stores. For island mementos, stop at the **Oriole Gift Shop** in the Montserrat National Trust complex, **Montserrat Ceramics** and the **Montserrat Arts and Crafts Association store**, both in Brades. If you're lucky, you may catch **Luv's Sea Island Cotton** open in Salem, where you'll find lovely placemats and other hand-woven goods.

Nighlife

Montserrat is known mostly for its peaceful, laid-back lifestyle. The liveliest it gets is on Friday nights when **Jumpin' Jacks Beach Bar and Grill** (☎ 664-491-5645, on Old Road Beach) is open for dinner, or the rum shops have a particularly good crowd. On Wednesdays, everyone gathers at the **Vue Pointe Hotel** (☎ 664-491-5210, Old Towne) for the weekly barbecue around the pool with live music.

Index